WHEN
GREED
TURNS DEADLY

by
DIXIE MURPHY

To My good friend Emily —
Best Wishes —
Dixie

Published by:

AZURE EYES PUBLISHING

Scottsdale, Arizona

DEDICATION

This book is dedicated to
Betty Lou Gray and Reeda Roundy

and to
JoAnn Buccola
for her determination for justice

ACKNOWLEDGEMENTS

This book could never have been written without those who gave their time by granting interviews which enabled me to tell this story as accurately as possible.

Without the dedication and determination of JoAnn Buccola this story would not have been told. I spent two full days in a California motel room with the tape recorder rolling while JoAnn told about her family, her sister and the terrible events that transpired which were the subject of this book. I have such admiration for her strength and resolve for seeing that her sister's killer was brought to justice.

There are so many others that I want to thank for telling me their stories; Jackson Police Lt. Dave Foster; Bonneville County Detective Victor Rodriguez; Tom Moss, attorney for the civil suit; and Michael Kane, Chief of the Idaho Attorney Generals Criminal Law Division.

Many thanks to Betty's best friends DeeDee Batson and Janice Roby.

Reeda's sister, Evelyn Hamilton, Leroy Leavitt, Vada Roberts and Jury Foreman Richard Schwartz all contributed valuable information.

And a special thank you to Donna Bowman who edited the early drafts and to whom I am most grateful for her patience and expertise.

Special mention and thanks to those who read and encouraged me to finish the book go to Sue Borman,

Sybil Ferguson, Sharon Murphy and Dennis Stevens.

I would like to thank my husband for his understanding and patience. Without complaint he survived with a wife who locked herself in the office and melted into her computer. It was for this reason I finally decided it was time for this book to be published for I did not want him to think all those hours were for naught.

Saralyn and Jeff declined to be interviewed and so their stories are told by others, newspaper accounts and transcripts of all the court proceedings including the trial transcripts.

The Roundy children, Ruth Ann, Paul and Clayton also declined to be interviewed.

Although all the events and quotes in this book have been taken directly from transcripts of taped interviews and trial transcripts occasionally I interjected my thoughts and assumptions based on the whole of the information. Obviously, I do not know what a person herein may have been thinking but can assume by their actions and statements that logically it may be so.

*NOTE: Some names have been changed where it is not necessary to disclose their involvement.

TABLE OF CONTENTS

1

THE EARLY YEARS

His legs were moving by sheer will, his heart pounding. The extra strength he asked his body to give was fueled only by the adrenaline pumping through his veins. Sweat poured down his neck soaking his dark blue jumpsuit, creating a steam chamber of almost unbearable heat. It had been a good many years since he had asked his body to meet such a demand. Not too far now, through the deserted mall parking lot, on to Channing Way, half a mile to go. No one would suspect. No one would suspect he was physically able to ride a bike even a few blocks, let alone more than seven miles. His doctor would confirm that. He should have followed her advice, but he could never have foreseen having to push his body to its limits again. Not now, not now that he had put his affairs in order once and for all.

As Officer Greg Black came upon the paunchy man riding a bike near the hospital at three o'clock in the morning he didn't think much about it. The night was exceptionally warm. This guy probably couldn't sleep, thought Officer Black, or maybe he was a shift worker on his way to work at the hospital.

Whatever, it wasn't anything particularly suspicious that needed to be checked out. The officer swung wide giving the bicyclist a comfort zone, glancing causally at him as he passed.

Born to parents Sara and William Gray in Devils Lake, North Dakota, on December 4, 1939, William L. Gray's early life was average, with the exception that he was somewhat sickly and accident prone. In the second grade he suffered a broken collar bone and a broken nose. By the time he was in the sixth grade he'd had pneumonia for the seventh time. William, known as Bill, was 14 when the family left North Dakota and relocated in Crestline, California. His half-sister, Beverly remained in North Dakota for a year before joining the family in California. Beverly was six years older than Bill, a child of his mother's previous marriage.

Sara and William owned and operated a small grocery store in Crestline. Bill worked in the store weekends and summers, claiming it was the only way his parents could get any time off. The grocery business was reasonably profitable and Bill's dad added to the family income by selling insurance which helped provide a better than average living for the Gray family.

A skiing accident added to Bill's list of injuries, but was more embarrassing for the teenager than anything else. His accidents combined with a sickly childhood, gained his parents' full attention and sympathy. Not feeling well was a favorite ploy of young Bill's to get out of doing something he didn't want to do. It worked well for him. His loving parents could find no fault with their son for any reason.

Still in high school, Bill began to dabble in cutting firewood for local residents which led his father to buy a truck and other equipment needed for the job. Tree removal from residential lots in the rapidly growing area was in high demand. Bill picked up some good jobs but would soon discover this line of work was very demanding physically, and recruiting help from his high school friends cut into the profits. But even at the young age of 17 Bill was a master at getting others to do the biggest share of the hard labor. With his father paying for more equipment and Bill merely directing his crew, it appeared that he was destined to be a successful businessman.

When Joseph Hales got out of the Navy in 1944, he returned to California and his family. Wife Dorothy, daughters Jo Ann and Betty, and son Dan were relieved to have their husband and father home safe from the war. A building contractor, Joe resumed his trade in the home building industry. Eventually, he began to buy homes in need of finishing or remodeling, fixing them up and selling them for a profit. There wasn't much Joe couldn't do. He was an expert carpenter, cabinet maker, plumber and electrician. Often the family would move into the home while Joe worked on it, then it was sold and they moved to the next project. It wasn't the most lucrative way to make a living but it afforded him a decent income and the opportunity to be near his family all day, not just evenings after work.

In 1952 Jo Ann then 16, married a dashing, dark haired young man, two years older, who won her heart and swept her off her feet. Joe and Dorothy were unhappy their daughter married so young without first finishing high school. They liked Dick Buccola but were sure it would never last. But forty-six years, two grown sons, and two grandchildren later, Jo Ann and Dick smile when they remember their favorite song in the '50s was, "Too Young To Fall In Love." Like pages out of a romance novel, they weathered the bad times and thrived in the good.

Joe had always been fond of the high country of south central California, so when he had an opportunity to buy a remodel in Crestline, he jumped at it. Their two teenagers still at home, Betty now 16, and Dan 14, weren't too happy about changing high schools but soon settled in and found Crestline to be to their liking. For Betty it became an especially great place to be when she met Bill Gray.

Having been hired by Joe to clear the timber from their yard, Bill quickly spotted his employer's pretty daughter. Bill, three years older than Betty, struck up small conversations and later started dating Betty on a limited basis. A year later the Hales sold their remodeled home in Crestline and bought an apartment complex to remodel in Long Beach. Delighted to be closer to her married sister, Betty spent a lot of time with the Buccolas, visiting often and occasionally babysitting for Jo Ann and Dick's two boys, Dennis and Don.

But distance didn't bother Bill. He drove often from Crestline to see Betty wherever she was. If Betty was at home he would drive there to visit her. If Betty was at her sister's babysitting, he would go there. Wherever she was he just had to be with her. Bill knew he wanted to marry Betty almost the minute he met her. Betty wasn't quite as sure in their early dating years, but grew ever fonder of Bill as time went by. But Bill didn't want to wait and was after her to marry him when she was just 17 and still a junior in high school.

This time Joe and Dorothy were very determined that their other daughter finish high school before she married. Joe himself had made the mistake of not graduating from high school and he always felt he'd missed something special, so he was very determined that at least one of his daughters would finish school. Betty promised her father she would. But two weeks before graduation and the day after her 18 birthday, Betty and Bill eloped. They were married in Las Vegas, June 13, 1960.

Bill's parents attended the wedding, but Joe and Dorothy had no idea when Betty got their permission to accompany Bill and his parents on a two-day trip to Las Vegas, that she would be getting married! Certainly one should question how Bill's parents could be a part of, and an accessory to, an elopement of a barely 18-year-old girl. But if it was what their son wanted, his parents would go to any ends to see that he had it.

Shocked by the elopement, and disappointed their second daughter married at such an early age, the Hales were consoled only by the feeling that she had married into a good family. Even though they didn't know Bill very well they had often remarked what a loving and close family he came from. They'd noticed while he was removing the trees from the Hales' yard in Crestline, Sara and William came by daily to bring his lunch. Every time they came, the parents hugged and kissed their son as though they had not seen him for years. If they came back that same day to bring him a snack, which they did frequently, they would go through the same routine all over again. To a casual onlooker, it seemed to be a loving family indeed. Joe and Dorothy felt confident that their daughter would always be treated with the same kind of love and respect.

In the early years of the young Gray's marriage, Bill seemed to get along fine with Betty's family, and they had no major problem with him, other than they wished he would settle into a job that would make a better living than the tree business. Dick had begun a commercial landscaping business which kept his and Jo Ann's average spending to a minimum, but occasionally allowed for a few extras. Betty, on the other hand, had nothing extra to spend. Whatever Bill decided to dole out was what Betty had, and it was never any more than enough for the bare necessities. This didn't stop the sisters from spending as much time as they could together, doing things that didn't cost too much.

When Sara and William came up with enough money for a down payment on the house next door to Betty's parents, Betty was elated. Before Joe and Dorothy moved to Buena Park it had to be a special occasion to go visit her parents. Now that she would be living next door she could see all she wanted of them and even more of Jo Ann and the kids as they often spent time with Grandma and Grandpa Hales.

To say the Hales family was a close family would be an understatement. Holidays were always spent together, including aunts, uncles, cousins and friends. No one they knew even remotely was allowed to spend the holidays alone. At Christmas there would be something under the tree for everyone, even if it was nothing more than a sack of candy.

Joe Hales was born on December 19 and as a child he always felt cheated out of a proper birthday celebration due to the Christmas holiday. He'd made a vow that when he grew up, every holiday would be celebrated to its fullest extent, on the exact day of the event. He kept his vow and his enthusiasm spilled into his families' hearts. They would always carry that same zeal and excitement for holidays.

When Bill married Betty, he and his parents were welcomed warmly by the Hales. But that family closeness wasn't a suffocating togetherness, everyone was busy tending to their own lives, and they made no undue demands on others. But when it came time for a family gathering, usually at Jo Ann's, be it a holiday or a birthday party, it was celebrated with all the fun and flair befitting a movie production. Marvelous decorating and extra special food preparation set the stage for every holiday gathering. Betty got so caught up in the excitement she began to make fancy cakes for whatever the occasion. Taking classes and perfecting her craft as the years went by she developed an extraordinary talent for design and decoration. Selling her cakes through word of mouth, Betty added a few dollars here and there to the Gray household funds.

When the Grays decided to start their family they didn't waste much time. Saralyn was born April 21, 1963, and 19 months later on November 30, 1964, Jeff joined the family. Now that Betty was a mother, Jo Ann and Betty had even more in common than they did before. They were constantly on the phone talking about the kids and spending hours poring over the Sears catalogue deciding what to get for birthdays and Christmas.

Saralyn was especially exciting for Jo Ann. She wanted to buy her clothes and dolls. Having two sons and no daughter, she was longing to shop for all the pretty girl things for her young niece. She explained to Betty that she needed some fun. "You have Saralyn so I get to at least buy dolls," she insisted, and by then Jo Ann had the money to spend on others. The Buccolas could enjoy the results of their labor and were steadily climbing to an above average financial status.

Money was something Betty didn't know much about. She hadn't the slightest idea how much Bill was making with his tree business. He controlled the checking account and paid all the bills. But the one thing she did know was they were darn poor. She was sad but thankful when her parents slipped her some money now and then, and Jo Ann bought quite a few clothes and necessities for Betty and the kids. It was the least they could do for her as they knew she needed help.

"Betty kept her kids clean and neat. She was an excellent housekeeper," Jo Ann recalls. "But they always looked kind of shop worn, they looked poor. The clothes were old faded hand-me-downs except the few clothes Mom and I could afford to buy. She never spent an extra dime on herself. If she had some money it all went for the kids. But I'll tell you one thing, she never complained. I never heard her complain about Bill. She always supported him, whatever he was doing."

In time, the Hales family wasn't as thrilled about Bill as Betty seemed to be. They were beginning to feel uncomfortable around Bill. The more they were around him, the more concerned they became. They sensed he was becoming very controlling over Betty, dictating her every move. She had to ask Bill about every little thing she wanted to do. Betty was scared to death to be late returning home for any reason. Like Cinderella, when her time was up she flew home immediately.

"I thought, give me a break. Everyone should be allowed some leeway in their lives," remembers Jo Ann. "But you couldn't talk her out of it. She wouldn't even make a phone call to tell him she would be late or ask for a little extra time. When it was time to go, she packed up the kids and she went."

Betty knew her boundaries because she'd been on the receiving end of her hostile husband's anger when she returned late before. Undoubtedly she found it much easier to comply with his demands than to make excuses. Purchases for almost everything had to have prior approval. It was quite simple. If Bill wanted something they got it. If Betty needed something for the house or the kids she had to convince her husband it was an absolute necessity. Only then would he give her the money. Often he wanted to see the receipt. If there was change left over, he took that into account the next time he gave her money for groceries.

Betty was a married woman, a housewife, the mother of two children but she had no say in daily events. Without realizing it, Betty Gray was going through life never being allowed to make any decisions of her own. Bill Gray was sole director of this household production.

Mood swings were not uncommon to Bill. No one knew if he was going to be pleasant and jolly or sullen and quiet. If anyone, even in a casual comment, tried to reason with him or kid him out of his dark moods he would throw a glaring look that truly unnerved them, a backoff or else, kind of look.

Jo Ann shuddered a little when she thought about it. "His eyebrows would turn down and those black eyes would stare right through you. I didn't want to be around him any more than I had to. It was obvious that he didn't care much for me either."

However, in spite of her inner feelings about Bill, Jo Ann always included him and her sister in functions held at her home, and Bill, probably somewhat subdued and intimidated by his sister-in-law, usually put his best foot forward. For Betty's sake Jo Ann would tolerate Bill but she much preferred to spend time with her sister when Bill wasn't around. It's quite possible Bill was a little jealous, at the very least envious, of his sister and brother-in-law. Dick's commercial landscaping was growing into a very successful business and soon the Buccolas were in a position to build their first home.

They chose a wooded, unimproved lot that needed to have some trees removed. By then Bill had sold off or lost most of his tree cutting equipment and had been working other odd jobs as he could find them. At least that was the understanding Dick had when he sought bids from three different tree removal companies. When Bill heard what they were doing, he went to his brother-in-law and asked for the job. Jo Ann was not in favor of dealing with Bill, she just didn't trust him, but Dick reminded her that Bill and Betty were struggling and needed the money. After all, this was family, and if they could help out they should.

Dick never expected Bill to beat the lowest bid; he was prepared to pay around the medium to higher range. A few extra dollars for family would not be a problem, he maintained. Over Jo Ann's nagging fears, Bill got the job. When the bill came in the mail, Dick couldn't believe what he saw. His brother-in-law had charged three times more than the highest bid Dick had previously received.

Expressing intent to pay only a fair price for the work received, Dick confronted Bill with this outrageous charge. As he had done in the past, Bill once again cried poverty, placing Betty's welfare somewhere in the middle of his justification. Dick made a silent vow that he would never allow his sister-in-law to go without food and necessities, but as long as Bill was controlling her life, he would never again enter into any financial dealings with Bill Gray. Although Dick paid the price, he made it known to Bill the charge was totally out of line. The fact that he and Betty were having money problems was no excuse to be dishonest in his business dealings. The only thing that kept Dick from punching Bill was he was family.

Although Dick thought it was over and to be forgotten, Jo Ann was furious. She called her sister over Dick's strongest persuasion not to.

"Don't involve Betty in this," he said, "I've learned my lesson."

A good hearted and trusting person, Jo Ann felt that people took advantage of her husband's gentle nature. If he wasn't going to stick up for himself, Jo Ann sure would. She called and made it clear to Betty that she and the kids were welcome in her home anytime but she did not want Bill Gray to set one foot inside her house again.

Bill drifted from job to job. He tried his hand as a heavy equipment operator and spent some time working in the quality control division at U.S. Rubber in the City of Commerce. Probably because his brother-in-law Dan had gone to work in the heating and air conditioning field, Bill started night classes to learn the sheet metal trade. When he eventually got a job, it wasn't long until he was the talk of the construction workers' pipeline. Bill showed up on the job but he worked only sporadically. He called in sick often. And even when he clocked in, his co-workers sometimes wouldn't see him all day until it was time to go home. Curious, they discovered Bill sleeping the day away under a staircase or in an area where no one was working. When he wasn't sleeping he was sitting on a step or bucket smoking cigarettes. Surprisingly, no one complained to the boss. Some felt that Bill Gray was best left alone.

There was something about Bill and his threatening attitude that held his co-workers at bay. Bill menacingly let it be known that people better mind their own business. There was obviously a violent side to Bill's behavior. His comments in passing conversation supported his big-man attitude. If someone complained they had a problem, Bill would boast, "That would never happen to me. Nobody would dare try that on me. Boy I'd go over there with my gun and blow him away. Want me go over there and take care of it for you?"

He was constantly bragging. "I fixed them but good." Or, "I sure put the fear in them, I told them where to get off."

He never gave anyone the slightest benefit of the doubt. He left the impression that if you crossed Bill Gray you would regret it. He would seek his revenge.

Although most thought he was blowing smoke when he talked like that, no one wanted to test him.

Dan wasn't comfortable with Bill's big-man attitude either.

It wasn't until Dan heard rumors that Bill was chasing around with a woman that Dan had to confess to his co-workers that Bill was his brother-in-law.

But Bill was the big man in his household and continued to rule over his subjects with no questions asked. Betty, ever naïve, was the mouse who went through her daily routine never questioning anything Bill said or did. It was that innocence of life that allowed her to do something out of the ordinary when she decided to take the kids to see their dad while he was working out of town and living in a motel room. Although he could have come home occasionally he made excuses and stayed through the weekend. Anticipating Bill would be happy to see them, she wasn't deterred when he didn't answer the door. Finding the bathroom window open in the back of his motel room, Betty lifted Saralyn up and through the window, sending her to open the front door.

The surprise was on Betty when Bill returned. Although he was alone, he was absolutely furious to find his family there. After cussing at her and reducing her to tears he sent them home immediately. From then on, Betty had suspicions her husband was seeing someone, but to anyone's knowledge she never confronted him about it. If Betty was beginning to realize the honeymoon was over and her marriage wasn't exactly what she hoped for, she kept it to herself.

Her husband was becoming someone she never knew before. Among other things emerging from this complicated personality, was the sneaky and controlling side of Bill Gray. There was nothing open and sharing about their marriage. There was no pulling together and working as a team. On the contrary, lies and deceit was what he based his marriage on.

Quite by accident, an attempted good deed by a co-worker turned into a nightmare when Betty found out how much money

Bill was actually making. Thinking he was doing a favor because Bill was out of town on a job when the paychecks were ready, a co-worker took Bill's paycheck and gave it to Betty. It was the first paycheck she had seen in more than ten years of marriage. She told Jo Ann how surprised she was to find out Bill was making such good money, and that's exactly what Bill never wanted Betty to know. Furious at his co-worker, Bill threatened bodily harm for what he had done. Then he raised hell with his boss, making a scene that should have cost him his job.

"I'm the man in my family. My wife has no business knowing how much money I make." he shouted at his boss, Larry Rice. Bill was determined that Betty not know anything about their personal finances. He did not want her to be aware there was more money available than the pittance he parceled out at his whim.

Bill should have expected to get fired over his ranting paycheck performance. But it didn't happen, probably because Mr. Rice was selling the company and would be glad to leave personnel decisions to the new owner. But even so, Bill could not stay out of trouble. He was acquainted with the buyer and they had never gotten along. Bill figured he was going to lose his job anyway and was assured of it when he had words with the future new owner and walked off the job.

The next day when Rice opened the shop he found some tools and equipment had been stolen. On a hunch, he drove to Bill's home and found the missing items in the garage. Just days away from the sale and not wanting to take a chance of further delay, he gave Bill a choice. Return everything immediately or face charges. To anyone who would listen, Bill professed he had made a deal with Rice to buy the equipment and Rice reneged. The items were returned, Bill cried foul, and Betty was left to believe Bill was just an innocent party to a deal gone wrong.

When Dan found out about his brother-in-law's burglary, it was too late. Dan had left his job and was consequently separated temporally from the construction pipeline. Dan was planning to start his own heating and air conditioning business because California was booming and the time was ripe for construction contractors. Bill begged, pleaded, and was finally accepted as a partner when he came up with some really needed cash to help get the business started.

But from the onset the relationship between Dan and Bill was doomed. Using a room in Dan's home as an office, Bill decided he should do the office work. It was all but impossible for Dan to get him to stay on the job and earn his pay. Dan's wife Karen was going crazy with Bill in-house all day. He sent her running for his coffee and expected her to fix meals and snacks when he was hungry.

The secretary was the final blow. Dan argued they didn't need, nor could they afford a secretary, but Bill hired one anyway. However, it wasn't just any secretary. It was the girl the construction pipeline had Bill linked to months ago. It was the final straw for Dan. He gave Bill the choice of buying him out, or he would buy Bill out, but one of them had to go. Bill said he would be glad to sell and named an outrageous price. If that's what Bill thought half of the business was worth, Dan wanted Bill to buy him out at that price. With the shoe on the other foot, Bill decided the business wasn't worth that much. Fed up, Dan told Bill he could have it all.

"I'll start my own damn business without you this time. You're not going to ruin my good reputation. But I'd like to know what you're going to do without your contractor's licenses, Bill. They're right there on the wall and you'd better get up and read whose name is on them. When I go, I'm taking them with me," Dan said angrily.

Bill quickly reconsidered and named a price that was still more than it was worth and Dan grudgingly bought Bill out of the business.

"I just wanted him out of my life. I couldn't handle it anymore," recalled Dan.

Whether Bill paid off his investment loan with the buyout money or left that to his father is unknown, but Bill didn't have the money to save his home.

Both the Hales and the William Grays had been helping out but there wasn't enough money to keep up the payments on the house in Buena Park.

Bill's dad had no idea that his son was as far behind on his payments as he was until it was too late. When it all came out the house had to be sold.

Totally unaware until the last hours that she had lost her home next to her parents, Betty was devastated. She just lost everything that kept her sanity. But Bill convinced her it was his idea to sell the home because they were going to buy a worm farm and sell live bait for a living. An avid outdoorsman and fisherman, Bill would certainly have some knowledge how to market his product. William helped once again and the young Gray family moved to Fontana, California to raise worms for commercial bait.

It was a miserable old place located in a poor and crime ridden area at the base of the mountains. The house was small and desperately in need of major repairs. The large shed out back that housed the dirt worm beds was in poor condition as well, but then, Betty would joke, you wouldn't necessarily need a very fancy place to raise worms. Few, if any white children attended public schools so Betty and Bill somehow managed to put Saralyn and Jeff in private school. Bill was thrilled to be

15

where he could hunt and fish more often, Betty was nervous and apprehensive. Fontana was a far cry from the safety of Buena Park with her mother and father living right next door.

Tackle and bait stores along the windy mountain roads were always in need of fresh bait to sell. Bill set up his clients and established a daily delivery route. Waiting for worms to multiply is not physically demanding. Since the whole family participated in counting and packaging, all Bill had to do was get the worms delivered in a fresh condition.

At first Bill made all the deliveries, but soon pressed Betty to learn the routine. She could fill in when he had something else to do, or on days when he was just too lazy to go. Bill had a lazy streak which he covered with his excuses of being sick. As a child his parents released him from his duties if he pretended sickness. It worked just as well with Betty.

She didn't mind making the deliveries. Since their move to Fontana, Betty saw very little of her sister. Jo Ann wouldn't go out there and her mother came only for support and to see the kids. Making deliveries was a chance to get away for a while and talk to someone besides Bill and the kids. But she was still nervous about traveling these back roads alone, more so since by the end of the day she would have accumulated a pocket full of money. Out of concern for her daughter's fears, Dorothy often went with her. But it was an additional burden on her mother so Betty pretended she was not afraid anymore to spare her mother the need to come help. Still, Betty was sure someday she would be stopped on the road and robbed or worse.

It was for this reason Bill gave her a gun and taught her how to use it. He'd always had a fondness for guns and started collecting them years prior to his marriage. An excellent marksman himself, he was as comfortable with a gun in his hand as he was with a can of beer. Bill would be a strong advocate of teaching his children how to shoot and understand firearm safety principles.

1971 was the beginning of Bill's real, and serious, medical problems. He'd made the deliveries that one day but had not come home for dinner and was still not home when a nervous Betty fitfully dozed on the couch sometime after midnight. Whether he had been out drinking is just a guess, but he claimed to have lost control of his truck when he dodged a coyote on a narrow road near Hemet about 2 a.m.

Bill spent the next sixteen days in the hospital recovering from multiple bruises and severe pain in his head, neck and back which turned out to be the lesser of his problems. Internal bleeding led to removal of his spleen and one kidney. The remaining kidney was slightly damaged but hopes were high it would mend itself. However, three months later doctors noted further deterioration and couldn't assure Bill this kidney wouldn't fail completely sometime in the future. With all the bad news they'd been given, a bit of good news was the insurance William had taken out for Bill and his family. The insurance paid all Bill's medical expenses and replaced the truck. There are many who believe that Bill's love affair with insurance began with this accident.

Six miles South of Yellowstone National Park, the nation's oldest and largest national park, lies the Grand Teton National Park. The majestic Teton Mountains rise sharply from the floor of the beautiful valley of Jackson Hole, Wyoming. The highest peak in the range is the Grand Teton which towers 13,766 feet above sea level. Some think a more beautiful place does not exist. The early history of Jackson Hole belongs to the fur traders, Indians and "Outlaws." Fabled, Teton Jackson, a colorful sort of a bad man, "holed" up from the law in this tiny frontier town. History has it that all sorts of outlaws found refuge in "Jackson's Hole."

Originally known as a winter paradise for snow skiers, it now beckons tourists year around. Nestled in a valley 60 miles long and 20 miles wide, is a mixed atmosphere of working cattle ranches, guest dude ranches and tourists. Each year at least a million tourists will pass through Jackson on their way to, or from, Yellowstone National Park. They stop to wander the wooden boardwalks that take them to quaint little shops, renowned art galleries, huge arches of elk antlers in the town square and the famous Cowboy Bar where the standard bar stool has been replaced with real western saddles. Hundreds of tourists gather to watch the Shootout between the good guys and the bad guys staged daily in the main street. Jackson Hole goes all out for their tourists and few leave without fond memories and pockets full of soon-to-be developed film.

The valley is everything an avid outdoorsman could wish for, rafting the Snake River, hiking high mountain trails, big game hunting and trout fishing at its best. Bill and his father made several hunting and fishing trips to Wyoming. They had friends in Laramie and Jackson which prompted the first few visits. After that they came because something about the area kept drawing them back. The 1977 trip would prove to be a turning point in the young Grays' lives. While in Jackson Bill found a small pawnshop that would soon be for sale. He'd always felt he had a knack for retailing stemming from his early days in the grocery store and later in his bait business. Bill was sure this would be the opportunity he was looking for. But there were a couple of problems he would have to work out. Finding the money to buy the pawnshop, and talking Betty into moving so far away from her family would be a real challenge. Then there was the idea of leaving the mild California climate for the sometime harsh and severe weather of Jackson, Wyoming. He had to convince Betty first, and took her on the only real vacation they had been on in 17 years of marriage.

After visiting Jackson, Betty had mixed emotions. It certainly would be hard to leave her family behind, but she too had a sense that this might just be the break they needed. Here in this beautiful valley might lay the chance for success and it would be a good safe place to raise their children. Anything would be an improvement over the worm farm, she told herself. No matter how long they raised worms, no matter how hard they worked, she knew they would never have anything to show for it. Betty was willing to try anything new and different.

Jeff at age 11 thought it might be OK, especially after his dad talked about the fishing and hunting they would be doing together. But Saralyn was a teenager and very tied to her friends, school and California lifestyle. She fought bitterly to remain behind with her grandparents until she finished school but her parents would not hear of it. If they moved to Jackson they would go as a family. Bill promised them all if they would give it a couple of years and were still unsettled, he would bring them back to California.

Putting the funding together to buy the shop was the biggest problem. Bill was determined to have the shop but did not have the money for the down payment. Understandably, he dared not approach either brother-in-law. He knew he could lean on his father for some help, but he needed more than his father could spare. Yet he worked out a deal with the seller, Gene Snyder, to hold it for him while he got his financing in order and settled his affairs in California. Bill wasn't the least bit worried about getting a loan once he had enough earnest money. He would simply use his father's collateral and credit rating. The bank would think they were dealing with William R. Gray, when in fact they would be dealing with Bill (William L.) Gray. A little scribble of the initial and no one would be the wiser. It worked before. Certainly it would work again.

Sure enough in his mind that he would get the money, and having been advised of the extreme difficulty of finding any kind of suitable housing in Jackson when he did return, he made arrangements to pay the rent on Snyder's soon-to-be vacant rental house, even though they would not actually be using it for almost a year.

Betty had no idea how they would get enough money to buy the pawnshop. When she questioned how they could do it Bill snapped back that he'd damn well get the money and with no thanks to her tightwad family. She knew his father had helped before and was most likely the first source now. If the worm farm would sell, and with William's help they could probably swing the deal. Betty secretly wondered who on earth would buy this run down excuse for making a living.

She needn't have worried about that very long. Less than three months after Bill's commitment to Snyder, the worm shed burned to the ground. Bill woke Betty up in the middle of the night to tell her he smelled smoke. Together they discovered the shed was completely consumed in flames.

Even though Betty had been sleeping soundly and would not have known if Bill had been up during the night, Betty was sure Bill had nothing to do with the fire. But Jo Ann certainly did and she confronted her sister about it.

"From everything I heard that farm wasn't worth much of anything except the insurance. They couldn't make a decent living with it because I know they were getting money from my parents and Bill's parents all the time. Then it burns down and it's well insured. I said, 'Betty don't you think this is a bit too coincidental? You can't sell it. It's worth practically nothing, probably way less than what you owe on it, and one night, ... boom ... it burns down. Now you've got the money to go to Wyoming. Don't you think that's a bit much?'"

But Betty couldn't understand why Jo Ann would think that. She stood steadfast believing Bill had nothing to do with it. "It was old dry wood framed and could easily have caught fire," Betty insisted. "Bill would never do something like that," she defended. "Maybe just once in our lives something lucky happened."

The Fontana police department was not as sure as Betty. The fire was a suspected arson and all suspicion naturally leaned toward Bill since he was the only one to profit from this timely fire. Unable to prove their suspicions, ultimately the insurance company paid off. The fire remains on the Fontana police records as an unsolved arson. Since the fire destroyed their livelihood the payoff was more than just the loss of a wooden shed. Bill had the money he needed for his down payment on the pawnshop when the family left for Wyoming.

Jo Ann knew she was going to miss her sister when the family left for Wyoming, but she was happy for her to be starting a new life that may allow them to have something other than pure poverty. Because of Dick's insistence, she tried to bury the hatchet with her brother-in-law. Inviting him into her house once again, she and Dick held a large going away party for Bill, Betty and the kids. They would all be welcomed to stay anytime they came back to California to visit.

When the Grays moved to Jackson in 1978 they joined 2,600 other permanent residents. The people who live there are a pioneer kind of people, friendly, always willing to help their neighbor, a sort of ruggedness born from living and working together in nature's sometimes harsh environment in the high country. Tourist survival is a common bond, and although the financial stability of Jackson depends on the tourist, the natives look forward to the off seasons, late fall and early spring. Only then can they walk down the street, see a familiar face, take the time to stop and visit and have their town to themselves for just a short while.

The Grays moved in, opened the pawnshop, and settled into their new community and new lifestyle. Everyone, that is, except Saralyn. Saralyn remained angry with her parents for over a year and promptly rebelled against anything positive her parents tried to get her to do. But Jeff was right at home. He took up skiing on the challenging and famous ski hills and snowmobiling in the winter, fishing with his father in the summer and hunting in the fall. Sharing one of his favorite interests, Bill taught both Saralyn and Jeff how to shoot proficiently. When they knew how to care for a gun, clean it and respect it, Bill bought them each a gun of their own. In fact, over the years, Bill gave his children several weapons, from hand guns to big game rifles. Although Bill insisted Betty continue to keep her small gun with her at all times she wasn't much interested in keeping proficient. She never felt threatened living in this peaceful, beautiful valley.

Located just a few blocks off the main street, "Gene's Pawnshop" was destined to become a successful business. It wasn't long until they changed the name to "Gray's Pawnshop." Later it would be officially called "Gray's Pawnshop, Antiques and Bail Bondsman." Saralyn and Jeff helped off and on in the pawnshop and Betty helped out when the shop was at its busiest or when Bill wasn't feeling well.

Bill was right. He had a knack for the retail business. He was good at striking profitable pawn arrangements with customers who needed a quick buck. Asked what a pawnshop really is, Bill said, "Well, it's kind of a poor man's bank. They would put up collateral to secure a loan. The person could pay some interest and renew their loan if they wanted. People would walk away from things of considerable value, they just wouldn't come back, expensive jewelry, guns, cameras, videos."

Since firearms are a popular pawning item at pawnshops, Bill applied to the ATF (Bureau of Alcohol, Tobacco and Firearms) for his Federal Firearms License as soon as he bought the shop. His license allowed him to take in used firearms as a pawn item, but also to sell new ones. This was Bill's favorite department. It not only afforded him the opportunity to wheel and deal but he was constantly on the lookout to add to his personal gun collection.

When someone wanted to talk guns, Bill knew what he was talking about. He stocked all the related equipment including everything needed for reloading ammunition, a popular hobby for any gun enthusiast. He took up the hobby himself setting a place aside in his garage where he could putter around with it in his spare time. Bill possessed an extraordinary amount of knowledge about all types of firearms and his gun department would eventually be considered one of the best in town.

Gray's Pawnshop quickly outgrew the Snyder building so in 1982 Bill took out a second loan so he could move and expand the business. He had convinced his bankers that he could make a large balloon payment in just three years. Business was good now. With a better location and a larger shop Bill had no qualms that he could meet his obligations later.

Bill moved his business to 560 West Broadway on the main street of town, adding a fishing tackle department, a large line of camping equipment, music department and more jewelry. He expanded his gun department which he felt was the most profitable department in the store.

The valley surrounding Jackson is home to more than 200 various type cattle, farm and dude ranches. All ranchers treasure their firearms. Living close to mountains and to Yellowstone and Teton National Parks, the natural and protected habitat of the grizzly bear, black bear, cougar, wolf and other predators, ranchers are always prepared to protect their families and their livestock.

Surrounded by forest abundant with deer and elk, hunting season is a special time of the year for the avid big game hunter. Wyoming has wide open gun laws. Anyone of age can pack a firearm just about anywhere. Almost every rancher's pickup will contain a firearm of some type year around. Bill Gray's shop was well stocked with guns, knives and accessories ready to supply these ranchers and hunters with most everything they needed.

With business flourishing, the Gray's lifestyle was rapidly changing. For the first time Bill could purchase a home for his family without his parents help. He bought a new two story home at 435 Stacy Lane, south of downtown Jackson. Unquestionably their financial status had increased compared to their previous struggle in California.

Proud of her first real home, Betty kept it neat and clean, planting pretty flowers outside in the spring, filling the yard with color.

In keeping with her family's traditions, Betty was still like a child when it came to holidays. She decorated the house inside and out for every major occasion. One need only drive by or step into her home to know which holiday was about to arrive. Christmas was her favorite. Betty started getting excited about Christmas when the first snow began to fall in September. By October she had made and frozen enough cookie dough to supply a large bakery. Anticipating she would be quite busy at the shop as the holiday approached, she wanted to be ready with her fun filled goodie baskets that she distributed all over town with a very sincere, "Happy Holidays." Presents for family and friends were chosen with care and love. Beautifully decorated packages were shipped, delivered and tucked around a magnificently decorated tree. Lights twinkled inside and out and Christmas music filled the air. This was always a happy time for Betty.

Topping off her delight in holidays was the baking. She still made cakes for every occasion and delightfully decorated every one with that professional flair. She'd gained the reputation in town as "The Cake Lady" and her specialty cakes were in great demand by the locals.

With her outgoing friendly personality and quick witted humor, Betty made friends easily. Most notable was Janis Roby. Janis's daughter Ronda and Betty's Saralyn were close in age and grew up together even though they did not always see eye to eye. Betty and Janis were typical best friends, sharing feelings, problems, recipes and everything else good friends do.

In the early '80s the Grays and the Robys often went out on the town for dinner and dancing and they spent many a cold winter evening playing cards. However, the more Janis's husband was around Bill the less he cared to have any association with him and so the husband participation waned over the years. But the two ladies remained close friends.

Bill's tough guy attitude and intimidating behavior was still present, doubly intensified by his owning a successful business in a small town, along with his self-appointed job as a bounty hunter. He told wild stories of tracking down bail jumpers and bringing them back at gun point. Always the bravest, most fearless, most proficient bounty hunter known to man.

Decked out in his gaudy pawnshop obtained gold and turquoise watch, gold chains and bracelets, he never ceased to brag of his wealth and prosperity. Even that could be ignored by considering the source, but few people who spent much time around the Grays were comfortable with the foul language Bill used, and more so his habit of always putting Betty down in front of them. His nasty, mean and vulgar remarks struck at the very core of their sensitivities. Betty tried to laugh it off and make excuses for her husband's behavior but inwardly Janis knew that she was deeply hurt.

The Robys weren't the only friends to wonder why Betty allowed Bill to treat her like dirt. Neighbors directly across the street, John and DeeDee Batson, raised their eyebrows on more than one occasion when Betty accepted Bill's crudeness without fighting back.

"When I first met Betty around 1984 we gradually became really good friends," DeeDee recalled. "Bill totally had her under his thumb. I mean she would have dinner on the table the minute he walked in the door. If she was working with him, she came home just a little bit before Bill so she would be sure to have dinner on the table when he got there. If she came over for a cup of tea, you could see her driveway from where we had tea, and if she saw him come home she would bolt and run for the door saying, 'He's going to be mad at me, I don't have dinner on the table.'"

Sometimes Betty, Janis and I would go to the Elks to play bingo. Let's face it there wasn't much to do in Jackson in the winter, but if Janis and I wanted to stay for a drink afterward she'd say. 'Nope, can't do it. Bill will be angry if I'm not home when I should be.' Sometimes I would think this woman is nuts. I'd never put up with a man like that."

Since all three couples were members of the Elks Club and attended most of the special functions, sometimes the husbands were forced to associate with Bill. But it was the women who nurtured and maintained the real friendships.

But Bill wasn't without friends. Lee Brown and Jack Hurley were considered good friends of Bill's. For Bill the definition of good friends might be someone you can use to his best advantage, but nonetheless both men made themselves available when Bill needed them.

Jack Hurley had known the Grays since they bought the pawnshop in 1978. Jack was a few years older than Bill but they enjoyed doing the same things. Over the years they had fished and hunted, snow machined, gambled in Las Vegas and occasionally gone for a cup of coffee or lunch whenever Jack was in town.

Jack, a typical cowboy boot, Levi-wearing valley rancher had a small ranch in Bondurant, Wyoming, 36 miles southeast of Jackson. Few small ranches can survive on their own so Jack supplemented his income as an electrical contractor. Bill used Jack's services often. But Bill used Hurley for more than his electrical skills. Quick to recognize a profitable deal, legal or not, Bill offered to come to the rescue of an acquaintance that was facing some serious money problems. When he told Bill he was about to lose his backhoe because he couldn't meet his payments, Bill immediately wanted to know if it was insured. Finding that it was, Bill offered to steal it. The owner could collect the insurance and Bill would sell it on the black market and make $15,000.

The owner of this particular backhoe declined Bill's offer, but Hurley did end up storing a backhoe for Bill at his ranch. How it was obtained, is unknown. It could very well have been an unclaimed pawn item. Nonetheless, Bill's fraudulent intentions were still clearly present.

Lee Brown began his life in Alabama and for the next 34 years worked his way west ending up in Jackson about the same time as the Grays in 1978. He worked on the Triangle X Ranch and later on Senator Hanson's cattle ranch. After ending his childless marriage, Lee went to work for the U.S. Forest Service at the Snake River Campgrounds as a driver for float trips, later becoming foreman of the campground. Lee and Bill met through the pawnshop and a casual acquaintance developed into a close friendship. With Lee's mechanical background, he could fix and mend almost anything and Bill reaped the harvest of Lee's abilities.

"If it could be fixed, Lee could fix it," recalls Lee's girlfriend, Cheryl Carson.* She and her two teenage sons lived with him for almost five years. Having had no children of his own, Lee seemed to enjoy his instant family but Cheryl and Lee couldn't quite put it together to make it to the wedding chapel. Occasionally their arguments ended with Lee moving out until they patched up their differences and he would move back in.

The Gray home was always open to Lee and he stayed with Bill and Betty on more than one occasion while he sorted through his personal life. Grateful for the refuge, Lee tinkered with Bill's vehicles and snow machines and did small house repairs for Betty that Bill never seemed to get to.

A cheerful and pleasant kind of person, as well as helpful,

Betty didn't mind at all having him stay with them. She liked Lee, and he was good to her, helping take out garbage or whatever he could do to show his gratefulness for their hospitality. Lee appreciated all the little things Betty did for him and told her so. He was fond of Betty and would cringe when Bill lit into her with his foul words. "You dumb bitch" or "fat cunt" seemed to be his favorite phrases. Lee saw no reason for it. Betty did not deserve to be treated like that. He never could understand what Betty had done to be on the receiving end of these brutal outbursts. In his mind she was the kindest, gentlest person he knew.

The general consensus of those who knew Lee was that he was a little slow mentally. He could hardly read or write. He had been a bit of a loner when he met Bill Gray and it would be reasonable to assume Lee was glad to have found a friend. It would also be reasonable to assume that Bill was quite aware Lee could be manipulated to do his bidding.

No one knows how willing Lee was to participate in Bill's unlawful adventures but there is no question that he was involved. Since he had never had problems with either the law or his previous employers, and was considered incapable of mentally concocting a plan of theft, it's quite unlikely stealing a snow machine was his idea. Nonetheless a snow machine belonging to the Forest Service ended up in Bill's garage. Without Lee's help Bill could not have gained access to it. And it would have been most difficult, if not impossible, for Bill to have loaded the 400 pound machine himself.

Not very mechanically minded, Bill needed all Lee's skills. In Bill's garage, they worked evenings and weekends building a new machine using parts from the stolen machine. Anything Bill couldn't use for his machine went into the pawnshop to be sold.

The shady side of Bill Gray was always present. He never missed an opportunity to put some quick, unearned money in his pocket. Claiming his Jeep was stolen, Bill collected the insurance when it was found stripped of its usable parts at the bottom of a cliff on Teton Pass. Lee had helped strip it then followed in another vehicle to the pass where they pushed it over the side.

Most people who knew Lee swear that he had no criminal tendencies. But then, most people did not know Bill Gray well either. The relationship between the two men was strengthened by the secrets they kept. Once Lee committed himself as a partner in Bill's thefts and scams, Lee could not easily disassociate himself from Bill.

Saralyn always had suspicions her father trashed the jeep. "He wasn't upset when the Jeep got stolen. Normally he would have thrown a fit. Nobody dared take anything from my dad. Then he made a remark that the insurance was worth more than the Jeep was," Saralyn said, recalling memories from way back.

But at the time Saralyn didn't know for a fact he did it and she would not have challenged her father if she had known. Her father was important to her and in her eyes he could do no wrong. Besides, she was a teenager caught up in the problems of growing up. Adult situations were best left to her dad to contend with.

Jeff knew about the Jeep. His dad had to tell him after Jeff overheard some conversation in the shop one day. Bill made up a cock-and-bull story about the insurance company being at fault, owed him some money as a matter of fact, and this was the only way he could get it back. Caught in his deceit, Bill told Jeff not to tell his mother. Bill had several lame reasons why Jeff's mother should not know about the Jeep. Undoubtedly, Betty would have quickly recognized this as insurance fraud and would have been very upset with Bill. But this little secret was something father and son would keep. Presumably, at his young age, Jeff wouldn't have known much about insurance fraud or even truly understand the full criminal intent of this action. But Jeff always did what his dad told him to do and he quickly forgot about it.

Betty wasn't the only one totally dominated by Bill. Saralyn and Jeff had great respect for his volatility although they were not afraid of him. He had never been cruel to them, gruff sometimes, but in fact he cherished his children. Even so, they knew they would not want to take a chance on the possible consequences if they were to cross him.

Bill's list of physical injuries rose dramatically after his snow machine accident. He remembers it well, saying,

"I was getting ready for the hill climb on a real lively snowmobile and lost control. I ended up with a steel plate down here under my knee. I had compound fractures in, I believe, eleven or thirteen places ... I'm just chuck full of nuts and bolts."

Betty rapidly came to the aid of her husband after his accident. She nursed and tended to his every need while managing to open and close the pawnshop on an almost daily basis. His legs had been the most severely damaged, resulting in an extensive recovery period. Bill could have resumed responsibility for the pawnshop much earlier than he did. Instead, he continued to rely on Betty to run the business while he lounged around at home under the pretense that his legs and knees were still bothering him.

Betty really didn't mind working every day, especially after

Bill's initial recovery, for it gave her some freedom from the constant demands Bill placed on her when she was at home. She knew eventually she would be relieved of her duties at the shop, but for now she was in charge. Betty was making some important decisions on her own for the first time in her married life, and it was a good feeling for her. It gave her a feeling of achievement and she'd gained the admiration of her friends, but most notably it gave her a sense of independence.

In California the Grays had been nothing, poor, insignificant and meaningless. Here in Jackson Hole they were somebody. They were known by most everyone in town and they had something to be proud of. They were respected business people. Although she missed her family Betty wouldn't have gone back to California to live for any reason.

Bill's sister, Beverly, passed away from a cerebral hemorrhage just before Bill and Betty moved to Wyoming. Devastated by their loss, the William Grays became even more attached to their son and his family. Jeff had always been special to his grandparents because he was quiet and always willing to please. But Saralyn, they thought, was way too headstrong and determined to have her way. It wasn't so much she would have her way as it was she knew the game and she didn't want to play.

Bev's daughter buttered up the grandparents and was always rewarded financially. Saralyn refused to be a "yes, yes" person and remained independent, consequently broke, and somewhat of an outcast in the eyes of her grandmother Gray.

Even though Betty didn't appreciate the partiality they showed to Beverly's children she got along well with Bill's parents. She was certainly grateful for all their help in the early years of her marriage. She was especially fond of Bill Senior and he seemed to care a great deal for Betty as well. In California they saw a lot of each other, almost daily, but after their move to Jackson their time together was reduced to occasional visits lasting up to two weeks at a time.

The difference between the California visits and the Wyoming visits was in Wyoming they stayed at their son's home as guests. From all accounts, Bill's mother certainly considered herself a guest. She seldom bothered to get dressed, and she lounged around watching soaps on television expecting Betty to wait on her hand and foot. She never touched a dish, made her own bed, nor offered the slightest help with food preparation or chores.

Presumably not unlike her son, Sara had a tendency to be a little on the lazy side. With Betty working more now, her mother-in-law was an added burden, but one she took on without complaint. It was Bill who had the complaint. He instructed his family to watch his mother for she had a tendency to take things from the house. On one occasion after Sara packed to leave, Bill instructed his children to go through their grandmother's suitcase and remove the items he knew his mother had carefully tucked away.

Neither Betty nor Bill was very happy about their daughter's decision to get married. Although Saralyn was almost 20, her parents were sure she wasn't mature enough for marriage. They tried to talk her out of it but it was her life, not theirs, she informed them. She insisted that she was ready and willing to spend the rest of her life with Alan.

"Alan was a bum," Bill declared. "I think he thought he found a meal ticket. At first I really didn't care for him. I got him a job in Kemmer and then he lost that job. From there they went to Salt Lake for a while. When they came home they stayed with us and then finally got an apartment. Alan seemed to settle down after that and got a pretty good job here with a cement company. Then (their baby) Cree* came along almost two years later and he really loved his son. When he (Cree) was little he would pick him up and play with him a lot. The kid picked up a hell of a vocabulary almost before he could walk. He (Alan) spent a lot of time with him. After that Alan and I became really good friends and I thought the world of him. When they broke up I blamed my daughter for it. I told her what she did to Alan was horse shit, so we had feelings over that."

Just like Betty's parents, Bill was disappointed that Saralyn chose to get married rather than go on to college. So he was quite relieved that by the time he graduated from high school Jeff was more interested in schooling than girls.

When he came home over holiday breaks or for the summer he stayed with his parents. On these occasions he worked in the pawnshop and in his spare time spent some quality time with his dad hunting, fishing, four wheeling and snowmobiling. Whatever the season called for, father and son were into it. Father and son had become very close. There seemed to be a special bonding and love shared between them.

When Betty found out she was going to be a grandmother she was absolutely thrilled. She couldn't wait to have a baby shower and invite all her and Saralyn's friends to share in their joy. The baby wasn't due until January so Betty made her plans for the shower in the off season when business was slow at the pawnshop and she could devote her full attention to the party.

Betty had returned to California several times since she left. Her father had passed away in 1983 and she had traveled their frequently during his illness and later when he died. But her sister Jo Ann had never been to Jackson. Betty was hoping she could entice her sister and mother to come for the baby shower. She wasn't disappointed.

Although Dorothy had visited her daughter in Jackson before, it wasn't the best time of the year to introduce her sister to Jackson Hole. It was a cold and exceptionally gloomy November in 1984. All the tourists were gone, the streets empty of activity. Some of the businesses were closed and boarded up for the winter. Some were just closed while the owners took a break before the ski season got into full swing. Snow had been pushed into parking lots and the streets were rutted with ice.

Jo Ann's impression of Jackson was none too favorable. She could not imagine what people would do with themselves in a town that looked to her like a ghost town. But she was happy to see her sister even though she told her if they were going to get together in the future, Betty would have to come to California. Jo Ann sure wasn't planning to come back to this God forsaken, miserable place.

The shower was exceptionally nice, highlighted by a special and extravagantly decorated cake for the occasion. Most all of Betty's friends were there to celebrate and meet Betty's sister whom they'd heard so much about. Jo Ann may not have cared much for Jackson but she certainly liked Betty's friends, especially Janis who she saw often during the week she was in town.

Although they enjoyed their time with Betty, it had been kind of a rough and enlightening week for Jo Ann and Dorothy. Bill had been acting like a spoiled child and it was obvious he resented Betty taking the week off to be with her family. His constant complaining how his legs hurt and he should not be working yet was a guilt trip aimed directly at Betty's heart. If he had to work, he would do whatever he could to make Betty's time with her family shorter and less pleasant. He made all sorts of excuses why she should come down to the store. She was constantly telling her mother and sister that she had to leave but would be right back as soon as she took care of whatever it was Bill needed.

When he was home, if the women were in the kitchen, he was in the kitchen. If they were in the living room, he was in the living room. Before their visit he seemed glued to his recliner chair, now he was constantly up and down like a child who was afraid he was going to miss out on something. Meals were a nightmare. If Betty forgot the salt he would say, "Where's the goddamn salt?" Betty would get it for him. He'd drink his milk then immediately out of the blue, "Well goddamnit, can't you see my glass is empty, get me some more milk." The tirades went on and on whether it be over coffee, food, dishes, anything he could find to complain about. Never did he get up and wait on himself and Betty always jumped to do his bidding. When Bill was on the peck Dorothy would quickly leave the table and start cleaning up something just to get away. She wanted desperately to intervene, but if Betty was accepting of his attitude what could she do?

Jo Ann described it as " unbelievable." "Something happened at every meal. It was even more unbelievable why my sister took that kind of abuse."

After a particularly bad morning at the breakfast table she confronted Betty after Bill left.

"My God Betty, how do you put up with this all the time?"

She laughed and she said, "You know everybody tells me that, even Bill's friends when they come over. I guess I'm used to it and just don't notice it anymore."

Everyone but Betty noticed. Even Saralyn once confronted her father asking if he was completely helpless. "Why can't you get up and do something for yourself," she once snapped at her father.

The day before Jo Ann and Dorothy left Jackson they were suddenly made aware that regardless of Bill's constant bragging of wealth and success, Betty was still broke. Seemingly, just as broke as she had been before she left California. She'd been in high spirits all week and never burdened her family with her personal problems. But on this day when they were in town and Saralyn decided she was hungry, Betty tried, unsuccessfully, to convince her to wait until they got home. Dorothy and Jo Ann had a sandwich while Betty had only a drink. Saralyn ordered a hamburger, fries, a drink and dessert which prompted Betty to remind her she shouldn't eat so much because she was gaining a lot of weight with the baby. Saralyn and her mother had words and Betty began to cry. She wasn't really upset with Saralyn for eating so much. She was upset because she didn't have any money to buy the food. She apologized to her mother and sister that she couldn't even buy their lunch.

"We work and work and there is never enough," she cried.

October 19, 1985, Jackson residents awoke to the smell of smoke and rumors that their town was burning down. In reality three businesses in different areas of town were on fire. At 4:04 a.m. fire fighters were called to Jackson Hole Hardware, located a half block off the main street in the center of town. The 60-year-old wooden building could not be saved but the valiant efforts of the 28 fire fighters from Jackson and Wilson saved the adjoining buildings.

At 5:43 a.m., a half a mile south of the hardware store the Virginian Lodge burst into flames. By 7 a.m. the firemen had it under control however more than half of the 150 motel units were destroyed. Gray's Pawnshop was the next. At 6:50 a.m. the pawnshop burst into flames. According to the front page of the *Jackson Hole Guide*, Bill was in the pawnshop when the fire broke out.

"Bill Gray Narrowly Escapes" read the headline followed by a picture of the burned out building. Fortunately the fire at the Virginian Lodge had been contained to the point that fire fighters could turn their full attention on the pawnshop. Although completely gutted with major damage to the building itself, a small portion of the pawnshop remained standing.

Ultimately, between 75 and 80 volunteer fire fighters from throughout Teton County responded to the fires. They came from Moose, Moran, Hoback Junction and Wilson. Only crews and equipment from Teton Village were left on call to protect the rest of the county. Within hours the chilling realization of the arsonist's intended widespread destruction came to light as it was discovered that two additional businesses, the Ramada Snow King Resort and the Pioneer Cafe had been targeted but had failed to ignite.

Bad as it was, it was not as bad as it could have been. The three fires erupted an hour or so apart giving fire fighters a chance to respond to each without being overwhelmed. The crude device used to start the fires was simple enough, a lighted cigarette burned down to set off a book of matches which then ignited containers of gasoline. This gave the arsonist enough time to safely exit the building before the fire erupted.

Fortunately it was not foolproof. The cigarette burned out before it could set off the matches in the two unharmed buildings.

Investigators felt that as much as 30 to 50 gallons of fuel was used in the five incidents. Neither gas stations nor distributors checked in the entire valley remembered selling that amount of fuel to any one individual nor had any residents reported theft of any flammable material.

"Whoever did this was very angry" said Fire Chief Ken Sutton. "This person had thought out the method very carefully."

Jack Killorin investigator with the ATF (Alcohol, Tobacco and Firearms), in a *Jackson Hole Guide* interview said, "Arsonists range from the rank of someone who throws some flammable liquid on a burnable surface and tosses in a match, to the very through professional who sometimes can disguise the fact that there's been arson at all. Somewhere in between you have the businessman who burns down his own place for the insurance, or a businessman who burns down someone else's to eliminate the competition. All of the motives that go into other violent crimes can come into play in arson, from murder, extortion, trying to put down competition, insurance fraud, revenge ... all of it. Any motive is possible in arson."

Jackson investigators followed up on dozens of tips and attempted to discover some connection between the five businesses. Obviously, the owners of the five businesses were checked out first. Having no single motive to make a connection hampered the investigation and ultimately no one was arrested.

Although investigators could not prove it, the fire at the pawnshop directed some suspicion toward Bill Gray. They questioned if the same cigarette-match ignition system was used. Discovery of the failed attempts and intensive investigation provided the assumption that the first two fires were started in the same manner. At the pawnshop however, the pattern of the fire tended more to appear that a flammable liquid was spread around the interior as opposed to the starter fuel being enclosed in containers until they ignited.

The pawnshop was the last fire to start, almost an hour after the second fire. Jeff and Bill were going fishing that morning. When they were getting ready to leave they heard the sirens. Out of curiosity they went to see what was going on. Only after he found out what was going on did Bill decide he should stop at the pawnshop and get some extra tackle for their trip. He told Jeff to wait in the car, he would only be a minute. Within a few minutes, Bill came running out of the shop just seconds ahead of a blast that almost knocked him to the ground. The pawnshop erupted in flames while Jeff and his dad stood and watched.

Could this fire be the type Killorin mentioned where an amateur simply spreads fuel and throws in a match? Was it possible that when Bill realized that other places of business were burning he decided to take advantage of this opportunity? The timing was certainly right. The balloon payment on their SBA loan was soon due and the Grays purportedly were having financial problems.

There was little doubt what Jo Ann thought. About two weeks before the fire Bill had called Dick wanting to get a loan to cover the SBA payment. He said he was desperate, and he must have been to call the Buccolas after what they had already been through with Bill. He went on and on about how much collateral he had to back up the loan. Dick told him if he had that much collateral the bank would surely loan him the money. But Bill insisted that it would take too long to get it done. He needed the money right away. He started out asking for $175,000 but before he was done he talked himself into needing $225,000. The good hearted man who can't say no said he didn't have that amount of money to loan but if it would help he could put together $50,000.

Jo Ann put her foot down, reminding her husband that he would never see the money again if he loaned it to Bill. Agreeing with that statement, but thinking it would be helping Betty as well as Bill, Dick could be talked out of it only after Jo Ann made a deal with him.

"If they can't make it there (in Jackson), if they lose the pawnshop, then they can come back here and we'll put them up and take care of them," she argued.

But Dick never had to turn Bill down on his offer. Bill called and refused the $50,000 offer. He said he needed much more and asked his brother-in-law to get him in contact with a lender. Dick said he would look into it but the Buccolas didn't hear any more from Bill and forgot about it until Betty called to tell them the pawnshop burned down.

"She was real upset, kind of hysterical I think," said Jo Ann. "All Betty could think about was the pawnshop was completely destroyed and they would probably lose their house and everything else they had. I don't even think she knew it was insured. If she did, she sure didn't think it would be enough to cover their loss. I didn't tell her then what we thought because she was so upset. But it sure seemed strange and most convenient to us that every time they needed money something happened to something they owned."

It weighed heavily on the minds of the investigators that Gray could have been responsible for at least his own fire. Jackson Police Detective Dave Foster felt strongly that Bill had set the pawnshop on fire but did not feel he was responsible for them all.

"Everyone who investigated these arsons felt he was responsible for at least his fire but I didn't think health wise he could have started the others."

The investigators were unaware of the suspicious fire in California for at that point Bill Gray had not had any problems with the law either in California or Wyoming. There had never been any reason to check on his past. The insurance company paid off, the pawnshop was rebuilt bigger and better and the Grays had money to spare. At least, Bill had money to spare. Betty was still left to only guess the financial status of the Gray household.

As predicted, Bill's remaining kidney progressively deteriorated and in early spring of 1987 it could no longer sustain him. To live, he would have to go on dialysis. Bill and Betty spent eight days at Salt Lake University Hospital preparing him for his life on dialysis. Not daring to spend money for a motel room, Betty slept several nights in a chair in Bill's room until Janette Glover, undoubtedly feeling sorry for her, invited Betty to come and stay at her home.

Mrs. Glover worked at the hospital helping transplant patients and educating them about their disease and how to take care of themselves. Over her years working with kidney patients she had helped hundreds of people through their crises. Some fared better than others, some she eventually lost. Educating the patient's family was as important as that of the dialysis patients. Many of her long hours were dedicated to the families.

Betty was no exception to the problem, but she was an exception to the rule. Mrs. Glover instantly liked Betty. She thought Betty was special.

"That's only the second time I have ever had any patients'

family stay with me in all the years I have been at the University," she said. "Betty was so delightful and energetic. Bill did not fare as well. He was in denial that this was happening to him and he had extreme emotional problems associated with it. It made him sick to his stomach seeing people hooked to machines that transferred their blood from the body through a filter system and back. He couldn't stand to watch. He got very weak when he went on the machines and after given more options Bill chose peritoneal dialysis."

Peritoneal dialysis offered the freedom from attachment to a machine for several hours three or four times a week. It would allow freedom to travel without having to stop and dialyze at kidney centers along the way or while at the destination. Although not without problems, it was the best choice for Bill at the time.

Betty was so upset and concerned for Bill she wanted to give him one of her kidneys right then and there. Besides her family being against it, she was advised to wait and see how Bill did with the peritoneal system. He was not in any immediate danger and would be placed on the waiting list for a donor kidney.

A permanently implanted catheter hose was inserted into his stomach. Four times a day he would attach a bag of dialysis solution to the catheter. The solution would drain into his abdominal cavity. When the bag was empty he would fold it up and tuck it under his clothing. His body wastes and excess fluids would pass from the blood through the solution residing in the stomach, cleansing and filtering the blood. After several hours the bag would be lowered to below his stomach so that gravity would then drain the waste-filled dialysis solution back into the bag. When it was full a new bag of solution was attached starting the process again. It would take about 30 to 40 minutes each time to fill the cavity and then Bill was free to do as he pleased for about six hours until it was time for a new bag.

Four times a day, seven days a week Bill would have to stop whatever he was doing and dialyze. Cleanliness was of the utmost importance and everything had to be in a sterile condition. Bill had an ultraviolet sterilizer which he used to sterilize different items he used and handled, especially the catheter hose. Whenever he handled the catheter or solution he would wear a disposable surgical mask and gloves. The slightest infection could be extremely serious, even fatal.

Naturally, having to dialyze himself every five to six hours brought on a change in Bill's daily routine. Everyone who knew of his problems felt sorry for him and no one more than Betty. Once again she tended to his every need and concern. She rubbed his back, washed and massaged his feet, waited on him like he was a king.

Millions of Americans experience some form of kidney problem or dialysis in their lifetime but Bill acted as though he was the only one. He wanted everyone to feel sorry for him, more so his family, and especially Betty. He demanded her undivided attention when she was not at the shop. She dared not make any plans with her friends and she sensed he resented his own grandson, Cree, taking Betty's attention when Saralyn brought him by. Still Betty never complained. She picked up the demanding pace, becoming very organized, managing to do everything expected of her and then some.

Within a few weeks Bill began go to the shop late mornings to prepare the bank deposits, sign checks for the bills, check the stock and leave a list of things he wanted Betty to do. Sometimes he stayed long enough for Betty to take a lunch break, deliver a cake she'd made the night before, or run an errand. Then he would leave to make the bank deposit and not return until late afternoon when he would check out the till and remove the money.

Once again Betty was working full time and she was gaining more confidence with every passing day. She was becoming quite good in recognizing the value of something brought in for pawn. Betty used to be more comfortable when Bill was there for she had been chewed out on more than one occasion when she had paid more than Bill thought she should have for an item. But now it was getting easier for her to determine value. Betty had a tendency to pay what she felt was a fair price. Bill on the other hand was harder in nature and it came easy to him to know when he could make a very favorable bargain for a good profit, often leaving the pawner in despair over the small amount offered for their pawn.

Although Betty's life was now even more demanding, she understood Bill's need to attend to his medical problems. It was only common sense that the healthy partner in this marriage takes the bulk of the responsibility. She was sure Bill would do it for her if the situation was reversed. But working full time was one thing. Being taken advantage of was another. With Bill's natural laziness to begin with, he found that no one could blame him for not attending to his business on a more constant basis. Betty was perfectly capable of running the shop. The money was coming in and about all he had to do was count it. Occasionally he went fishing for an afternoon. He even managed a couple of trips to Las Vegas.

Las Vegas was like a magnet, drawing Bill to the town and the tables even when his health was at its worst. Caught up in the glitter of the city and in keeping with his portrayed image of wealth, Bill would deck himself out with all the jewelry he could wear ... usually two gold neck chains, several gold bracelets and an exceptionally large turquoise watch. When Bill saw the picture of a man's spinner ring he had to have it at all costs. The ring was a gift to Dick from Jo Ann. But Dick thought it was gaudy and wouldn't wear it so Jo Ann sent a picture asking Bill if he could sell it in the pawnshop.

This unusual ring was an oval shaped diamond that floated on the mounting. With movement the diamond would spin flashing brilliant sparkles in all directions. This fit Bill's personality to a tee. The ring was added to his gambling costume.

Bill's Nevada trips were puzzling to outsiders. It was the hooked gambler who would go alone specifically to gamble, more so one who was in extremely poor health, hauling suitcases full of dialysis equipment. Most wives would be concerned if their husband was a habitual gambler, but Betty never worried about Bill, in fact she looked forward to his trips. There was seldom a time he didn't return home flashing rolls of money, passing out cash to her and the kids, "proof" of his victory at the tables. Betty may have bought it hook line and sinker, but Jo Ann and Dick were very skeptical.

"Neither Dick nor I could believe he won every time he went. Those big casinos weren't built on winners," Jo Ann recalled. "I thought he might be dealing guns on the black market. Dick thought he could be dabbling in drugs. We always had a feeling his attachment to Las Vegas was more than just gambling."

Although still having to dialyze himself every four to six hours Bill finally fell into familiarity with the procedure and resumed a somewhat normal routine except for resuming full responsibility for the pawnshop. Instead of being appreciative of Betty for taking over for him in his crisis he was growly and on the peck about anything and everything.

More so than anyone else, Betty's best friend Janis knew what she was going through and tried her best to lighten her load. If Bill's pickup was at the shop when Janice drove by she would try to get Betty out for a cup of tea. It was seldom an easy thing to do. Bill scowled when Janis came in the door. He just couldn't let Betty go without first making some crude remark such as, "Jesus Christ what do you have to go to tea for," in a voice that sounded to Janis like, "What right do they have to go to tea." Janis thought Bill resented Betty leaving the shop for even an hour. Although it wasn't much of a pleasure to be confronted with Bill's foul mouth and attitude she stopped as often as she could.

Recently Betty had more on her mind than Bill and the shop. She was extremely worried and concerned about Saralyn and Cree. Saralyn and Alan had been married for four years and then divorced. Still unsettled with her life and with promises of travel and unyielding love, Saralyn took her son and went to Florida with a new boyfriend.

Bill remembered it well, "I guess he just beat the shit out of her, threatened her life and everything else. Once in a while he would let her call me. I'd tried to find out where they were and asked her if she wanted me to come and get her." I said "Where are you? And she said, 'I can't.' That's all she said, 'I can't,' because he was right there by the damn phone. Finally she got away from him. She left everything there, I mean everything. She sold all the guns that I'd given to her in a pawnshop to scrape together plane fare. She put enough money together to get a taxi out to the airport and a room for her and Cree until her flight left. She was petrified as shit that he was going to find them at the airport. He called, I can't even remember what the hell his name was, and he calls and asked if I had heard from Saralyn. I said what do you mean, heard from Saralyn and he said she had taken stuff. I guess a couple of suitcases, and she was gone. He thought I had sent her a plane ticket, and I says, 'Mister,' I says, 'If I'd known where you were, I'd been down there a hell of a long time ago. Your ass would be in jail.' When she got home I didn't know about it. She stayed with some friends for a few days. When she called I said honey this sounds like a local call. Why won't you tell me where you are? Our home is always open to you. And she started crying. I wanted to go get her but she had a friend bring her home. We all had a good bawl in the driveway. The neighbors must have thought we were all nuts. And then we proceeded to find out the living hell she'd been going through."

Although Betty was greatly relieved to have Saralyn home and safe, mother and daughter continued to experience their differences. Bill gave her everything she wanted, and now that she was home she could do no wrong. There was no question Saralyn was a daddy's girl. Saralyn loved her dad and went straight to him when she wanted something and she always got it. But then unlike her father, her mother was trying to get Saralyn to take some responsibility for her life.

Even though Betty wasn't one to share all, or dwell on personal problems, Janis was sure Betty was very troubled inside. Any form of a social life, such as it was, was almost nonexistent now. Betty had to have missed those fun times at the Elks Club, if nothing else enjoying a meal she didn't have to cook. The Elks Club was a hideaway for the locals from the tourist filled town and the Grays knew almost everyone who went there. It had always been their favorite place to go with their friends.

"They always seemed to have fun together" Janis recalls. "But Bill wouldn't take her out as much after he got sick. Their daily lives seemed centered around Bill's health and her working every day in the shop. I think overall Bill was good to Betty. I don't think he ever hit her or anything like that. He was just very unresponsive to Betty's needs."

Betty needed fresh air and a change of scenery. She longed to go places, see and do things. She needed Bill, at the very least, to acknowledge that her life changed too when he got sick. She was slowly sinking into an unnoticeable depression, a life of circumstances in which she could not foresee any change.

On the surface the Grays appeared to be doing quite well with their business. Occasionally if a piece of jewelry came through the shop that caught Bill's eye Betty would get it for a holiday present. He didn't mind spending for jewelry and pushed her to wear it constantly. The jewelry, consisting of gold and amethyst bracelets, gold chains, diamond earrings and rings, was unclaimed pawn jewelry of mediocre quality, but it served the purpose for which Bill wanted it. He seemed determined to impress others that he was successful, even if he had to embellish the truth a little.

"We had a lot of coins, half dollars, dollars, ten dollar gold pieces, Krugerrands, silver ingots, gold ingots ... you name it. We had so damned many that when we had the fire we had to haul 'em out with a backhoe. We had to make several trips to get them all out." he bragged.

But with all this display and bragging of wealth Bill kept a tight rein on Betty's financial activities, still holding her accountable for almost everything she spent, still controlling her and the checkbook. Even with all her added responsibilities she could not sign a check.

Betty wanted to have all the nice things her sister had but fell well short in the long run. Most of their furniture was Jo Ann's hand-me-downs given when they lived in Buena Park 18 years ago. The few nice accessories scattered here and there were presents from her sister.

"There was always enough money for Bill to get what he wanted," Janis remembered, "but Betty was always broke. If we went shopping I might buy a few little things but she seldom bought one thing. She said she just enjoyed looking. She begged Bill to recarpet the house, she begged him to get some new furniture, she begged him to paint the house, but he would do none of it."

Betty's close friends knew the truth. Everyone else in town thought the Grays were very well off.

Bill's work habits continued to be sporadic. Some days he worked, some days he went fishing, sometimes he went to Las Vegas. There were fewer and fewer days Bill paid any attention to the shop except to pay the bills, handle the money and order merchandise.

One of their largest suppliers for fishing tackle and camping equipment was Fanning Wholesale. Fanning Wholesale was located approximately 100 miles southwest of Jackson in the city of Idaho Falls, Idaho. Although sporting a population of only 45,000 people, Idaho Falls is the business, shopping and medical hub serving the small farming communities dotted throughout the Snake River Valley. Supporting its population growth and stimulation is the Idaho National Engineering Laboratory (INEL) contingency of scientists, engineers, technicians and high technology government subcontractors. More than 50 nuclear reactors have been built at the facility and in December 1951 the EBR-1 reactor generated man's first useable electricity from nuclear energy.

A stone's throw from the downtown business center, the clear water of the Snake River rumbles through the town providing electrical energy to the city, as well as numerous sporting activities for its residents. The closest major metropolitan city to Idaho Falls is Salt Lake City, Utah which lies 225 miles south, or Boise, the Idaho capitol, 300 miles due west. Northwestern Wyoming residents drive to Idaho Falls frequently for shopping and medical needs provided only in the larger city environment.

Gray's Pawnshop was a good account for Fanning Wholesale. As the pawnshop flourished so did friendships between the Grays and Fanning salesman, Leroy Leavitt. Roy, as everyone knew him, called on the shop on a regular basis. Over the years he and Bill struck up a friendship which led them to an occasional lunch and some fishing at nearby trout streams in the Jackson area. They'd taken their wives wild asparagus picking, went on a float trip down the Snake River and dined together when the Grays were in Idaho Falls for the Fanning Trade Shows.

Overall however, most of their friendship was based on a working relationship and that was the way Roy really wanted it. Like other people who were around Bill very long, Roy was uncomfortable with the language Bill used and how he roared and swore at Betty. Roy was a quiet and mild tempered individual and did not appreciate the way Bill treated his wife. Thinking back, Roy remembered the real Bill Gray.

"I always thought he was abusive toward Betty. In my presence he called her a bitch, using the four letter word on several occasions. He would sometimes get irritable and ignorant with his customers too, but then sometimes he was really cheerful and pleasant. Guess it depended on how he felt on any given day."

Roy had been working off and on in sporting goods stores for a little more than 10 years. He truly enjoyed his work. Selling fishing tackle and camping equipment was a natural for him, as he was an avid sportsman and thoroughly enjoyed the outdoors. His choice of living and working in southeast Idaho afforded him easy access to all the outdoor sports Mother Nature had to offer. In 1970 he went to work for Fanning Wholesale stocking shelves in the warehouse. Within months he was promoted to sales where he traveled an established route calling on customers and filling their orders. He began calling on the Grays when they first bought the pawnshop in 1978. Roy had three sons from his first marriage and two sons with his second wife LaDeana. They were married in 1971, two years after Roy's first marriage ended with a mutually agreed to divorce.

She was a quiet person, a little overweight, and some would describe her as plain. She did not wear makeup nor did she care to invest in good fitting, better quality clothing. She worked a full time job, was a marvelous cook, kept a neat and clean house and was always there when her family needed her. She was a good wife to Roy but her life centered mostly on her teenage sons. She preferred to stay at home more than anything else.

She would go with the family on weekend camping trips since they had a travel trailer with all the comforts of home, but only if Roy's co-workers wouldn't be there. She really didn't care to associate with them because when they got together she always felt left out. All they did was talk about business. She didn't understand, and she didn't want to. In that group she felt totally ignored and for that reason turned down most outings if they were going to be there.

It was certainly the men putting their heads together which resulted in the few outings the Grays and Leavitts had together. To appease Roy, LaDeana went along, but she and Betty had little in common, not much on which to base anything more than a passing acquaintance. And now that Betty was working in the shop she was just as guilty of talking business as all the others.

In 1985 Roy had an opportunity to buy into the Fanning Wholesale Company and he jumped at it. This was his life. He was good at what he did and above all, he enjoyed it. To become a partner further solidified his keen interest in, and loyalty to, Fanning Wholesale. Having been a longtime friend, as well an employee of the major stockholder, Gary Roberts, Roy was even more comfortable with his decision.

Fanning Wholesale was an aggressive, productive company, selling everything from paper clips to fishing tackle. The highlight of the year was their annual buying show held for their customers from all over the Snake River Valley and beyond. Salesmen from various factories were on hand to show the customers the newest products and offer special show pricing. Store owners and purchasers of Fanning merchandise were invited to come meet the reps and see what next year's hottest items were going to be. The Grays always came to the show and there, through Roy, met Reeda Roundy.

Reeda came to work for Fanning Wholesale as a buyer in 1984. She had worked for a sporting goods wholesaler in Denver and Salt Lake City but when she heard there was a position open in southern Idaho she jumped at the chance. She'd been in Idaho before and was well aware of what it had to offer for outdoor sport enthusiasts. If ever there was a woman who truly loved and enjoyed outdoor sports it was Reeda Roundy.

Reeda LaRene Roundy was born on March 10, 1940. As a child, growing up near Nephi, Utah, she was her daddy's little fishing partner. They went fishing more often than her mother cared to remember. She learned from her father how to tie flies. At the age of ten she could cast a fly as well as anyone.

Reeda had two older sisters. Evelyn was 12 years old when Reeda was born and Renee was 15. Since the girls were so far apart in age Reeda did not feel very close to them. She spent more time with her grandmother Hensen – so much so that eventually she lived with her even though her older sisters remained with their parents. Grandma lived only a half a block away, so Reeda had two homes to go to whenever she pleased.

The Roundys were a poor family. Reeda's father was a miner who worked long hard hours and brought home very little money. They raised rabbits and chickens for food and her mother canned vegetables and fruit, most often given by neighbors who had extra to share. Helping to feed a large family of aunts, uncles and parents as well as his own family, Reeda's dad relied on nature's resources regardless of the season. More often than not, a poached elk or deer carcass could be found hanging in a hidden place in the old barn.

"Dad almost got caught when he was cleaning a couple of pheasants and the game warden stopped by," remembered sister Evelyn. "Thank goodness the warden was an old friend. I guess Dad knew it was against the law but without that food we would have been darn hungry because we didn't have any money."

After Evelyn and Renae married and left home, Reeda became her father's hunting and fishing partner. She learned to be very proficient with a rifle, proudly bringing home her own deer when she was still just a teenager.

Just out of high school Reeda took a job in a sporting goods store in town. She could talk hunting and fishing with anyone who came in. She knew just which lure to use for the big ones and knew when and where they were biting. It seemed even then she was destined to pursue a career in the sporting goods field.

She moved to Provo, Utah after she got married in 1960. There she worked off and on at various jobs in between raising three children Clayton, Paul and Ruth Ann. After divorcing in 1977 and remarrying a year later, Reeda moved to Tucson, Arizona with her new husband. Ruth Ann, Clayton and Paul still in high school, elected to finish school with their friends and remain in Salt Lake with their father. Maybe Reeda was too independent,maybe she was unable to accept the responsibilities of marriage, or maybe she just chose the wrong men, or a combination of all three. But, by the time she moved to Denver in the early '80s she had been married and divorced for the third time. This time Ruth Ann stayed in Utah attending nursing college while Clayton and Paul dabbled in the house building business, and ultimately started their own construction company in Provo.

Reeda was a large woman, big boned and on the heavy side, yet very attractive. You would hardly notice her weight because she had good taste in clothes and was always nicely dressed. Dark brown hair surrounded a narrow face with deep dimples in each cheek. Her smile was radiant and infectious. Reeda was everyone's friend. She was like a mother to the younger Fanning employees, in fact many of them called her mom.

Everyone cared a lot about Reeda and she cared a lot about them. If anyone was down, needed a ride, needed a little money, needed anything within her power to give, she was there to help.

She instigated company picnics, invited her co-workers to dinner at her home and in the summer months she shared fresh vegetables from her big garden. The garden was her pride and joy. Living alone she certainly did not need rows and rows of corn, peas, carrots, onions and the like for just herself but she planted enough for a large family. She spent numerous hours in her garden motivated by the chance to share the vegetables. Reeda's heart was as big as the great outdoors she loved so much. Sharing and caring could best describe Reeda Roundy.

Reeda was the head buyer for Fanning Wholesale. Her knowledge of sporting goods was outstanding. Her expertise in the field was mainly concentrated on the purchase of fishing tackle and camping gear. She was a godsend to her boss, Gary Roberts. Reeda took a tremendous load off his shoulders when she came to Fanning. As president of the company, he was then free to concentrate on the company itself, purchasing only the firearms and ammunition and leaving all other categories to Reeda.

Several times a year the Fanning buyers attended trade shows in large cities all over the country. These shows were put on by major manufactures and they offered hundreds of booths to visit and thousands of items to inspect. A good buyer has a knack for purchasing merchandise that will sell quickly, keep prices competitive and above all not overstock the company. Reeda was well respected by the reps for they quickly learned she was not a pushover and would not succumb to high pressure sales tactics.

Taking owners and buyers out for dinner to show appreciation for business they'd already received, or in anticipation of favorable results the next day on the sales floor, was common practice for manufacturers reps. Over the course of an evening the reps would have an opportunity to pitch their latest items in a quiet and more intimate atmosphere compared to the busy frenzy at the show. It was at one of these dinner occasions in 1969, fifteen years before Reeda came to work for Fanning, that she met Howard Wilson.*

Howard was well known and respected by the wholesalers in the 13 states he'd covered for so many years. His wife and two children were accustomed to him being gone a lot. Life on the road with such a large territory was demanding but Howard wasn't ready to give it up and settle down with his family in Seattle. He knew his being gone so much had certainly been a strain on his marriage, but he loved his work.

Howard and Reeda became very good friends over the years. Their paths crossed frequently at the shows, and in between when he called on the companies Reeda worked for in Denver, Salt Lake and later in Idaho Falls. Although Howard was nineteen years older than Reeda they seemed to have a lot in common. Howard was just as avid an outdoorsman as Reeda. Not long after Reeda moved to Idaho Falls their relationship became more than just friendship and there was talk between them of Howard getting a divorce so they could be together.

Gary Roberts, President of Fanning Wholesale, and his wife Vada had known Howard long before Reeda came to work for them. Howard had called on Fanning for more than twenty years and was one of the reps who came to work their buying show every year. Gary and Vada had always liked Howard and eventually came to know about his and Reeda's affair, but they ignored it, maintaining it was none of their business.

Roy Leavitt also had known Howard a good many years. And it wasn't very long until he also knew about Reeda's affair, in fact she told him about it. She wouldn't hide anything from Roy for they had become the best of friends. Something between them just clicked and they thought of each other much like brother and sister. Reeda had gone camping with Roy and LaDeana a couple of times and there were occasions when Roy would go with just Howard and Reeda.

Roy was somewhat in awe of Reeda's abilities as he spoke about her. "When it came to going hunting she was, so to speak, one of the boys. We went elk hunting on several occasions. She was as good as or better than anybody I ever hunted with."

Roy had always liked Howard but didn't trust him when it came to Reeda. She was getting anxious about his divorce and Roy felt that Howard was being less than honest with her about it.

"I'm a good listener," said Roy, "and sometimes she would talk to me about Howard. She wouldn't come out and say it, but deep down she knew he might be stringing her along but she didn't want to believe it. At one time he told her he was divorced but she found out that wasn't true. He also told her he had cancer and it was hard for him to chew and swallow. He put lots of effort into every swallow he took as though it was really hurting him. He said he was going to Texas for treatments but we never saw any hair loss or other effects of treatments. Later we found out he didn't have cancer. I didn't know what to think of it unless he was stalling for time or just wanted her sympathy."

It was a distressing time for Reeda. One day Howard was supposedly packing to move to Idaho and the next day he had some excuse. Undoubtedly, Howard wasn't sure what he was going to do. He was serious enough and had apparently thought about it enough at one point to tell Gary and Vada that he was planning to leave his wife and run his business from Idaho Falls.

When he bought land in Island Park, a resort area in the mountains 85 miles north of Idaho Falls, the Roberts were sure they would eventually put it together.

Reeda and Howard spent several weekends camping on the land, clearing brush, cutting and stacking the dead trees for firewood. Howard told everyone he was going to build a cabin on that land for Reeda. Together they hunted in the fall and fished in the summer and it seemed that they were made for each other, but several years went by and Howard was still returning to Seattle and his family.

Howard's home life didn't appear to have been all sunshine and roses. For one thing his wife knew of her husband's infidelity.

"Oh you're the Reeda my husband's been dating," she accused when Reeda called on the pretense of business. They talked for a while, absent of screaming or crying. Later Reeda told Roy she thought Howard's wife was a very nice person.

Reeda called several times after that for legitimate business reasons and everything seemed all right, but she never could figure out why his wife hadn't thrown him out. Reeda wasn't happy about being "the other woman" however she felt she could justify it since Howard's wife knew about her and had taken no action. She was convinced Howard must have been telling her the truth when he said that he and his wife were no longer in love and had been living many years together only for convenience.

Shortly after divorcing her third husband, Reeda started receiving phone calls that were most disturbing. She was getting phone calls from a man who told her he had been hired by her ex-husband to kill her. He toyed with her, telling her he knew where she was at all times. Reeda began to believe it so she would not leave a forwarding address when she moved, nor would she list her phone number in the telephone book. But he always seemed to be able to locate her. His calls were spaced as much as a year apart. He told her that even though he was hired to kill her he was not going to do it. He thought she was a nice person, he would really rather date her. He sent candy and flowers and signed his name C. J. Walker.*

When Reeda asked her ex-husband about this hit man, her husband answered exactly as one would expect. No, definitely not. He had not hired anyone to kill her. There is no record of her contacting the authorities but she told Howard and her children that if anything ever happened to her they should have the authorities check out a C. J. Walker.

The whole scenario didn't stack up. Reeda was sure he was some sort of a crackpot. She was convinced he was somehow involved in the sporting goods business. She thought he might be someone who knew her through the shows she attended even though no one she asked knew of a C. J. Walker.

Reeda had always rejected Walker's invitations to meet with her. But several years later when her curiosity finally got the best of her, she agreed to meet him in a restaurant. Still concerned just enough to be cautious, she enlisted the help of a male friend who would be there if she needed help. Entering at different times, her friend observed the two in conversation for about a half hour. There was no shouting or loud voices, just a quiet conversation, then they left. Reeda did not share the content of her conversation with her friend or anyone else.

Neither the face-to-face meeting nor the passing of time seemed to lessen Reeda's concerns about her safety. In

November of 1988 Reeda approached Vada Roberts with an envelope she wanted Vada to keep for her.

"The first time she told me about it was at a buying show in Denver. She handed me an envelope and asked if I would keep it for her and if anything happened to her I was to turn it in to the authorities?' I said, 'Well Reeda what is it?' She said it was very serious, and then she told me about Walker and his threatening to kill her, the phone calls and how it unnerved her that he could find her so easily. She said she had met with him out of curiosity, wanted to see what he looked like. I kept the envelope, but then I thought and thought about it overnight and told Gary about it the next day. He said we shouldn't keep it. It should be with a lawyer or someone official. So I gave it back to her and told her just that. She said she was going to see about putting it in the safe at Fanning's. What was in the envelope I don't know, I didn't pry."

After Roy introduced Reeda to the Grays at the Fanning show, Betty and Reeda gradually became good friends. Whenever Betty was in town to pick up merchandise for the pawnshop they would go to lunch and occasionally went shopping. A few times Betty brought her car to the "The Falls" for servicing and the two women spent the entire afternoon together, sometimes just out at Reeda's house talking and relaxing. Betty even talked Bill into letting her accompany Reeda to Utah to visit Reeda's kids.

Bill and Betty had stayed overnight at Reeda's home and Reeda had spent a few weekends with the Grays in Jackson. Early in their friendship there was no indication that Bill did not like Reeda. She and Bill were friendly but distant. Just like everyone else, Reeda was uncomfortable with Bill's attitude toward Betty, his demanding attitude and ever-present foul mouth. Bill, always cautious of anyone interfering with his dominating control over his wife, would have preferred Betty to not have any friends, but he tolerated and accepted Reeda more as a business relationship than for any other reason.

As a child Bill was used to getting his own way. As an adult he could control his wife, family, finances and every aspect of his life, but he was powerless to control his own body. Bill and Betty made several trips to Salt Lake for tests to monitor his deteriorating condition. Twice he had been hospitalized with serious infections at the catheter opening. He was very careful with the sanitation surrounding his dialysis but day in and day out, sometimes hurried, the chance of infection seemed ever-present.

After one of his hospital stays Betty and Bill stopped in Rexburg, Idaho on their way home and ended up staying overnight with former neighbors John and DeeDee Batson. Rexburg was only 60 miles from Jackson but any distance was too far for Betty to travel to see friends, given Bill's angry reaction to her being away. She'd felt a deep sense of loss when DeeDee moved from Jackson, so she was quite happy when Bill agreed to stop in Rexburg.

What should have been a great visit between close friends turned into a shouting match leaving bitter feelings. Although Betty had always been a little squeamish about bloody wounds she'd been taught in Salt Lake how to cleanse and care for Bill's infected catheter opening. When Bill announced it was time for her to wash out his wound, Betty, for the first time, accidently picked up something other than the saline solution she was to start with.

"You dumb bitch, you dumb fucking cunt. You stupid bitch, what do you think you are doing?" spewed from his nasty mouth. It was more than DeeDee could take and she snapped back.

"What in the hell are you doing? Goddamnit Bill, don't you talk to her that way. This woman is trying to take care of you. You can't do it yourself. You're lucky to have someone that will do it for you."

Betty didn't cry but she was close. She was used to that kind of abuse but it was painful when he did it in front of her friends. She finished cleaning the wound and the women retreated to the kitchen, Bill to a comfortable chair and John wondering what in the hell was a nice person like Betty doing living with this creep.

By Christmas of 1987 home dialysis alone was not sufficient to keep Bill's system clear of infectious waste. His ankles were swelling and he was tired and sleepy most of the time. Supplemental dialysis on a kidney machine was required and he underwent treatment in the kidney center at the Eastern Idaho Regional Medical Center (EIRMC) in Idaho Falls twice a week. His condition was deteriorating daily and he was placed higher on the waiting list for a donor kidney.

As Bill's health worsened Betty's responsibilities at the pawnshop escalated. Now Betty literately took complete charge of the pawnshop. For the first time in their married life, Bill had to relinquish his hold over the money and allow Betty to have her name on the checking account giving her the authority to write checks.

She begged Bill to allow her to hire someone to help in the store, receiving permission only after she reminded him that she might have to leave suddenly to take him to the hospital or rush home to tend him if he needed her. He finally gave in and allowed her to hire a part-time employee, Eric Hoffman. Eric was perfectly capable of selling merchandise but had not yet learned how to deal with the pawns. Thus Betty was very reluctant to leave him alone for very long unless it was an absolute necessity or an emergency.

Life was changing rapidly for Betty. She was happier when she was at work but she still had to come home and deal with Bill's demands, in addition to the meals, housework, laundry and yard. Sometimes she would still be up baking cakes at midnight, and up at five in the morning to decorate them before opening the store.

But the one thing she missed the most was tending to her grandson. Although Saralyn would bring him by the store to see her, it was not the same. She wanted uninterrupted quality time. Cree was the apple of her eye and he loved his grandma. Anytime he saw Betty, if she was near his little play school or if she got out of a car, anywhere, anytime Cree saw Betty he would come running as fast as his little legs would take him. It was a major undertaking for Saralyn or anyone else to pry him loose. Sadly, Betty could seldom find much time to take him.

True to form, Bill used his sickness to keep Betty's full attention. If she hadn't had to go work he would have tried to keep her confined at home waiting on him hand and foot. Having no choice but to allow her to work he wanted her to be just as captive at work. He tried not to let her make many choices, but sometimes she had to. Then he made it as difficult as he could.

Making her feel guilty usually worked the best, illustrated by a simple request to take a short break with DeeDee whom Betty hadn't seen since the blowup in Rexburg over a month ago. Bill was at the store on one of his rare visits when DeeDee came in.

"Bill, can I go get a cup of tea with DeeDee?" Betty asked.

Immediately his face paled and he slumped over, "Well I just don't know if I can handle this place," he said in a low sickly tone.

"I'll only be gone 30 minutes," Betty begged.

"I just don't know if I can handle this place," he whined. "I just don't know if I can do it, but I'll close up if I can't make it."

Mustering some strength over guilt Betty went anyway.

"If he closes up, he closes up," she said. "I have to get away or I'm gonna explode," she confided to DeeDee.

In full charge of the business, Betty needed to learn everything there was to know about buying and selling retail. She wasn't sure what to buy, how much to buy, or even how much she should mark it up for a profit. Since Fanning Wholesale salesman, Roy Leavitt, was a friend as well as a business associate, Betty tended to ask Roy when he came in on Tuesdays about what she should do. Roy knew she needed a little help so he was careful not to let her buy too much of one thing or too little of another. He was not a high pressure salesman tending to overload his clients just to sell more merchandise.

"She really had the whole thing dumped on her and I wanted them (Bill and Betty) to be successful in the future, as well as now, so it was important that she learn the trade. When Bill got sick and she had to take over the pawnshop she had no idea what to do or what the product knowledge was all about. I gave her my 800 number in Idaho Falls and told her anytime she ran across something she didn't know about to give me a call and I'd help her. She would get merchandise and she didn't know what to sell it for, and I said, 'I'll tell you your cost, you tell me how much markup you want on it and I'll figure it for you.' Then she would call up and say, 'Well I sold it.' and I'd say, 'Gee that's great.' That builds up her ego you know. She was really pleased to be doing something."

Betty was appreciative of Roy's help and unlike Bill he tended to make her feel good about herself and her accomplishments. She was growing very dependent on Roy to help her make some of the business decisions.

Envious that Roy's schedule sometimes took him to different places, especially to Island Park and the area around the town of West Yellowstone, Montana that she had not seen in all the years they had lived in Jackson, Betty constantly reminded Roy of how much she would like to see that part of the country. Even though it was routine and somewhat boring to Roy, it was something Betty longed to do. She wanted to drive away, anywhere, get away from Bill's constant complaining, her worries over Saralyn and the pawnshop. She wanted some space, some quiet time, some time for herself free of the nagging daily routine.

Surprisingly her opportunity to get away, if not alone, came on a beautiful September day when Roy came in the shop on his regular Tuesday. Bill and Eric were both there when Roy mentioned he was headed to West Yellowstone, to cover an account for another salesman. Betty once again mentioned her desire to go.

Roy remembered, "Maybe it was one of Bill's good days, I don't know, but he said, 'Why don't you take Betty with you today, she could use some time away from here.' I thought it a little strange as he never seemed to care one way or the other about Betty's needs, but I took her and I enjoyed showing her the different areas she hadn't seen before. She made me stop to take pictures when she saw something that caught her eye. She was bubbly and happy. We had a real nice day."

Several weeks after the Yellowstone trip, Betty was in Idaho Falls to pick up merchandise from Fannings. It was the lunch hour and Reeda was gone but Roy was there when she went in so she jokingly told him he should take one of his best clients to lunch.

"We talked about business mostly but she told me that she didn't think Bill was as sick as he claimed to be because he was well enough to just up and leave for Las Vegas and be gone three or four days and then come home only to be sick again. After that I was more aware of what was going on and I really felt sorry for her. He just stayed home when he went on dialysis. He'd come to the shop for an hour or two and then say 'I'm sick' and go home.

"She was left basically to run the whole nine yards. She was doing everything. She was keeping up her housework, doing her cake business, running the store and tending him ... being a nurse to him. Yea, and all that time he was running her down like how she didn't know how to do nothing. When she started to cry I put my arms around her and hugged her. She said, 'Oh Roy, it's been so long since anyone has held me and comforted me. At least you seem to care.' She began to call me more often and I was really beginning to care for her a lot and really looked forward to Tuesdays so I could see her."

To Betty, Roy was a light at the end of a long dark tunnel. In total contrast to Bill, he treated her with respect and tenderness. He encouraged and acknowledged the accomplishments she made. His kind and gentle nature was indeed refreshing to someone who had been verbally beaten for years. Yes, there was a better way of life and Roy had stirred emotions in Betty she had not felt for many years.

By the fall of 1987, Roy and Betty's relationship developed into a love affair. They tried to keep it a secret from all their good friends except Reeda. Having confided in Reeda, Betty prompted her to cover for them if Bill ever happened to call or attempt to check up on her. Bound by her friendship with both Roy and Betty, Reeda would not reveal their secret. The two lovers would be left alone to seek their own destiny.

1988 didn't start out promising to be a good year. Betty had been having stomach cramps coupled with excessive bleeding and in February had a hysterectomy. Just before that, one of Bill's lungs was punctured accidentally while he was undergoing dialysis and that landed him in the hospital two days prior to Betty's surgery, so both Grays ended up in the hospital in Idaho Falls at the same time.

Knowing he would be discharged much earlier than she, Betty worried about whether Bill could get along without her. Jumping for his every need since he'd been sick she had come to think of him as literally helpless. She prevailed upon her mother and was grateful to Dorothy for coming from California to take care of Bill and the house while she was hospitalized and through her recovery.

Dorothy had been a little worried about how Bill would treat her. Sometimes he could be so abrasive and foul, but this time he was pleasant and seemed to be genuinely appreciative that Dorothy came to help out. He even took her with him one day to see her daughter in the hospital while he went in for dialysis.

Betty was recovering well and seemed in good spirits. She had reason to be happy. Roy and Reeda, two of her favorite people, had come to visit bringing flowers, candy and funny get well cards.

With her mother there to help, Betty's doctor allowed her go home early if she would promise to get lots of rest. He strongly advised her not to go back to work for at least three weeks. Her surgery had been extensive and she should not lift anything over five pounds for a month.

After a week Betty was at the shop a few hours a day and in two weeks she was back working full time. Fortunately it was the slowest season and not as demanding as the summer months. Even though Eric had been working every day, Bill had been forced to oversee the shop while Betty was hospitalized. The added responsibility had taken a toll on his already poor condition and his legs and ankles continued to swell. The only way he could relieve the pressure was by sitting in his recliner and elevating his legs. After Betty went back to work, Bill stayed home all day watching television and sleeping. He seldom left his chair.

Fortunately for Bill, Betty took immediate action when she came home one day and found him bloated and unresponsive. His skin had taken on a yellowish color and was hot to the touch yet he was shaking with cold. Sensing something was terribly wrong she rushed him to Salt Lake University Hospital where he was treated for another serious infection. Gone untreated, this one certainly could have killed him. It was the third episode of serious infection Bill had contracted but this was by far the most dangerous.

Betty had no choice but to leave him as she had to come home to work. Bill came home a week later. Although he was back to fairly good health, he remained at home propped up in his recliner smoking cigarettes, watching television and listening in on all phone calls.

The problem with being a bail bondsman was receiving phone calls at any hour of the day or night. For this reason the shop phone and home phone were connected to the same line. When the phone rang at the shop, it also rang at the house. Now that he was home so much he began to listen in on all the phone calls that came to the store. As soon as the phone was answered at the shop he would quietly pick it up at the house taking care not to breathe into the phone and hanging up only after the connection was cut off at the shop.

Betty was aware he was listening; he'd been doing it for many years. She cautioned Roy never to call her unless he was to talk only about business. If they were to discuss anything privately she would have to call him and take the chance that Bill would not pick up the phone on a whim. Ever fearful Bill would find out about Roy, and cautious about using the phone, she began sending notes and cards back to Roy with the Fanning Wholesale driver who delivered her orders on Thursdays. They were usually in a manila envelope or in a small box marked Attention Roy. The driver would either give them to Roy personally or put them on his desk.

"She'd send me notes and then she wanted an answer back. I told her I wasn't much of a note writer, but it seemed to be important to her so I'd pick up an I Love You-type card and send it up in the freight. When I didn't get down to pick up a card she would ask me to send her a note anyway and I said, O.K., I'll try to come up with something. I never kept any of her notes and cards but it didn't surprise me that she kept mine. You know how women are and sometimes the littlest things mean a lot to them. She gave me her picture. I kept it in my wallet, and she told me she kept one of me in her wallet. I think it was one she had taken when we went to West Yellowstone."

And so, the notes passed back and forth sprinkled with X's and O's for hugs and kisses and the romance blossomed. Inevitably their talk turned to marriage and Betty was certainly ready to change her life. Any spark of love and affection she used to feel for Bill had long ceased to exist. Their marriage had gone downhill faster than Bill's health. Instead of appreciating her for tending to his every need he seemed to resent her.

"You sleep on the couch," Bill would say. "Dobbie [the dog] is a better companion than you, you fucking cunt." They were words that fueled her determination to leave. No one could really love someone then belittle and degrade them like he had done to her all these years. She was nothing more to him than his nurse, cook, maid and employee.

Their sleeping arrangements had changed when he started home dialysis. She moved to the downstairs bedroom while he stayed in the master bedroom upstairs. They told themselves and their family that it was because of his dialysis equipment and the need for him to be up and down at night. Secretly Betty cherished the privacy of her bedroom. Even if Bill got well she would not willingly go back to his bed. Understandably Bill's sickness had curtailed their sexual activity. Under the circumstances it was for the best.

Betty knew Bill would be extremely angry if she left him. She had never crossed him in all their married life because she dreaded the volatile outbursts and threats that would follow. Leaving him would surely cause a major confrontation. Betty hoped she and Bill could end their marriage peacefully and without hurting the kids, but deep down she was sure Bill would fight for everything they had. She would be willing to settle for less, just to get out quickly and quietly, but she could not just walk away without anything.

She had put her whole adult life into this marriage and its assets. She was entitled to something. But no, she knew he would not send her on her way with his blessings. She would be lucky to get out with the shirt on her back until the divorce was final and the assets forcibly split.

Although she wanted a commitment from Roy that someday they would be married she needed some time to prepare. She also had real concerns about Bill's health. No matter how desperate she was to be free, she would not leave him until he was well enough to take care of himself. If he couldn't ever go back to work they would just have to sell the business. Roy and Betty would just have to wait it out.

Roy had his own problems to contend with. He had two sons at home, still in high school. He needed time to get them at least through school. He wanted to save enough money to begin his new life and take care of LaDeana too.

He was concerned about LaDeana. She certainly didn't deserve to be hurt, but he was sure he loved Betty. He was drawn to Betty because, unlike LaDeana, she was really interested in him, his business and his friends.

"I didn't want to hurt LaDeana's feelings, plus I did not want to hurt my boys' feelings, and I wanted them to be more or less on their own before I left. I really dreaded the day I would have to do it, but we were talking about waiting a few years so I kind of put telling them out of my mind. I thought I would wait until she got her divorce and then I would get mine."

Roy became the spark Betty needed to lift her spirits. She was willing to wait, no matter how long it took, until the time was right. Her first goal was the determination to lose 60 pounds. She would watch what she ate and by gradually losing weight she would be comfortable enough with her appearance to have Roy proud to have her as his wife. But Roy told her he loved her regardless of her weight.

"If you love me like this ... this isn't Betty," she said. "This is a depressed woman living in a shell. I've never been this heavy. I'm going to show you what I really look like."

"She may have been considered heavy to some people but she wasn't to me." Roy recalled. "I never thought much about her weight one way or the other but it bothered her and she really was determined to lose it."

Betty had always maintained her weight near 115 pounds until just before moving to Wyoming.

"When they left she had put on a few pounds and I attributed it to her nervousness about the worm farm and their money problems," said Jo Ann. "One other time she had gained a little weight but when she made up her mind to take it off, she did. She was 5'2" and by the time the pawnshop burned down I think she weighed close to 175 pounds which is a lot of weight for that height."

Betty recruited Janis to walk with her. Weather and time permitting they took to the streets and were a familiar sight, winding their way around town.

"I guess Roy was the incentive she needed because she was serious about losing that weight and really stuck to it," recalled Janis. For Betty it was the one thing she could do now, while she waited for Bill to get well so she could leave.

But Betty wasn't the only one in the family to have weight problems. Bill had soared close to 230 pounds which was a big load for his short 5'7" frame. He tried to hide it in the one piece coveralls he wore every day. The coveralls and men's sandals worn with socks were Bill's trade mark and seldom would anyone see him wearing anything else, unless he went to work or the weather prohibited him wearing the sandals.

His hairline was rapidly receding on top but he still had

ample hair on the sides. As with a lot of men that start losing their hair he'd grown a full beard. The dark brown beard also helped disguise the acne scars left when he was a teenager. Now in his upper forties, the gray color of aging was beginning to appear in his hair and beard. When angered, his eyebrows would turn downward and his staring dark brown eyes could penetrate your soul. When happy, his eyes twinkled and his smile was jolly. Lately though, Bill had little to be happy about. Although he had not been in good health for years, real or imagined, Bill was a sick man now and Betty was extremely concerned for him. Both of them knew if he didn't get a kidney soon he wasn't going to make it.

Still totally against the advice of her family, Betty flew to Salt Lake and was tested to see if it was possible she could donate one of her kidneys. Even though she knew their marriage was over and she was planning to leave him, she was willing to place her own welfare in jeopardy, or at the least disadvantaged, to save his life if she could. But the decision was taken out of her hands when a kidney fitting Bill's requirements suddenly became available.

When the unexpected call came that a kidney was waiting for Bill in Salt Lake, the major problem was how to get him there. Salt Lake was a good six hours from Jackson and Bill was too ill to drive himself. Betty was committed to the fullest extent to finish two wedding cakes that evening. Bill remembered it well.

"When the phone call came that I had a kidney she couldn't take me to Salt Lake. She had some wedding cakes to set up the next day and no one else could do it. First I called Janis to take me down but she had something going on with her kids the next day so I called our pastor, Roy Plummer and he took me. I paid for his lodging down there. Well, I paid for all his expenses. He stayed the night coming in and checking on me and praying with me. He stayed until my folks got there. Betty came down the next day for four or five hours but the weather was bad, especially on the pass and she had to get home to open the shop the next day."

Bill received a new kidney at the University Hospital in Salt Lake City on April 22, 1988. Fortunately for Bill, he had applied for Indigent County Aid when he started his dialysis in the spring of 1987. The county paid all his dialysis bills as well as the transplant. All Bill needed to get the aid was proving he did not have enough income to pay his medical bills. It was an easy thing for Bill to do. He was his own bookkeeper.

Within two weeks Bill was home and on the mend. Medicated to the hilt with anti-rejection drugs, water pills, blood pressure pills and anti-inflammatory medication, Bill began to learn how to live without dialysis, and with a transplanted kidney. Blood had to be drawn at least every three days. The results were telephoned to Salt Lake where they closely monitored his condition.

A transplant recipient cannot actually feel, or get any indication within themselves when an organ is rejecting. A constant monitoring, blood tests and biopsies are required to insure that the kidney stays healthy and that the recipient has not gone into the rejection stage. If it starts to reject and not caught quickly it can be fatal for the organ and subsequently the recipient.

For several months he went to Salt Lake every two weeks for biopsies and a check up. It was an exhausting routine for a man who was out of shape and in poor health. After his transplant, Bill began developing blood clots in his legs. He was put on yet another medication to thin the blood. For the next eight weeks, other than his trips to Salt Lake Bill stayed home recuperating and regaining his strength.

His doctor in Salt Lake, Dr. Karen Servilla, was pleased with his progress. There were no signs of rejection. He was in overall good condition except for his weight and Dr. Servilla recommended that he begin some sort of an exercise program. She saw no reason why he could not go back to work and resume a basically normal life even though he would be on anti-rejection medication for the rest of his life.

The medications main purpose was to slow down the immune system. The body's natural tendency is to attack any foreign object within. The new kidney would trigger the immune system to fight it. Slowing down immunity to the point where the body would accept the new kidney also slowed it down to accept infections and other diseases. For the rest of his life he must be cautious about his environment but he could function normally in every other respect.

Bill seemed to be grateful for a second chance at life. He told everyone he felt better now than he'd ever felt. Full of promises, he told Betty they were going to get away and spend some quality time together just as soon as he was up to it. He promised he was going to close the shop in the off season, take Betty on a cruise, something she had always wanted to do. But Betty didn't need lavish expensive trips and cruises. She would have been just as happy going camping if Bill would have ever taken her.

At first Betty was really encouraged. She wanted Bill to have his health back. But as the months passed she became increasingly angry. Bill was not taking good care of his new kidney. Overeating and doing nothing but lying around were exactly what his doctor had told him not to do. His weight soared. In part, the medicine he had to take had a tendency to induce puffiness and bloating, but this was controllable with exercise and diet.

The donor kidney came from a healthy 19-year-old male who never smoked, drank alcohol or used drugs. Betty felt very lucky and grateful for the kidney, but was concerned that Bill's continued abuse might destroy this precious gift.

She encouraged him to walk with her and Janis in the evenings but he refused. He bought an exercise bike and a Nordic Track, made a futile attempt to exercise, but soon abandoned the idea saying it was just too hard on his knees. However, Bill's knees were in great shape the day Jeff got married in August.

A large wedding was held at the church as the Grays welcomed Kim to their family. A pretty, petite Wyoming girl, Kim met Jeff at school where she was studying to become a nurse. The two of them were perfect for each other. Making this wedding cake was a very special joy for Betty. All the Grays friends were on hand to help celebrate the occasion including Roy, LaDeana, and Reeda who drove up from Idaho Falls. Dorothy flew in from California but Jo Ann, true to her word, sent her gift with her mom.

After dancing all night at the reception at the Elks Club, Bill had good reason to retreat to his recliner the next day. Betty had been concerned all night that he may be overdoing it but no one was going to stop him from celebrating his only son's wedding day.

But well after a reasonable recovery from the wedding celebration Bill remained at home. Bill had been a self-diagnosed sick person all his life. Now more than ever he could use his health as an excuse. Constantly complaining he didn't feel well he went from bed to recliner, recliner to bed. He wouldn't even bother to fix himself something to eat. Betty had to be sure she had a fresh lunch prepared for him every day before she went to work and the first words out of his mouth when she walked in the door after work were, "What are you going to fix for dinner tonight?"

His health would improve rapidly when his friends came by saying it was too bad he didn't feel well enough to go fishing or snowmobiling with them. Just maybe he felt well enough on that day, he would say, as he jumped up to get his gear. But when he came home it was back to the recliner complaining that he must have overdone it and quickly fell back into the same routine.

Betty knew he was faking. She had caught him in his act on more than one occasion when she came home unexpectedly and found Bill up puttering around then rushing to his chair when he saw her. As usual his defense was to put her on the defensive and he found everything he could to complain about from his meals to the cleanliness of the house. Nothing she could do would please him. And nothing except money could propel him from his chair. No matter how sick he professed to be each day, he went to the store every evening to check out the till and count his money.

Betty really wasn't quite sure how much the pawnshop was worth or how much debt was against it. Bill had made all the financial decisions in their marriage. All these years Betty's checks from her cake baking went into their bank account and for all these years when she needed groceries or anything else, she had to ask her husband for money. About all she had known was they never had enough. The IRS forms she was required to sign showed no or very little profit. Bill kept very poor records and juggled his books to be favorable to himself and less favorable to the IRS. He took cash from the business freely, often pocketing cash exchanges thus not having to report all the income. All those years she'd had only Bill's accounting to rely on, which was nothing more than he wanted her to know. Now she was finding out for herself things were much better than she ever dreamed. She just had to call and share this news with her sister.

Even though Bill was just as driven to make sure Betty did not know the full extent of their financial affairs as he had been 20 years ago when Betty accidentally received his paycheck, he was losing ground now.

Not the dummy Bill had labeled her, she found she could make decisions on her own and was developing into a sharp business woman. Ever so slightly emerging into her own person, Betty was gaining the strength needed to release herself from Bill's unrelenting dominance.

Betty clung to thoughts of her future with Roy and her notes and cards through that fall and winter stepped up her need for assurance of his love. "Will you marry me? Do you still love me? You haven't changed your mind? Until we are united in marriage."

Roy's responses were warm and loving, confirming his feelings for her. That was all she needed to make it through the winter but not without remorse for her actions. Eventually she confided in DeeDee and Janis about her relationship with Roy and often cried with shame. She was concerned Saralyn and Jeff would be really upset if she left Bill. They cared a great deal for their father. He gave them everything they wanted that he could give. He openly shared a love for them, a love he never shared with Betty. But rationally, Betty consoled herself in the knowledge that her two children were adults with lives of their own. They would not lose either parent in whole ... just the visiting place would be different.

Rumors spread rapidly in a small community and Saralyn heard rumbles that her mother may be seeing someone. Direct and to the point, Saralyn confronted her mother with what she heard. She wanted her mother to confess and say, "Yes I am having an affair" and explain it to her, but her mother denied it.

"Don't believe what you hear from your girlfriends," she told Saralyn.

But Saralyn wasn't quite ready to believe her mother. She felt her mother was holding something back. Rapidly Saralyn went to the defense of her father. She became short and snippy with her mother, blaming her for every little thing that happened. She seldom brought Cree by the store to see his grandmother where she used to stop in frequently. Saralyn and her dad often went to lunch and Saralyn made a point to make sure her mother knew how much time they were spending together. This was Saralyn's way of silently saying, "If what I heard is true and you and Dad get a divorce it will be your fault and I will take my Dad's side." Saralyn was a fighter, headstrong and determined. Some say she had a volatile personality not unlike her father's. But she could be tender and loving and sensitive like her mother unless threatened. When threatened, or deceived, she became hostile and vindictive.

By spring Betty was jokingly signing her cards to Roy "B.L.L." which was a play on her initials, the B and L for Betty Lou and the extra L for Leavitt. She had made up her mind to stay through the busy summer season and would leave Bill in September. He could either go back to work or sell the shop. Selling would be the best for her. She would get her half of the money which she intended to use to help Roy settle his financial affairs with his wife when he got his divorce. But was he really ever going to divorce LaDeana? DeeDee poised this question to Betty, "What would she do if he didn't?"

"I really needed to know inside me. Was Betty finding this strength to leave Bill based solely on the fact she had Roy?" I challenged her. "What if Roy decided not to leave his wife? What if he chickens out when it's decision time?"

She finally said, "I would leave Bill anyway."

"I didn't want her leaving Bill for another man. I wanted her leaving Bill because it was the right thing to do. Because it was the one thing that would make her the happiest."

This totally dominated, subservient woman had reached deep inside and found she could survive without Bill. Before taking on the responsibility of the pawnshop, her self-worth had been at its lowest. Now in the mainstream, meeting people, running a business, her self-esteem had risen to a level she didn't even know existed. Her desperate desire to be free drove her to set her plans in motion. Slowly, methodically, she would prepare.

She thought out her needs, then determined how she could fulfill them. She would take money from the store a little at a time so that Bill would not miss it. She could not consider it stealing. It was half hers anyway and she felt that as hard as she had worked these past few years she deserved the equivalent of a pay check. If there was plenty of money for Bill to gamble with, there should be enough for the small amounts she intended to set aside. Possibly having taken a page out of Bill's book, Betty did not account for cash transactions as diligently has she had in the past. Twenty dollars here or there, less than one roll of the dice, would be tucked away. It wasn't much, but to her it was the beginning, the beginning of her freedom.

After Betty accumulated around $200 her problem was what to do with it. Where could she keep it safely hidden from Bill? Discussing her plans and problems with Reeda resulted in Reeda opening a safe deposit box at an Idaho Falls bank. Given access to the box, Roy deposited various amounts of money Betty gave him when she saw him, usually on Tuesdays. Following her plan, Betty put several household items on layaway and made lists of personal items she anticipated taking when she left. This was a happier time for Betty. Something positive was actually happening toward her long term goal.

On the surface everything appeared normal in both households. The Grays spent a day in Idaho Falls with the Leavitts picking wild asparagus and at the invitation of Bill. Roy spent a night at the Gray's home in Jackson. Bill and Roy maintained their same casual friendship and the days ticked by.

True to her convictions Betty slimmed down to a petite 114 pounds. Bill bought Betty a white 1988 Subaru station wagon which was one of the few things Betty had ever had that was new and considered hers. It was her pride and joy and she wouldn't allow Bill to smoke in it nor would she allow their dog Dobbie to ride in it.

Bill took Dobbie with him almost everywhere he went and even though Betty loved Dobbie as much as Bill did, she did not think her new car was the place for a good-sized dog to scratch the interior and shed his hair. Since she transported her large wedding cakes in the car she was paranoid about its cleanliness. A dog in her car was just not permissible.

Although Bill's health was improving daily, his personality was not. Bill had always had a menacing temper that flared instantly when angered. Sometimes his volatile reactions coupled with his eternal filthy mouth presented a picture of a man possessed. Bill's tolerance level for dealing with life's little annoying problems was apparently on low when he was disturbed one evening by a noise at the front door.

"Betty and I were watching television. It was about 9:30 in the evening when we heard this noise. It sounded like somebody tried to pull the front door off the hinges. The dog started barking. I jumped up immediately, ran over to the closet and grabbed a pistol, ran downstairs, flipped on the light and told the dog to get 'em. There was nobody there. I couldn't see anybody. But what I found was a pizza deal on the door knob. You know like coupons. Well I was furious 'cause I went down there to protect my property and all, so I called the pizza place. I asked for the manager and told him what happened. I says, you people are nuts. You don't know how goddamned close he came to getting killed."

The manager adds that Bill threatened to "fucking blow him away" if his employee ever came back.

Was Bill all mouth and no action? His mother-in-law knew him to be a big talker but she wasn't totally convinced he wouldn't back it up. Dorothy writes, "Through the years I have heard him boast that he knew how to evade the law. He often said that he could cover his tracks so that he would never be accused of any crime."

Backing that statement was a chilling conversation Bill had with John Batson when John and DeeDee still lived across the street. After an evening of dinner and cards, Betty and DeeDee were immersed in conversation as were John and Bill. John was complaining about his ex-wife's alimony. Making the payments kept him and DeeDee so strapped that they couldn't do as many things as they would like to. His ex-wife had money of her own but she still wanted everything, John complained. He was sure it was more vindictive than anything else.

Bill, who always had the answer for everything, boasted, "Well that would never happen to me. I'd hire a hit man for $1,500 and have her knocked off."

Shocked, John said, "Bill, don't say anything like that. I don't even want to hear anything like that."

Since John knew Bill was a bit of a bragger with a big man around town kind of attitude he didn't think much more about it. Theft and insurance fraud were not the only crimes Bill Gray had thought about.

Betty was extremely upset the day she found one of Roy's cards laying on the floor in front of the closet where she thought she had them safely hidden among her cake decorating utensils. Her mind raced back, could she have dropped one the last time she was in there? No, she was sure she hadn't. That was quite a while ago and she would have noticed it before now if she had. She had been so very, very careful. There was only one conclusion, Bill found the cards and now he had to know about her affair with Roy.

She was visibly shaken and somewhat puzzled. She had never known Bill to get in her cake things. He wasn't above being nosey, but if he found these cards he was doing more than just being nosey. She wondered why he had not confronted her about it. She'd always thought that if he ever found out about Roy he would blow his stack. And why would he have left the card on the floor? He was way too sly and sneaky not to put everything back in its place exactly like he found it unless ... unless ... he wanted her to find it.

Yes, he wanted her to find it out of place so she would know that he knew about Roy. She was sure he knew about her affair now, but as the days passed she was almost relived when he hadn't mentioned it. She was not quite ready to face him.

Although Bill's parents visited their son and his family several times a year, Betty had seen little of her family since Bill had been sick, except her mother who had come to help while she was in the hospital. True to her word, Jo Ann had not returned to Jackson since Saralyn's baby shower five years ago. In that five years Betty had gone to California to visit a few times but they mostly stayed in touch between visits via the telephone. In the fall of 1988 and spring of 1989 Betty's calls were becoming more frequent.

"My sister was getting more and more depressed all the time," Jo Ann recalls. "It was getting worse and worse whenever I talked to her on the telephone. She would cry more than she would hardly ever talk. I said, 'Betty you've got to get out of this situation, you can't keep doing this to yourself.'

"But at the time I had no idea she was seeing Leroy Leavitt either. She said she couldn't handle this anymore. Bill wasn't helping. He wasn't doing a damned thing. She was wearing out and said she was just going to have to quit baking cakes even if Bill would have a fit. She was upset because she couldn't take care of Cree very often and she loved him so much, but she was just too tired after working all day, keeping the house and baking half the night. Finally she did tell Bill she was quitting the cakes and I guess he got real upset because it was really good money."

Indeed, Betty was beginning to fall apart. On a beautiful

spring Sunday in early April Bill was out fishing and Betty was home alone. Jeff and Kim were still in Portland, Saralyn and Cree were spending the day with Saralyn's friend, Janis was busy with her family and Betty felt abandoned. Her thoughts turned toward Roy. She knew he would be spending the day with his family but Bill would never do anything with her. When he felt good he was gone, when he was home he was always sick. Unusually emotional she called Jo Ann. Immediately breaking down and crying when she heard Jo Ann's voice, Betty poured out her frustrations of being terribly lonely and bored, not only at the moment, but everything that had been building her depression.

"Get on a plane and come see me" Jo Ann pleaded. "It's still the slow season so you can get away for a while."

Betty initially resisted, citing all the reasons why she couldn't get away, until Dick got on the phone. By the time he got through talking to her she was laughing and convinced to go. When Bill came home he was not happy to learn of her plans. Bill had built up a degree of animosity toward Jo Ann over the years, most likely stemming from his jealousy, and therefore didn't want Betty to spend any time with her.

"Stay with your mother while you are there, stay away from your rich bitch sister," were his orders. "Every time you come back from there you are impossible to deal with."

But Betty would not stay at her mother's; she would stay with Jo Ann whether he liked it or not. Betty had gained a new found confidence since Roy had come into her life. If she couldn't stand firm on this, how could she ever hope to stand firm when the time came for her to ask for a divorce. Recognizing her mind was made up, Bill asked her to stay until after his previously scheduled Las Vegas trip. Then she could leave the Monday after he got back. When Betty called to tell her sister when she was coming she told Jo Ann, "Plan something for every minute of every hour. When I get home I will rest. I just want to keep my mind off of things."

Betty arrived in California on April 17 and busy they were. Dick rented a limousine and took the girls out to dinner and plays. The sisters went to movies, shopped and stayed up half the night talking. Betty told Jo Ann about Roy, showing her the picture she kept in her wallet, and confided that they were in love and had talked of marriage but she was going to be sure that Bill was well enough to take care of himself before she could leave.

"She had not told Bill yet about wanting a divorce but was going to when the time arrived to where she was comfortable," Jo Ann recalled. "She felt Bill already knew about Roy because he found Roy's cards hidden in a closet and she was concerned that he hadn't mentioned it to her."

Two days after Betty arrived in California, Bill called. When she hung up the phone she was crying.

"I knew it," she said. "I knew something would happen to ruin my trip. Before I came out here Bill was telling everyone that came in the pawnshop that I was going to California when I didn't really need to."

Wanting sympathy Bill had claimed he didn't know what he was going to do, or how he was going to manage without her. "If I got too sick to work, I will just have to close the doors," he'd whined.

"He was trying to get everybody in town to feel sorry for him and make me look bad," Betty told Jo Ann. "He kept thinking I would back down. I didn't, and now he's put himself in the hospital. He's got a blood clot and has to stay there from three to six weeks. I guess I have no choice but to go home."

Once again Dick talked to her. "Didn't you tell us this was

your slow season? You've already paid for your plane ticket. Stay the rest of the week, a week isn't going to hurt that business," he pleaded.

"O.K., I'm not going back," she said after thinking about it. "I know that's what he wants me do. He probably did this on purpose. I'll stay the rest of the week."

Betty called later to be sure he wasn't lying to her and found he really was in the hospital. But she may have been correct when she thought he landed himself in the hospital.

The Saturday night before she left, he was angry. He drank heavily at the Elks Club and danced all night. Betty had warned him he should not be dancing so much. He was well aware he'd have to pay the price. He knew his legs could not take that kind of abuse without consequences. He complained all day Sunday, but Betty refused to cave in and left as scheduled on Monday.

A week later the two sisters held each other tightly as they gave their good-bye hugs. Tears were present in both sets of eyes as Betty walked down the ramp to her plane. It had been a roller coaster fun and emotional week. But compared to previous visits Jo Ann had never known Betty to be so uptight and nervous. When Betty walked down the ramp to her airplane and out of sight Jo Ann had an unexplainable strange and empty feeling. She felt she should go after her and tell her not to go home.

Jo Ann called her sister two days later to find out if it had taken Betty as long to recuperate from their exhausting week as it had taken her. "I was absolutely shocked when he answered the phone. I said, 'Bill, what are you doing home? I thought you would be in the hospital for three to six weeks.'"

He laughed and said, "Well Betty is home now so I figured I could lie in bed at home just as well as I could in the hospital."

And he did, while Betty picked up the same dismal routine

of running the business and waiting hand and foot on Bill the rest of the time. Beginning to deviate from her normally calm resignation to her situation she was flighty, frustrated, anxious and upset. Inward anger consumed her as she watched Bill languish around the house day in and day out. Having talked to his doctor, Betty knew the way to good health and a speedy recovery was a mild exercise program, but Bill made no visible attempt to even try. It was going to be a long summer for Betty.

Nothing seemed to pull her out of her depression, almost anything set her off. She lost it when she was mowing the lawn after a long day at the shop. A rock flew up and broke the windshield in her car and she began to cry uncontrollably. As usual Bill was propped up in his recliner watching television when she stormed in and shouted at him, "Why won't you get off your dead ass and help me out around here?"

Having just come from her sister's home where love and respect were abundant, Betty felt a sense of loss for the years that she had lived with a man who treated the family dog better than her. She desperately wanted to run, anywhere, to be free, to build a new life and most of all to be held and loved and cared for.

It was doubtful Betty could hold on like this until September. She'd talked to Bill before about selling the pawnshop and he'd said he would consider selling the business but not the building. That was fine with Betty she was tired of the whole responsibility. But that was months ago and he'd done nothing about it. Once again she brought up selling the pawnshop. Once again she thought her suggestion fell on deaf ears.

Bill had everything the way he wanted it and Betty realized that it was going to take more than a suggestion to force him to take action. She would have to tell Bill she wanted a divorce. It would then be his decision to keep the business or sell it. If he kept it he would have total responsibility for it. His choice, but his workhorse would be gone.

"It was at least three weeks after she came home from California. We had gotten up in the morning and she was getting ready to go to work. I approached her. We had relations the night before, and I snuggled up to her and said, 'How about a little?' She withdrew and I asked her what was wrong. She said she wanted a divorce, or that she thought she wanted a divorce, I can't remember which. That was around May 13.

"We worked that day and went out to dinner that night and I asked her if we could talk. We talked a little about how we would handle it and I said that I wouldn't quit trying. We talked about how we would split things up, we both cried. She said she was going to stay until the 15th of September and then go to her mother's for a while. I asked her if there was another man and she said, 'No Bill, no one but you.' I had no reason not to believe her."

It's doubtful that Bill accepted this news as graciously as he claims. One could only imagine that he would have jumped all over her, shouting and swearing, but she told Roy only that Bill knew she was divorcing him and he was OK about it. Roy later learned from one of his accounts that Gray's Pawnshop was up for sale, it was listed in the Wall Street Journal. Betty had no idea.

On June 3 Jo Ann received a collect phone call from Betty. "She had never called me collect before. They had lived there 12 years and she had never called me collect. Bill had just stepped out and she apologized for calling collect but for some reason Bill was going through all the phone bills. She had just told him she wanted a divorce. He asked her if anyone knew about her wanting a divorce and she told him no. So she wanted to be sure that it not be known that she had already told me. In all the time Betty lived in Jackson, unless my brother-in-law was out of town, I was never privy to a private phone call with my sister because he would always get on the extension line and listen."

Bill had insisted that Betty not tell anyone about their getting a divorce. Not Saralyn and Jeff, her family, her friends, no one. In fact he told her they would split everything they owned down the middle so there would be no reason to involve lawyers either. It was certainly the reverse from what she expected of him and she dared not tell him she had already mentioned it to Jo Ann.

Betty could understand Bill's pride might be hurt if his friends found out they were splitting up but what on earth would it hurt if her mother knew. Now, more than ever, she was quietly preparing for her departure. Aware that her mother was moving out of her big house into a smaller place closer to Jo Ann, she wrote a letter to her mother asking her to save household items that she may not need after the move.

Obviously she had to tell her why, and thus she wrote that she would be leaving Bill in September. Betty completed her letter, addressed it, sealed it and placed it in the pile of outgoing mail which Bill immediately scooped up saying he was going by the Post Office and would take the mail.

Agreeable as Bill may have appeared to a quiet and friendly divorce he had begun to rummage through everything including Betty's letter. He took it home, steamed it open and read it. Absolutely furious, he jumped all over Betty when she came home from work. Cussing and shouting he reduced her to tears and a firm promise to keep their divorce a secret.

If Jeff had been around more he may have detected something was wrong just as Saralyn had. But Jeff was taking part-time summer jobs to help support himself and Kim through school. When they did come to Wyoming, half the precious little time they did have was split between his family and his wife's family.

Jeff knew his mother wasn't the happy bubbly person she used to be but he chalked it all up to her having to take full responsibility at the store because of his father's illness. Certainly his dad would be well soon and things would get back to normal. If there was one thing Jeff was sure of it was that his mother would come to him if anything more serious was happening. They had been way too close over the years for her to withhold anything important from him.

Jeff was correct. Betty wanted desperately to tell him she was going to divorce his father. Somehow she knew he could understand where Saralyn would undoubtedly blow up and vent her anger, pushing her even further to her father's defense. But she promised Bill she would not tell them and after what she had been through before, she was going to keep that promise.

Jo Ann couldn't get Betty off her mind. Something kept nagging at her to call her sister.

"I called her again on June 22. Betty said it must be mental telepathy because she was just going to call me collect, but if Bill woke up she'd have to hang up. She said he was extremely angry and that he was blaming me for her wanting a divorce. He thought I persuaded her to do it when she was in California. When he found the letter he demanded to know who else she had told, and she finally admitted she'd told me. She said she was really nervous about the whole thing, and said she was kind of scared of him now."

Betty was in better spirits when she walked with Janis a few days later.

"It's remarkable," she commented, "Bill is coming in every day helping me. He's working out on his Nordic Track and has lost some weight."

This was good news as Betty had frequently voiced her concerns over Bill's abuse of his new kidney. Now it appeared that he was getting himself in shape and for the first time in years showed an interest in going back to work and taking charge. Finding out his wife was going to divorce him may have been the wakeup call Bill needed to get himself out of his recliner. It also prompted him to launch a campaign of extreme interest in everything his wife was doing. Nothing would escape his scrutiny.

When Bill caught Betty with a couple of boxes he was more than just curious. He was hostile.

"I noticed that things were missing. When she came home from work she brought two empty boxes. She went directly downstairs and when she came up she didn't have them. I thought it was strange. The next day I went looking for them and found them full and taped shut. Betty was working but I didn't look in them. A few days later they were gone and I assumed she took them to Janis'."

Bill confronted her about the boxes asking what was in them. She said, "Oh, little things."

"Betty, don't goddamn lie to me," he shouted at her. "I don't want anything taken out of this house. If you wanna keep this peaceful and have a no problem divorce I want this shit knocked off. In four or five days the boxes came back."

Unfortunately, that wasn't the worst to come. When Betty was out walking with Janis, Bill started going through her purse and wallet. He found that various amounts of money would build up, close to $200 and then it would be gone. He made notes as to how much each compartment of her wallet contained each day and recorded the date when the bulk of it disappeared.

He found her layaway slips from the department stores. Surely he found Leroy Leavitt's picture hidden in one of the compartments. He mentioned none of this to Betty, however she must have had an idea that Bill was snooping in her purse for she told Janis that she had to hide her purse in the washing machine or take it with her everywhere she went.

Alarmed, Janis warned Betty, "Get that picture out of your wallet, no telling what Bill would do if he found out about Roy."

The picture remained hidden in the wallet but all of Roy's cards and notes were taken to Reeda's.

For the first time in all their married life Betty did not have to, nor did she ask for permission before she could plan something. And so when she collaborated with Reeda to be her alibi, when she was going on a two night camping trip with Roy, she simply told Bill that she and Reeda were going camping with some of Reeda's relatives. Bill asked a lot of questions as he watched her pack. He wanted to know who they would be with, where they were staying and every small detail. He asked if she was still planning on leaving and she said, "Yes, you can see I'm packing."

"No," he said, "I mean are you still planning to get a divorce?"

"Yes, why are you bringing this up now? Are you trying to ruin my camping trip?"

Now that she was not hiding the divorce she found the courage to stand up to Bill. She would not let him stop her from this weekend she had planned for so long, but she couldn't keep from looking in the rear view mirror several times as she drove to Reeda's house in Idaho Falls to meet Roy. She had good reason. Later Bill drove to the Island Park recreational area in Idaho where Betty said she was going to be. His pursuit was futile for Roy and Betty had camped near Spencer, Idaho, a totally different area than where she told him she would be.

No one knows exactly what went on in the Gray household the next two weeks. Bill's version seems to differ from Janis' and Jo Ann's. Bill claims he was bending over backwards to win her back. "Treating her like a queen," were his words. Everything was just fine between them he claimed. They were calling each other "honey" and had resumed having sex.

However, Janis recalls that frequently Betty called her and said, "Call me back in a few minutes and ask me to go somewhere. I've got to get out of here."

Janis is positive there must have been severe dissension between them at that time. Betty was certainly edgy. Bill had begun to follow them when they walked in the evenings and Betty confided in Janis that Bill was acting so strange she wasn't sure she could make it until September to leave.

On July 19 Jo Ann received a second collect phone call from a very nervous Betty.

"She called me in the morning and told me that she had made an excuse to Bill that she wasn't quite ready for work yet and he would have to go without her. Not thinking that this was going to be what it was, I started rattling off things I wanted to tell her, and my sister being the way she was just waited for me to get through.

"But I could tell in her voice she was in a hurry and then she finally said, Jo Ann you can't keep telling me these things, I've got to get off this phone in case Bill gets to the pawnshop and would decide to pick up the phone. I just want you to know Bill is saying bizarre things and he is acting really weird, and if anything is to happen to me I want you to know I have a safe deposit box in Idaho Falls and it's under Reeda Roundy's name and the only people who know about it are Reeda, Roy, me and now you.

"I told her she was scaring the hell out of me and asked what was going on and what was in the safe deposit box. She said she was taking a little money so she could have it for the first and last month's rent to get her established until she could find a job and that she had some coins, some loose diamonds and some gold chains. She was very nervous and apprehensive and I could tell she was scared. I asked her to please go to a pay phone and call me back collect and let me know what was going on. She said she would, but she never did." ...

2

Shock & Suspicion

It was a clear, calm, summer morning. Idaho Falls summers are to be envied for the warm days and cooler evenings. Early mornings have a fresh, clean feeling about them, but Monday, July 24, 1989, was promising to be warmer and muggier than most. The town was beginning to awaken, but at 6:30 a.m. primarily the joggers and site workers catching the morning bus out to the Idaho Nuclear Engineering Laboratory (INEL) were the only ones stirring.

It was the usual time for Patti Donbeck to be out jogging. She took her normal route, the back roads behind the Shopko store and on to the large covered shopping mall on East 17th Street. Nearing the mall Patti heard several sirens which she believed could be either police or ambulance. Although it was not unusual to hear sirens in that area since the hospital was just blocks away, it was unusual to hear that many sirens at one time. Probably a bad accident Patti thought as she continued on her way. She didn't even think much about the strange looking guy on a bike coming toward her where they confronted each other with that "which way are you going to take" exchange. It would be almost a year later when Patti would think much more about that morning.

Roy Leavitt arrived at Reeda's house about 7 a.m. A few minutes early, but better early than late, he thought. He might have time to visit with Betty before taking Reeda to the airport. Pulling into the driveway and parking behind Betty's Subaru, Roy went to the front door and rang the bell. The door was open, the screen door closed. It had been unusually warm the past few days and even the nights offered little relief. A brick home could get quite warm in the daytime sun, retaining the heat throughout the night. Roy was not surprised the door was open.

He rang the bell a few more times without response then went around to the back door. The double sliding patio door was open, the screen door closed. Crime is so rare in Idaho Falls that little thought is given to leaving doors and windows open and screens unlocked. He called out the girls' names and received nothing but silence. This was puzzling to Roy as he knew Reeda was always prompt and timely. Since she would be catching a flight soon he was sure she would be up and ready to go.

He walked back to the front of the house, noting that Reeda's car was there, next to Betty's in front of the garage. Clearly if the girls were not home they did not leave in either car. If Reeda had decided not to go to Las Vegas she would surely have called him at home to tell him. He'd visited with the women just the night before about 7:30. Nothing was said that indicated any change in plans then, so if something came up it sure did so in a hurry.

Roy stood in the driveway for a few minutes wondering what to do. He looked up and down the road. Maybe the girls took a morning walk and were a little late getting back. No sign of anyone on the road. They probably overslept or are in the back packing and can't hear me ringing the door bell, he thought.

The farthest thing from Leroy Leavitt's mind was murder. It just didn't happen in Idaho Falls. Once in a while a domestic dispute resulted in a homicide, or the Mexican farm workers battled it out among themselves with knives and guns, but with the exception of a psycho who killed two convenience store clerks and kidnapped and killed a local school teacher a few years back, this town just did not have crime like you hear about in the larger cities. Besides, things like that just don't touch your life, it always happens to the other guy. And so when Roy went back around the house to the patio door and entered the house through the unlocked screen door he called out their names and proceeded toward the back of the house wondering ... where are they, what's going on?

Stepping into the bedroom hall he first noticed Betty in her bed, peacefully asleep. A few more steps and he saw Reeda sitting up in her bed, her head tipped back against the head board, her neck protruding forward. At first glance he thought she appeared to have a red bandanna across her face. He instantly thought Reeda may have had a heart attack as she had been seeing a doctor for heart problems. Wheeling around he called out to Betty, "Wake up; wake up, Reeda needs help."

An eerie silence and absence of stirring confronted him. A knowing feeling came over him as he stepped further into Betty's room. Although looking very much as though she were asleep, Roy could now see there was a large amount of blood under Betty's head. Her color was grey blue and he knew in an instant she was dead. He did not touch her, although this was the woman he loved, he could not bring himself to touch her.

Bolting for the telephone in the kitchen, in his extreme shock he dialed 119 instead of 911 and could barely get his hands steady enough to try again. After what seemed to him like forever he reached the 911 dispatcher and shouted, "I need the police and an ambulance. It looks like there's been a murder ... two people." As the dispatcher was trying to get an address and more information Roy blurted out, "It's written in blood on the kitchen, it says Satan Loves You."

Roy had walked around the center island on his way to the rear of the house. He'd noticed some red substance in some bowls but briefly thought Reeda had been canning red jam. Only when he came back to the phone did he notice the writing.

The dispatcher continued to press for the address and identification of the victims but as he was looking around the room he again interrupted, "They're both in their beds dead and there is stuff all over the house. Looks like there's candles and blood written, written on the stuff Satan Loves You." Asked if he was absolutely sure neither one was breathing he told the dispatcher, "I didn't check their pulse, but there's blood everywhere."

In her calming voice the dispatcher got his name, the names of the victims and assured him the police were on their way. She asked him to go back and check to make absolutely sure that neither person was alive. Roy went to each room confirming what he already knew. His best friend and his future wife had been shot to death in their beds while they slept.

Roy was grateful to the dispatcher for keeping him on the phone and keeping his mind occupied until the authorities arrived. "I can hear the ambulance coming ma'am. Do you want me to go out and wave them in?"

Police were summoned to a modest, typically middle class home in the country. Located about three miles from the city of

Idaho Falls, the house was on three acres of land surrounded by fields of grain and famous Idaho potatoes. Reeda didn't own this home, nor did she rent it. She was a house sitter.

Idaho Falls is home to a large number of Mormons whose ancestors crossed the plains in covered wagons in 1847 to escape persecution for their beliefs. These Mormon pioneers founded the town of Salt Lake City and from there many migrated north to Idaho. Often older couples whose children are grown and gone from home were called to go on missions for the church. These couples would leave their homes for a minimum of two years and re-root in other states or foreign countries to work for their church. Whenever possible it was always desirable to have someone live in and take care of their homes while they were gone.

Reeda was the perfect one for the job. She was a tidy housekeeper, kept up the lawn and garden, treating the home as though it was her own. She would pay the utilities and minor repairs but otherwise did not pay rent. The home on Crowley Road was the second home Reeda had cared for while their owners were away on missions. Roy and a few of the Fanning employees, using company trucks and their labor of friendship, had helped Reeda move into this home just seven months ago.

Upon entering this brick ranch house from the front, the formal dining area and the living room were on the north end of the house to the left. Straight back from the entryway passing the entrance to the living room and basement stairs was the breakfast area. The open kitchen, divided from the breakfast area by the center island was to the right. The large sliding patio door was located on the east wall of the house just behind the kitchen table. Beginning at a point from the living room, the main hall led to the south past the kitchen toward the bedrooms. At the end of the hall was the master bedroom and bath. The door to the master bedroom was a large double door cut at an angle which would not allow you to look directly in the room until actually stepping into the bedroom wing alcove at the end of the hall and looking somewhat back. However, if the door on the second bedroom was open, the eye would naturally look more forward toward that room, allowing a person to see directly into that room while still in the hall. This was why Roy saw Betty first, but thinking she was asleep did not become alarmed until he reached the entrance to the master bedroom and then saw Reeda.

The guest bathroom was at the end of the hall between Betty's room and a third bedroom. The full basement had one finished bedroom, a laundry room and a furnace room. Wood framed but not yet sheetrocked partitions divided future anticipated rooms, now used for storage.

Outside a large gravel circular driveway curled around the front of the house and a small canal supplying water to the farmer's fields paralleled the road. Two bridges over the canal allowed access to either end of the driveway from the main road. Large mature shrubs surrounded the front of the house on both sides of the entry steps and a variety of additional shrubs and trees helped fill in the large front yard. The two car garage and parking pad where the two cars were parked was located at the north end of the house.

Reeda's weekend hunting and fishing vehicle, a Dodge Ramcharger was parked in the left space of the two car garage while a stack of unpacked boxes occupied the other. The back yard was large with a good sized vegetable garden, fruit and pine trees and a small patio just off the kitchen sliding door. The lawn was well maintained and one would have to look hard to find many weeds in Reeda's beloved garden.

Sheriff's Deputy Kevin Cox and Sergeant Andert were the first officers to arrive at the Crowley Road home. Leavitt came rushing out from the back of the house, flagging them into the driveway. Deputy Cox reported Leavitt was extremely excited, using rapid, stuttering speech.

Roy took the officers into the house via the rear patio door and showed them where the two women were. Deputy Cox picked up the phone to tell the waiting dispatcher that officials were on the scene. She advised that another ambulance was on the way, but Cox simply stated "That won't work." and the saddened dispatcher replied, "Yea, didn't sound like it." and they signed off.

Within minutes the first of the paramedics arrived and entered the house. As they started down the hall Leavitt pointed out to Officer Cox a series of strange prints embedded in the carpet. Thereafter, Cox led all persons entering the house through a path that would avoid destroying these unusual prints.

As the two officers prepared to secure the scene, Leavitt waiting nervously but patiently outside, noticed another similar footprint in the gravel near the parking pad at the rear of Betty's car. Pointing this out, one of the officers found a box in the garage and placed it over the print to protect it from the ensuing influx of investigators and analysts yet to arrive. Having had an opportunity to study the print for a few moments, Leavitt sensed he'd seen that type print somewhere before.

A second ambulance and several more police and official cars converged on the scene. The media was arriving too as their scanners picked up radio messages from Cox to the station. Soon the scene was secured and authorities from the Bonneville

County Sheriff's Office began an investigation that would become one of Bonneville County's most lengthy and frustrating cases. The time was 7:20 a.m. and the city of Idaho Falls awoke to shattering news that two women had been killed while asleep in their beds and Satanism was involved. Otherwise open, doors and windows now were shut and locked tight.

Sergeant Kent McCandless and Detective John Cowden of the Bonneville Sheriff's Office were the first investigators to arrive at the Crowley Road home. After a quick inspection of the scene and information exchange with the patrol officers, McCandless returned to the office to request assistance from Bob Kerchusky, state fingerprint expert, and Don Wycoff of the state Forensic Lab. He was also offered the services of John Kotrason from the Idaho Bureau of Investigation (IBI), who was based in Idaho Falls.

Agent Kotrason whose job it was to assist smaller agencies with major crimes arrived early at the scene. His first task was to interview Leroy Leavitt. Leavitt told Kotrason of finding the bodies and why he was there. He told him Reeda worked for Fanning Wholesale, the same company that he worked for, and he often took her to the airport when she went on business trips. He had visited the women the night before and they were in good spirits when he left about 8 p.m.

Yes, he and Reeda were good friends. Reeda had gone camping and fishing with Roy and his family on several occasions. Asked if he knew the other woman, he acknowledged that he did. Betty and her husband had a business up in Jackson and were good customers of Fanning Wholesale. In fact, he was the salesman that called on the Grays and sold them their fishing tackle and camping gear. Yes, he knew Betty quite well, but when asked if he was having a relationship with either woman he denied it.

Kotrason didn't keep him long. They would get back with him later that day after they had a better chance to look at the situation and Roy had a chance to calm down a little. This normally quiet and gentle person was now left to sort through his thoughts, emotions, and to somehow deal with his pain.

When Delta Air Lines announced the final boarding call for passengers to Salt Lake, Vada and Gary Roberts reluctantly boarded the aircraft. They couldn't imagine why Reeda was not there. They had taken numerous flights together over the years and Reeda had never been late. She would have notified them if something had come up and she wasn't going to make the flight. However, after they took their seats and the door was closed the plane remained sitting at the ramp.

"I know that airlines don't hold flights for late passengers but in the back of my mind I kept thinking that they just might be waiting for Reeda," recalled Vada. "Even Gary said, 'Well maybe we're going to be 10 or 15 minutes late because she called and said she was on her way.' I think both of us had a feeling that something was wrong. Then when they called for Gary to come to the cockpit I was sure it had something to do with Reeda. When Gary came back he said it was a phone call from Sheriff Dick Ackerman and there was a problem with Reeda. Ackerman hadn't said what it was but we were to call his office when we changed planes in Salt Lake.

"Immediately after arrival Gary went to the nearest phone. I was standing next to Gary when he called and he went as white as a sheet and kept saying 'I should come back then, I should come back,' but the Sheriff said, 'No, we want you to go on to the show. We want you to be our eyes and ears.'"

The Roberts were asked not to tell anyone at the show about Reeda's death until they heard from him. The Sheriff wanted them to watch anyone who might have had a personal relationship with Reeda and report back if anything was said that was out of the ordinary or suspicious.

"That was a hard thing to do. Everyone knew Reeda and inquired about her. We went through that whole day of that show trying to explain where Reeda was without saying she was dead. The first day there we didn't have an appointment with Reeda's boyfriend, Howard, so we didn't talk to him. He was busy, I mean you'd glance around and you could see him but he was always busy. We didn't talk to him until the next day. By then Sheriff Ackerman had given us permission and Howard came up and said, 'Where's Reeda?' Gary said, 'There is a problem and Reeda won't be here.' 'Why?' he wanted to know. 'We have a dinner date tonight with a customer of yours and mine.'

"When Gary told him that Reeda had been shot and killed, he could hardly stand up. He grabbed a table where we were standing and kind of held on to it. He just shook his head. He looked like he had been hit in the belly. He asked all the questions, who, what, where and why but all we could say was that we didn't know," Vada said trying desperately to hold back her tears.

They avoided Howard the rest of the show because every time they saw him they thought of Reeda. It was too painful and the fact that Roy found his girlfriend and best friend dead, hurt Vada even deeper. "He really loved Betty and it was a terrible, terrible shock to him. If it hadn't been Roy it would have been us, because sometimes we picked her up when we go on these trips."

Vada couldn't help but wonder if Reeda's stalker, C. J.

Walker, had been much more serious about his threat than they had thought.

Chief Investigating Officer of the Criminal Division of the Bonneville County Sheriff's Department, Detective Victor Rodriguez, was designated by Sergeant McCandless to be the lead investigator and case officer. The son of a Mexican immigrant came to the small farming community of Burley, Idaho with his parents when he was six years old. His father was a farm hand for many years, and then went to work for Ore Ida Foods as a general laborer. A hardworking, dedicated man, Mr. Rodriguez later became a reserve for the Burley Police Department, mainly working as an interpreter for the department which dealt constantly with the swelling number of Mexican farm workers. Within a short time he was hired full time, gaining a reputation nationwide for his 162 homicide investigations which produced 100% convictions over a 30 year career.

After Victor left college his father helped him get a job with the Rupert Police Department as a patrolman. A month after he started there was a homicide and he picked up on some small clues which culminated in a conviction. From that he felt he had a knack for homicide investigation and eventually ended up learning the trade in the Detective Division in Caldwell, Idaho.

After much persuasion by Bonneville County Sheriff, Richard Ackerman, Victor moved to Idaho Falls in 1982. Hired mainly to be the link between the Spanish community and law enforcement, dabbling only briefly in homicide, it wasn't long until Sheriff Ackerman realized that every homicide case

Rodriguez was involved in, an arrest was made within three days. Quickly promoted to the Detective Division of Bonneville County, Detective Rodriguez's record stands at 23 arrests and 23 convictions which he claims would not be possible without the guys who have worked with him. "They're good," he said, "damn good."

As he stepped into the death rooms, he first noted the absence of any type of struggle or attempt to flee. Neither woman had been given an opportunity to fight for her life. Detective Rodriguez instantly felt these killings were executions, cold blooded and premeditated. Whoever they were looking for had not killed in a moment of spontaneous anger nor had they come to torture, abuse or rob. It was quiet, it was clean. Although Leavitt, in his shock, shouted to the dispatcher that there was blood all over, other than the likelihood the words on the center island had been written in blood, the only blood to be found was at the death beds. Nothing was unnaturally disturbed, nothing had been turned over or appeared out of place.

Reeda's king-sized bed was located in the left center against the north wall of the master bedroom room, facing toward the door. The entire west wall was decorated with designed mirror tiles. Investigators determined only one shot had been fired. The bullet had entered above Reeda's left ear, passed through her head, exiting on her right side above the ear, smashed into the mirrored wall, bounced off the mirrors and was found under the bed. Several particles which appeared to be bone fragments and flesh were lodged in, and surrounding, the hole in the mirror.

The investigators could not find the expended shell casing in the death room. The wall heater located on the west wall was eventually totally dismantled and every inch of the room searched. The shell casing was gone. Undoubtedly, the killer took it with him.

Reeda had been sitting up in bed when she was shot, her legs crossed, her arms crossed at the wrist, resting on her lap. She was wearing a nylon short sleeved nightgown. The bed covers were pulled over her lap as were some papers she had apparently been working on in preparation for her business meeting the next day. The blankets on the side of the bed nearest the mirrored wall were pulled back as though someone had thrown the covers back and stepped out of bed. Reeda's head was slammed back against the headboard, tilted slightly to her right, causing her throat to protrude grotesquely forward. The red bandanna that Leavitt first thought he saw was actually blood that had settled in and around the mouth. All other blood had drained down the back of the headboard. There was no spattering of blood on the wall behind her head, nor was there blood all over the bed, indicating Reeda had not lived long enough to move and scatter blood. She had died instantly.

Detective Rodriguez is confident that Reeda had fallen asleep while sitting up reading and was not aware someone was in the room. Had she been awakened she would have either turned toward the intruder and been shot in the facial area or turned away and been shot in the back of the head. The killer had the time and the patience to place this shot fairly close to her ear at a rather straight angle.

The room had not been disturbed. The dresser top was cluttered with feminine toiletry items, the drawers closed and unruffled. Two packed suitcases were in a chair. Reeda had gone to bed with every intention of catching her flight to Las Vegas the next morning.

Betty was lying on her stomach, her head on the pillow turned to her right. Her right arm was extended upwards across the pillow, her left arm straight down at her side. She was nude from the waist up wearing only under pants on a hot July night. The covers were tossed over her from the shoulders to just above the knees leaving her head and legs uncovered. The investigators felt the covers had been placed over her after she was shot.

Her feet were in a position unusual for someone sleeping on their stomach. Normally the legs would have been bent slightly in the direction of the head, one slightly ahead of the other. Seldom does one sleep on their stomach with the legs straight out, but if they did the feet would also be straight out, flat and somewhat separated. Betty's legs were straight, her heels were together and her toes were pointed straight down. This indicated to Detective Rodriguez a great degree of tension. They were not so certain she had been asleep when she died. Reeda was more likely to have been shot first and Betty may well have been awakened by the sound of that shot, forced to lie back down, then shot. Rodriguez was thoroughly convinced Betty knew what was coming.

The gun appeared to have been fired just inches from her head. The bullet entered the back of Betty's head and had exited into her pillow. There was a large concentration of blood under and around her head and trailed down the left side of her body. A portion of the blood alongside her body had been smeared outwardly as though something had been dragged or scraped through it. Again, only one shot had been fired and again the shell casing could not be found. Betty's suitcase, packed for a one-night stay with her close friend, was lying open on the floor in front of the closet.

Bed covers in both rooms were disturbed in a manner felt to

be inconsistent with normal behavior given the 90 degree temperature in the house. Special attention was given to what appeared at first to be covers thrown back as though someone had tossed them back as they got out of bed. The pillows and areas where someone would have been sleeping were examined for indentations and there were none; then vacuumed for hair and fibers. However, detectives were certain that no one else had been in the beds and that the covers were purposely placed that way to give the appearance both women had bed partners that night.

Of particular interest were the footprints embedded in the carpet. All other areas of the carpet appeared to be freshly vacuumed and relatively undisturbed except the path investigators followed. The prints appeared to have been made by shoes having a knobby type sole, similar to a sport shoe with round cleats; certainly not the common type tennis shoe or style of shoe women would normally wear. No shoes that would leave the same type print were found in the house. The prints left on the carpet were not complete enough to produce an exact size but the detectives felt the prints were large and especially larger than the women would have left. These were photographed and sections of the carpet removed for further analysis and comparison.

One set of footprints was found to enter Reeda's bedroom, going to the north side of the bed, the side from where Reeda was shot, then around the bed near the mirrored wall where they crisscrossed over each other showing a considerable amount of activity, and then exited the room. The killer either went looking for the bullet and shell casing, or to stage the bedcovers, or both. The carpet in the second bedroom was a tightly weaved commercial type and would not reveal any prints leaving the detectives to only theorize the activities of the killer there.

Following the footprint trail, detectives found them entering the living room, going directly to the recliner then exiting. Detectives were sure that at one point, either before or after the women were shot, the killer had gone into the living room and sat in the recliner. The recliner was vacuumed for clothing fibers and hair samples in anticipation that what they might find would not match other fibers or hair that would normally be in the home. The recliner also contained small particles of cheat grass which was a prevalent weed found anywhere in the area.

A third series of prints was discovered on the throw rug in the hall bathroom. The toilet seat was in the up position as a man would normally leave it indicating to the investigators the killer was male and had used the bathroom. Common sense would prevail that if Leavitt or any other invited male used the facilities the previous night while the women were still alive, surely at least Betty would have used it last thing before retiring and would have habitually left the seat in the down position.

The L-shaped center island separated the kitchen area from the small breakfast table next to the patio door. The four burner cooktop was located on the end of the smaller portion of the L, across from the phone and parallel to the main hall. Eighteen small saucers had been placed in a pattern of six each, on three sides of the island, down each side from the cooktop and across the corner of the L where it turned and divided the room.

Each saucer contained red wax and small metal bases of burned down candles. The words "SATAN LOVES YOU" had been printed on the counter top between the saucers in capital letters. A steel wool scouring pad with dark brown stains was found in the sink. Detectives concluded that the scrape marks in Betty's blood had been made by the killer scraping her blood into a bowl or container with the scouring pad; then setting about leaving his grisly message.

Besides the writing, the connotation of six saucers with candles in three rows was meant to lead investigators in the direction of a ritualistic killing designated by 666, the mark of the blasphemous beast in the Bible's Book of Revelation. Detective Rodriguez and Detective Sergeant Morgan Hendricks were the department experts on ritualistic killings and quickly dismissed any consideration of satanic involvement.

"That was easy," said Detective Rodriguez. "It was lacking a lot that would have led us to believe that. We dismissed it as a means to throw us off track. The key though was using Betty's blood. Whoever that person went to kill, Betty gave it away. We were sure it was targeted at Betty. If the killer would have been that smart he would have used Betty's and Reeda's blood and he would have made a star on each forehead. Or he would have put blood all over the place. Dismemberment or mutilation would have been another clue to Satanism."

Agent Kotrason set out to interview as many neighbors as he could find. Although there was a home across the street, Reeda's house was set back off the road far enough that a person would have to be paying particular attention to see, or hear, what might be going on across the street. The next closest neighbor was a half mile north. Not surprisingly, no one had heard or seen anything out of the ordinary the previous night.

Kotrason then proceeded to measure the rooms in the house in order to prepare a scaled diagram of the murder house. As he was measuring he found a bundle of letters tucked away in the front closet. Upon closer examination he determined that they were love notes and cards sent to Betty Gray from Leavitt. Leavitt would definitely have some explaining to do. He had previously denied having anything other than a friendship and these notes and cards certainly indicated otherwise.

The house was thoroughly photographed and videotaped

both inside and out. When that was completed, the counter top of the center island was cut off and removed for further testing. Detectives found two partially filled bottles of liquor and a glass saucer containing nine cigarette butts on the kitchen table.

Leavitt had said neither woman smoked and were very moderate drinkers. A black purse identified as Betty's sat on the table near the liquor bottles. Reeda's purse was found on the far end of the center island, her briefcase in a chair. No paper money was found in Betty's purse while Reeda's contained a fair sum of money. Noting that other valuables in the house were left undisturbed, investigators knew robbery was not the motive behind these murders.

A search of the basement yielded several of Reeda's hunting rifles in an unlocked gun cabinet; her prized .30-06 lay on a bed. None of the rifles had been fired recently.

Leaving two officers to guard the premises, investigators left the house near 11 p.m. They took with them boxes and bags of potential evidence, including bedding from the death beds, jewelry from the dresser in Betty's room, three mini cassette answering machine tapes, five handguns that also did not appear to have been fired recently, and a .38 Smith and Wesson revolver found in Reeda's Ramcharger.

What was the motive for these wanton murders the detectives pondered? There is always a reason for a homicide. It can be as simple as a killing in the rage of the moment, or obvious if committed in the commission of a burglary or sex crime. Even the most outrageous, senseless slaughtering of an individual, or a group of people, will have motivation behind it regardless of how diabolic it may be. The rule of thumb is to determine the motive and the killer will be somewhere behind it.

Until the autopsies were complete, detectives wouldn't know for sure if either woman had been sexually assaulted but there was absolutely nothing at the scene to indicate sexual motivation. Burglary was ruled out immediately. Too many things that could have been taken; jewelry, money, electronic equipment, automobiles had been left in their place. The presence of a satanic symbol didn't fit the scene. Someone wanted these women dead. He didn't want anything from them, he just wanted them dead.

Every officer involved with a homicide agrees the most difficult part of their jobs is to notify families of their loss. A death from illness gives a family time to prepare, an accident is sudden and traumatic; murder however, is so senseless the shock is unbearable. Investigators pay particular attention to reactions of family members when notified of the non-accidental death of a loved one. Statistics prove that family love, hate, relationships and money, are most frequently the force behind murder. Homicide detectives have found that most often the killer sat at the same kitchen table with the victim for many years.

When the Bonneville County Sheriff's Office called the Jackson Police Department to have their officers notify Bill Gray about Betty's death they requested that the officers pay particular attention to his reactions and what was said when they told him. Lt. Dave Foster and Chief of Police, Dick Hayes prepared to do the notification. "I was shocked when they said who it was, I would expect a number of other people but Betty Gray certainly was not a person I expected to get a call on," Lt. Foster said as he thought about seeing Betty walking around town with her friend Janis Roby.

A veteran police officer, Foster started his career in Pasadena, California in 1976. Working patrol, later advancing to detective status, he's worked more homicides than he wants to remember. While working with the Special Enforcement Team he became quite proficient at interviewing suspects and recognizing when two and two didn't quite add up to four. Having been with the Jackson Police Department 12 years, Lt. Foster came to know most of the local people. Bill and Betty Gray were no exception.

Both Foster and Hayes had been in Gray's Pawnshop on numerous occasions checking for stolen merchandise. Bill didn't like it. If items were found that were proven as stolen they were confiscated. Obviously Bill didn't appreciate losing merchandise he had paid good money for. Sometimes a customer will pawn something for much less than its value when it's stolen. They just want their money fast.

Most pawnshop operators tend to recognize suspicious merchandise and avoid it but not Bill. It was generally assumed by the officers who checked the shop that Bill had no qualms about taking in stolen merchandise. But he complained loudly when caught with it. He didn't like the officers and he didn't like them checking his shop. His attitude was rude, he was uncooperative, and his language was as foul as bad breath. He was furious when they took a stolen chain saw claiming he didn't know it was stolen and he had paid good money for it.

Having worked in the pawnshop for so many years, Betty had a pretty good idea when something came through that was suspicious and called the police on a few occasions to report it. Not once in 12 years had Bill made a report.

The Jackson Police Department will readily agree pawnshops are a proven dumping ground for stolen goods and no matter how honest or careful an operator might be, inevitably stolen merchandise will end up on their shelves. The department was working on a special ordinance that more clearly defined responsibilities of pawnshop owners, police intrusion, and subsequent confiscation. They'd been in the shop just lately to talk to Bill about this ordinance. As normal, Bill was quite belligerent and uncivil toward them even though they were there to help.

Since the officers knew Bill personally and had always known him to carry a gun, they decided to have two patrol officers wait outside while they did the notification. "Precaution," Foster said, "if there was possible guilt who knows, he might run for it or worse yet, start shooting." They established that Bill was at the pawnshop and then called for Gray's pastor who was out of town. Substitute pastor, Don Fuller of the First Baptist Church, readily agreed to be there in the event he would be needed.

At 12:15 p.m. on July 24, 1989 the two officers arrived at the pawnshop to tell Bill his wife had been murdered. While the two patrolmen and Pastor Fuller waited outside, Detective Foster and Chief Dick Hayes entered the pawnshop and were somewhat startled at Bill's initial reaction to their presence. Unlike previous visits when Bill would all but ignore them and leave them waiting until he was darn good and ready to talk to them, he came right over.

"We came in and told Bill we needed to talk to him. A couple of customers were about to leave and Bill went immediately to the door, let them out and locked the front door." Bill said his employee was at lunch and offered for them to go to the back room. The officers followed him to the back of the store.

This is strange, Lt. Foster thought, for all Bill should know is we are here to check the shop or discuss the ordinance. Why does he now want to talk in the back room? Why lock the front door, he's never done that before, he acts like he is expecting us.

Bill took their suggestion to sit down, and then was told Betty was dead. She and her friend had been murdered in Idaho Falls. Immediately Bill started wailing, a high pitched wail; "Ohoooo, Ohoooo. Oh no, oh no, not Betty." Again, Foster's suspicions were somewhat aroused.

"Reaction to a notification varies so much, but the quickness of the reaction was what seemed suspicious. It takes most people a few minutes to register what they have just been told; sometimes they just sit in disbelief for a few seconds before it really hits them."

When Bill rather quickly recovered, he asked what happened and was told they didn't know yet. The boys in Idaho Falls were still sorting it out. He wanted to know where it happened and when it happened, but he did not ask how they were killed. On the average, a relative of a homicide victim wants and needs to know how their loved one died; stabbed, shot or strangled, what? Did their loved one suffer before they died? Bill did not ask these questions.

On the contrary, Bill seemed to feel he was the one who suffered by his poor me remarks. "Oh God, the only thing I have ever been proud of is my marriage and my children. Why do things keep happening to me?" and "What's that old saying, if it wasn't for bad luck, I'd have no luck at all."

Although the officers were not yet aware that Betty had asked Bill for a divorce, if they had been, they may have thought more about his next rehearsed-sounding statement;

"When we get the place sold, we were going to sit back and clip coupons and enjoy what we had left." In a crying voice Bill said he, " ... woke up this morning was a good day, was happy and then get hit with that," then added, "Hope they catch them bastards."

They talked briefly about the last time he had seen Betty, and yes, he knew Reeda. Bill volunteered he'd been home nursing his swollen legs in the recliner most of the night. Just then the pawnshop phone rang and Hayes answered it, telling Bill it was the doctor's office and they had his lab results. But ultimately, the officers had to get down to the unpleasant, but necessary, business left to do. Lt. Foster advised Bill that they would have to get fingerprints, hair and blood samples from him. Bill wasn't considered a suspect at the time but samples had to be taken, for elimination at the crime scene if nothing else. Everyone who was close to the victims would have to go through this. Having to give samples didn't seem to bother him much, or maybe he wasn't listening, for Bill changed the subject and was compelled to ask about Betty's jewelry, grossly inflating its value.

"Christ, what about all the jewelry she had on?" Foster didn't know and asked if she tended to wear a lot of jewelry. "Oh shit, $40,000, $50,000 worth," replied Bill.

Chief Hayes offered to notify Saralyn but Bill said it was something he would have to do himself. For a few moments Bill was worried what to do with his dog before he went with officers, but decided Dobbie could stay with Eric until he could come back for him later that day.

Mentioning that Bill was in no shape to drive, more so to keep Bill with them than because of his physical condition, Foster and Hayes took Bill to the police station for fingerprinting and then to the doctor's office for the body samples. But blood wouldn't be one of them. Gray had given blood earlier that morning for his medical checks and his blood was hard to get so the doctor warned against taking more blood at that time. Since Bill was still not actually a suspect they took the doctor's advice. Then they drove Bill to Saralyn's house.

Saralyn was just leaving to go back to work. When she saw two men get out of the car followed by her father she sensed something was wrong. Saralyn instantly knew it was the police in an unmarked car and her first thought was that of Cree who was at day care. But when told it was her mom, who she knew had gone to Idaho Falls, she assumed it was an accident and her mother had gone off the pass.

"Where is she? Where did she go off? Is she alright," were her instant questions.

"No," Bill said, "Your mother has been murdered. She's dead Saralyn."

After fielding several more questions from Saralyn, Foster and Hayes left Bill with his sobbing daughter requesting that as soon as Saralyn's boyfriend, Kent Hoffman, could get there, Bill should come back to the police station.

Saralyn had previously made arrangements with her mother to bring Kent and Cree over to her parents' house for dinner that evening. She had something real special to tell them. Now as she sat on the couch with her father she wanted to tell him what it was.

"We were going to tell you and Mom tonight that Kent and I are going to get married and that you were going to be grandparents again. Now she will never know she was going to be a grandma again."

Bill raised his hand palm up and slapped himself on the forehead. "Oh my God," he said, "If I had only known. I am so sorry, if I had only known." Then he reached for her and hugged her, holding her tight. The true meaning of what her father just said was lost on Saralyn in her shock and emotional state. Her only reaction was to comfort.

"Dad, don't be sorry. It's not your fault. There's nothing you could have done."

Lt. Foster, who had been on numerous notifications through his many years in law enforcement, was disturbed with what he had heard and observed at this notification. His intuition told him something didn't smell right and as soon as he returned to the station he called the Idaho authorities.

"Hey," he said, "there's something wrong here. This guy's putting on a real good act. You really need to get over here and talk to this guy."

The detectives in Idaho Falls were working on Leavitt and weren't interested in going to Jackson, but because of Foster's insistence, decided to go later that day. At the moment though, Leroy Leavitt was in the hot seat. He was a serious suspect in the minds of the detectives. He'd been caught lying and that doesn't sit well with homicide investigators.

Detective John Cowden and Agent Kotrason confronted him with the cards and letters. Roy said that he misunderstood Kotrason's question thinking he asked him if he'd had a relationship with either woman, that weekend. One would have to know Roy to understand that to him, having a relationship was a nicer way of putting, having sex. Roy had trouble admitting, even to himself, he was having a sexual relationship with Betty. Sex was not, and never had been the driving force behind Roy's love for Betty. She was genuinely interested in him and the things he liked to do. She was cute and bubbly, with a great sense of humor and through business they had a lot in common. No, Roy truly loved Betty and sex was just a confirmation of that love.

Through Roy, detectives learned of the intended divorces. Betty had already told Bill she wanted a divorce but Leavitt had not yet told his wife. One would suspect Roy may have felt somewhat sorry for Betty considering her situation at home.

"I was really just a listening post and helped her with her

problems. She told me how lonely she was and she just wanted to be held. That's when I fell in love with her," he said in his interview.

Further probing produced an admission from Roy that he was dreading the day he would have to tell LaDeana he wanted a divorce which indicated he was in no hurry to hurt or leave his wife and family. Roy's answers to Betty's notes depict her growing need to confirm his intentions, witnessed by his responses of, "No, I haven't changed my mind." "Of course we will always be together." and "We will be together soon." Quite possibly Roy was under pressure to get his divorce much before he was ready, and that is precisely what Cowden and Kotrason wanted to know. If Betty had been putting undue pressure on Roy that could certainly be a motive for murder.

Pressed for more information, Roy told officers about the safe deposit box. No, it wasn't his and Reeda's deposit box. It was really supposed to be Betty's and Reeda's but Betty never got in to sign for it so he had been putting things in it for both of them. He was not sure what all was in the box or exactly how much money was actually in it. Roy answered all the officers' questions even though he didn't think he knew anything that could help them. They would interview him at great length the next day.

Around 4 p.m. Detective Rodriguez and Detective John Cowden arrived in Jackson. Saralyn, her boyfriend Kent and Bill were already at the police station. The detectives talked to Saralyn first. She was very emotional and still in a state of denial. She talked about her mother and father, she loved her mother and father very much. Her father was good to everyone in the family and her parents were definitely very happily married. They had a nice family, she thought. She knew of no one who would have reason to harm her mother. The detectives couldn't talk to Saralyn very long. The more she talked the more emotional she became and the detectives said they would come back another time.

Their initial insight into Bill Gray was rather sinister. He was armed with a small caliber pistol which they immediately took from him before starting his interview. Still not considered a suspect, but certainly in the running, detectives would pay close attention to everything about Gray. Detective Rodriguez noted that Bill appeared to be worn out, tired, complained about his legs, knees and back. He had bloodshot eyes and said that he didn't feel good. Yes, he would have had a very stressful and emotional afternoon. Understandably he would not feel very good after he heard about Betty, but if he had been in Idaho Falls the previous night he could also be worn out from a lack of sleep.

Sympathetic to his loss, but having to do their job, he was told they wouldn't keep him long but they needed to ask him questions to gain information which would help them find Betty's killer. They wanted to get into Betty's life. They wanted to know about the divorce and they wanted to know where he was Sunday night.

Showing no signs of emotion Bill talked to the detectives. He said Betty wanted the divorce. She had gone to California and when she came back she wanted a divorce. He was sure it was "That million dollar rich bitch sister" of hers that started it all. He suspected another man but when he asked Betty about it she denied having another man. She was not planning to leave until September and Bill was confident they would have patched things up by then. He would never have quit trying. He would always love her.

His recollection of the last time he saw Betty was Sunday morning. He and Betty had planned to go to the Wilson Chicken

Fry with the Robys, but then she changed her mind and decided to go stay with Reeda in Idaho Falls and take her to the airport the next morning. Reeda and Betty were real good friends. Betty had stayed overnight with Reeda before and they had fairly recently gone on a camping trip together.

She straightened up the house and made a salad for his dinner before she left. He asked her why she was going so early and she said they were going to do some shopping and she would help Reeda pack. He went to work about 9 a.m. and thought Janis said Betty left for Idaho Falls around 11:30 a.m.

His health had been a real problem for the family and had been very stressful on Betty because he almost died. He would have if he hadn't gotten a donor kidney. He thought Betty had been kind of depressed because he hadn't been well enough to work very much, and she had been working and taking care of him. His legs always gave him a lot of pain but had been especially bad this past week.

On Sunday he worked at the pawnshop until about 3 p.m. then went home to get his swollen legs up for a while. He fell asleep in the recliner until 10 p.m. then went down to the shop to check out the till. He was home by 10:45 or 11 p.m. and again fell asleep in the chair until Dobbie woke him up to go out. He let the dog out and crawled into bed. Monday morning he'd had blood drawn for tests about 8:30 a.m. at the hospital and went to work from there.

He couldn't think of anyone, or any reason, someone would want to kill Betty, but Reeda had a boyfriend who was married and he thought Betty had mentioned that they'd been having some problems. Bill still did not ask how the women were killed, if they had been raped or the condition the bodies were found in. He was only curious about the time of death.

Bill was very cooperative and friendly with the detectives.

He took them to the pawnshop and allowed them to take ammunition and guns from the glass case and cigarette butts from his truck's ashtray. He certainly gave the appearance he had nothing to fear or hide.

Kim and Jeff just got back from their after dinner walk when the phone rang. Jeff talked to his dad frequently on the phone, so it was a bit odd when Jeff answered the phone and his dad abruptly asked to speak to Kim. Within a few seconds Kim had Jeff get on the other phone and Bill said simply, "Mom's dead." Jeff's first thought was an accident but Saralyn, who was also on the line, said "No, they murdered her." Further inquiries provided only that Betty and her friend Reeda were killed in Idaho Falls, the police were not saying much and there were no details yet.

Thirty to 45 minutes later, Jeff and Kim were driving out of Portland. They'd made some phone calls, packed some things, including a couple of Jeff's guns, and left. They would drive all night and arrive in Jackson early Tuesday morning.

Jo Ann got home around 10:30 p.m. Monday after a day of shopping in Los Angeles with her girlfriends. Dick had been home less than five minutes when Jo Ann walked in the door. Dick had gone to dinner with his friends knowing Jo Ann would be late returning from her day with the girls. Traditionally, they would stay for dinner while waiting for the big city commuter traffic to slow before starting home.

"We had two really strange phone messages on the recorder," Dick said to Jo Ann when she came in the door. The first message was from Bill and his voice, as well as his message, seemed odd to Dick. It was as if he was leaving a message for a stranger who wouldn't recognize his voice or know how to call him back. Bill left both his name and phone number on the answering machine. The next one was from Jo Ann's brother Dan, and he was downright demanding. He didn't care how many phone messages they had, they were not to call anyone until they called him first.

Both messages had been directed at Dick and he was just about to call Dan when Jo Ann came home. Unconcerned, Jo Ann began putting her day's purchases away while Dick called Dan. But Dan was on his daughter's phone line and his daughter, Shari, answered her parent's phone.

"Uncle Dick," she said, "Dad's on the other line but it's really important. He wants you to not call anybody and keep your line open. He will call you right back."

Within seconds of Dick hanging up the receiver the phone rang. "You better answer this Jo Ann," he said. "Dan doesn't want me to talk to anybody until I talk to him first." It was Shari again.

"No! Aunt Jo Ann, Dad wants to talk to Dick, Dad wants him to keep this line open, stay on the phone so nobody can talk to you until he gets off the other phone."

A bit more inquisitive than Dick, Jo Ann wants to know what's going on and why she was to stay on the line. "He'll talk to you in just a minute. He just wants your line left open. He will be right here."

Holding the phone, Jo Ann could hear some unclear voices and mumbling through the line. Now, having a few seconds to think and assemble these strange phone calls in her mind, suddenly she knew what Dan was going to tell her. She started to cry, throwing the phone at Dick she said, "You take this. I don't want this call. I know what it's going to be Dick! Betty's

126

dead, Bill killed her!"

Jo Ann had been extremely apprehensive about Betty since the collect phone calls and planned to call her that next day, even if Bill would be listening on the phone. Now Jo Ann knew she would never talk to her sister again. Not unlike Roy Leavitt who was secure in the belief that tragedies of this magnitude could never enter your life, she never dreamed murder would be the end result of Betty and Bill's problems. Too late she realized the collect phone calls had been the key, a plea from her sister that her life was in danger. Jo Ann would always carry the burden of inaction to the phone calls even though she could have changed nothing. But that last phone call from Betty would propel her energy and determination giving her strength for what was yet to come.

When Dan got on the phone with Dick, he confirmed what Jo Ann already knew. He'd just gotten off the phone with detectives in Idaho Falls. Bill's strange phone call to Dan previously was unfortunately, the truth. Shari had answered the phone and Bill wanted to talk to her mother, not her dad. When Karen got on the phone Bill then told her to get Dan on another phone. But after both Dan and Karen were on the phone there was silence. Bill said nothing. For some time this family felt Bill had a gangster-type personality. His fondness for guns, bragging of being a bounty hunter, his "don't cross me" attitude, combined with a strong suspicion he burned down his worm farm and pawnshop to collect the insurance, gave rise to an underlying sense of danger.

Since they had just found out the week before from Dan's mother about Betty's plans for a divorce, Karen and Dan had talked at length about their concerns of how Bill would accept Betty divorcing him. They were well aware of his possessive control over Betty and had even discussed if there was anything they should or could do.

This knowledge prompted Karen to become very concerned with the continued silence on the other end of the phone. She suddenly had the strangest feeling Bill had left the phone to get Betty and was going to kill her, or threaten to kill her on the phone for them to hear. Karen waved, getting the attention of her girls, as well as Dan who was still on the phone in the next room. Trying to convey her fears she curled her fingers to make the form of a gun and pointed it at her head.

Expecting any moment to hear a gunshot she shouted, "Bill, Bill are you there?" After a few more terror-filled seconds of silence, Bill began to laugh.

"Put your goddamned quarter in the machine if you want some information," he chuckled. "You don't get phone calls like this for free."

Relieved because he was laughing, and fed up with this nonsense, Karen fired back. "I beg your pardon Bill, you called us we didn't call you, this isn't a pay phone!"

"Well I've got some news for you. Betty has been murdered," Bill said his voice flat and unemotional. "Her and her goddamned girlfriend are dead."

Since the beginning of this phone call Dan was extremely anxious. Now he wasn't sure if he heard him right but understood his sister and her friend were dead. Thinking it was an accident he began to question what happened.

"Shot," Bill said, "murdered. Someone took them out, probably her boyfriend. He found the bodies."

"Where is she? Where is she right now?" Dan demanded. Dan kept Bill on the phone long enough to find out his sister had been killed, not in Jackson, but in Idaho Falls, then hung up on him.

Dan was on the phone with the Idaho Falls Sheriff's

Department when Dick returned his call. It had taken quite a while for Dan to get the confirmation he so dreaded hearing. The Sheriff's Department passed him back and forth to various people and wouldn't give him any information.

"Don't you hang up on me, don't you dare hang up on me, Karen could hear him shouting, I've got to stay on this phone until I get to the right people and find out what's really happening."

Eventually he was turned over to Detective Paul Wilde. Blurting out his story and that he was calling from California, Wilde asked Dan for his sister's name and the date of her birth. Dan's mind went blank.

"Oh, God, she's three years younger than me. Help Karen, somebody help me. When is Betty's birthday? I know, it's June, June 12," he finally remembered.

Dan went on to tell Wilde his brother-in-law was Bill Gray. They owned a pawnshop in Jackson. "I've got to know," he said. "My brother-in-law just called me and I don't ever believe a thing he tells me and I have to check this out myself."

The information Dan had given Detective Wilde was sufficient for him to know he was talking to the brother of one of the murdered women. Wilde confirmed they did have a double homicide in Idaho Falls and Betty Gray was one of the victims.

The first thing that came to Dan's mind was Bill. "You'd better check out my brother-in-law. I wouldn't put it past him to have done this," he told Wilde. "Betty was planning to divorce Bill and Bill was the kind of a person who could do something like this."

Wilde wanted to know if Betty had recently been in California. She was, Dan confirmed, but he hadn't seen her on this trip. He'd been so busy he was only able to talk to her on the phone.

"You need to talk to my other sister, Jo Ann. Betty stayed with Jo Ann and she could tell you what you need to know," Dan offered. Wilde asked him to have Jo Ann call him back that night.

Dan would be forever saddened by the fact his busy life had kept him from seeing and hugging his little sister one last time. He searched his mind to remember the things they talked about on the phone when she was in California. He remembered how happy she was, telling him all the things she and Jo Ann had been doing and what a good time she was having. For such a short time Betty had forgotten her problems and was happy. He would have a little empty place in his heart for a long, long time, probably forever!

Jo Ann wasn't sure she could pull herself together long enough to call the detective. Her first thought was to call him back in the morning. Her mind was racing. How was she going to tell her mom? What plans were they going to have to make? It was her need to know what happened to Betty that gave her the strength to make the call.

"I know now I was kind of in shock and the full depth of what I was told hadn't sunk in yet. Paul Wilde asked me a lot of questions about Betty being out here. I ho-hummed around and really didn't tell him much of anything. This was the first time I ever had to talk to the police on a serious matter and I wasn't thinking straight. I didn't know what Dan might have told him and I didn't know how much he already knew, or how much I should tell him without telling my family everything before they heard it from somebody else. Betty asked me to keep her secret about Roy and since he was married I didn't know if he had told the police about the affair. I asked Wilde questions and I know he was being as evasive with me as I was with him. He did tell me there were suspects and I told him, I said, I hope you don't overlook my brother-in-law. He said Bill was one of them. The spouses are always suspects in these kinds of cases.

"When I asked him for Leroy Leavitt's phone number he wanted to know how I knew, and what I knew, about Leavitt. Not sure how much I should say I told him I knew Roy sold merchandise to my sister's pawnshop and I understood he's the one that found my sister. I wanted to talk to him to see what he could tell me."

Jo Ann got Roy's phone number but Wilde advised her Leavitt was also a suspect and would prefer it if she didn't talk to him until after they had more time to check him out. That wouldn't be a problem for at the moment Jo Ann was more interested in talking to her family. She would need Dan and Dick's advice before she talked to anyone else or told the police anything more. Jo Ann had little to report back to Dan. He probably knew as much, if not more, than she did at this point.

Because Bill also called Jo Ann's aunt, the decision was made to notify their mother that night. They didn't want her to be alone if she heard it from anyone else. Jo Ann would bring her mother back to her house to stay until they left for Wyoming. By midnight they were en route in Dan's motorhome to tell Dorothy her youngest child had been murdered.

It was time now for Jo Ann to tell her family a secret, a secret she once promised to keep but could not keep any longer. So during the hour drive to San Bernardino Jo Ann informed her husband and brother that Betty was going to divorce Bill because she was having an affair with another man. The affair had been going on for two years. Betty didn't intend for it to happen, it just happened. She was so depressed and crying all the time. It's kind of understandable how something like that could happen under the circumstances; Jo Ann defended her now dead sister. Dan and Dick learned of the collect phone calls, how Bill didn't want Betty to tell anyone about the divorce and his rage when he steamed open the letter Betty had written to her mother. Jo Ann talked and talked, telling them everything she could think of and asking for advice on what to tell the detective. It was her only defense, for when she stopped talking she knew she was going to be hysterical and she must be strong for her mother who would need her now more than ever.

It was close to one 1 a.m. when Jo Ann, Dick and Dan arrived at their mothers' home. Knocking on her bedroom widow, with Jo Ann calling her mother's name saying "Mom, it's Jo Ann" to keep from frightening her, they finally aroused her from her sleep. Dorothy instantly knew something was terribly wrong but her first thoughts were those of her grandchildren.

"No, Mother, it's Betty." Clinging to each other for support they allowed their emotions to release in total despair.

Dorothy refused to allow herself to believe it. This could not have happened, not her daughter, not this way.

"I immediately placed a call to my son-in-law Bill. I wanted to hear from him exactly what happened to my daughter and her friend. Crying, I asked Bill to tell me what he knew. He said, 'You mean you don't know? Haven't Jo Ann and Dan told you?' Then he laughed. I couldn't believe this was real. I said, Please Bill, tell me what you know.' Again he laughed. I asked him if my granddaughter Saralyn was there. I asked to speak to her. 'You want to speak to Saralyn?' he asked. Then he laughed again. I tried to ask questions and he continued to laugh. Finally, I told him I couldn't handle his laughing anymore and hung up on him."

After driving all night, Jeff and Kim arrived in Jackson close to 9 a.m. Tuesday. Bill and Saralyn were on their way out the door. They were going to see Janis. Tired from their all night drive, Jeff and Kim tried to sleep but couldn't. They were anxious for Bill and Saralyn to get back and fill in the details they'd wondered about all night.

"Details," Bill said when he returned, "were still sketchy and he really didn't know any more than what he'd told them the night before on the telephone except for the news he'd just gotten from Janis. Your mother," Bill informed Jeff, "was having an affair. She was going to divorce me and marry her lover." Saralyn helped fill in the blanks while Bill went into his emotional act putting on a good show for his family. But Bill was very preoccupied with Janis' news. If she knew, who else knew? He was driven to find out. He called Betty's close friend, DeeDee.

"Boy was he mad," she remembers. "He cussed at me calling me every name he could think of. He said I should have come to him, I should have told him I knew about the affair and Betty wanting a divorce, but what he really wanted to know was who did I tell, who else knew."

"I kept going over and over with him. Look Bill, I was Betty's friend, she confided in me, she asked me not to say anything, and I told no one. I didn't even tell John. I told no one I knew anything. He was so angry and I was so scared that John finally took the phone away from me. When I thought more about it, I felt he was really mad at Betty. I think he was angry because she broke her promise by telling Janis and me. She'd always followed every instruction he gave her and then he finds out that probably for the first time in all their married life she disobeyed him."

Tuesday would prove to be a busy day at the Idaho Falls Sheriff's Department. After calling DeeDee, Bill called Detective Cowden in Idaho Falls.

"Betty's best friend, Janis Roby, came over last night. She was all broke up. I wanted to talk to her last night but there was just too damn many people around. There were people here until one in the morning, I think. So this morning Janis called and wanted to talk to Saralyn. Saralyn went over there and she came back and told me what was going on. Do you have a pencil handy? This is really hard on me but like I said, I think I've cried my last tear. Do you know who Roy Leavitt is? My wife has been seeing him. Do you remember that camping trip I said she and Reeda went on? Well, Reeda stayed with relatives at a different camp. Roy and Betty were together there."

He went on to tell Cowden that DeeDee Batson knew about it, as well as Janis and Betty's sister Jo Ann. There was a pause while Bill looked up and gave Cowden DeeDee's out-of-state phone number.

"I confronted Betty about it. She said there was no one else. I loved her so goddamned much that I'd have believed anything she told me. Now the way that Janis found out was she walked in the store one day, see in the wintertime I love to gamble, I'm a good gambler, I make money at it, and this year Betty really pushed, you know, 'Why don't you go? Why don't you go?' Well I was always gone on Tuesdays. Tuesdays is when Roy came, okay, to do business, monkey business I guess. Well one of the Tuesdays I was gone, Janis just walked in and Roy walked in with a rose and gave it to Betty. Well Janis is no damned dummy. Now here's some more shit, okay; you still writing? Janis told me that Reeda has a box of cards that Roy gave to Betty. They'll be at Reeda's house someplace."

Cowden listened patiently, asking questions when Bill took

a breath, letting the tape recorder take his notes. When he thought Bill was finished, Cowden said he was coming to Jackson the next day and he would bring back the gun they had taken from Bill the night before at the interview.

"I'll give you a call and we can sit down and talk."

"Okay," replied Bill, "but I've got more. Deanie, that's Roy's wife, knew nothing about this, they were going to get a divorce when Betty divorced me, and Roy and Betty were going to get married. And she's been buying all kinds of stuff on lay-away, household utensils, furniture."

Cowden asked if she had her own bank account.

"She shouldn't have her own bank account, but I think she did because she's been stealing money from the store and I never said a damn thing to her about it. I figured it was fifty percent hers anyway. She's never had to do that. Christ, I treated her like a queen. I bought her everything she ever wanted. If she wanted money, I didn't care if she wanted a $100 or a $1,000; I just whipped it out and gave it to her."

Detective Cowden asked about ownership of the business, the land, vehicles and insurance policies.

"We're both on them as ... we're beneficiaries on each other's insurance policies."

"When you went in for your operation, or when you found out you were going to have your operation, did Betty take out any more life insurance on you," Cowden asked?

"Nobody will insure me. I'm not insurable." In a crying, emotional voice Bill now rambles on, how he felt she would come to her senses, he never thought she would go through with the divorce; he was so surprised to hear that from Janis yesterday. Cowden again reassured Bill he would be over and they could iron all this out then.

"I hope you've got some more news for me when you come,"

Bill said.

"I do too," replied Cowden.

Later that day, Cowden and Kotrason interviewed Leroy Leavitt at length, only this time they read him his rights. Leavitt signed the forms confirming he understood his rights and readily agreed to answer all their questions without benefit of a lawyer. The detectives wanted to know everything about Betty and every detail of their affair. Again Leavitt had problems facing the questions about, and use of the word, sex.

Leavitt: And the last year or so, I got to know her real
   close.
Cowden: By real close, you mean intimately?
Leavitt: I don't know what you mean by "intimately," but
   I would have to say ...
Cowden: Did you have sex relations with her?
Leavitt: (Pause). Yes, I loved her very much.

The detectives dove into the affair, how they met, when did it start, where they had sex and how often. Asked how she was dressed when they slept together, "She wore only underpants; she said it was too warm. She said she never wore a nightgown," confirming that when she was found, she had gone to bed in her normal attire.

Kotrason: What about going and meeting her at Reeda's
   house and just jumping in the sack? Did you do that?
Leavitt: No. I would meet her there at Reeda's and kiss
   and hug her but nothing more.
Kotrason: Did Reeda know you were doing this?
Leavitt: I assume she did because she gave Betty a key to

her house.

Kotrason: But you never had an opportunity to go to bed
with her there at the house? Or you didn't take that
opportunity?

Leavitt: I didn't take that opportunity, no.

More questions from Kotrason. Was Betty unhappy at home
and why? Divorce plans? Were you actually planning to get a
divorce?

"Yes," he feebly admits.

Getting around to Sunday and Sunday night Leavitt said that
"He and his family had spent the weekend at Buttermilk
Campground in Island Park and returned to Idaho Falls around
5:30 or 6 p.m. He and the boys were cleaning out the camper
when Reeda called and asked him to come over. She wanted to
show me something about the sprinkler system since I told her
I would water the lawn and garden while she was gone. I'd done
it for her before when she was gone so I knew all about the
sprinkler system but she was insistent that I come right over.

"I got over there about 7:30 p.m. and I was really surprised
to see Betty there. She had called and told me she would be
coming over on Monday and we planned to go to lunch, but I
never expected her to be there Sunday night. I sat on the chair
in the kitchen and Betty sat on my lap. They offered me some
tea and I said, 'No,' I had to get going. I'd had a flat on the Jeep
and wanted to get that taken care of in addition to finish
cleaning up from the camping trip.

"I left a little after 8 o'clock. I took the tire to get it fixed
and spent the rest of the evening at home. LaDeana and I went
to bed about 10 or 10:30 p.m. I had a restless night and so did

LaDeana. It was about 3 a.m. and I was tossing and turning; felt like something was wrong. And in the morning, when we got up I said, 'I had a restless night.' LaDeana said she didn't sleep too well either."

Cowden: Did you ever at any time, suspect in your mind that Bill might suspect you?

Leavitt: No, never crossed my mind.

Cowden: Did you ever stop and think of what would happen? What would be the consequences? How would Bill react if he should find out?

Leavitt: The only thing I thought about was, if it came to that situation, I'd lose an account.

Cowden: And that's all? You'd lose an account?

Leavitt: And lose, you know, a friend and everything.

Cowden: What do you think Bill would do now if he found out?

Leavitt: I really don't know.

Cowden: You made a comment that you really didn't want to call him. Don't you think he might wonder? He might wonder why?

Leavitt: It's like myself, I wonder why he hasn't called me, you know. It's like he hasn't called, I wonder why he hasn't called me. I've wondered that. And I thought, well with the turmoil and everything, maybe in the latter part of the week I'd give him a call or something like that. But I never went through anything like this before, so I don't know what to do and what not to do.

Cowden: It's kind of a bad situation.

Leavitt: Yeah, it sure is.

Kotrason: Betty confided in Janis and Janis laid it out to Bill and you can probably write your account off.

Leavitt had both keys to the safe deposit box. "I have the only keys to it because Reeda didn't really want to keep the key. Reeda put in a bag, I don't know what. It looked like coins, but I'm not sure what it was. And then she gave me this other stuff to drop off. Some of it was in an envelope, some of it wasn't. I'd just go down and drop it in the box there. I don't know how much is in there. I would say a couple of thousand dollars. Betty was supposed to be the other person to have access to it but she never got down to sign it and she didn't have a key. She'd usually give it to me on Tuesdays when I was up there, sometimes other days when I saw her."

Cowden asked why Betty was doing this. "She just said for when she got her divorce. She wanted it there so she could use it. No, I never thought about where she might have gotten it. She just gave it to me and said, 'You can put this in the box,' and I did."

Winding down the interview Leavitt was asked if he would voluntarily submit to a polygraph test, which he readily agreed to do. Leavitt told them he had brought in his tennis shoes and a sole print had been taken. He also volunteered a key to the safe deposit box which the detectives accepted after having Leavitt sign forms giving them consent to have possession of the key and search the box. Leavitt was asked to give samples of, pubic and head hairs. Since Leavitt had recently been in the house it was possible his hairs might show up in the bedrooms. Everything found had to be identified and tagged as to who left a trace of themselves in the murder house.

Now that this was all out and the police knew everything, Roy would have to tell his wife everything that evening.

"I have to do it before she finds out from someone else. I think she's an understanding gal. I think she'll stand by me."

When Roy left the station he was going home to face his

infidelity and ask his wife to somehow understand.

When Kay Gunderson learned of the murders he was stunned. He thought he may have been the last person to see them alive. He was right. Kay's brother and Reeda had been dabbling at raising worms for bait and he'd asked Kay to drop off the worms and also give her some raspberries. Betty answered the door and Kay thought it took quite a while, longer than normal, for her to come to the door.

The front door was locked and she peered out through the window to be sure who it was before she unlocked it and let him in. No one else was in the house. There hadn't been any phone calls. He thought the women had been drinking Long Island Iced Teas which may have accounted for the liquor bottles on the table and Roy's thinking that there was less liquid in the bottles that morning than there had been the night before.

Neither woman smoked nor did he remember seeing cigarettes or cigarette butts on the kitchen table. Kay said the women were in good spirits and everything seemed normal when he left about 10 p.m.

While the Sheriff's Office was buzzing with activity downtown, criminalists were back at the Crowley Road home. Detectives Byington, Dixon and McCandless placed their priority on the outside of the house. A plaster cast was made of the footprint in the driveway and the grounds were searched inch by inch. The murder weapon could not be found in the house, yard or the canal. Their search produced few items deemed to be of much importance. A wet wipe wrapper, a Salem Light cigarette package and an empty Mountain Dew soda can with the pull tab missing were among the few items found. Detectives would return to the house many times before they would take down the tape and allow the Roundy children access to the house and their mother's possessions.

Howard Wilson flew directly from the sporting goods show in Las Vegas to Idaho Falls for questioning. He openly shared details of his and Reeda's relationship with the officers and was extremely distraught. They'd been friends and business associates for more than 15 years. In 1984 or 1985, just after Reeda moved to Idaho Falls, their relationship became physical. They got close while on a fly fishing trip together.

"She was a person who loved to hunt and fish." he told the detectives. "We did that together. She loved the outdoors."

Investigators wondered if this relationship was as comfortable as Wilson professed. Some of the answering machine cassettes, removed from Reeda's home, were recorded conversations between Howard and Reeda that suggested she was pressuring him for a much stronger commitment. For some time he had been telling Reeda he would get a divorce but the tapes showed he wasn't able to do it. On the tapes he told Reeda he had already divorced his wife and was loading his belongings, preparing to move. But later he acknowledged that he had not divorced his wife, had not packed and couldn't make up his mind.

"You've lied to me about so many things," Reeda said, like a voice from the grave. "Yea, I guess I have," responded Wilson. But he couldn't bring himself to end the relationship despite Reeda's pressuring him to make up his mind. His business had taken a downward turn and his wife knew of the affair. Could these kinds of pressures drive a man to commit murder? It was certainly a possibility.

Wilson had fought in World War II and was in the first wave

of Americans to storm the beaches at Normandy. When asked if he had killed a person before he had to say yes. But Wilson's alibi was virtually unshakable. He'd been home in Seattle, Washington with his wife and family cooking for a barbecue, substantiated by his wife and friends. He took a polygraph test, and submitted hair and blood samples. The five handguns found in Reeda's home were his. He'd asked Reeda to keep them for him. Howard Wilson was eliminated as a suspect.

Several Fanning Wholesale employees were interviewed, among them co-owner Vada Roberts. Her account of C. J. Walker and his threats to kill Reeda immediately got the detectives attention.

Walker was located near Seaside, Oregon. Sergeant Allen Creech from Seaside had personally known him. Creech said he would be very surprised if Walker killed someone. He thought he could possibly kill on the spur of the moment but he doubted he could form intent to kill, travel as far as Idaho Falls and still have the intent. Walker was a loudmouth and very opinionated. He used to drink too much, came across as a tough guy, liked to wear camouflage and combat boots, read "Solider of Fortune" magazine, but he was unaware of any mercenary work that Walker could have done. His alibi of being at a birthday party for a friend on the evening of July 23 was confirmed. Having passed a polygraph test and with his strong alibi, C. J. Walker was also eliminated as a suspect.

Four possible suspects, four passed polygraph tests and four strong alibis; Roy Leavitt, LaDeana Leavitt, Howard Wilson and C. J. Walker were taken off the list. The Roundy children had been eliminated, they were in Utah and there was nothing to gain from their mother's death. Her insurance would barely cover her funeral expenses and her assets were few. But Detective Rodriguez felt even stronger that the target had been

Betty and the one with the most to gain from her death had the poorest alibi of all.

Steven Mackley, security guard for the Eastern Idaho Regional Medical Center in Idaho Falls, learned about the double homicide on the Monday evening news. He pondered quite awhile if what he had seen that morning may have any connection, and then called authorities.

He had worked the 11 p.m. Sunday to 7 a.m. Monday shift. About 3 a.m. he'd finished checking the South Parking Lot, parked his car at the emergency entrance and was about to go in when something caught his eye. Coming from the north toward the hospital was a single light bobbing up and down. Thinking this was a little unusual he stood and watched.

As the light came into the parking lot Mackley could see it was a bicycle. He had to step around the building a little more to see the rider pull up to a Suburban-type vehicle, put the bike in the back and get in the front seat. If the vehicle would have left immediately he wouldn't have had an opportunity to check further and would have gone on about his business. But the man laid down in the front seat with his legs extended out the open driver's side door. This prompted Mackley to think he may be attempting to hot wire and steal the vehicle.

As Mackley approached, the person sat up and closed the door. Mackley motioned for him to roll down the window which he did, part way. The man slumped down in the seat and peered out at Mackley over the top of his glasses. He could see that the man was sweating profusely and out of breath, so much so, it prompted Mackley to ask if he was alright. The man said he was

OK, he'd just been riding a long way.

When asked for his name, the man gave one, but Mackley could not remember what it was. When asked for identification he was shown a medical-alert bracelet on the man's right wrist but the light was too dim for him to read it. The man mumbled something about being there to pick up the vehicle for some friends.

Mackley described the man to be in his late 40s or early 50s, with pock marks on his face, like acne scars. Mackley said he could remember him having very little hair, although his only source of light was his flashlight which he did not shine directly in the persons face. He thought the man was wearing a dark colored jumpsuit. The vehicle was described as an older International-type van with big box windows, lower to the ground, gray or olive green. It wouldn't start on the first try, on the second it started but was running very rough.

The fact that the vehicle had Wyoming plates is what inspired Mackley to call authorities. The news said one of the murdered women was from Jackson, Wyoming. The 26-year-old security guard told officers, "I just don't know if what I saw will be of any help."

The Wyoming license plates were certainly of particular interest to the Bonneville County detectives. On a slight chance, they called the Jackson Police Department requesting that they look for a vehicle matching the description given by Mackley.

Patrolman Chris Brackens first stop was the pawnshop and he need look no further. An olive green 1971 International Travelall was parked at the side of the pawnshop. There were no plates on the vehicle. Officer Bracken returned to the station and notified the Idaho authorities of his find. Taking a camera he returned to the shop, took several photographs of the Travelall and recorded the vehicle identification number.

Although there had been no mention to Bracken of a bicycle when he went looking for the vehicle, when the pictures were developed a bicycle could be seen through the windows of the Travelall, leaned up against the wall of the pawnshop. Detective Rodriguez and his team would quickly turn their full attention to Bill Gray.

When Leroy Leavitt got wind that Bill may have been in Idaho Falls that night he wasn't surprised. He had thought about it continuously since it happened. The detectives had asked him if he had an opinion as to who may have murdered these women and he told them he had no idea.

"I didn't suspect anybody, 'cause in our world it's just not done you know. So I really didn't suspect anybody, but before that first night was over I had to think it could have been Bill. I told the detectives that those footprints looked familiar. I'd seen that up in Jackson. I said that looks like Bill Gray. We had gone ice fishing and Bill was wearing these shoes and he kept slipping and I said something like, those shoes sure are slippery and he lifted up his foot and showed me the knobby sole and said. 'Yeah, when I bought them, because of this knobby tread, I thought they would be good in snow and ice but they're not worth a damn.'" Leavitt didn't want to believe it even happened, but when he came to terms with it he couldn't rule out Bill as the killer.

The town was both shocked and saddened by the news of Betty's murder. The house on Stacy Lane was soon buzzing with activity. People were coming and going, bringing food, offering their condolences, asking if there was anything they could do.

Jo Ann called wanting to know about services. William and Sara Gray arrived, and Cree was asking where his Grandma Betty was.

Somehow this tiny four-year-old knew something was terribly wrong. He was continually crying and asking for his grandma over and over again. Finally Saralyn sat him down and explained that his grandma was an angel now. She told him a story about beautiful angels and how wonderful it was to be an angel in heaven. He seemed to accept that it was alright now. Thereafter, when anyone came to the house and Cree was there he would tell them, "My Grandma Betty is an angel now, isn't she beautiful?"

Bill wasn't in agreement with Cree. Showing a display of emotion in front of his family he cried a brief time and then his emotions turned to anger and hatefulness. Verbalizing his outrage, he never let up on condemning his wife, calling her every derogatory name he could spit out. He detailed how he searched the basement looking for Betty's purse until he found it. His subsequent inventory provided the proof she had been stealing from him. Bill's father had always been fond of Betty and said very little, but Sara joined her son in the bashing contest. In time, even Saralyn and Jeff were voicing displeasure with their dead mother.

Vulnerable to begin with, Bill preyed on his children's emotions. Rather than being allowed to deal with the shock of their loss in a loving, understanding, atmosphere, they were placed on the defensive and reduced to feeling sorry for their father with a strong need to protect him. Because they perceived their dad to be very emotional and upset, they vowed that he couldn't be left alone. One or the other must be with him at all times unless he was with his father.

But the continual Betty bashing was not the only thing that

146

distracted their attention. Solidifying their decision not to leave their dad alone was his insistence that Betty wasn't the only target. Bill had planted the idea his life could be in danger. If someone took out Betty and Reeda no one in the family was really safe he kept reminding them.

Adding more fuel to the fire, Bill had everyone convinced the phones were tapped and the house was bugged. He'd seen someone climbing a power pole near the house so he was sure of it, he told them. The phone was almost taboo. Limited calls were allowed but nothing could be discussed about what was going on in the house. If conversation came up in the kitchen Bill would jump up and turn the water on in the sink full force to muffle the voices. If someone came by to visit, or the family started to talk about the murders, he immediately ushered them out to the patio. Everyone had that prickly feeling of an unknown presence. Shadows in the yard had an ominous feeling. They were certain the police had started a plot against their father that would put the CIA to shame.

Bill was clearly running the show. Although Saralyn and Jeff were curious when they would be able to get their mother home, and if the police had any more information about who may have killed her, Bill did not want his children to contact the police for any reason. He insisted he should be the only one to talk to the police. He would get all the information and let them know what he found out.

This time it was Bill Gray who was given his rights before starting an interview. IBI Agent John Kotrason and Detective John Cowden returned to Jackson Wednesday morning, July 26, armed with a great deal more information and a chilling scenario on their minds. The cat and mouse game begins when the detectives approach this interview with a plan to let Bill do most of the talking. Put him at ease with small talk and see what he would have to say.

Killers who think they have committed the perfect crime relish the game. They seldom ask for their lawyer to be present for this would indicate they had something to be afraid of. They would want to help the detectives in their search for the real killer and their curiosity to find out what the authorities knew would be overwhelming, compelling them to be cooperative and chatty. Cocky and self-assured he could outwit them, Bill was no different.

This man, who was spoiled by his parents as a child, who bullied and dominated his wife as an adult, who was never held responsible for his insurance frauds and thefts. that loved to gamble and was good at it, was confident he could play the game and win. But he was going to insure his bet. He brought his own tape recorder to the interview. Detectives found that highly unusual. Why would a supposedly grief-stricken man who lost his wife to a homicide just two day ago, think about bringing a tape recorder to his interview? Perhaps he intended to keep a record of what he told the authorities so he couldn't be tripped up later.

Before the detectives could start the interview Bill wanted to know if they had found any checking or saving accounts that Betty may have opened either in Jackson or Idaho Falls. He was advised they had not.

After the preliminaries for the record were completed, the three-hour, 78-page interview began with the detective's inquiries and Bill Gray attempting to put the focus of blame on his wife.

Gray: I do all the book work. Betty didn't do those at all; even when I was in the hospital, once in while I could get her to, to remember to go to the bank. Usually when I got out of the hospital I'd be going through the mail and, uh, I'd have a whole goddamn stack of deals from the bank. Where I was overdrawn on my regular reserve and Christ, there's thousands of dollars lying in the safe and she wouldn't even go to the bank.

Cowden: You indicated to me on the phone that your wife was taking money from the business. When did you discover it and how did you discover it?

Gray: Well, she's always left her purse, ya know, laying around. We never hid anything from either one of us. And uh, if I needed her nail clippers, I'd say, "Honey, where's your nail clippers? "In my purse." I says, "Well, where's your damn purse?" She says, "Hanging on the door." If we discovered we needed some milk or something, ya know, something from the market, and uh, I might have just $100 or $50 bills in my pocket. And I'd say, "You got a couple of bucks?" And she'd say, "Yeah, it's in my wallet." So I'd go and get it. Well I noticed this change and I can't really pinpoint how long it's been going on. I can tell ya how long I've been doing it because I've kept a record of it. But I don't have it with me. Matter of fact, my son's sitting out there. I can have him go get my briefcase.

Kotrason: Where would the money be that she was taking out of the till?

Gray: You tell me. I have no goddamn idea.

Cowden: Did you ever ask her about it?

Gray: No, hell it was half hers. She was stealing from me. It was ironic 'cause, ya know, we had agreed everything was gonna be peaceful. We were gonna split everything down the middle. I still think we would have worked it out.

Cowden: So, you're saying, this pending divorce, you, you believe would have been worked out?

Gray: Yeah, yes I do. See, I knew nothing about the other man. She'd lied to me. She told me there was no other man and I didn't want to make waves over a piddly goddamn $15, $20, $25, $50 or $100 a day to blow my chances of putting things together.

Cowden: Did you ever suspect her of taking anything else out of more value?

Gray: Yeah, that's what I was getting to. I know she took home these two boxes. And uh, it struck me funny. Ya know, because when she brought them in I was already home and she stopped at the market. When she came in, she went back downstairs with these boxes. And I saw her carry 'em in from the car. So when she went walking that night, I went down and looked and the boxes were in the closet and I still didn't think anything of it. And uh, the next morning, I think it was ... It wasn't the next morning it was the following morning, I went down and looked at the boxes again and they were still there, but they were full.

Cowden: What was in these boxes?

Gray: I don't know. I have no idea. So, I made an excuse to come home for, for some damn thing that afternoon, and I checked 'em and the boxes, like I say were full. Well I had to get back down to the store so I figured that night when she went walking I would check 'em then. But that night they were taped shut with nylon tape. So I just, well, ya know, thought what the hell's going on? The next morning I checked, they were still there. That night when she went walking they were gone. So when she came home from walking we watched TV until about 10 p.m. I told her, I says, uh, you mind if we have uh, uh, another talk? She says, "No," so I turned the TV off and I says, uh, Betty, I says, you brought some boxes home, I says. Uh, they're gone. She says, "What do you mean they're gone?" I says, Betty, I says, don't goddamn lie to me, I know they're gone. I says, I want this shit knocked off. I says, I want those boxes back in this house and I don't want anything removed from this house until where it all comes down to where it's cut and dried, that we are getting a divorce.

Bill went on to say Betty started crying and apologized saying she would return them and in a few days the boxes came back. When I saw 'em, they were all unpacked. I asked her, I says, what's in 'em? She says, "Just little things that I thought you'd give me a problem over taking." Now when I talked to Janis yesterday and found out all this information, I confronted Janis with it. I says, Janis, I says, I've been hurt so damn bad already, I says, you can't hurt me anymore. I want the truth and I want it all. She says," Bill," she says, "Betty hasn't been giving me any money." I says, don't lie to me Janis, I says, I know you hid two boxes over here for her. She says, "I haven't hid anything for her." She says the stuff she's taken out of the house is at Reeda's.

While Bill thought he was having detectives understand Betty was doing things she shouldn't have been; cheating on him, a thief, stealing from him, poor me; in reality he was painting the picture of a sneaky, greedy, controlling side of himself. A man so greedy that he would become extremely upset over the removal of two small boxes that may have contained nothing more than a few household items or Betty's personal things. This didn't sound like a man who thought he could still put his marriage back together.

Cowden asked Bill if he took care of the freight when it came into the pawnshop, specifically to find out if Bill may have discovered some of the cards Roy sent to Betty in the freight.

Gray: Usually Betty did. I always did before, but I've been so sick. It's just the last three months that I've really started to be able to participate in the business somewhat.

When Cowden asked him if before that, had he seen any cards or letters in the freight, Bill said he had not and quickly reminded detectives again that he had not known about Roy until Janice told him the day before.

Cowden: You noticed the change in Betty as far as being depressed and all, and you attribute that to the fact that she had the whole business and the worry about you being sick and things like that. Any other type of change, mannerisms, dress fads, dieting?

Gray: She was on a diet. She was a pretty big gal. She got up there pretty big.

Kotrason: Did you notice though that she was losing weight?

Gray: There was no secret about it. Thought it was great, 'cause she's been heavy before. She's always been very trim. When we lived in California she got very heavy. She went on a diet and she got down skinnier than when we were married. She stayed that way for years and then we moved here and over a period of time she started putting on weight and it just kept coming and coming. I know she'd go at 240 and possibly 260. [Betty had never weighed more than 175 pounds.]

Cowden: Geeze, how much weight did she get down to?

Gray: Probably a 114.

Cowden: Let's get back to business a minute. On Sunday, this last Sunday, do you remember what time you closed the store?

Gray: Uh, Sundays I try to close by 3 p.m. I'd say we were probably out of there by, oh by 3:30 p.m. probably.

Cowden: Did you go right home or where did you go?

Gray: Yes, I think I went straight home because my legs and knees and calves; my knees, calves and my ankles were just, ya know? My ankles were about that big around. (Indicating a large circle with his hands) I can't stand on my feet for more than an hour and a half. Two hours sometimes and then I'm in agony. Three years I was on death's doorstep. The last two years I almost crossed over.

Cowden: So you got home about 3:30 p.m. Where did you go Sunday night?

Gray: Sunday night I didn't go anywhere. Set there in the recliner with three pillows, with the recliner rocked up as high as it'd go, and three pillows and a heating pad.

Discussing what else he did Sunday night he related his story about going home and falling asleep in his chair. He said he tried to call his son who was away at school in Portland, Oregon and his parents who were visiting his mother's brother, also in Portland, but couldn't reach any of them. They'd gone on some excursion of some type and then to a movie. Monday morning he got up about 7 a.m., had blood drawn at the hospital and opened the store. No questions were asked about his leaving the house about 10 p.m. Sunday to go down to the shop and check out the till and Bill didn't offer anything in that regard.

Cowden: As far as vehicles, you own that blue pickup and a white uh ...

Gray: Subaru.

Cowden: Okay.

Gray: And that's all.

Cowden: What time did you open the store?

Gray: Probably anywheres from a quarter to 9 a.m. to 10 minutes to 9 a.m.

Cowden: Was anybody there?

Gray: Uh, Eric. Eric was there and there was probably two or three other people waiting for me to get back.

Cowden: What kind of car does Eric own?

Gray: It's a black car. It's a little black pickup up with a camper shell.

Cowden: Does he own a bicycle?

Gray: I have no idea.

Cowden: Do you own a bicycle?

Gray: I had a bicycle. I haven't ridden a bicycle since I screwed my knees all up four years ago, snow machining. I was getting ready for the hill climb, on a real lively snow machine. And I got a little out of [inaudible]; fly me out in a helicopter and I haven't been able to, to uh, I haven't even ridden a snow machine since then because I can't take any pressure on my knee. And this one, pointing to the other knee, I fucked up in high school skiing. And it's never been any good. My knees are just ... and then the Prednisone. Since I've been on Prednisone, they're even worse than they were before.

Cowden: You stated you went to Las Vegas quite a bit. Do you like to gamble?

Gray: Oh yes. I'm a good gambler.

Cowden: When was the last time you were in Las Vegas? Can you remember?

Gray: Just before the season started. The only time I can go is in the winter. Summertime we're too busy. And I've been sick. Last time? Jack took me down when I was sick. Jack took me to Jackpot once, and I gambled a little down there.

Cowden: Jack?

Gray: Jack Hurley. We go gambling together quite a bit. He does all my electrical contract work. And we made several trips to Las Vegas while I was still real sick.

Cowden: Where do you usually stay?

Gray: Well I like to stay at Bateman's but one time I went down by myself, I stayed at the Sahara. An I, uh, got so goddamn bad there I thought they were going to have to airlift me back to Salt Lake. They had to come and pick me up in a wheel chair at one place, take me out to a taxi and then they wired the Sahara I'd be in the taxi with a wheel chair, and took me up to my room and uh, I think the whole trip I was down there four or five days. I bet I didn't get to gamble more than, shoot, 12 hours.

Cowden: What were you playing, poker?

Gray: No, I'm a, I'm a crap shooter, and a baccarat player. I've made a hell of a study out of it. Thirty years. Yeah, if you don't know what you're doing, you got no business putting a penny down.

Cowden: Do you remember when that was, when you got sick?

Gray: I was on dialysis at the time. Because I felt sorry for the porter, uh, I give him, I give him $5 bucks to haul all the shit into the room. Uh, hell, I had, uh, probably ten cases of dialysis solution with me, my dialysis machine and all my other medications. I requested a room as close to the casino as they could give me, because of my condition.

Asked again when the last time he was in Las Vegas, Bill gave a rather long accounting of having carts waiting for him and being shuttled between planes at the airports, renting a car with Hurley driving, getting tired of hitting other casinos, "cause Jesus, ya know, used to be you could, your big games developed from 3 a.m. to 5 a.m., 6 a.m. And it was getting to the point to where, to find these big games, God we'd have to hit five or six casinos." So they started staying at the Bateman because they had 16 tables, the rooms were close and Bill could gamble for a while and then go to his room and rest. "I'd expend a hell of a pile of energy gambling. I might only gamble for 20, 45 minutes, and I quit. When that energy is gone, it's time to leave the table."

Cowden: There's one question I want to ask you and I'm sure you've probably thought about this after our visit Monday. In your mind, why would someone want to kill Betty and Reeda?

Gray: I have absolutely no idea. Betty never hurt anybody in her life until I found out she was screwing around.

Cowden: That hurt didn't it? That cut you.

Gray: You don't have to ask that do you?

Cowden: I know. When you first found out Bill, how did you feel? Rage, uh, hurt, uh ...

Gray: I didn't believe it. I told you, you were full of shit.

Cowden: ... not from me, but from Janis.

Gray: When I heard it from you, I was pissed at you.

Cowden: But I'm asking, how did you feel when it was actually told to you by someone else?

Gray: I was infuriated.

Cowden: You were pissed, right? You were angry?

Gray: Yes, matter of fact, when I talked to you, I think I told you I was done crying, but I wasn't. I don't think I ever will be. I loved her so goddamn much. She was my whole life. Her and my children. I just prayed to God when I woke up it was gonna be a bad dream, but the next day it was still there. Oh God, I don't know. There ain't any ... There is a reason for me to go on, and that's my children. If it wasn't for them I wouldn't be sitting here talking to ya, I'd be with Betty.

He couldn't think of why anybody would do that to Reeda and his wife.

"Somebody did it," he said. "If I knew who did it I would take care of it myself. I could never let anybody hurt my wife. Never in a million years."

After further small talk Cowden asks Agent Kotrason if he had any more questions.

Kotrason: Yeah, I've got a couple of questions and I'm gonna be blunt. Did you kill her?

Gray: Does that deserve an answer?

Kotrason: I expect one.

Gray: No, I did not.

Kotrason: Okay, will you be willing to take a polygraph?

Gray: I think it's horseshit, but yes. I have to clear it through my doctor.

Cowden: We have to eliminate people and that's part of the process of finding the person that did it. And part of the process, since you were married to one of them and you were going through a divorce.

Gray: There was no, there was no papers filled out, there was nothing done. Here's what it was. When she came home from her sister's and that was when I discovered there was definitely a problem. Okay, when she came back from her sister's she brought back a piss pot full of costume jewelry and started wearing that shit. And I asked her, I said, "Betty," I said, "What do you screw with this for," I says, all the goddamn diamonds and emeralds and, ya know, good jewelry that I bought her, I says, "What do you wear this crap for?" She says, "Well it's the fashion." And I says bullshit. I says, it's your sister's fad fashion. I says, your kind of jewelry is always in fashion. Her sister is mega-bucks. She isn't her old self when she comes back 'cause she's been wined and dined at the best, and uh, usually after, you know a few days back to the regular grind, everything's normal. And it, uh, didn't seem to be coming around. And uh, I ain't gonna lie to ya, I'm gonna tell you the whole damn thing. Uh, we had sexual relations and one morning we're starting to get ready for work and what not, and I grabbed her and started clowning around and I says, how about a little before, ya know, work? And Jesus, she got rigid as a board.

Cowden: And that was out of character?

Gray: Oh, out of character, Christ Almighty, it had never happened in all the years we been married. I says, something's wrong here and we should talk about it. And oh hell, how did she put it? She just let me know that she didn't feel like it at the time. And it had never been that way before, ya know. When I was ready, she was ready. Uh, I told her, I says, okay, I says, when you're ready, I says, you're gonna have to let me know. I says, 'cause I won't lay a hand on ya.

Cowden: Did you sleep in one bed or separate beds?

Gray: No, we slept in separate beds since I've been so sick.

Cowden: You were together one night, and then the next morning ...

Gray: We were together more than one night. And uh, in the mornings, hell, she'd come up and crawl in bed with me, ya know? And we'd snuggle and get it on.

He went on to explain how she'd changed and again, he reminds detectives that he didn't know about Roy until Janis told him, and how heartbroken he was that she lied to him. He'd ask her time and again if there was another man but she said, "Bill, nobody but you." He never thought they would ever get a divorce. Bill went into great detail how he wined and dined her, buying her jewelry, flowers and cards to win her back.

Gray: I was just busting my ass trying to get things back to normal. But she stayed firm on wanting a divorce. She told him she planned to leave in September. And I asked her, I says, why September? She says, "Because I know you need help through the summer.

You're not strong enough to take care of the store." She says, "So I figured I'd stay until the busy season was over." And I asked her, I says, well what are your plans then? She says, "I'd like to go to Mom's and spend a month with my mother." And I told her, I says, I think that'd be the best thing you could do. Get away for a month, get your head on straight and then make a decision. I told her, I says, If that's what you want after the 30 days, I says, I won't fight ya, I says, I want you to be happy. Then she's crying again, she says, "Well I don't want to hurt you." And I says, well Betty, I says, you've already hurt me. I says, I won't quit trying. I says, I know I've got until September and a month to go after that, I said. I can't quit trying. I love you too much to quit trying. I felt very positive, ya know, that we would solve this problem and everything would be hunky-dory.

Then he talked at length about the camping trip and how he found out Reeda had been with her relatives but Betty had been with Roy.

Gray: If I'd a known about that, I'd hired a taxi and gone up there. And I'd a broke every fuckin' bone in his body, with a baseball bat, believe me. So I got lied to again.

Bill had been rambling on and on and the detectives just let him go, interjecting a pertinent question here and there. What he said now would give them information to sort out and check out later. A strange personality was emerging. Bill would go from a loving, kind and understanding person to a volatile, frightening, foul-mouthed bully.

Cowden: Let me ask you something here, is that a medical-alert bracelet you wear?

Gray: Yes.

Cowden: Can you take it off? Can I look at it a minute? How long have you had this?

Gray: I can't get it off. I've had a medical-alert bracelet ever since I've been on dialysis.

Cowden: And you wear it all the time?

Gray: Yes, you see I have to, ya know. I have that on every day 'cause if I got the wrong medication, I'd be dead.

Bill and the detectives worked at trying to get the bracelet off his wrist. Finding it to be a major undertaking they gave up.

Cowden: Boy, that thing's really on there ain't it? You just don't get that off very easy.

Gray: No, they're made not to come off.

Cowden: Well now, Sunday, what was your conversation with her, Sunday morning before she left?

Gray: Okay, Sunday morning, did you find out when she left? I did I guess.

Cowden: No, when did she leave?

Gray: 11:30 a.m., Janis saw her just before she left town.

Cowden: OK, good. That's great.

Gray: That help ya?

Cowden: You bet. What was your routine that morning? What did you and she do Sunday morning?

Gray: Okay, Sunday morning? Got up and talked a little bit. Uh, when she got out of the shower, I was still getting dressed in the bathroom there. I was brushing my teeth when she got out of the shower. That was the day of the Wilson Chicken Fry which we usually go to, the firemen's benefit. Uh, she was going to go to that and I asked her, I says, who are you going to the chicken fry with, 'cause I figured Janis, uh probably a couple of others got together and go out. That's usually what we did, we'd pretty much stick [inaudible] together and we go out to the chicken fry. And she says, "Well, she says, It looks like it's gonna rain." She says, "I don't think I'll go to the chicken fry." She says, "I think I'll just go on over to Reeda's." I said, OK. She says, "Before I go," she says, "I wanna uh, clean the house up and take care of some washing." and uh ... Oh I know what she did that morning while we were talking. She was fixing my dinner, or lunch if I wanted something to eat. I usually don't eat. But she was fixing me a special uh ... salad she makes up with um, tuna fish in it and then she makes a fresh salad oil. There's lettuce and cheese stuff in it. It's tasty, very tasty. So she was mixing that up and putting it in bowls where I could just take what I wanted if I wanted something for lunch when I came home, before she got home. And uh, got that stuff all ready. And uh, then I left for work at the store. We hugged each other. Give each other a kiss. That was the last time I saw her.

Cowden: Bill, I've really only got one more ques ...

Gray: Uh, the only part of it was, the day before Janis was in the store and just, just pleaded with her not to go. She says, "You've been wanting to go floating all summer long." She says, "Come on it will be fun, we'll have a ball." And Betty says, "No I don't think so. I'm going to go down to uh, to uh Reeda's." And she says,

"You can go down the next day." She says [inaudible] "Go down the next day." She says, "Come go floating with us." I mean she literally pleaded with her. If she'd only listened, she'd still be here.

Cowden: What, what do you think about the person that killed her?

Gray: Low life, scum-sucking son-of-a-bitch, I guess.

Cowden: What do you think ought to happen to him?

Gray: I think he should be hung.

Cowden: Eye for an eye?

Gray: Ya damn right, that's what it says in the Bible.

Cowden: Speaking of that ...

Gray: What is Idaho's ... Pardon?

Cowden: Speaking of that, did you guys go to church much?

Bill was curious, and about to ask what kind of death penalty Idaho had but was interrupted before he could finish his sentence.

They used to go to church a lot but he couldn't be in crowds now that his immune system was so low. "I can't take a chance on rejection. If one of you guys sneezes, I'm leaving. My chances for rejection are still very, very high."

Seemingly relaxed now and sure that he had fielded any tough questions successfully, Cowden hits him with a big one.

Cowden: I have one question. Why would someone say that they saw you in Idaho Falls on Sunday night?

Gray: Huh?

Cowden: Why would someone say they saw you in Idaho Falls on Sunday night?

Gray: Nobody would have any reason to say that because

I wasn't in Idaho Falls.

Cowden: You weren't there?

Gray: Hell no.

Asked when was the last time he was in Idaho Falls Bill told them he had gone down to pick up a lawn mower, would have to find the receipt to recall the date and he'd taken Betty's Subaru. This reminds him of another possession he must get control of and to solidify that he could not have gone to Idaho Falls because the Subaru was already in Idaho Falls and he had no means of transportation to get there.

> Gray: I got a little Subaru. It's the only thing we've got in a long time. When will that be released? Because, if I have to make a trip to Salt Lake to the hospital, that's the only transportation I have.

At this point, Jeff returned with the briefcase and Bill produces a couple of layaway tickets and proceeds to educate the detectives about a very deceitful wife.

> Gray: Okay, on 6-13, layaway ticket, I think from Pamida. There was a crockpot, wash cloths, an iron, some more wash cloths, towels and sheets. On 6-30 the layaway ticket was for a toaster for $9.99, a can opener for $9.99, a Revere cook set for $69.99. That was on the night of 7-3, that I found that, okay? And the layaway came to $89.97 total.

He described another layaway ticket and then showed them a hand written paper with his dated and dollar amount inventory of money he found in Betty's purse.

Gray: On 6-30, okay, 6-30 is the first time that I looked in her wallet. Yeah. She had $85 in one compartment, $12 in another compartment, $2 in the top, $20 in another compartment, for a total of a $119. You get a little smarter as you go along but it was unusual for her to carry that much money, unless she was going shopping. If she went shopping, hell, I might give her, ya know, if she said she needed $600 bucks, I gave her $600 bucks. Okay?

On 7-3, she had ... huh? Okay I must of checked it two times. I checked in the morning and I checked it in the evening on 7-3. There was $158. Next time I checked it on the same day, there was $264.

Okay. On the night of 7-4, there was a new $20 added to it for a total of $33 and there was a total of $250 gone. By the way, was 7-4 a Tuesday? She could have given that to Roy when he came up on Tuesdays. That son-of-a-bitch. Also on the 4th, in my main cash drawer, my $100 bills had been changed by one bill. My $50 bills had been decreased by $100, so she went in and got larger bills.

Now, this is a list that she had complied of things she was still gonna get. She had down a: steam basket, can opener was already on layaway, pots and pans were already on layaway. The toaster was already on layaway, a four-sided grater, spatulas and scrapers, spoons, whips, steak knives. Now this one really rings home after finding out what I found out. Coffee pot, question mark. Roy does not drink coffee. Okay, that's uh, 7-5, uh [inaudible] 7-3, 7-4, $250, 7-5, have you got that one?

Okay, 7-5 she had $1 up in her little top compartment, she had $25 in the lower compartment. Uh, minus $33 that she had the day before, she must've stole $42 that day.

Bill continued the inventory of Betty's wallet, entry by entry, day by day, compartment by compartment. The first entry was made on June 30 and the last, the morning of July 23. His notes clearly showed that Betty had $230, plus $20 she had asked Bill for in her purse when she left for Reeda's Sunday morning. The change had not been overlooked either.

Gray: Quarters mostly, that she scarfed up from the soda pop sales. The next day in the top she had $6 and her coin purse was loaded. That was at night. Let's see, the morning 7-7, where is that? The store till was off $50. Evidently she juggled so much money through there she forgot how much she had. Twice a day he rummaged through her purse noting every detail.

On 7-11, night time, lots of big change, $8 in the top compartment, $11 in the bottom compartment. On 7-12 she had two $100 bills in the bottom, and $50 still tucked away down inside. She had a $20, two $10s, and two $5s for a total of $281 ahead of what she had the day before. So she had a big day that day. I know you guys are gonna find this hard to swallow with all this shit that I'm still, ya know, busting my ass trying to get her back. But it just ... money means nothing to me. We're very rich. Very rich, and uh, love is blind.

Kotrason: If you are very rich why would she take money if she figured she was going to get half of everything? Or was she going to get half of everything?

Gray: Yes, we would split everything right down the middle. Well, hell, 29 years, she earned it the same as I earned it. Another thing that comes into view here since, ya know, Roy came into the picture. Roy knew my financial status. Okay? 'Cause he came up to me one day and said "With everything you bought at the show and everything you've got you must be a millionaire." I just looked at him and laughed and I says, well we're, add to that, let's say multi. I didn't tell him how much, I just said multi. Roy must have gone after her for my money. I, I wouldn't be a bit surprised, because he knew how I treated her. Christ Almighty, just ya know, all the time new jewelry. Whatever she wanted she got. I treated her like a queen.

Kotrason: Why would she steal this money though?

Gray: Okay, I'm thinking this. She wanted to sell everything, and I told her, I says, definitely not. I says, I will not do that. I says, I'll sell the business because of my health.

At this point in the interview the detectives ran out of tape for their recorder. Bill offered to lend them one of his but they declined and would now rely on their notes. But Bill's recorder kept recording, recording his every word, and the inflection in his voice as he swore and laughed and came unglued when he found out about the safe deposit box.

He went on to explain that he wanted to keep the land and

building and rent it out. In 20 years it would be paid for. He told Betty she would get a check for the rentals every month.

"We'd split it down the middle 50-50."

He said she was agreeable to that, but he guessed she wanted to sell the business to where she would get a large sum of money to get started in her new life.

Asked if he thought Roy could have killed the women he thought it was very, very possible. He volunteered that Reeda had a lot of boyfriends and one of them could have done it.

"I know Reeda, but I don't know Reeda, if you know what I'm saying. I think Reeda got around [laughter] a little."

Gray: You said the other day you had something to tell me. So far, [laughter] you haven't told me anything.

Cowden: I'm gonna tell you something now. We haven't let any grass grow under our feet and we located a safe deposit box.

Gray: You did? In Idaho Falls? Was Betty's name on it?

Cowden: Yes, and we've secured those contents.

Gray: Can I ask what was in it?

Cowden: Yeah. There's money in it.

Gray: How much did she unravel?

Kotrason: There was about $3,000, somewhere in there, don't hold us to that.

Gray: So I'm going to get it back?

They told him that loose coins and coins in plastic wrappers as well as some women's rings were in the box in addition to the money. Bill inquired if there was any chance a great big man-size ring with four beautiful half carat diamonds was in it? No, there were no men's rings.

"Damn her." he replies.

Kotrason: Are you missing any silver dollars?

Gray: Mister, I could be missing 600 and, no, uh, $264,000 worth of coins.

Kotrason: What about gold pieces?

Gray: Yes. Anything from half dollars, $5, $10 gold pieces. Krugerrands, uh, gold ingots, silver ingots, silver one-ounce rounds, you name it.

Kotrason: She had envelopes with cash, a brown paper sack with cash in it, $100 dollar bills, and $50 bills.

Gray: That's why my goddamn pawn account was screwed up. I'll tell you I'm in total shock. I'm beyond being hurt anymore."

The wife he loved so much, the wife he treated like a queen, the wife he would kill himself to be with if it wasn't for his kids, had stolen from him, and two days after her death the self-professed multi-millionaire is no longer going to grieve for her.

The detectives are ready to terminate the interview but Bill's interest in the safe deposit box's contents compels him to ask numerous questions about the jewelry and coins until he is satisfied that he knows exactly what was there.

Gray: $3,000 bucks plus gold and silver dollars, and ...

Cowden: Well, don't hold me to that figure. It may be off.

Kotrason: There's only one gold piece and 29 silver dollars.

Gray: No, no, no, I'm not gonna hold you to anything.

Kotrason: Bill I just want ...

Gray: Approximately $3,000 in cash. One $5 gold piece. How many silver dollars?

Cowden: Twenty-nine I believe.

Gray: I bet she hygraded those too.

Cowden: And then there was some plastic. There was only five of those if I recall.

Gray: Plastic containers about that tall? They hold 20 apiece.

Cowden: No, no, this is a square, single individual pocket-type plastic. Individually wrapped [inaudible]

Gray: She hygraded. Do you know what she probably has in those 29 plus, how many packages? She probably has anywheres from $3,000 to $30,000 right there.

It had been a long session. Detectives were finished but Bill said he had more to report on the layaway slips and the inventory of Betty's purse. After listening to several more minutes of his detailed report, detectives made copies of his papers in case they needed to refer to them again and terminated the interview.

Bill was glad they had enough interest in his plight to take copies. A picture was taken of the medical-alert bracelet on Bill's wrist. Asked if he would mind if they took a couple of pictures of him, the good guy, with nothing to fear said, "I don't mind. I've got nothing to hide. I told ya."

While Bill Gray was being interviewed in Jackson, Idaho authorities were working with security guard, Steve Mackley. Mackley had helped draw a composite sketch of the man he had seen in the early morning of July 24. The picture emerged of man with similar characteristics to Gray, including a pronounced receding hairline, however it was absent of any facial hair. Bill Gray had a full beard, had a full beard the night of July 23. In fact had been full bearded for a good many years. This was disappointing for the detectives but understandable given the conditions and length of time Mackley had talked to the man. Making a full report for the investigators, Mackley searched his memory for every detail he could remember about the man and the vehicle.

Upon hearing the rumors around the station about the possibility of a bike being connected to the murders on Crowley Road Patrolman Greg Black had a talk with the detectives. At 3:05 a.m. Monday he'd checked out some kids in an area not far from the hospital. From there he drove south on Channing Way toward the hospital where he noticed a man on a bicycle riding the same direction. Channing Way had several street lights and he observed a man in dark colored clothes with a salt and pepper beard, wire rimmed glasses, about 50 years old with middle age spread. He didn't remember seeing a light on the bike as he had just looked straight across at the rider as he passed.

The man was sitting more upright than a person would be if hunched over the curled handlebars of a ten speed so he thought it was an older style bike with what he thought to be a chrome front and dark back. He did not notice any other thing on the bike such as a basket or sack. He thought the rider could have had a backpack but just wasn't positive. Officers were grateful for this piece of information. This substantiated Mackley's reporting of a man on a bike in the same area that night, and the time he talked to the man in the Travelall.

After Bill learned he'd been identified as being in Idaho Falls it prompted him to make the comment that he'd been thinking about shaving off his beard. Saralyn and Jeff were horrified. It took a lot of persuasion to talk their dad out of it. He'd been bearded for the last 12 years. They couldn't imagine him without it. Why, all of a sudden would he think about this, three days after his wife's death? Saralyn and Jeff didn't know their dad had been accused of being in Idaho Falls Sunday night. No one thought anything more about it.

On Wednesday evening close to 10:30 p.m. when Bill went to check out the till at the shop Jeff stayed home since his grandfather was with his dad. But when they didn't come home by midnight and then 1:30 a.m. Jeff became very worried for their safety with all his father had been saying. He called the shop and did not get an answer. He loaded a gun and was about to go down to the shop, about half scared he would find bodies, when they finally came home. Greatly relieved they were home safely, Jeff didn't even ask what took them so long.

Lloyd Laker, a veteran Jackson Police Officer of 25 years, knew Bill Gray well. They'd played cards together and he and his wife socialized with the Grays on several occasions over the years. On duty, Laker was driving around town close to midnight Wednesday evening. He noticed two vehicles leaving Gray's Pawnshop. A new model white Cadillac was following an older green Travelall headed south. Aware of the recent investigation in Idaho Falls he drove up behind the Cadillac and noted the California license plate number, then pulled alongside the Travelall and saw Bill behind the wheel. They didn't wave or exchange nods as Bill did not turn his head in acknowledgment that Laker was next to him. Laker pulled away and continued his route around town. About an hour later he checked the Gray home but neither the car, nor the Travelall was there. Laker filled out a report and made a mental note to mention it to the guys first thing the next day.

Officer Chris Bracken checked the pawnshop early Thursday morning. The Travelall had not been returned. Since the last time the Travelall was seen it was headed south, Bracken had a hunch he might know where it went. Not only did officers know most of the townsfolk they also had a pretty good idea of who associated with whom and what was going on in this small tourist town. Bill Gray was known to be a good friend of rancher, Jack Hurley and Hurley's ranch was about 35 miles south of Jackson in Bondurant, Wyoming. If Gray was trying to stash the Travelall, that would be a logical place to look.

Bracken rented a light plane and flew out to Hurley's ranch where he spotted the Travelall backed in among some farm equipment and other vehicles. Later that day he drove out to the ranch and identified it by its identification number as the same one he had taken a picture of the day before at the pawnshop. When Bracken ran a check he found that the Travelall was registered to a Ron Mitchell. The Cadillac seen the night before following the Travelall out of town was registered to a William R. and Sara Gray, Bill's parents.

Ron Mitchell's address on the registration was P.O. Box 3706 and the post office box was registered to Jackson Hole Security Patrol, William L. Gray. Later when they probed deeper into Gray's buying and selling automobile activities they found 14 vehicle registration transfers all to P.O. Box 1871, Gray's Pawnshop. The Travelall was the only one to have been registered to P.O. Box 3706.

As soon as the autopsy was finished on Wednesday, Reeda's body was released and she was taken back to Utah where she was born 47 years ago. Arrangements had been made while waiting for her return, and her funeral in Nephi was held on Thursday July 27. The attendance was small, just close family and a few friends, including Roy Leavitt.

There was a private family viewing prior to the service which enabled Reeda's children to see their mother for the last time and say their personal good-byes. Now, their healing process could begin.

Flying into Jackson Hole, Wyoming is an awesome experience. Approaching the valley from the south requires a higher approach altitude than most commercial airports, to clear the high mountain ranges. Upon entering the valley, passengers can see some of the most spectacular scenery in North America. Ten mountain summits tower more than a vertical mile above the valley floor. Crystal clear, blue lakes nestled in the high mountains sparkle in the bright sun. Passengers are treated with an eye level glimpse at the peak of the Grand Teton with its barren sheer cliffs. Snow remains on the mountain year round nestled in glacial crevices near the peak. Once clearing the mountains, commercial jets will rapidly lose altitude, traverse up the valley past the airport, then turn around and line up with the runway. The airport is small and modern and the runway is short. For commercial airliners the runway has one of the shortest minimums allowable.

Dick, Jo Ann and Dorothy expected to arrive at their hotel close to 2 p.m. Thursday. However, when landing at Jackson Airport, their pilot came in hot, overshooting the touch down markers. The plane ran out of runway and skidded to a stop in the dirt and sage brush well beyond the end of the pavement. Shook up a little, but without injuries, the passengers were detained in the aircraft for over an hour and a half while ambulances and fire engines surrounded the plane. No doors were allowed to be opened on the aircraft and in the July sun the airplane was intensely warm inside.

After several passengers became ill from the heat and authorities were sure it was safe, the doors were opened allowing fresh air in the cabin. All passengers deplaned 30 minutes later, hot and miserable but otherwise alright. By the time the Buccola's and Dorothy's luggage was unscrambled in the chaos, a car rented, and a six mile drive to town, it was close to 5 p.m. when they checked into their motel.

It had been a long day. Dorothy needed to eat before taking her medication, Dick was hungry and Jo Ann knew she should force herself to eat something, and then they would go and see the family. Jo Ann was nervous about seeing Bill. It wasn't that she didn't know what to say, on the contrary, she knew exactly what she was going to say. It was her phone conversation with Janis after their arrival that caused her concern.

Bill had let it be known that Dorothy was welcome to come, and stay at the house, but Jo Ann would not be welcomed at the home on Stacy Lane. She knew Bill was blaming her for Betty wanting a divorce, but she had something to say and was going to make every effort to talk to him.

"One way or another he's going to hear me out," she vowed, "I'll not leave this town until he does."

There was a newer Cadillac with California plates, which they assumed belonged to Bill's parents and another car in the driveway when they arrived. After ringing the bell several times without response Dick suggested they leave.

"Come on Jo Ann, they just don't want you in there," Dick said. "We'll try again tomorrow."

But just as they were stepping off the porch Bill opened the door.

"We stepped into the little entry area and naturally I started crying because of my sister. I looked at Bill and said, 'I'm so sorry what happened, but you and I really have to sit down and talk. I've already talked to the police and I want to tell you what I told them.' Mention of the police undoubtedly allowed her acceptance into the house. Bill had to know what had been said.

Jo Ann, Bill, Jeff and Kim sat at the kitchen table to talk while Dick and Dorothy joined Bill's parents in the living room. Jo Ann was relieved that her niece had already left having heard from Janis that Saralyn was blaming Jo Ann for her mother's death. If Jo Ann would have told her about the divorce she thought she could have prevented her mother's death.

"There was nothing Saralyn could have done to prevent what happened. She had no control over her father. But I wish Betty would have told the kids. I knew Bill didn't want anyone to know about their divorce. I'm sure it was all part of his plan that we would all be shocked to death when we found out and would have all been on his side rather than Betty's."

For now, it would be easier to tell Bill what she was going to tell him if Saralyn wasn't present.

Clearly Bill Gray's behavior through the many years the Hales family had known him, had left them respectful of his volatile and dangerous personality. For Karen to jump to such an irrational thought that Bill was going to kill Betty while they were on the phone and Jo Ann's instant statement to Dick, "Betty's dead, Bill killed her," before she knew any of the circumstances, proved they felt there was something in Bill that would allow him to kill.

Solidified by Betty's recent fears and knowing what he was thinking, Jo Ann was unquestionably afraid of Bill. So much so, that she started out by telling Bill she had already told everything she was going to tell him now to the police, when in fact, she had not talked to any officials other than the brief and uninformative conversation with Detective Wilde Monday night.

"I hadn't talked to the police yet but I wanted him to think I had because I was scared of what he might do. If he thought I had already told them everything he would have no reason to come after me. I said, 'I'm sure I'm not your favorite person being as you blame me for everything that happens. I like you OK. Bill, you're probably an alright person, but not for my sister. I just don't like the way you possessed her. You told her everything she could do. Excuse me, but you told her when she could go to the bathroom and when she couldn't. You treated my sister like dirt. I am going to tell you everything I told the police and I told them I thought you killed Betty. It's going to be tough, but try and put yourself in my shoes as Betty's sister. Everything is real fresh in my mind and I've got to tell you why I think what I do.'"

So Jo Ann began with everything she could think of that Betty had told her while she was in California, about wanting a divorce, about Roy and their plans to marry, the cards and collect phone calls.

"Do you remember a day last week when Betty made an excuse not to go to work with you? Betty called me collect again and she said that you were acting real strange and that you shoved her. She was afraid of you Bill, and she must have been afraid something was going to happen because she told me about her safe deposit box so I would know about it. She thought you already knew about Roy because you found a card Roy had sent her. She was totally convinced you knew about Roy, and I'm convinced you knew about Roy."

Defending himself, Bill insisted he never knew about the

cards and in fact was totally surprised when he heard it was Roy. He thought it was someone else from Fanning Wholesale, giving away the fact he had known for some time Betty was having an affair.

Jo Ann went on to tell Bill how concerned she was that he might find out. That she strongly advised Betty to get the picture of Roy out of her wallet and to stop seeing him until the divorce was final.

"Frankly, Bill, I was very scared of what you might do if you found out. Bill said he couldn't have handled it if he'd have known, which I already knew. That's why she's dead."

Kim and Jeff just sat and listened while Bill asked questions and accused Roy and even Roy's wife of killing Betty. When they were through talking it was almost midnight. Before they left, much to Jo Ann's surprise, Bill put his arms around her. He said, "I'm really glad we had this talk Jo Ann. Now I know why you feel the way you do."

He never came out in defense of himself, Jo Ann remembered. He never said, "Jo Ann, I didn't kill your sister." An innocent person would have thrown me out of the house if I would have openly accused them of something like that, but it was obvious he wanted to find out what I told the police.

After the Travelall had been slipped out of town the night before, Jackson authorities thought it possible Bill might take further actions to cover his trail. They decided to keep surveillance on his activities Thursday night. Lt. Dave Foster and Officer Scott Hughes, along with two Bonneville County Officers, spent most of the night watching Bill's house. If he decided to take off or move anymore possible evidence they would know about it and take appropriate action. It was an uneventful night. Bill was home all night with the family. Although they didn't know who they were then, they observed the late departure of Jo Ann and her family. The lights went out at 1:30 a.m.

In Jackson, as well as Idaho Falls, the double homicide was front page news divulging the innermost family secrets. "HOMICIDE VICTIM BETTY GRAY WAS HAVING AN AFFAIR" ... "BETTY GRAY WAS GOING TO DIVORCE HER HUSBAND." There was nowhere to hide. The town was small and most everyone either knew the Grays or knew of them. Morning coffee klatches lasted longer, the speculation was rampant and Bill was furious. He called Detective Foster threatening to go down and raise hell with the newspaper.

"I told him I'd look into it but they were just repeating what the Sheriff told them so it really wasn't the paper's fault," said Foster. "They were only printing what they had been told and there wasn't anything a person could do about that."

Steven Mackley stared long and hard at the six photos the investigators laid out in front of him. He knew immediately which man he had talked to the early morning of July 24, but he was puzzled as to why he could not remember the beard. His reporting that the man had light colored hair, when in fact Bill Gray had dark brown, almost black, and a slightly grey mixture, was understandable considering the light. He could only attribute not seeing the beard to a combination of things. In addition to the poor lighting conditions, the man was slumped down so low in the seat that Mackley's view was downward. Given the balding and pronounced receding hair line and the glasses low on the nose he could get the impression that the man did not have facial hair. Nonetheless he was positive the man he saw that night was #3 in the photo lineup, Bill Gray.

Officer Black, the patrolman that passed a bike and rider on Channing Way early Monday morning, was not as certain. He looked closely at the photo lineup but could only say that #3 looked "most" like the man he saw that night.

By Friday morning Detective Rodriguez was sure he knew the identity of Reeda Roundy and Betty Lou Gray's killers. Step two was to gather sufficient evidence to get an indictment. Regardless of the disappointing composite sketch that showed no facial hair, the Travelall was the key. It was too much of a coincidence for Mackley to describe this very unusual Travelall bearing Wyoming plates and then find one fitting that same description in the possession of the husband of one of the murdered women. The detective didn't believe for one minute that Gray did not know about Betty's affair prior to her death. Gray was too sneaky, proven by his own account of going through Betty's purse without her knowledge. Certainly he would have found Roy's picture in her wallet as he searched through every compartment. The detective was sure he had his man and he was sure he had the motive. He just had to prove it.

Rodriguez prepared a fifteen page affidavit for search and seizure warrants on the pawnshop, the Gray home and the Travelall. In particular the warrant listed clothing, guns, bullets, tennis shoes, candles and various documents. Having heard a preliminary report from the Ballistics Lab in Boise they first thought they were looking for a .357 or .38-caliber revolver. Then, knowing the killer walked around the room looking for the shell casings the idea came out it could have been an automatic, a 9mm or 10mm. The warrant would list both possibilities. Detectives Rodriguez and Cowden drove to Jackson to have Teton County 9th District Judge, Terry Rogers execute the warrants.

Before a judge will issue a search warrant he must be convinced there is sufficient reason for the request. The procedure is designed to protect civilians from having their premises or private property unreasonably searched on a whim that whatever they find will incriminate. Law enforcement must lay a valid foundation that the evidence already in the possession of the authorities is incriminating enough to substantiate further search and seizure. Therefore, when preparing an affidavit requesting a search warrant the affidavit must contain quite detailed information about the case up to that point. It must list specifically the items they are looking for and tie those items to the facts they have. In essence, the affidavit contains most all the information investigators have on the case to that date.

Search warrants are public record open to anyone to examine and thus, a prime source for reporter's information. When prosecutors have reason to withhold information from the public for various, and sometimes obvious reasons, they request the judge to seal the records. Bonneville County Prosecutor Kimball Mason requested Teton County seal the search warrant affidavits on the Gray case. Through this action, reporters would be limited to information discovered on their own and what authorities felt could be shared without contaminating their case.

Bill didn't know where Betty was, or when they could expect to bring her home. He told everyone, including his children, the police would only tell him when he called that she had been taken for an autopsy and they would let him know when her body would be released. In fact, he had been calling the detectives wanting to know when he could get Betty's Subaru, her jewelry and the contents of the safe deposit box, but had not once asked where Betty was.

Jo Ann couldn't understand why it would take so long for an autopsy. She was fed up with Bill's family, the way they were acting, slamming Betty at every opportunity. She was anxious to see her sister one last time to say her goodbyes. Her mother was still in a semi-state of shock and would just sit as though in a trance relying on Jo Ann and Dick to make the decisions. Dorothy needed to get away from Jackson and go home to deal with her pain, in fact they all needed to go home. Jo Ann wanted to call the police herself and ask where Betty was and when they could have her, but if Bill found out and thought she was going behind his back she was afraid he wouldn't allow her to attend her sister's funeral. She had managed to exercise a great deal of patience with Bill these past few days but by late Friday afternoon she had enough.

Calling the Bonneville County Sheriff's office, Jo Ann spoke with John Cowden asking him if he had any idea where her sister's body was. She told him her brother-in-law said they had not released her body yet and she wanted to know if he had any idea when they would be doing that. When Jo Ann was told the autopsy had been finished on Wednesday and the Sheriff's department could have released the body any time after that she was shocked.

"My brother-in law said he called you every day wanting to know where she was and you never tell him anything. You always tell him you don't know."

"No," he said, "Bill has called us several times but he has never asked where his wife's body was. You are the only person that has called wanting to know that."

Still cautious and afraid of Bill's reaction Jo Ann asked Cowden to call Bill and tell him.

"I don't want to be the one to tell him. I don't want him thinking I'm doing something behind his back. You've got to call him." Cowden wouldn't be calling Bill. He would tell him in person.

At the request of Detective Rodriguez who was en route to Jackson to get the search warrant, Lt. Foster set up another interview with Gray. Since Foster had been present at the notification, Rodriguez wanted Foster to sit in on this interview along with John Cowden, who had been present at all of Gray's previous interviews and had been fielding his inquiries. If Gray told a different story than he had before, these detectives would know it and challenge him on the spot. It wouldn't be as friendly of an interview as Gray had encountered before. This time they would get right to the point. The goal of the interview was to commit Gray to a story.

"We knew there had been a Travelall identified in Idaho Falls and one found at the pawnshop and then he tries to hide it a couple of days after she's killed," recalled Foster. "But Mackley, Mackley describes a pock marked face, looking over the top of his glasses slumped down, a medical-alert bracelet. He just described Bill Gray. He had a pock marked face and he always looked over the top of his glasses. We've got a photo taken in this office where he's slumped down in the seat peering over the top of his glasses. Put it all together and it really pointed to Gray. We'd see what he had to say and go from there."

Bill was still fuming over the newspaper articles. He wanted to know if Foster was able to get them to print a retraction, but Foster again explained they were only printing what they'd been told.

Gray: Well hell, half that shit wasn't true.

Foster: They were just quoting the Sheriff.

Gray: Son of a bitch.

Cowden: Anything you say can, and will, be used against you in a court of law. You have the right to talk to a lawyer before we talk to you. And if you can't afford to hire a lawyer one will be appointed to represent you before any questions can be answered. And if you decide at any time to exercise these rights and not answer any of the questions [inaudible]. Do you understand these rights as I have explained them to you? Having these rights in mind, do you wish to talk to us now? Sign it with your birth date, and we'll witness it and we'll get down to business.

The date was Friday, July 28, 1989 and the time was 7:35 p.m. Bill Gray had his tape recorder on the table next to Foster's ready to go, and Cowden got right to the point.

Cowden: I found out some things in town that make me a little bit unhappy.

Gray: Like what?

Cowden: Well, uh ... you own a green Travelall?

Gray: No, I don't.

Cowden: Do you drive one or have you had one?

Gray: I had one that I sold. I didn't own it. I bought it for a guy and sold it.

Cowden: Oh. How long ago was that?

Gray: Uh ...

Foster: Has it been quite a while, or ...

Gray: Oh shit, I don't even know.

Gray went on to explain that he had bought the Travelall for another man. The man wanted some work done on it and Bill had it repaired. The man paid him $200 down and when he came to pick it up he wasn't happy with it. Bill told him as far as he was concerned it was his. He'd wanted it, Bill had the work done and the Travelall was his whether he liked it or not.

Gray: He went over and had it uh, registered and everything. And I held open title on it, and he finally finished payin' for it and picked it up.

Foster: Okay. How long ago was that?

Gray: He picked it up, uh ... oh, when in the hell. Oh, he had the keys ... uh ... I think it was ... I'd have to look at the tapes. I think it was Saturday he finished payin' for it, Friday or Saturday.

Foster: This last Saturday?

Gray: Uh huh.

Foster: So a week ago, approximately. And then he came and got it?

Gray: Yeah ... Oh, I don't know ... [inaudible] and it's gone so he's picked it up. I don't know. I couldn't tell you when.

Foster: Okay. So it wasn't the car you drove at all.

Gray: No. Well, I drove it from where I bought it to the garage that did the work on it, next door to the pawnshop. I can't remember if they brought it back over, or if I drove it back from there. We're right next door to each other.

Cowden: So that's the only time you've ever driven it?

Gray: Yes, sir.

Foster: And that was about a week ago when he came and got it, at some point, and that's the last time you drove it was a week ago?

Gray: No. I hadn't drove it for ... since it had been repaired. You'd have to check and see what the date was on the repair ticket.

Foster: I see. Do you remember who you sold it to?

Gray: It's ... I think he worked down in Pinedale on one of the ranches. So when he went to get the title on it, I had him mail the title to me. And he came back and he was bitchin' about, you know, he wanted more work done to it. And I told him, I said, hey, for $400 bucks, I says you know, I've already paid, I think the, the wheel bearing and the master cylinder and it cost me $64 dollars, and uh, I made about oh almost a $140 off the vehicle and I says, Hey, I ain't puttin' anymore goddamn money in it. When you get the rest of the money you can pick up the vehicle.

Foster: Okay. So he picked it up and it's down in Pinedale somewhere, then?

Gray: I have no idea.

Foster: You're not sure? Do you have his name?

Gray: It's ... let me think. I'm so bad on names. I had open title on it. I just give him the open title. He went to the courthouse and got his uh title, paid the taxes and what not. He had all the receipts for that shit. And then like I say I had him mail me the title. Then when he came back in I had him sign it 'cause he still owed me the $200 bucks that he was bitching about, and I uh, I had to sign it and we had it notarized and uh, when he came in either Friday or Saturday, one or the other I think it was and uh, I give him the title and shit back.

Cowden: Do you remember his name at all?

Gray: Ron, Ron Miller or Ron Mitchell. I think it's Ron

Mitchell.

Cowden: And that's in Pinedale? Where is Pinedale?

Gray: Pinedale's about uh, 64 miles from here. About an
hour and 20 minute drive. He is working on a ranch
down there.

They talked about Bill selling cars and that sometimes he
took them in as a pawn. "We pawn anything that's legal and has
some keys," he laughed.

Foster took him into his activities on Sunday afternoon and
evening and Gray related the same story of going home and
putting his feet up, returning to the pawnshop later to check out
the till and returning home, staying until Monday morning when
he went to get blood drawn, then opening the shop.

He said he went down to the shop every night to check out
the till and last night he didn't get down there until almost
midnight because Jo Ann and Dick had come in and they talked
for hours and hours. He said Jeff went with him to help him out
because he hadn't made a deposit since Saturday and it was 2:55
a.m. this morning when he crawled into bed. But was this true?
Foster had been on surveillance of Bill's house most of Thursday
night and no one saw him leave. Bill was either blowing more
smoke or he left very late after the officers did.

Cowden: What about Sunday? What time did you go
down there?

Gray: Sunday? I really don't know what time I went down
there.

Cowden: Was it early or late?

Gray: No it was late. Now what rang my bell was Shawn,
who lives downstairs in an apartment below the
pawnshop. He was living down there then and he saw

the truck there 'cause I went back down to close up and set the alarm there at uh, 5:30 p.m. So that's when my help leaves. And Shawn comes in and uh, says, "I saw your truck out there," he says, "I been wantin' to come in and, you know, pay my respects and tell you how sorry I am about Betty and everything."

Foster: When ... I'm sorry. When was this? Was that last night?

Gray: Yeah. I told him, you know, what the hell has been going on. And uh, I was, you know, really gettin' wore out and angry over it. Because, you know, it's takin' so damn long and I wanted to get Betty home and get that part behind us and what not. "Well Jesus Christ, Bill," he says, "We hear you every night when you're in here." And he says, "We hear you come and we hear you go." So, I told him I was gonna have you call him and he says, "Well, hell," he says "I'll call him if you want." And I said, Well thank you very much, Shawn. I said, I really appreciate it. He says, "I'm gonna go down and see Jason [Shawn's roommate] now." So he went down to where Jason worked and checked his time card. Jason checked out at 10:32 p.m. and it takes him 10 to 15 minutes to walk from where he works back to the apartment. And Jason says my truck was still setting out front. I hadn't left yet at that time. Now can you tell me, since the autopsy is all done, what time was Betty killed?

The detectives couldn't give Bill a positive time for Betty's death stating that they were still waiting for reports to come back and then led him into the Travelall issue where again he said he had not driven the Travelall since he bought it about a month ago.

Turning the conversation toward how he and Betty had been getting along since she told him she wanted a divorce he was adamant that nothing had changed, everything was the same as before, they still went out to dinner and once again, like he had in every other interview, went through the story that he asked if there was another man and she said, "No one but you." and he had no reason not to believe her.

Getting around to his health, Bill had lots to talk about. He said before he got his kidney he may have had 30 days left, 45 at the very outside. The blood clots were worse than the actual kidney surgery; his legs hurting and swelling where he couldn't do anything around the store. Asked if he did any therapy for it he said there wasn't any therapy for it. Walk, maybe. But he couldn't walk, his knees were too bad.

Foster: Do you ride on an exercise wheel or bike or whatever the hell they call those things?

Gray: No. I bought one of those Nordic Tracks and that's the best thing I ever did because it's smooth and doesn't jar my knees. The pressure of pedaling would flat kill me.

Foster: Well, there has been some problems that have come up over in Idaho Falls.

Gray: Explain that.

Foster: Well, I will. It comes from Idaho Falls and some of the information these fellows have developed is really not heartening to hear. John, it came from the Falls, you tell him.

Cowden: Yeah. One fellow uh, told us that he witnessed a man down by the hospital on a bicycle.

Gray: No sir.

Cowden: He put the bicycle in the back of a green Travelall. He talked with him and he did see Wyoming tags on it.

Foster: The problem we've run into is that he described you very, very detailed. And we've gone a step further with a photograph that they took of you and we showed it in a lineup. He identified you as the person he saw.

Gray: It's impossible.

Cowden: He ID'd the Travelall.

Gray: [laughs] He may of ID'd a car but ...

Cowden: No. He identified both you and the Travelall.

Gray: It isn't, definitely, because it isn't true, John.

They went on to tell him that a deputy in Idaho Falls had seen a man on a bike riding toward the hospital and that he also picked Bill out in the photo lineup. Bill admitted that he had been to the hospital in Idaho Falls before, but not that night, not for some time now.

Gray: Dave, I'm telling you I wasn't over there.

Foster: Well, why would two people who have nothing to gain by trying to hurt you, why would they pick you out?

Gray: I don't know. How many people look like me?

Cowden: Nobody.

Foster: Now they positively said that's the person, right down to the medical-alert bracelet on the right hand.

Gray: I'm telling you he's wrong.

Foster: Well, is Lloyd Laker wrong when he tells us that you were driving a green International Travelall yesterday morning just after midnight?

Gray: Yes he is.

Foster: When he runs the second vehicle that's driving behind him, which he knows is your father's, when he runs the plate, which is identified as belonging to William or Sara Gray?

Gray: Uh huh.

Foster: So he's wrong?

Gray: Dad went down and got gas.

Foster: OK and he didn't follow a green International?

Gray: I have no idea.

Foster: That's down at Jack Hurley's house being searched pursuant to a search warrant. Bill, now is the time to start telling the truth, because you're not. God, it hurts me to no end to say that to you, but now is the time, Bill. You gotta look at it from our side and the things that we're seeing, the things that we're learning. These people aren't all wrong.

Gray: I wasn't over there.

Foster: We'd like to hear it from you and hear the truth from you Bill. Bill, these people aren't going to make these things up. One of, two of them were police officers. One of them knows you as well as anybody in this town. He said it was you. There is no doubt in his mind it was you, followed by your father's car. Now what are we to think, Bill? Are all these people lying?

Gray: I told you, I went down and got gas.

Just a few questions previously Bill said his father went and got gas. Now, against the wall, he went and got gas. Foster read Officer Laker's report word for word and advised Bill they were towing the Travelall in "as we speak."

Cowden: You know you can't keep that bottled up in you. You, you should tell us.

Gray: I have told you.

Cowden: No. What you told us is what you want us to hear.

Gray: I've told you the truth. If you guys aren't going to believe me I guess I need to talk to my attorney.

As far as the detectives were concerned that was the end of the interview. When Bill mentioned the word, attorney, they were done.

Foster: If you change your mind, Bill, you'll need to contact us. We won't be talking to you anymore about it.

As Jack Hurley was driving from Jackson to his ranch in Bondurant he passed a tow truck. The vehicle being towed was the green International Travelall Bill brought out to his ranch the night before. Tucked in the latch on the front door of Hurley's home was a roll of papers advising the owner of the premise that the vehicle found on his property had been seized by the Teton County Sheriff's Office. He called the Sheriff's Office wanting to know what was going on and was told the Travelall was evidence in a crime in Idaho Falls.

William Gray answered the phone when Hurley called Bill's house. When told the Travelall had been seized William replied, "Oh my God, Bill is at the police station right now. He is with the authorities."

William drove to the police station and was waiting when Bill and the detectives terminated their interview. William asked to speak with his son and they were given a private room in which to talk.

They talked for 45 minutes to an hour and when they came out, Bill wanted to talk to the detectives again. At 10:58 p.m. both recorders were turned on and Foster went into great detail that Bill asked to talk to them again, without benefit of counsel. And once again they went over Bill's rights and his wanting to talk to them without his attorney present.

Cowden: What is it you want to tell us?

Gray: Okay. I did take that car out of town that night. We had gone down to the store and made up the till for Eric to open the next morning. And the guy did come in and finish paying for the car and I wanted the repair bill on it. I took it down to Bondurant and he, 'cause he had a set of keys to it, 'til I got the balance of the final repair.

Cowden: Why would you want to hide it then?

Gray: He had a set of keys. I didn't want him to take it until I got the repair bill. Now as far as you guys thinking I took that thing over to Idaho Falls, uh, the mileage should verify that on the registration when he registered it.

Foster: It's not registered. It hasn't been registered in months.

Gray: It is registered.

Foster: To who?

Gray: To ... it's registered to that guy, uh, I sold it to. I said it's either Ron Mitchell or Ron Miller.

Foster: Why wouldn't you have told us that, Bill? That's no big deal. I mean, so what?

Gray: You had told me that the vehicle had been seen over there. You told me that it had been identified in Idaho

Falls.

Detective Foster lays it on the line. The first mention that he was seen in Idaho Falls was the interview on Wednesday, July 26. The Travelall was not mentioned at all. Around midnight that night he attempts to hide the Travelall. Then in this interview he is asked if he owns a green Travelall, which he denied. He then said, "Well I had one but sold it." Emphatically he stuck to his story that he had not driven it since he bought it about a month ago. When faced with the fact that he was identified, indisputably, as driving it two nights ago, he continues to deny. Now he comes back in and tells them he lied because they told him it was seen in Idaho Falls and Foster abruptly reminds him they had not mentioned the Travelall had been seen in Idaho Falls until well after he had denied again and again he did not own one, nor did he drive one.

He argued the fact as to when they first told him the Travelall was seen in Idaho Falls to the point that Foster told him to listen to your tape. "Our tape is going to say the same as yours."

Bill changes the subject.

Gray: How many damn vehicles that color are there around? I don't even know if it was the same one.

Foster: An incredible coincidence! The issue is, that the vehicle was over in Idaho Falls on Monday, and you've been identified as being over in Idaho Falls on Monday also. They identified your bracelet. Bill, not everybody is talking to a person that looks like you, that has that bracelet on, in a green Travelall with Wyoming plates.

Gray: Do you think I'm that stupid to ...

Foster: I don't think you're stupid, I think you're very upset and I think you were distraught, and I don't think

194

you were Bill Gray that night.

The sparring continues and the officers throw out more substantiation for their accusations.

Cowden: You told us that the Sunday before Betty left you checked her purse. You had it written down. There was $230 and when she left she asked for $20 more, which made it $250 bucks. When we examine the crime scene it was quite obvious right away that robbery was not the goal. There were two purses in that house. One purse, one lady was getting ready to leave the next morning for Las Vegas. The money she had in her purse to go to Las Vegas was there. Betty had a little bit of change. The $250 was missing. Now we caved Roy in really bad, that's how we got the safe deposit box. We put him on the polygraph. She didn't give Roy any money. What happened to the $250? Who would have known that money was in that purse? You were the only one besides Betty.

Interrupting, Bill offered that she probably went shopping and his suggestion was countered that there were no recent purchases or receipts found in the house or in Betty's car. Again, Bill wanted to know the time of death and began to review his alibi.

Gray: I can prove that I was here 'til at least ... quarter to 11 p.m. because when he, Jason, came home and saw my vehicle out there.
Cowden: No. He told me on the phone. You got there about 10 p.m. and you left about 10:30 p.m. He said your habit was to get to the store at 10 p.m. or a little after. And then he said sometimes he's heard you there

at 10:30 p.m. He said that night you came around 10 p.m. or a little after. I asked him if he saw you, he said no, he didn't see you but he hears the dog walking up there.

Gray: Yeah ... pretty much the same. But uh, would you please talk to him again about that?

Cowden: I already did that. I've got it all on tape.

A little more sparring about his alibi and Bill said, "I just wish to hell I'd come clean with you on that first time."

Cowden: Well, I guess we can stop this thing here.

Lt. Foster tries to put what he just heard in perspective. "He buys a Travelall for a man he doesn't know. He has some repairs done on it for $64. The man eventually pays the full original price of $400 which included the repairs and takes the Travelall. Then the man brings the Travelall back wanting more repairs on it. Bill isn't going to do any more repairs on it because he already put out $64 which cut into his profit. The man just walks away, leaving the Travelall and $400 behind.

"Two days after his wife is murdered, when all his family is there, Bill decides at midnight to beat this man out of the $64 that he really doesn't owe, and he drives the Travelall down to Bondurant to hide it from the man because this man had a set of keys. I would think that most people, while there are grieving families there a few days after a murder, are not going to be thinking about hiding a vehicle from a guy, especially when he doesn't owe you any money in the first place.

"I told Bill to wait here after the interview, and I went to the guy from the Bonneville County Prosecutor's Office who was there because I wanted to take him to jail, and I would have. If that crime had occurred in Jackson, Teton County, he would have been in jail that night. He didn't want him taken into custody until he had a chance to review these past events with the Idaho Prosecutor and we had to let him go."

Officer Lloyd Laker came into the police station just as Bill was leaving. Having known Bill for a lot of years it was especially hard on Laker to have provided damaging evidence against his long-time friend. Conversing briefly in the hall, Laker was even more disheartened when Bill told him, in reference to Laker's report, of seeing the Travelall leave town,

"We have known each other too long and this can't go any further."

Now, having to report this statement, Laker admitted it was hard on him, "Yes, but I know what my job is."

When Dick, Jo Ann and Dorothy went to Bill's that night to confront him with the fact that Betty's body could have been released two days ago, Bill was not home. Lee Brown and his girlfriend Cheryl were there with Bill's parents. Saralyn had gone home to check on her son, Kim and Jeff had gone with their dad. When they asked where Bill was his mother said, "Oh, they're interrogating him again. Do you want something to eat?"

Declining the food, they left the message to tell Bill to call them when he got home and they would come back. Bill didn't call that night. He was to be kept quite busy arguing with officers while they searched his home and business.

The search of Bill's house was already in progress when the interview at the police station terminated. Although he knew a search warrant had been issued, Bill was furious to find the officials going through his house. He cussed at them and challenged everything they touched or took. The searchers went about their business bagging, tagging and removing items in spite of Bill's constant interference.

"We were obviously running short on sleep by this time after being up most of the night before watching his house, then going through that lengthy interview and then back to the house working the warrant," recalled Foster. "Some of us were talking about putting someone to watch the pawnshop and doing that the next day when we could have had at least two or three hours sleep. None of us had slept in 30 hours and we were beat.

"Bill overheard our conversation and started ranting about who was going to pay for the business he would lose while we had his shop closed. So we wouldn't have to put up with any problems he might raise we decided to go ahead and do it that night, but one of our officers was in the garage and pulled this box off the shelf and it was a box of crystallized dynamite. So my attention, his attention and the attention of a few others, was focused on that dynamite and what we were going to do with it.

"Our bomb tech was gone and so we had a bomb tech from Idaho Falls come over and blow it up. We had to move it in a dump truck and oh it was a pain, so all of our attention went to that. I was over at the pawnshop later but I finally gave up, my body finally gave up, so I went home to get some sleep."

The home at 435 Stacy Lane contained an inordinate amount of weapons and ammunition. Searchers found box after box of shells, several boxes of 9mm 125 grain bullets, 9mm shells in a sack, boxes of 9mm Lugar empty cartridges and one box of 9mm Lugar empty shell casings. Several handguns were taken including a 9mm Executive Arms handgun in a holster, a Browning 9mm in a leather case and a Smith and Wesson 19-2 handgun fully loaded with six rounds.

Several light and dark blue and denim jumpsuits, red colored candles, insurance papers, Betty's will, notes written by Gray, a flashlight, gloves, hairs, fibers and the lint from the clothes dryer were also among the many items taken from the house. Tennis shoes, even remotely resembling the pattern left at the scene, were not found.

Mary Lou Royce, Teton County crime scene analyst, was working the search warrant and had noticed disposable surgical gloves and wet wipe packets along with other medical supplies but they were not taken. They were not listed on the search warrant. The refrigerator contained several cans of Mountain Dew soda pop.

By 2:30 a.m. Saturday, officers had completed their search of the pawnshop. Among the items taken there were hair and fiber samples from a bicycle seat, a bicycle, additional samples of Bill's handwriting, film, keys and three 9mm handguns.

Mary Lou Royce would later examine the Travelall and find that parts of the interior appeared to have been wiped off where other parts remained dirty. There were no fingerprints found in the Travelall, "Not even smudges," she reported. Bill had admitted that he drove the Travelall over to get it serviced when he first bought it and again to Bondurant just two nights previous. The question was, if he was merely hiding the vehicle from a man who had a key, why would he have taken the precaution to wipe the interior free of fingerprints?

Vegetation and soil samples were taken, in particular the driver's seat and floorboard. Cheat grass of the same variety found in the recliner at the Roundy home was found in the Travelall but it was common to Wyoming, as well as Idaho. Although this information further confirmed investigators suspicions, it could not be considered foolproof evidence that it came from the Roundy yard. Hair found in the Travelall matched the hairs found at the scene but forensic experts would later say they could not positively say it was Bill Gray's hair. It had the same characteristics as Gray's, but hair fibers are not positively identifiable as are fingerprints.

Saturday morning Dick was furious. He called the Bonneville County Sheriff's office to get the number then called the mortuary Betty had been taken to.

"I'm from California and I'm sitting in this motel room with Betty's mother and sister," he explained. "We have to get back home and we just found out she has been released and I would like to bring them down so they can say goodbye before we go."

If Dick thought he was mad, the man on the other end of the line erupted.

"Do you know that I have been in charge of this body since the homicide? The Roundys immediately called us that night, but I have yet to hear from one person from the Gray family to let me know what to do with this body. We have had no instructions as to how to treat her, what to do with her, or anything else."

The mortician Reg Ecker and Dick talked for several more minutes. Finished with his call, Dick said he would take Jo Ann and her mother to Idaho Falls but he doubted they would want to actually see Betty now.

Still upset, Dick said, "We're going over there. I don't care if he thinks I've gone behind his back or not. This is beyond anything I have ever heard of. I'm going over there and tell him what I've done."

Bill was still ranting over the search of his house and

pawnshop when they arrived. Shoving his copy of the search warrant at Jo Ann he complained that he didn't know why the police were constantly questioning him, why were they searching his property. Then he held up his arm, shaking his medical-alert bracelet at her, and began rambling something about "This bracelet is going to hang me."

When Jo Ann questioned what he was talking about he reached out and snatched the search warrant papers out of her hands and muttered that she wouldn't understand. Quickly changing the subject he started in on Reeda.

"That bitch is nothing but a tramp and a slut," he remarked. "She had so many boyfriends, running around sleeping with them all the time. One of them was married so she didn't think anything about letting Roy and Betty use her place. She probably encouraged it."

Within a few minutes he regained control and was now ready to give the family some fresh news.

"OK, now I want everyone to come in this room and everybody sit down. I've got some real bad news."

Jo Ann remembers it well. "Everybody get in here, everybody sit down, and he was acting so important. He starts to tell us about Betty being released and he's telling a whole different story and a different mortuary to boot. Then he said, 'You can't see her, she's not viewable, we can all go down but nobody's going to be able to see her.' Then he puts on this fake cry that he's got. I mean it's so phony it's unbelievable."

If Bill didn't have a clue where Betty was, it's highly probable he still hadn't called anyone. He found out from the detectives the night before at the interview that her body had been released but he did not bother to find out for sure where she was, and he was undoubtedly trying to convince the family that he had been in touch with the mortician and it would be a waste of time for them to go to the funeral home with him.

Dick said they were going, but they would go to the mortuary where Betty was, not the one Bill was telling his family about. Dick told Bill what he had done and that he came over to tell him. He gave Bill the name of the correct funeral home, the phone number and Reg Ecker's name.

"You'd better call him Bill," he said. "He wants to know what to do."

When Bill got off the phone he informed everyone that if they were determined to go, they had to leave immediately. Dick, Jo Ann and Bill rode with Bill's parents in their car and Saralyn went with Kim and Jeff. Dorothy and Janis elected to stay behind and wait for Dan and Karen who were expected to arrive from California anytime.

"I was almost ashamed to face the mortician because of what happened," Jo Ann said. "But the minute we arrived the mortician wanted to know which one was Dick Buccola. Then he came over and took my husband's hand and said, 'I want to thank you very much for our phone conversation this morning and for getting this family here.'

"Bill came in with his sad face but it didn't last long. The first thing Bill wanted to know was the time of death. He wanted to know what time had been put on Betty's death certificate. When told there was no specific time listed yet he said, 'Oh hell, it looks like the bastards are going to arrest me and the time of death is the only thing that will save me. I need to know what time they think she died.' He pushed to see the autopsy report but was advised only the Sheriff's Department had that information.

"Reg Ecker sat the family down and explained that Betty had undergone an extensive autopsy and even though she had been in refrigeration he would not recommend that the family view her. Now that the family was here he could prepare her for a funeral but because she had been there so long and he had not been given advance instructions he didn't think even then she could be viewed. Bill would have none of it. 'She's to be cremated,' he demanded."

Although Jo Ann had promised herself to be calm and stay in Bill's good graces she couldn't stop herself from arguing with him now.

"I knew Betty didn't want to be cremated because we talked about it when our dad died. Although Betty had made a wisecrack years ago in Bill's presence that she guessed she would have to be cremated when she died because they were so broke they couldn't afford a funeral, I knew she was just kidding and I knew Bill knew it. It was the money that influenced Bill's decision. I offered to pay all the expenses including the casket and funeral but he wouldn't budge. I've never felt so helpless in all my life. I wanted for Betty to have what I knew she would want but her husband was the final authority and he wouldn't listen to anyone. Please Bill, Betty didn't want this." Jo Ann begged. Jo Ann and Dorothy's tears would not change his mind. Saralyn and Jeff's pleading would not change his mind. Betty would be cremated and her ashes would be left to Bill's whim as well.

Saralyn insisted someone from the family should view Betty to be sure it was really her. Since Roy was the one that identified her to the police how did they know it was really her mom in there? For all they knew it was someone else and with Roy's help maybe her mother had just ran away. No one wanted to do it. Everyone wished they could see her one last time and some had just the slightest curiosity, but if she was in the condition the mortician indicated she was, they were sure they didn't want to remember her that way.

Primarily in protection of her husband, but also because she was an RN and had dealt with the unpleasantries of life, Kim volunteered. When she came back out to the family Bill took her aside and told her not to tell anyone what she saw.

"Don't you ever tell my two kids what you just saw in there."
Kim promised that she would not.

The real fireworks started when Reg started talking about the expenses Bill was obligated to pay. Bill refused to pay for the extra refrigeration claiming he only needed refrigeration for one day since he had just been notified. The state or county was going to have to pay for everything else. It was their fault she had been here so long. He sure as hell didn't tell them to keep her that long. Then he refused to pay for the body bag saying it was the cop's decision to use a brand new body bag, not his. They used it in their investigation and they could damn well pay for it.

Jo Ann remembered how embarrassing this was. "Everyone was so embarrassed. I wanted to say this is absolutely ridiculous, we'll pay for it. I knew Dick wouldn't care but he didn't want me to say any more in front of Bill and his parents if I wanted to stay in their favor until I could attend Betty's services."

The family's ordeal and embarrassment that day was far from over. Ecker gave Bill a small clasp envelope containing the jewelry Betty had been wearing when she came to him. After Bill opened it and pulled out the contents his face got red and he demanded to know where the rest of her jewelry was. Instantly on the defensive, he would not accept Ecker's explanation that everything Betty had on her body when he got her was in that envelope.

"She had a heart shaped bracelet and a gold necklace, I know she was wearing them. They're not here and I want to know where they are. I'll not pay one dime of this bill until they're found." he said belligerently.

Bill reached for some paper on the desk, wrote something down and drew a diagram of the heart shaped bracelet then shoved it at Ecker telling Ecker to sign that he had not given him the bracelet and necklace. Once again Jo Ann couldn't hold herself back. She knew Bill was going to the police station when he left the mortuary. They probably had what he was looking for. Betty had a habit of taking off her jewelry at night and putting it on a dresser or night stand. Probably what was lying around would have been taken by the police and not have gone with Betty's body.

"Bill, would you leave this poor man alone?" she pleaded. "You're going to get the jewelry when you go to the police station."

"He's going to sign this first." Bill proclaimed. "I know Betty had this bracelet, I saw it on her and he hasn't given it to me. Somebody's gonna pay for this," he threatened.

Hoping to change the subject, Ecker suggested if the family would want to say their private goodbyes to Betty he would put a drape over her and bring her to the viewing room. Sometimes, he told them, it is consoling if you can stand beside her even if you cannot actually see her face; a time to say your prayers. If she was to be cremated this would be their last opportunity to be close to her and instill in their minds and hearts that she was truly gone. Deciding to wait for the rest of the family to arrive, Saralyn, Jeff, Kim and Bill went to the police station while Bill's parents elected to get something to eat. Jo Ann and Dick went with William and Sara but were too upset to eat.

After the family left, Reg Ecker called the Sheriff's Office.

"The morgue called us and said this guy's over here talking about some kind of bracelet she had on. At first I didn't know what he was talking about because I'd spaced it. I thought we'd better find that bracelet or he's going to sue us for stealing stuff, which he did accuse Foster and I of taking $20,000 in coins from his house at the search warrant," recalled Detective Rodriguez.

"And he made such a big deal about that bracelet. I mean it's a $200 bracelet. It's gold, but not real gold. It's pawn stuff. But he said Betty had it on her and he wanted it from her body. So I looked at the photographs from the scene and there it was right there, on her right wrist. Who'd know that but Bill Gray?"

Bill wanted his wife's jewelry and he knew exactly what he was looking for. The officer gave him the jewelry they had taken from the dresser in the bedroom where Betty died. What he was looking for wasn't there. This time Bill was angry.

"My wife wore that heart shaped bracelet all the time. I know she had it on. I'll sue you sons-of-bitches if you don't find it and quick."

Betty's jewelry, he told the officer, was worth in excess of $30,000. Helpless because they couldn't find the missing jewelry they promised to do some more research. At the moment there was little they could do. At least he could have the keys to the Subaru but he would have to go to the home on Crowley Road to get it.

Janis and Dorothy were at the mortuary when everyone returned. Dan and Karen had driven straight through from California and were too exhausted to come back to Idaho Falls. They stayed in Jackson assuming they would still be able to pay their last respects at a funeral.

Bill elected to go into the viewing room with Betty alone. Whether he pulled back the drape and viewed his wife or said anything to her, is pure speculation. Jo Ann always felt he did something when he was alone with her. His insistence that he go alone was not believed to be fear of losing control in front of the family, for when he returned neither his face or voice showed the slightest emotion.

There were many tears when the rest of the family stood beside the gurney with a red velvet drape covering Betty's body. Other than the sound of sobbing, they stood in silence as each one dealt with their own private feelings, saying their own silent prayers. It was a lousy way to say goodbye. There could have been a viewing if the man arguing with the mortician again had cared enough to find out where his wife's body had been taken after he killed her.

Bill wanted the cremation to take place the next day. It would take some special arrangements. The crematorium was in Blackfoot, Idaho, 25 miles south of Idaho Falls and it was normally closed on Sunday. Bill's insistence prompted Ecker to make the phone calls that would open the door to his demand. Then Bill said he wanted to watch the cremation.

"Mr. Gray," Reg Ecker said somewhat horrified, "It is a sight that few people can take much less a close member of the family. I have only had one family that wanted to be in attendance and they were so shaken they had to leave."

He went on to explain what to expect. Although there was little to see but flames through a small glass door, it was an uncomfortable and very unpleasant situation. It would take from four to six hours and they would stop and stir the remains periodically. Against Ecker's advice Bill insisted he was going.

"Who wants to go with me?"

Always in support of their son, Bill's parents said they would go. The rest of the family had all they could take and retreated to the parking lot.

Bill guided the three car caravan to Reeda's yellow brick home on Crowley Road. Stopping in the circular driveway in front of the house, they could see Betty's white Subaru parked slightly off the edge of the driveway. With the Subaru keys the police had just given him in hand, Bill went directly to the front porch of the house. When he fumbled a second as though he was looking for a certain key then opened the screen door someone said, "He's going in that house!"

Saralyn leaped out of the car and ran to the porch grabbing her father's arm, pulling him away. She was mortified to think he would go in the house. She didn't know what it might look like inside, but if two people were killed in that home less than a week ago her mind raced to bloody scenes she had seen in the movies and she wanted to spare her dad from seeing something terrible.

Jo Ann wasn't thinking that at all. Not realizing it would have been impossible for Bill to have access to the house until all the evidence had been collected and the police were finished, she thought he was going in to help give himself an alibi in case the authorities found something to connect him to the house. However, it's a fair assumption that he wanted to look for items Betty had recently purchased. He'd made a list and when he couldn't find them at his home he had to assume they were stashed at Reeda's. He may well have also planned to look for the missing jewelry he had seen on Betty that Sunday night when he put a gun to her head and pulled the trigger.

What Jo Ann should have thought about was the fact that Bill knew there was a key to Reeda's house on Betty's key chain. There were two theories tossed about as to how the killer entered the residence. Based on a Jackson witness, Paula Lesinger, who swore she saw Bill Gray in a green Travelall that appeared to be going south out of town about 7:30 p.m. Sunday night, some thought Gray may have gone to Idaho Falls early in the evening, snuck into the house and hid in the basement when the women might have gone out for dinner.

In fact, if Gray left Jackson around 7:30 p.m., drove to the EIRMC and rode his bike to the house, he would have arrived about the time Kay Gunderson was leaving around 10:30 p.m. It's highly unlikely the women went out after that giving him no chance to sneak into the house before they went to bed. Where the witness saw Bill in the Travelall was actually between the pawnshop and Bill's house. It's highly possible Bill was checking out the Travelall, getting gas and preparing for his trip. Further, the two renters who lived in the apartment below the pawnshop, definitely placed Bill at the pawnshop between 10 and 10:30 p.m. because they heard him unlock the door and come in with the dog.

The more probable theory was that the killer entered through the unlocked patio door. The screen was closed, but the patio door was open when Roy arrived and it had been hot that night. Investigators surmised the girls had gone to bed with the sliding patio door left open to help cool the house and the killer came in and left through that door. But how could Bill have known for sure the doors wouldn't be locked when he got there?

Much later, when Jo Ann was talking to the police, she never thought to mention this incident because there had never been an issue raised of how the killer got into the house. Jo Ann tended to put much more thought into Bill's wild idea that someone had purposely fixed the tires on Betty car to cause an accident.

"Look! Something's wrong with the car. The tires don't look

right. Someone's been screwing around with them," Bill remarked as soon as he approached the Subaru. Everyone looked but it was hard to tell if anything was wrong since the car was sitting quite tilted on uneven ground. After pulling the car onto the driveway he walked around the car and looked at each tire. Saralyn and Jeff walked around and looked at each tire. Dick walked around and looked at the tires. The tires appeared to be normal to them.

"I'll take Saralyn with me," Bill told the family. "She's pregnant so we're going to stop and get something to eat."

By now no one else had eaten either except Bill's parents. Food sounded like a good idea, but the last thing Jo Ann and her family wanted to do was to spend any more time with Bill.

The Buccolas decided to ride home with Janis and Dorothy. Kim and Jeff were relieved to ride home alone in peace and quiet. Everyone followed Bill back to town so he could show them how to get on the right road to Jackson. Dick volunteered to drive Janis's car and he watched the Subaru intently to see how it was riding. There appeared to be nothing visibly wrong with the tires, so when Bill stopped to give Dick final directions no one thought anything about leaving Bill and Saralyn behind.

Although Jo Ann would have much preferred to have gone to the motel, they decided to wait at the house for Saralyn and Bill to come home so they could discuss a memorial service for Betty.

"We were sitting out on the patio waiting for Bill and Saralyn to come home because my mom and I were both very uncomfortable in the house. I don't know, it was Betty's home and she wasn't there. It was just kind of strange. They didn't come and they didn't come, and we were beginning to get worried. We knew they were going to get something to eat but we stopped and ate. Bill's parents said they stopped to eat, so they shouldn't have been that far behind. When they got home two hours later it was absolutely crazy."

Saralyn was extremely hyper when she came in. The entire ride home with her dad had been a nightmare. He told her the tires had been deliberately fixed by putting more air in the left front and right rear tires and releasing air in the other two. If he hadn't noticed it and would have reached speeds of 55 mph on the pass they could have been killed.

After the family parted in Idaho Falls and gone their separate ways, Bill said he wouldn't be surprised if someone hadn't planted a bomb in the car. She was terrified to be in the car but everyone else had left so there was nothing else she could do. She decided if her dad was still going to ride in it she would have to take her chances with him. They went to a gas station and Bill added some air to the tires then he started looking for a bomb. He looked under the hood, in the trunk, under the car, and everywhere else he could think of; then told Saralyn it was probably alright because he couldn't find anything. Her father had been ranting and raving about the fingerprint dust that was all over the interior so they went looking for a car wash. The only one they found was already closed so they got a hamburger at a drive-thru and started for home.

Saralyn was tense, thinking they could be blown up at any time if there was a bomb and her dad hadn't found it. She cringed every time they hit a bump. Approaching the Swan Valley junction, a little road not far from the Wyoming border, Bill got Saralyn's attention and put a finger to his lips.

"Shush," he whispered. "I don't want you to say anything. When we get out of the car I'll talk to you. Don't say anything else."

Saralyn quickly obeyed until he stopped at a road side restaurant. Getting out of the car Saralyn started to say something but Bill grabbed her by the arm pulling her away from the car.

"I don't want to discuss this in the car because the car might be bugged," he said, "the police have been in the car, they have searched the car and they have planted a bug in hopes we might talk on the way home. Now I need to make a phone call to a friend of mine."

Saralyn wanted to know why he couldn't wait until they got home.

"Because the house and the pawnshop are also bugged," he replied. "I need to make it from a pay phone out of state."

Saralyn got a Coke while Bill got change and went to make his call. Waiting patiently, Saralyn stood next to her dad while he talked to his friend Jack Hurley in Bondurant. Just a little curious when he hung up she asked her dad what that was all about. Putting his arm around her he said, "Honey, I'm sorry but I can't really tell you right now. Someday I will explain it to you. But right now you can't tell anybody, including Jeff, about this call."

If Saralyn had not been so brainwashed she would have found that phone call to be very peculiar, but with all that had been happening the only one she felt she could trust was her father. She was confidant he had a good reason for what he was doing. After all, the police were trying to frame him and he had to do something to protect himself.

All the rest of the way home he started in on the car again. He kept telling her the car wasn't driving right. Can't you feel this, can't you feel that, can't you feel the front end is loose? She really couldn't feel anything but after a while he had her convinced that she could and she was scared to death they were going to lose control and go off the pass. Between that and her father telling her somebody was out to get him, they got Betty and now they're after him, Saralyn was in shambles by the time they got home.

Seizing the opportunity, Bill told everyone they must check their cars make sure they weren't tampered with. Go out, look under them every time you go somewhere, he was saying. Now everyone felt somehow sinisterly involved. Was someone planning to kill one of them next? That's certainly what they were beginning to think.

Jo Ann looked at the whole fiasco very differently.

"When he started in on how the tires had been fixed so they would go over a cliff if he drove too fast, I said baloney. I said, Bill, nobody would know you were going to be driving that car home. If what you're telling us is true, that wasn't meant for you. That had to be meant for Betty. Somebody wanted her to go over a cliff on her way to Idaho. When she didn't die in an accident somebody, probably you, went down there and killed her."

Jo Ann and her family left, but Janis was still there when Bill unnerved the family once again. Bill, Jeff and Kim had gone out on the balcony to smoke. Everyone else was just beginning to wind down and settle in for the evening. Saralyn had finally calmed down and was about to go home when Bill came running in the house shouting.

"I gotta get my gun, somebody's out in the bushes, I gotta get my gun."

Saralyn went out to look and Jeff said he thought he saw someone too. Saralyn wanted her dad to call the police which was the last thing he wanted to do. He tried to put her off but she insisted. There is no question Saralyn believed her dad's life, and maybe everyone else's, may have been in danger and now she was really scared.

Bill called the Jackson Police Department wanting to know

if they had someone watching his house. He said there was someone sneaking around in the bushes outside his house and if it was the police they better tell him because he would do whatever he had to do to protect his family. The police assured him no one was watching his house and offered to send someone over to look around.

If he was intentionally trying to scare his family, he succeeded. Kim was absolutely panicked. She was still concerned about someone tampering with their cars, and then it had only been hours since she had to look at the unpleasant dead body of her murdered mother-in-law. Now Bill was telling them someone was out to get the whole family.

"Betty isn't the only target," he had said so many times.

Janis couldn't believe what was happening. Anyone in control of their emotions could see what Bill was doing to his family.

"For God sakes Bill, what have you done to somebody that would make them want to come after you? You think someone killed Betty and now they want to kill you and the rest of this family? What in the hell have you done?"

"Remember the guy I thought set those fires?" he said. " I ran him out of town and I'll bet he's the one."

Janis just shook her head. The whole thing was ridiculous. Kim was so upset she was shaking. Bill had to give her one of his Valium pills to calm her down. She slept fitfully knowing Jeff was going to stay awake all night for Bill cautioned them to sleep with one eye open and to keep their guns by the bed.

"We got all the guns out; made sure all the guns were loaded. We had, I don't know, all kinds of guns. There were guns within reach wherever you were," remembered Kim several years later.

Following his father's instructions, Jeff loaded two of his guns and set them on the night stand while he guarded his sleeping wife. The next day he had to take his wife to stay with her parents in Riverton. She couldn't stay in that house any longer; not until she could get herself and her emotions under control.

Early Sunday morning Bill and his parents left for Blackfoot and the cremation of Betty's body. Saralyn spent the day with Kent and Cree. The Buccolas and Hales walked around town visiting the quaint shops and exquisite art galleries. It didn't take long for the local pipeline to pass the word that Betty Gray's sister was in town.

Besides the slight resemblance between Jo Ann and Betty, the Buccolas stood out from the crowd of tourists. Having only been in Jackson once before during the winter when the town was quiet and empty, Jo Ann didn't stop to think when she packed that the tourists that filled the streets, and piled out of their motor homes, were comfortably dressed in their summer shorts and cotton t-shirts. Jo Ann and Dick were always well dressed, regardless of what they were doing, but since they were coming for a funeral they had brought some of their better clothes. Everywhere they went they were quickly identified.

"I couldn't get over how nice and friendly the people in that town were," Jo Ann recalled. "I guess I can understand now why Betty liked living in Jackson so much. People came up to us and told us how sorry they were about what happened and they all had something nice to say about my sister. That's why there had been so much food brought over to Bill's. Everyone wanted to do something for Betty because if anything happened to someone else, Betty was right there. She would take the whole meal."

There was an enormous amount of food brought by the good people of Jackson. The last thing they could do for the person who had been so good to them was help her family get through their crisis.

Although it was always difficult for Jo Ann and Dorothy to be at the house it was particularly distressing Sunday night. Bill came marching in carrying a small plastic box containing Betty's ashes, the proud hunter returning with his kill. There was no emotion, in fact he was laughing as he announced that he left his cheating wife sitting in the front seat of the car when they stopped to eat on the way home. He asked if anyone wanted to look in the box. When no one did, he offered that there wasn't much to see anyway, it was just a few bone fragments and ashes. He placed the box on the coffee table.

Jo Ann wanted to leave immediately but she had to find out what Bill intended to do with Betty's ashes. She wanted desperately to take them back to California where she thought her sister would have wanted her to. But Bill refused to even consider it.

"I'll keep her right here until I decide what I'm going to do," he said.

Jo Ann was heartbroken to have to leave her sister's last remaining shred of existence with the man who she knew killed her. But that wasn't the only thing she had to deal with that night.

Reinforced by Bill's cheerleading, suddenly everyone was mad at Betty. Bill had been stirring the pot for several days. The hatefulness he had been displaying was just as prevalent as it had been earlier in the week. Bill was calling his wife a whore, Saralyn was calling her mother a slut and Jeff said he despised her. Janis and her husband just sat, too stunned to say anything.

Jo Ann leaped to the defense of her sister reminding them how warm and loving she had always been with her family and how she had worked so hard and taken such good care of Bill when he was sick. She lashed out at Saralyn, reminding her who had saved the money for the down payment on her trailer house and at Jeff, telling him his mother had gone without a lot of things to keep him in school. She tried to explain Betty's side of the story but it was falling on deaf ears. Dick had to caution her to bite her tongue if she didn't want to be turned away from the family, which would include being turned away from going to her sister's services. It couldn't happen soon enough for Jo Ann. She desperately wanted to attend her sister's service, but she just had to get away from this weird family.

What Bill was doing to his family was interesting. He instilled fear in their minds to draw them closer to him for protection. Keeping them on edge and confused, they had little chance to think rationally. He played mind games with them continually bringing up Betty's faults, never giving way to her good side. He placed all the blame on Betty. Everything that had happened was her fault. The police became the bad guys and they were trying to frame their father. He told them anything and everything that would help his cause. Under this type of pressure they were confused and unable to apply common sense to what he was doing to them. Only the outsiders could see what was happening. But the one thing Bill was counting on worked for him. His children loved and trusted him. No matter what, they could never allow themselves to believe their father could have killed their mother. That would have been one shock too many just now.

Saralyn had been quick to react to her father's brainwashing. She was still upset with her mother's denial of her affair. With Saralyn's everything up-front personality, she had little tolerance with anything but the truth and now she knew for a fact her mother had lied to her.

Jeff was particularly hurt that his mother had not confided in him, if not about Roy, at least the divorce. He and his mother were very close and it hurt him that she wouldn't have come to him with this news.

Dorothy tried to explain that his mother did not tell him about Roy and the divorce because she had promised his father that she wouldn't. She broke that promise once and the retribution was more than she could handle. Betty always felt when she would be allowed to tell him, she could make him understand. Of the two children, it was Jeff she wanted to tell. But that Sunday night, a week after his mother died, when he sat with his Grandmother Hales on the balcony he was deeply confused.

Unbelieving of what she'd been hearing about her daughter, Dorothy said "Jeff, you don't really hate your mom do you?"

"She's not the mother I knew." he retorted. "My mother is dead. The lady that was murdered was not my mother."

When the phone in the Buccola's motel room rang at 7 a.m. Monday, and it was the police, Jo Ann was startled. She didn't know they even knew who she was let alone how to find her. The caller wanted to know if she would go downstairs and talk with an officer who was waiting in the motel parking lot. Alone, since Dick and Dorothy had gone to a coffee shop down the street, Jo Ann asked brother, Dan, who was in the next room to go with her.

The officer, who was a personal friend of the Grays offered his condolences then wanted to know if they would come to the police station and talk with detectives. Apologetic, because they were meeting the family within the hour to finalize Betty's memorial services, she promised to come to the station later that day.

Dick and Dorothy returned before the officer left and Dorothy gave way to the extreme duress she had been under since she had arrived in Jackson. Softly crying, she told the officer, "My daughter was a good girl. She wasn't what they're trying to paint her to be. She was a good mother and a good wife. She wasn't responsible for what happened."

The pressures of the family and news articles had worn her defenses down and she felt the need to defend the daughter she so loved, and now lost. Putting his arms around her for comfort, the officer told Dorothy not to worry. "Betty was very much liked in this town. She had a lot of friends in our department as well. We know she was not responsible. Whatever she did, she must have had good reason."

Surprisingly, the family was able to come to agreement on the services. Bill gave a little and allowed his children and Betty's family to participate in scheduling the program. But when the funeral director asked for a picture of Betty to display at the service Bill decided to use his and Betty's wedding picture. Jo Ann had brought recent pictures from Betty's California trip which the newspaper was going to use. Jeff and Kim said they knew of recent pictures they could find which could be blown up, but Bill insisted on the wedding picture.

"That made me so mad," remembered Jo Ann. "That picture was taken 29 years ago. It was Betty that was dead not him. All he wanted was for everybody to see him and Betty together so he could get some sympathy."

Assembling the obituary for the newspaper Bill wanted donations to the Kidney Foundation in lieu of flowers. This was to include the family. Once again this pushed Jo Ann's buttons. "I said, Bill, Betty's going to have flowers." I didn't mind the Kidney Foundation. I know that's a good cause, but everything he was doing seemed like it was for him. The Buccolas and Hales went directly to the florist and ordered flowers for friends and family in California, as well as for themselves. Kim, Jeff and Janis followed, ordering a nice spray, a final tribute from her children and good friend.

A nervous Dick and Jo Ann parked their car several blocks away and walked so their car would not be spotted in front of the police station. They still had at least 24 more hours to stay in this town and their respect for Bill's volatility was overwhelming.

"I've never been able to look at Bill in the eyes because he scares me," recalled Jo Ann. "I've always felt this real uneasiness ... I mean scared. But with all this happening I was even more scared of him. I didn't want him to catch us talking to the police even though he thought I already had. We didn't know what he might do and we didn't want to find out."

More or less sneaking into the police station, Jo Ann was better prepared and assured than when she talked to Detective Wilde one week ago. With the tape recorder on, she recounted for Detective Bracken the events leading up to and surrounding her suspicions of her brother-in-law's involvement in her sister's death.

Not only did Jo Ann give information, she received it. She learned the authorities had linked her brother-in-law to a green Travelall and someone identified Bill as being in a Travelall at the Idaho Falls hospital the night Betty died. The Travelall had Wyoming plates and the person in the Travelall was wearing a medical-alert bracelet. Now Bill's statement of "This bracelet is going to hang me." made sense to Jo Ann. Now Jo Ann's suspicions of Bill were solidified. She knew without a doubt, who had killed her sister. So did the Jackson Police.

Nine days after her death, August 1, 1989, a memorial service was held for Betty Lou Gray at the First Baptist Church in Jackson. Family and friends gathered to pay respects and remember the loving mother; the once happy, spunky, vibrant woman who died so violently and suddenly in the prime of her life.

The pastor, who had been on leave, came back specifically to conduct the services. It was something he wanted to do. Betty had always been a special person to him. He had so much information about Betty's life in Jackson that Jo Ann was sure a lot of people must have talked to him before the service and related their fond, and sometimes humorous, stories about Betty. His eyes seemed to fall more often on Betty's mother, brother, sister and children than her husband. Perhaps there were other people at the service who had unsettling suspicions.

It was what they came for and stayed for. It was time to say goodbye. Even under sedation, Dorothy was so distraught she could barely maintain control. Jo Ann fought to be strong for her, but lost the battle. It was especially hard on Dan. He'd always been his little sister's protector when they were young. He couldn't help but feel he must have let her down somewhere along the line. Saralyn and Jeff clung to each other and their father for support. Even Bill Gray cried a few real tears.

Jo Ann was mindful of the large attendance at the service, thinking how well liked her sister must have been. She was also aware of the plain clothes detectives that were as unobvious as a herd of elephants. The police officer she had met in the motel parking lot was there in uniform, just enough presence to remind mourners that this was a death that did not have to happen.

As they were leaving, a familiar face came up to Jo Ann and reminded her that she was DeeDee Batson, Betty and Bill's former neighbors. Jo Ann remembered her being at Saralyn's baby shower several years ago. DeeDee wanted Jo Ann to call her after she got home. She had information she wanted to share. Jo Ann promised she would and they exchanged phone numbers. Although the Hales and Buccolas had been invited to come over to the house and eat, Jo Ann had accomplished what she came for. She paid her last respects to her sister. Now she wanted nothing more to do with Bill Gray and his two spiteful kids.

Also invited over to the house for something to eat after the service, Janis and DeeDee went first for coffee. There they discussed each other's thoughts. Thoughts they'd been struggling with since they first heard how Betty and Reeda died. Both were quite sure it was Bill Gray who pulled the trigger. Having these thoughts in mind probably added to DeeDee's uneasiness when she went to the Gray home. Bill seemed to follow her everywhere.

"Every time I turned around he was there," she said. "I took his little grandson out into the yard and we were talking and looking at different things. Bill was right behind us. I was very uncomfortable. He was so strange. He kept following behind me apologizing for that conversation on the phone. It was like he had really fouled up by showing his anger towards me and he was trying to apologize. Then, when I was sitting at the table with his mother and father he asked if I was going to stay overnight. I said no, I was going back to Rexburg. 'Well the bedroom next to mine is available,' he said with a hint of suggestion. It gave me the creeps. He gives me the creeps. He knows I loved Betty with all my heart. She was like a sister. But it wasn't the first time he had made little flirty, repulsive remarks. He'd say things like, 'I sure miss not looking over in your yard and seeing you in your bikini.' He made me sick to my stomach. I gotta get out of here, was all I could think about, and I left."

Having finished packing and about ready to leave the motel room, something made Jo Ann decide to call Saralyn. She was her sister's daughter. She knew her sister would want her to help Saralyn through this. Jo Ann wanted her to know she would be there if Saralyn needed her. Luckily, Saralyn was still at home.

"She answered the phone and I said, before I leave Saralyn I want to talk to you and see how you are doing. She started crying and I started crying and then she stopped and immediately started blasting me. 'Aunt Jo Ann, I can't believe you. Why didn't you let me know about Mom and Roy. I could have saved my mom and Reeda.' All these things were going through her mind and I said, Saralyn calm down, there's nothing you could do to stop this. If it was going to happen, it was going to happen. She started asking me a lot of questions and then she started in calling her mother some of the most horrendous names, asking how could she do this to our family and on and on.

"Then she called Roy a bunch of names. I started crying again and I said, Saralyn, don't you dare call your mother those names. You know your mother was not the type of person you are saying. She just fell out of love with your father and Roy happened to be there. We started screaming at each other and I said, Saralyn I don't want to talk to you anymore right now and she said, 'Don't you hang up, I want to finish telling you.' I don't want to hear anymore, I shouted. You're going to make me say something I don't want to say and I'm going to try to hurt you as much as you're hurting me right now. Saralyn kept on and I lost it.

"I'm gonna tell you something right now, your mother went to her grave thinking you hated her. I told her how it hurt her mother when she was acting like she was going to lunch all the time with her dad, thanking him for the down payment on her mobile home; real sarcastic in front of her when it was her mother who saved all the money for it. All those snippy innuendos she was throwing at her and the things she was saying. I said, she definitely went to her grave thinking you hated her. I hope you live with that.

"Oh, I was so angry. We were screaming back and forth and Dick came running down the hall and my mother was yelling, 'Stop it, stop it, you've got to stop it. Dick, get her to stop.'

"I said, this little witch is going to get it. My last words to her were, where in the hell was your father when these murders were committed? You tell me where he was. I want to know.

She said someone was at her door and she would call me right back but she didn't. We left town 20 minutes later."

The next day the *Jackson Hole Guide* published a brief statement about the memorial service and the readers learned that a man on a bicycle had been observed in the area on the night of the murders. A man driving a green Suburban or Travelall-type vehicle with Wyoming plates had also been seen in the area. Both men were observed between 10 p.m. and 5 a.m., the article stated. The department requested anyone with information on either the person, or the Travelall to call the department.

The same day, Reeda Roundy's sons Clayton and Paul were in Idaho Falls cleaning out the house where their mother last lived and died. Previously contacted by the Idaho authorities they were aware Bill Gray would be stopping by to pick up items belonging to his wife. They would have much preferred to pack Betty's things and leave them with the detectives but Bill was insistent that he come to the house.

Bill and his father were greeted at the door, invited in and offered refreshment.

"Bill broke down for a moment, showing his sympathy and said he was sorry this happened and that he sure hoped they caught whoever did this, Clayton remembered. We sat there in the living room for maybe five minutes while Bill smoked a cigarette and then he got up and went down the hall to the bedroom where Betty had been. I followed him down there because he was leading the way. He opened the closet, checked the top and drawers of the dresser and looked in a cedar chest. He asked us if we had seen a heart shaped bracelet, a necklace and some other things."

Bill produced a list of items he was looking for. He'd received Betty's credit card bill and was seeking to track down all the charges that were on it. Since he had not found them at home he was sure they would have been at Reeda's, but the boys had found only one large shopping bag containing towels, wash clothes and an iron. This they knew was Betty's. The credit card receipt with Betty's signature was still attached to the bag.

Bill asked about other jewelry, money and a silver set worth $48,000, he bragged.

"The whole discussion struck me as kind of odd. Most of the

items on his list were worth less than $10. It seemed like there was more of an issue on material items than there was on the murders. Even though Bill showed sympathy when he first came in, it lasted only a few minutes, then it was, 'Have you seen this? Have you found this?'"

Undoubtedly in the 10 days since his wife died Bill Gray had invested a good deal of his time searching, inventorying and making lists of his lost assets. The Roundy boys had already packed most of the household and admitted they may have overlooked something that they thought belonged to their mother. They promised to take the list and as they unpacked would look for the missing items. Weeks later they found, and shipped to Bill, a Revere Ware pot and pan set and a toaster.

Detectives met Bill at the Roundy home and accompanied him to the hospital where he was to have blood drawn. He'd slipped through their fingers the day of his notification, in part because he was not a suspect then, but more so on the doctor's advice since he'd already had blood drawn earlier on that day. Now that he was definitely a suspect, blood had to be taken. Anticipating retribution from Gray if any problems would arise, officers took the precaution of having it drawn in a hospital rather than a doctor's office.

Bill and the plain clothes detectives were standing at a counter when Steven Mackley came around the corner. He stopped in his tracks when he saw Gray. There he is, he thought. What is he doing here? For the second time Mackley positively recognized Bill Gray as the person he talked to that night in the Travelall. There was not the slightest doubt in his mind.

While Gray was in Idaho Falls, Detective John Cowden and Sergeant Paul Wilde were in Jackson interviewing Jack Hurley. About midnight on July 27 Hurley received a phone call from Gray which woke him up. Bill said he wanted to come out and talk to him. Hurley knew what happened to Betty and thought that Bill couldn't sleep and needed someone to talk to, so he said, "Sure, come on out."

Bill showed up at Hurley's about 1 a.m. with two vehicles, a white Cadillac and a green Travelall. He recognized William Gray as the driver of the Cadillac. When Hurley asked Bill how he was doing since the death of his wife, Bill said he was being framed and he needed a favor, asking to leave the Travelall at the ranch. Since Hurley had stored other things for Bill he didn't think much about it, and said it would be no problem. Bill left the Travelall in the driveway of the house with the keys in it.

The next morning Hurley moved the vehicle about 75 yards and stored it in back with other vehicles. Yes, he most likely was wearing gloves because he was going out to do chores. The Travelall was hard to start and was running very rough. He did not remember if there were plates on it. He didn't think Bill had brought it out to hide it. If that was so, there were some large buildings it could have been hidden in.

After the Travelall was seized he called Detective Foster and proclaimed he didn't know what was going on, had nothing to do with any of this. He was upset that Bill brought the Travelall out to him under the circumstances. Yes, they were good friends. They had gone to Las Vegas together in May or June of that year. Bill liked to play craps but he played just a limited amount of time because he couldn't stand for very long. Detectives felt Hurley was somewhat reluctant to talk about this and quite sensitive about his possible complicity.

When detectives tried to talk to Saralyn, she wouldn't even consider the possibility that her father had anything to do with her mother's death. "Ridiculous," she said when she was told her father may have ridden a bike from the hospital to Reeda's house.

Based on what she knew about her father's health she didn't think he could ride a bike a mile, let alone 12 miles round trip. When they continued to suggest it was possible her father was responsible for her mother's death and tried to reason with her, Saralyn became very hostile toward the detectives. They couldn't deal with her. Every time they tried to talk to her she'd get right in their face.

"Leave my dad alone," she threatened, "he would never, never hurt my mother. You don't know my mother. You don't know my father."

To Saralyn these detectives were threatening her entire life. "My mother's gone. You're not going to take my dad."

She refused to consider what they implied and refused to talk to them again. Saralyn was on the defensive. When Saralyn got this way, anyone that knew her well cut a wide swath around her path. Detectives would not try to contact her again.

Eric Hoffman, Gray's Pawnshop employee, said he would have been surprised if Bill had not known about Roy. It was certainly obvious to him as he observed Roy and Betty together in the shop on Tuesdays. Recounting the events of Sunday, July 23, he had worked from 10 a.m. to 3 p.m. Bill had been there all day. About noon, Bill complained about his knees and ankles hurting. He pulled up his pant leg to show Hoffman how swollen they were. Hoffman could see that they looked like they were swollen and he offered to let Bill go home, but Bill declined and his truck was still at the shop at 4 p.m. when Hoffman drove by.

On Monday he came to work at 10 a.m. Bill had opened the shop earlier and was still there when Eric went to lunch. When he came back about 1 p.m., the door was locked and Police Chief Dick Hayes informed him about Betty's death. Bill was always in and out of the shop and frequently went home early complaining about leg pains. Yes, this was the first and only time Bill had ever rolled up his pant legs to show Eric any swelling.

Detective Cowden's interview with the two men who rented the apartment below the pawnshop confirmed that no one had actually seen Gray on that fateful Sunday night. Shawn Jamison heard the door open to the pawnshop about 10 p.m. and the sound of the dog walking on the floor. Sometimes he hears Gray shuffling papers but couldn't be sure if he heard anything that positively placed Gray in the pawnshop after 10:00 or 10:30 p.m.

When Jason Perry came home from work he noticed Gray's pickup was at the pawnshop and just assumed if his pickup was there, so was Bill. He usually parked his Fastback on the side of the pawnshop next to a Travelall-type vehicle that hadn't been moved for a long time. When he came home from work Sunday night about 11:30 the Travelall was not there. Both men specifically remembered hearing the dog walking around until at least 1 a.m.

While Gray was counting on his renters as helpful to his alibi, detectives looked at it quite differently. They surmised that Gray had gone to the pawnshop about 10 p.m., then left in the Travelall about 10:30 p.m., leaving his pickup parked in its normal place. Gray had his dog with him almost everywhere he went and it was most unlikely that Gray would have gone home leaving Dobbie alone overnight in the pawnshop. He would have taken the dog with him if he was going home. If Shawn and Jason heard the dog in the pawnshop as late as 1 a.m., Gray was definitely somewhere other than at his home through that period of time. Because the renters didn't hear the dog past 1 a.m. does not mean he was not there. Certainly the dog would quiet down and go to sleep as did Shawn and Jason.

The time sketch matched quite well to the information they had. Leaving Jackson at 10 or 10:30 p.m. Gray could have arrived at the hospital around midnight. Allowing a full hour bike ride, which could include a short stop or two to catch his breath, he would have arrived at the Roundy home about 1 a.m. Giving him a full hour in the murder home, which is probable given the amount of cigarettes left on the plate and the fact he rested in the recliner, he could have left around 2 a.m. An hour for his return to the hospital would place him there at 3 a.m., the approximate time Steve Mackley saw him. Several variables could apply but the overall time frame of 10:30 or 11:00 p.m. Sunday night to around 3 a.m. Monday morning was not only possible, but very probable.

When interviewed July 26, Gray told Detectives Cowden and Kotrason that he would take a lie detector test after checking with his doctor. He'd been using his health problems as an excuse to get out of doing anything he didn't want to do most of his life. Once again it worked to his advantage. If he had just said yes, he would have been polygraphed that day. If he had said no, he knew the detectives would think he had something to hide. He wanted them to believe that he had nothing to hide and was not afraid to be polygraphed but he could not do it right then. Bill placed the decision on someone else. It was not his fault he couldn't take it.

Although the officers advised him a polygraph was used more for elimination of a suspect than it was used to find guilt, Bill remained firm under the ruse of doctor's orders. A few days later when he knew he was in trouble and needed a lawyer he again put the decision on someone else. Now he refused to take a polygraph on the advice of his attorney. Bill Gray would not step forward and prove his innocence. Somehow that didn't surprise anyone.

Detective Rodriguez's record of an arrest within three days of the crime had been broken. He was certain he had his man, but could not place him under arrest. As much damaging evidence as they'd gathered these past days, Bonneville County Prosecutor Kimball Mason didn't think it was enough to justify an arrest. He wanted the gun. He wanted fingerprints from the scene. He prompted the detectives to get some concrete evidence that Bill Gray had been in the murder home the night of the murders. Granted, Gray's activities had been strange and suspicious, but Mason was convinced that alone would not be sufficient evidence to prosecute and win. He would take no action unless the detectives had much more to give him.

If Gray was not wearing a backpack when Patrolman Greg Black saw him riding the bike near the hospital, he still had to have transported at the very least, the gun, the candles and the can of Mountain Dew found in the Roundy yard. It may have been as simple as tucked in his shirt and pockets, or a fanny pack around the waist. Officer Black and security guard Steven Mackley had not ruled out a backpack, they simply didn't remember specifically if Gray had one that night. Regardless, he'd planned well enough to remember to bring some liquid for his laborious ride. The Mountain Dew can was deemed most likely to have come from Gray's refrigerator. It certainly was his brand of refreshment and officers were sure it was more than just a coincidence.

Bill had to drink large amount of liquids due to the medication he was taking for his kidney problems. He may well have drunk something from the murder house, some liquor, water or liquids from the refrigerator, as he sat in the recliner, rested and smoked.

Nonetheless he had to relieve himself before leaving the house and didn't think to leave the seat down in the female position. The candles found in the Gray home during the search were the same size and type, but not the same color, as those left on the center island. The metal bases were similar but not identical, thus not positively connectable. Detective Rodriguez felt sure Gray brought the candles with him. The cult connotation he left was not a spur of the moment thought. He couldn't have counted on finding 18 candles, all matching, in Reeda's house after he got there. The house was not disturbed in any manner that would indicate someone searching. No, that was too many candles to hopefully find. He had to have brought them with him.

Surgical disposable gloves were the reason prints were not found in Reeda's house. Bill had plenty of them in his home left over from his days on peritoneal dialysis. Tighter fitting and less bulky than cotton or leather, he would not have needed to remove them for any reason while he was in the house, or the entire night for that matter. Everyone knows that fingerprints are the single most damaging and convicting evidence that can be found at a crime scene. A killer, who has given a great deal of thought to the crime and subsequent cover up, will place high priority on not leaving fingerprints behind. That certainly would have been first on Bill's list of not to do's.

Detectives were somewhat surprised that Bill didn't put priority status on separating himself from the Travelall and medical-alert bracelet almost immediately after his encounter with Mackley in the hospital parking lot. On the surface it seemed to all boil down to not having enough time. Bill had been up all night, a strenuous and exhausting night. He couldn't have possibly gotten back to Jackson before 5 or 5:30 a.m. Monday. If he stopped to rest after he was more or less forced to leave the hospital parking lot prematurely, and if he stopped to dispose of the gun and clothes en route, he may well not have gotten back until much later.

Bill must have taken into consideration the possibility his clothing could get blood on it when he shot the women. He had no way of knowing for sure the women would remain sleeping after he entered the house. Had one or both awakened and fought, or his first shot had not killed them instantly, blood could have been spattered everywhere. Scraping Betty's blood to write the message would also heighten the possibility of contaminating his clothes as well as his shoes with blood. Bill would have thought this out and anticipated having to change his clothes and shoes, then hide or destroy the ones worn when he killed the women.

It's a good bet he stopped along the way to rid himself of all evidence that could incriminate him. Whether he stopped at his house when he arrived in Jackson to clean up, get his medicine, feed or get food for Dobbie, or any numerous reasons, before or after he parked the Travelall back at the pawnshop is just a guess, but it's probable he did return home before he went to get his blood test. Once he got to the store he needed to stay there and go on with business as usual giving the appearance that it was just another day when someone came to tell him about Betty.

Certainly Bill did not anticipate the vehicle being seen at all, let alone someone confronting him face to face while he was in it. That had to be an unexpected event so he had never thought out an alternate plan. But Bill was very confident he could commit the perfect murder. He had taken great measures to create a phantom Ron Mitchell and falsify the documents which led him to believe he had distanced himself from the Travelall. However, the most popular theory is that he never considered the security guard would put two and two together and it would lead them directly to him. He wore the medical-alert bracelet all the while he was being interviewed by detectives that first week. He had no problems with a picture being taken of it on his wrist.

Detective Rodriguez probably put it in the best perspective. "He's so smart, so intelligent, and so damn dumb. The train of thought is the smarter you are, the easier it is to get caught. The dumber you are, the harder it is to catch you."

Although they could not positively place their man at the scene, detectives diligently continued working on the case. They continued interviewing and checking every possible lead. They held a meeting every morning to exchange information and kept in constant contact with the Jackson authorities. The Jackson Police and Sheriff's Department shared their offices, equipment, phones, expertise and man hours with the Idaho officers who were spending a great deal of time in Jackson. No one was clamoring to be the big shot. They all had one goal in mind and that was to prove that Bill Gray shot and killed two defenseless women while they slept peacefully in their beds. All of them were certain of his guilt. All of them wanted Bill Gray to be held accountable for what he did.

One of the first items a crime scene investigator wants to

find is the murder weapon. Everyone wants the murder weapon. Detectives want it in hopes it can be traced directly to the suspect. Possession, maybe some fingerprints, even better if it has some of the victim's blood on it. Easy arrest, easy conviction. Prosecutors want it so they can wave this sinister object in front of the jury and dramatically point out we have the weapon that killed, and if we have the weapon that killed, we have the killer. The jury wants it. If it bears all the hard evidence and is traced to the defendant they can convict without doubt and remorse.

Unfortunately, it's seldom that easy. The weapon is not always found, and if found, it must be linked to the killer. If the weapon bears no fingerprints, no blood or provable connection to the suspect it is simply the weapon that killed. The more premeditated the crime, the less likely to find incriminating evidence on a weapon or even the murder weapon itself.

The Idaho and Wyoming authorities wanted the gun that killed Betty Gray and Reeda Roundy. They would be looking for a needle in a haystack under the circumstances. Their suspect was very familiar with guns, he carried them in his possession most of the time, he bought and sold them and he was knowledgeable enough to dismantle and exchange parts which could hinder or hide the obvious.

In this case there were guns everywhere. Reeda's home had guns, Gray's home had guns, the pawnshop had guns, Gray's children had guns and it was days after the murder that they knew for sure which type weapon they should be looking for. Officers poured over the pawnshop gun register checking on guns that had been pawned and sold, or pawned and reclaimed after the murders. They checked repair shops. They looked, but they did not find.

The most obvious place to look for the 9mm Lugar was

along the route between Idaho and Wyoming; an impossible task. There were three possible routes Gray could have taken to and from Idaho Falls, all passing through some of the most rugged wilderness area to be found anywhere. Two of the three routes would have required taking on Teton Pass which climbs sharply to an elevation of 8,431 feet. Newer and more powerful cars and trucks are reduced to a crawl on this dangerous pass loaded with S curves, sharp switchbacks and steep drop-offs. Investigators thought it would be the less likely route taken by Gray in the poorly-running Travelall.

The mileage over the pass, and the shortest of the two routes, was 88.2 miles from the pawnshop to the hospital. In view of the slow-down on the pass, it would have taken as much, if not more time, than the longer southern route around the pass. This route, the most logical, was 106.4 miles of winding road which follows the south fork of the Snake River through the mountains, passing a large reservoir after entering Idaho, continuing through the valley's farm lands and into the city. The possibilities for hiding a weapon were unlimited. It could have been taken miles into the forest via the numerous service roads, buried, or simply tossed in the wilderness, the reservoir or the Snake River, never to be found.

Although this would have been very probable and highly convenient for Gray, Detective Rodriguez leaned toward the idea that Gray still had the gun.

"He could have dismantled it, changed barrels, fired it, brought it back out and it wouldn't have the right barrel. But I don't think he would sell it or throw it away, because that man is so cheap. If you've got a penny in that corner over there, Bill Gray's gonna jump on it and ask if you have any more. He's got it, that's a trophy to him. That gun's a trophy to show what he did."

On August 16 the *Jackson Hole Guide* headline read, "Truck Seized from Victim's Husband." Readers learned that a witness placed a Travelall in Idaho Falls in the early morning hours of the murders and a similar Travelall had been tied to Bill Gray. The Guide reported that the lab work was going slowly.

"Right now, there's only myself working on the case in the lab," Donald Wyckoff, of the Idaho Forensic Bureau said. "There's so much to go through. It's a question, with all the amount of evidence collected, what is important evidence. You have to prioritize, based on what you think occurred and what evidence you think is important. We may do analysis of evidence right up to trial time, if there is a trial."

Spokesman from the Bonneville County Sheriff's Department, Paul Wilde, related that four suspects had been given lie-detector tests. Final autopsy reports, although they had some information from the autopsies, had not yet been received, and he confirmed that the Travelall had been impounded.

"No additional information on the murders will be released until Sheriff Ackerman calls another news conference," said Wilde. "There are too many conflicting stories and too much speculation. We don't want it interfering with the investigation."

Readers, thirsty for an arrest, would be gravely disappointed.

Sixty members of the Bonneville County Jeep Patrol went back out and thoroughly searched the roadside between the Roundy home and the hospital but found nothing of value. Armed with more information regarding the bike and the Travelall they knocked on doors once again and interviewed every person along the routes the killer might have taken.

Pictures of the Travelall were posted at the hospital in hopes an employee may have noticed it the night in question. No one, besides Mackley and Black, had seen the Travelall or a man on a bicycle late Sunday night or early Monday morning.

Cunning as he was, smart as he thought he was, by parking the Travelall in a place where people come and go at all hours, where an out-of-state vehicle parked in a lot with other automobiles would not stand out, turned out to be the worst decision Bill Gray made. Had he parked the Travelall alone, in the dark on a country road, no one would have seen it at that time of night, or if they had, there would have been no eyewitness face-to-face encounter, no medical-alert bracelet connected, nor is it likely the Wyoming tags would even have been noticed. Clearly the neighbors were tucked in for the night and no one was stirring in the vicinity that early morning of July 24.

Compounding any possibility of placing Gray in the murder house Sunday night, Leavitt reported that after a day of asparagus picking earlier that spring, Betty and Bill stopped by Reeda's for pie and ice cream before returning to Jackson. Reportedly Bill had been in Reeda's home on at least two other occasions Leavitt was aware of. Thus it was not all that disappointing when the report came back on the hairs found in the recliner. The report stated the hairs had characteristics similar to Gray's but no positive link was possible. The hairs were much like Gray's when examined with the eye and through a microscope. However, unlike fingerprints, human hairs can't be used to positively identify someone.

Since Bill Gray had been in the home previously, a sharp lawyer would make a point that the hair could have been left in the home before the murders, or because fibers and hairs transport rather easily, could have fallen off of Betty's clothes while she was in Reeda's home.

There was not enough saliva on the cigarette butts found on the kitchen table for a positive DNA test and the print of the shoe that left the knobby pattern in the carpet was not clean or complete enough to determine an exact shoe size. The print was partial, the toe was missing, and the shoe that made the print could have ranged from size 5 to 13½.

Law enforcement officers from both Wyoming and Idaho were placing every priority on this homicide. The clocked man hours were rapidly rising and both departments' budgets were heading toward shambles.

Wyoming officers were making it their business to keep a watchful eye on Gray, his movements, his whereabouts. They were checking all the ranches in the valley looking for a Ron Mitchell. Public records, driving records and utilities were checked thoroughly. All the Ron, Ronald and R. Mitchells were checked out but none were the Ron Mitchell who bought a green International Travelall from Gray's Pawnshop. Their search started with Teton County, spread to all of Wyoming and bordering counties in Idaho. In all, 130 Mitchells with variations of initials and first names were found. Most were eliminated rapidly due to the age and the description given by Gray. The officers were not surprised Mitchell could not be located. They thought Gray's story was a bunch of hogwash the minute he started telling it. But they, and ultimately a private investigator, would not quit looking for some time.

As more informants were found, their stories served to strengthen the information given by others. Bill told detectives he hadn't ridden a bike in years, yet Richard Oetting, owner of Frontier Texaco, said different. His business was just a couple of doors down from the pawnshop and Bill had been in before, so Oetting knew who he was.

A week or two before the murders Bill came riding into his gas station on a bike. He was exhausted and sweating. Oetting got a five gallon bucket out for him to sit on while he caught his breath. Bill said he must be getting old and that he hadn't ridden a bike in 10 or 12 years. The boys had borrowed the bike and broke it and he was out for a test ride, he added. As Oetting filled the bike's tires he thought to himself, no wonder it's hard to ride, not much air in the tires. I was also going to tease him about riding a girls bike because the bike had a larger than normal seat padded in sheepskin. In about 10 or 15 minutes Bill left, riding up a slight incline in the road. After Oetting was interviewed he went over to the pawnshop. The bike he saw Bill riding was leaning against the back wall of the pawnshop.

This information tied a bicycle to Gray and further substantiated the security guard's account of the man in the Travelall lying down in the seat sweating profusely. Bill was out of shape and not in particularly good health at the time of the murders. It was logical he would have been extremely exhausted after his ride from Reeda's house.

Only a killer, who was so totally drained of energy that he had little choice but to rest, could sit and relax in a recliner in a murder home for any amount of time. Theory as to whether he rested before the killings or after the killings has been batted back and forth numerous times. Some feel he would have been much too tired and so out of breath that his breathing could have been loud enough to wake the victims if he had gone directly to the bedrooms and shot the women. If this is true, he slipped into the house, rested and then walked down the hall to kill his unsuspecting victims.

If he did sit in the recliner first, he had one last chance to think about what he intended to do, one last chance to search his soul and his conscience, one last chance to change his mind.

On the other hand, if he went directly to each bedroom, shot the women and then rested, the thought that he could sit and rest at all after killing two women was unconscionable. Either scenario was extremely chilling. The speculation continues. The answer is unknown.

Tracing ownership of the Travelall led investigators to a Michael and Sherril Coy. The Coys lived in a small crowded trailer court south of town. Prompted by the manager's complaints that they had too many vehicles for their allowable parking space, the Coys decided the Travelall would have to go. Mrs. Coy had pawned several items at Gray's Pawnshop in the past and thought it might be a quick way to unload the Travelall.

Reaching Bill on the phone she told him they would like to pawn it for $200. Bill said he didn't loan on automobiles but if they wanted to bring it down he would take a look at it. When he saw it he didn't want it because it wasn't four-wheel drive. The Coys took the Travelall home and forgot about it so they were somewhat surprised when Bill came knocking on their door about 5 p.m. that afternoon. He had changed his mind. He said a friend of his who worked on a ranch came in looking for something to haul fence posts with and he thought the Travelall might work for him.

Although Bill wanted to drive it, Coy wouldn't let him because of insurance, but he took Bill for a ride discussing its various problems as they went. Coy told authorities, "The Travelall vibrated enough to shake your teeth out. It was all over the road. The brake shoes were shot and it was a gas guzzler. But it would go 80 mph." Bill wasn't all that interested in the condition of the Travelall but did want to know how to switch the gas tanks.

Because of its poor condition the Coys sold the Travelall for $150. Bill wanted a receipt and the title made out to a Ron

Mitchell. Coy would have the title notarized the next morning and Bill would bring his friend Mitchell out to drive it.

However when Bill came back the next day Mitchell was not with him. Bill said his friend couldn't make it but he would go ahead and take care of all the title work for his customer. Bill was angry with Coy because he took the plates off, but he left with the Travelall and the notarized title that bore neither a name of a buyer nor the current mileage recorded from the Travelall odometer.

The Coys had more interesting information to share with investigators. Sherril worked an early morning shift at the Virginian Cafe. Michael, who was in poor health and not working at the time, drove his wife to and from work. Their daily routine of going for coffee before going to work took them past Gray's Pawnshop sometimes twice a day, almost every day. As the previous owners of the Travelall they had a slight interest and noticed it had been parked by the side of the pawnshop, always in the same place, for a couple of weeks. They recalled commenting to each other as they passed each day that Gray hadn't sold the Travelall yet.

On Monday morning July 24, at 6 a.m. when they went by, it was gone. The Coys decided that Gray probably got it sold. However, when they passed the pawnshop that evening the Travelall was back. This time it was parked in a different place, more towards the back of the shop. The Coys decided Bill hadn't sold it after all.

When officers got a look at the Travelall certificate of title, dated June 22, 1989, the mileage recorded at the time of the sale was 73,406.9. The actual mileage on the vehicle when it was seized was 73,551.9. Therefore if the mileage was correct on the title at the time Gray purchased it, the Travelall had been driven only 145 miles. This would not have been enough miles to have taken it from Jackson to Idaho Falls and back, and then to Bondurant.

In his July 28 interview with Foster and Cowden, Bill encouraged them to check the mileage on the Travelall. It would verify that there were not enough miles on it since it came into his possession to have been driven to Idaho Falls and back to Jackson. But as Bill was formulating plans for the perfect crime he failed to take into account that when a vehicle is serviced, it is standard procedure for the mileage to be noted on the work order and the Jackson Service Center did just that. On July 7, 1989, when they serviced Bill Gray's 1970 International Travelall, James Corman, mechanic for the Service Center, recorded the mileage at 73,158. In fact, the Travelall had been driven 393.9 miles since it had been repaired. The distance traveled came out almost perfect for the Travelall trip to Bondurant and either two trips to Idaho Falls, or one trip to Idaho Falls and another to Island Park.

Detective Rodriguez was convinced Gray went looking for Betty at least once before, more probably the weekend of her camping trip. He feels certain Bill was prepared to kill Betty then if he would have found her. There was no other logical reason for Bill to have taken the Travelall that many miles when it was barely drivable and of questionable reliability.

When Gray registered the vehicle he wrote in the mileage he felt would cover his tracks if the Travelall was ever connected. Obviously, Bill Gray knew when he bought the Travelall he would use it for the sole purpose of carrying out his plan to murder his wife, and the murder would take place somewhere other than Jackson Hole.

Whether his plan was complete enough at that time to include parking the vehicle at the hospital and using the bicycle to transport him quietly and unobtrusively to the murder house is unknown. But certainly this scheme was devised at the very least, a few weeks before the murders when he was seen riding a bike and making sure it was in good condition for his midnight ride.

The bits and pieces of information gathered by the officers painted a picture of a man completely consumed by greed. His wife was having an affair he did not confront her about when he found out. Instead, he snooped and waited until he was satisfied she had every intention of leaving, suspected first by her advance planning for her financial welfare and confirmed when she finally told him she wanted a divorce. There is no question he wanted their divorce kept a secret witnessed by his immediate demand for Betty not to tell anyone, then his anger when she did. There would be no motive if he could have everyone believe they were still happy and comfortable in their marriage. Totally incapable of accepting the fact his possessions and assets would be split equally between them, he had to be assured that Betty could never divorce him.

Betty may well have had a feeling Bill might be checking up on her. The front door on the Roundy home was open and unlocked when Roy came by Sunday evening. They were expecting Roy and had the doors open for him. However when Kay Gunderson came by a few hours later the front door was locked and it was Betty who answered the door. Normally, Reeda would have answered the door to her own residence unless whoever they thought was at the door would have been someone Betty might have been halfway expecting. The simple act of taking so much time to answer, then peering out the window cautiously prior to opening the door, indicated a degree of apprehension and possible fear of the person she thought might be there.

Investigators found no sign of forced entry into the house.

Roy said the front door was open, the screen door locked. The rear patio door was open, the screen door closed, but not locked when he arrived. The preferred hypothesis was that the killer entered and exited through the unlocked patio door. However, if the women were having apprehensions that Bill might come around, and they had taken the precaution to lock the front door after Roy left, surely they would have locked the patio door before retiring. Roy had said the lock on the patio door was broken and Reeda placed a stick in the slide to lock it, but nonetheless it was securable.

This scenario deepens with speculation when one asks how Gray intended to enter the house after he arrived. Certainly he could not have totally depended on finding one of the doors unlocked. Even if the women did leave the patio door unsecured Bill had no way of knowing for sure they would do that. Was he planning to leave, if he couldn't get into the house quietly through an unlocked door? Not likely, considering the amount of planning and effort it had taken him to get there. Was he prepared to scale a wall and enter the upper bedroom windows that would most likely be, and were, open? Hardly, with all his extra weight and his poor condition. He was too much of a coward to break a basement window or make any noise that could alert the women to his presence giving them a chance to fight for their lives. No, Gray had to have had a plan, before he arrived, that would guarantee him easy, quiet, access into the house.

Could his pockets have contained a key? Could he have discovered the key Reeda gave Betty in her purse and taken it Sunday morning when he checked her purse that last time? Could he have discovered the key much earlier, had a duplicate made and gone to Reeda's when he knew they were on the camping trip to make sure it was the key to Reeda's house?

Detectives do not remember seeing an odd key in Betty's purse. But they did not check out all the keys on her Subaru key ring. If Jo Ann thought Bill was attempting to go into the house that day after their visit to the mortuary, and Saralyn pulled him off the porch before he could, it is highly probable Bill knew there was a key to Reeda's house on Betty's key ring. The various scenarios could be batted around forever. But the fact remains, no one but Bill Gray knows how he entered the house that night.

Further speculation has one wondering if his plan had not included his urging Betty to go to Idaho Falls and stay with Reeda that Sunday night. Roy was very surprised to see her there that evening. He knew she was coming to Idaho Falls Monday. They had planned to have lunch together, but he had no idea she would be there Sunday night.

In Bill's July 26 interview he said Janis came into the pawnshop on Saturday and pleaded with Betty not to go to Idaho Falls on Sunday. "Let's go floating, you've always wanted to go floating, don't go to Idaho Falls." Then Betty said to Janis, "No I don't think so, I think I'll just go on down to Reeda's."

Bill tells detectives he heard this conversation in the pawnshop and relates it to them complete with all the statements made between the two women. But just one statement before, he'd told detectives he didn't know that Betty was going to Idaho Falls until after she got out of the shower Sunday morning. He thought she was going to the chicken fry with Janis until he asked her and she said. "It looks like it's gonna rain. I don't think I will go to the chicken fry. I think I'll just go on over to Reeda's."

He stammers through these parts with many uhs and pauses as his mind races to give any explanation that will be believable and non-incriminating. But he can't have it both ways. He either knew Betty was going to Reeda's on Sunday because of the conversation with Janis, as he told the detectives; or he learned for the first time Sunday morning that Betty was not going to the chicken fry, but to Reeda's instead, as he also told the detectives. Most likely neither of Bill's versions were correct.

Bill knew Betty had planned a trip to the Falls on Monday. He may have encouraged her to go on down to the Falls Sunday afternoon so she could spend some time with Reeda before she left, then do her business on Monday and come home. One could assume Betty would have been interested in this suggestion. A freebie more or less, without the argument usually attached when she wanted to do something. Not only could she get away from Bill for a while, but she might be able to spend some time with Roy. She certainly had this on her mind, for it is known Betty prompted Reeda to get Roy to come over to her house on a ruse. Undoubtedly Betty thought it would be fun to surprise Roy that she was there.

Bill was not going to murder his wife in his own back yard knowing full well authorities would descend on him immediately. What better place than a home out in the country miles away from Jackson. He had the Travelall, he had forged the mileage, the bike was ready to go and he was fully prepared and committed to his plan. The only thing left to do was to get Betty in the right place.

When the detectives really thought about the extreme amount of premeditation that went into Gray's plan they could only conclude that Bill Gray was absolutely devoid of any form of emotion. For weeks, possibly months, he lived with his wife, observed her feelings, her laughter, her sadness, her love for her children and grandson, caring of others and caring for him. He was in daily contact with this vibrant human being he knew so well, who would have donated one of her own kidneys to save him, who shared all the bad times as well as the good. Yet even as he lived with her, looked at her, watched her, touched her, talked to her, he knew he was going to murder her.

Why Reeda, why would he kill Reeda? Was she in the wrong place at the wrong time, as many believe, or did Bill hold a vengeance against her for her complicity and acceptance of Betty's affair? Logically, based on the inordinate amount of preparation and thought given to covering up his crime, coupled with the satanic implication, Gray intended for investigators to believe it was a double homicide committed by crazed cultists picking a target at random, or targeting Reeda for her interest in astrology and tarot card reading. At the very least he wanted suspicion directed toward Reeda, her house, her boyfriends; placing the bed covers in a manner to suggest male companions, lovers, illicit affairs gone wrong.

Reeda's murder was included in his plan from the onset. Reeda had to die too, for he fully intended for investigators to think it was Betty who was in the wrong place at the wrong time.

3

DOUBLE TALK AND DECEIT

Everyone who knew Betty well suffered a deep loss, as did her good friend DeeDee.

"If I could describe Betty it would be, America and apple pie. She was the sweetest, most loyal human being I have ever met. Not a streak of malice in her. She never had a grudge. She totally, totally did everything Bill asked her to do. And, when she came to me and told me she was having an affair with Roy she said, 'I don't want you to condemn me. I don't want you to tell me to stop. I just want you to listen. Roy takes me for a ride and we look at nature. It isn't anything big. He spends time with me and he is so kind.'

"I think more than anything sexual in that relationship, I think Betty was just looking for companionship; somebody who appreciated her, for who she was, something she never had with Bill. When she finished telling me her story she said, 'He's not the kind of person anyone would think to have an affair with, he's not real good looking, but he's just perfect for me!'"

Jo Ann's love for Betty was deep, deeper and closer than average sisters. When Betty was slim it was easy to tell they were sisters. Betty's hair was more of an orange red where Jo Ann's tended to be more auburn red. Betty usually wore her hair shoulder length, full and curly. Jo Ann's was longer and she often wore it pulled back with a few wispy soft curls falling loosely around her face.

Jo Ann's freckles disappeared when she was a teenager but Betty's remained, blending nicely with her red skin and hair tones. Betty at 5' 3" was only an inch taller than Jo Ann and six years younger. Both sisters had a fun sense of humor, a radiant smile and a happy-go-lucky attitude that drew people to them. Only by choice of mates and environments did they differ.

Betty lived in a small western, tourist town in the high mountains where blue jeans and t-shirts were the normal dress code; chicken frys, BBQs, rodeos, dinner and dancing at the Elks Club were Betty's forms of entertainment. In Jackson Hole the pace of life was slow and easy. Jo Ann on the other hand, lived in sunny California abundant with shopping, fine restaurants, entertainment and designer clothing; a fast-paced life style in the upper circles of the affluent. Although they lived in two different worlds, hundreds of miles apart, the sibling closeness prevailed.

Jo Ann was devastated over the loss of her sister.

"Everybody liked my sister. She hardly ever got mad at anyone and if she did she wouldn't say anything. She was a real easy going person. She made everybody laugh because she was always joking around. She was a real cut up. I always wished I had her sense of humor. She would come off-the-wall with some dumb thing, really quick witted. She's always been that way. I guess I'll always have my memories. It's not enough, but all I have left."

Jo Ann experienced all the normal emotions associated with the violent death of a loved one. First the deep sense of loss and remorse, then the guilt. Why didn't she see what was happening? What should she, or could she, have done to protect and save Betty? Why did she let her leave California? But when she finally came to terms with the fact that nothing she could have done would have prevented what happened, her final, and also normal emotion was anger.

She didn't contact the Jackson police for several weeks after she got home. Jo Ann already told them everything she could think of while she was in Jackson and they'd given her every indication, even though they had not said it outright, that Bill was the only suspect, and they were satisfied Bonneville County would soon file criminal charges.

Bill knew he'd made some major mistakes. His well-thought -out plans had gone amuck. He called Jo Ann several times leaving a message for her to call him back.

"I talked to him the whole time I was in Jackson. I got everything out in the open. But once I left my sister's memorial service I said that's it. I'm never talking to that man again unless I absolutely have to."

Getting no response from messages left at the Buccola home he started calling Dick's office. Dick left instructions to say he wasn't in, but the phone calls kept coming. Finally after Bill said it was an emergency and he must talk to Jo Ann immediately, Dick returned the call.

When Dick told Jo Ann what Bill wanted she was stunned. He wanted funding to retain a lawyer. Not just any lawyer. He wanted Gerry Spense who had never lost a case and gained national recognition for some well publicized cases he'd defended including the Karen Silkwood and north Idaho's Ruby Ridge Randy Weaver trials.

Spense, a resident of Jackson, who has a deep voice with a western-type drawl, wears a leather fringed western jacket in place of a suit and requires a $350,000 up front retainer fee. The mention of his name instills fear in the average prosecutor.

Jo Ann couldn't believe it.

"Do you mean he was hinting to you for Gerry Spense's retainer fee and he thinks I'm going to let you pay for his defense when I think he killed my sister?"

When she called the pawnshop the next morning, high on emotion and ready to unload, she reached Jeff. Bill had left at midnight the night before for Cheyenne.

Accompanied by Saralyn, who was still making every attempt not to let her dad be alone, they drove in the night to make an early morning appointment with an attorney. Not wanting Saralyn to think he was worried that he would be charged with the murder of her mother, Bill gave her the excuse that he thought the Roundy children might be planning to file a suit against him and he needed to talk to a lawyer just in case they did.

Clearly Bill was sure criminal charges would soon be filed. He was well aware authorities had some very damaging evidence against him. Wanting a lawyer but not wanting Saralyn or anyone in Jackson to know he was worried enough to retain a lawyer, his decision was to consult an attorney from out of town.

He was fuming about money when he picked Saralyn up at their motel. Much of the discussion on their ride home centered on what he could do to get a lot of money right away. He knew his sister-in-law had the bucks to help him, but would she do so voluntarily? Add to Bill's list of criminal thoughts ... blackmail.

He would get the money from Jo Ann. If she wanted Betty's remains so goddamn bad she would either give him the money or he would flush her sister's ashes down the toilet.

Years later Jo Ann learned of this remark and commented that she would never have paid Bill a dime for the ashes.

"I'd never have gotten Betty's ashes from him. He would have sent something, but it would not have been hers. He would have a big laugh over that."

The days began to pass and what had been front page news was now reduced to a small column on the second page saying investigators were still checking out all possible leads. Soon there would be no mention of the double murders at all. No one in the know could understand why an arrest had not been made and no one was more upset about it than Jo Ann. There was not the slightest doubt in her mind that Bill killed her sister. Not only did she harbor an understandable, unrelenting hatred and anger directed personally toward Bill Gray, she found herself angered and totally frustrated with the Bonneville County legal system.

The Jackson police were always appreciative to hear from Jo Ann when she started calling with information she either remembered or learned from constant contact with Janis, DeeDee and others. They added everything she told them to their file but advised her that Bonneville County was in charge of the case.

Changing her direction to Idaho she went first to Sergeant Paul Wilde. Wilde took her phone calls and made notes as she poured out her reasons why she knew Bill killed her sister, for there was trouble in the Gray marriage. She related the collect phone calls when Betty told her she was afraid of Bill and that he was acting bizarre, flashing a gun and threatening Betty to keep their divorce plans a secret.

During the final collect phone call Betty must have had a premonition when she said, "If anything happens to me I want you to know about the safe deposit box."

She sent copies of her phone bills proving the collect phone calls. She related past events which revealed Bill's shoddy work habits and shady business practices; the timely, mysterious fire at the worm farm, his explosive reactions when angered or crossed, his controlling influence on Betty, his greed. Oh yes, his greed. Wouldn't there be a substantial motive for murder when his wife was planning to divorce him and he would have to split their assets, not to mention the good-sized insurance policy on her life?

Was Bill telling the truth when he said he and Betty had sexual relations the night before she went to Reeda's?

"No way," Jo Ann insisted. "She was leaving Bill and he knew it. She was getting a divorce. My sister would not have had sex with him. In fact, Betty said, they hadn't had sex for a long time. Why would they just happen to have it then?"

Within a short period of time Jo Ann was on a first name basis with just about everybody in the Idaho Detective Division since she'd called them so often. In the beginning, answers to her constant inquiries of the investigating officers were always the same. They were waiting for lab reports on fiber and hair samples, final autopsy reports and bullet analysis. They were looking for a Ron Mitchell, the murder weapon and were still investigating all possible leads.

Always assured they were making progress pacified her for a while. She'd always been so sure Bill would be arrested quickly, but her confidence began to wane when weeks, then months passed, and there had been no arrest.

Her constant perusal of the status of the investigation finally came down to the realization that there would be no arrest. The Bonneville County Prosecuting Attorney, Kimball Mason, refused to bring charges against Bill Gray for the murder of his wife and her friend.

Although Jo Ann was of the understanding that the investigating officers were confidant there was sufficient evidence for a grand jury to bring an indictment, Bonneville County Prosecutor Kimball Mason was not. He stayed steadfast that without the murder weapon and being able to positively place Bill at the scene on the night of the murders he would not go for an indictment. Mason said he was not going to prosecute without further evidence and what they did have was all circumstantial. As far as he was concerned there was no case against Bill Gray.

Idaho law addresses evidence as direct and circumstantial. "Evidence consists of testimony of witnesses, writings, material objects, or anything presented to the senses and offered to prove existence or non-existence of a fact." Evidence is either direct or circumstantial. Direct evidence is evidence that directly proves a fact without the necessity of an inference. It is evidence which by itself, if found to be true, establishes that fact. Defense attorneys often portrayed circumstantial evidence as dirty words to a jury, implying a weak, weak case.

Direct evidence is if someone actually sees the murder and can testify, "I saw him shoot the gun and kill the person." or if the witness is in the next room and hears the victim screaming and saying, "Please don't shoot." He hears a person say, "I'm going to kill you." and then he hears a gun shot. These scenarios are direct evidence because the witness was hearing it when it happened, or seeing it when it happened, or in some cases, even smelling. The witness perceives it through some of his natural senses. That is direct evidence. Anything less than that is circumstantial.

Circumstantial evidence is evidence that, if found to be true, proves a fact from which an inference of existence of another fact may be drawn. It is not necessary that facts be proved by direct evidence. They may be proved also by circumstantial evidence or by a combination of direct evidence and circumstantial evidence. Both direct evidence and circumstantial evidence are acceptable as a means of proof. Neither is entitled to any greater weight than the other.

First degree murder charges are generally sought when deemed to be premeditated. When a person plans in advance to commit a murder, takes caution to cover up the murder and carries out that murder, it is considered premeditated which generally carries life in prison without parole or the death penalty. A person who murders with premeditation will almost never commit the crime if another person is present, therefore almost every first degree murder case will be prosecuted on circumstantial evidence.

Fingerprints are circumstantial, confessions are circumstantial. Hair samples, fibers and blood are all circumstantial. Most prosecutors prefer to prosecute with circumstantial evidence. It can't forget, it can't be swayed, it can't be confused, as can human eye witnesses, and it establishes fact.

Defense attorney Gerry Spense, whom Bill first wanted to

hire to defend him, best put it in perspective when he said, "Each piece of circumstantial evidence constitutes a thread. Enough threads will make a rope. A rope has the strength for conviction."

Jeff quit his part time summer job in Portland so he could stay with his father through the summer. He took his mother's place in the pawnshop working almost every day. Understanding Jeff's need to stay and help his father through his crisis Kim went home to Portland shortly after the memorial service to resume her nursing job. By fall Jeff was relieved to go back to school, away from the investigators, newspapers and sympathy looks from the townsfolk.

But Saralyn held tight to the only parent she had left. With her mother gone she felt it was her responsibility to protect and take care of her dad. She married Kent in a quiet wedding with only a few family members and close friends in attendance. Saralyn couldn't help but think of how happy her mother would have been with this new grandchild on the way and her marriage to Kent. Betty had liked Kent. She particularly liked how good he was to her grandson. It was important to Betty that Saralyn marry someone who would treat Cree with love and kindness. Both Kent and his parents fit those criteria.

Wanting to keep the family ties open, Jo Ann succeeded in patching her problems with Saralyn and they talked occasionally on the phone. Jo Ann was determined to keep in touch with her sister's children and refrained from saying anything to Saralyn regarding her father or the investigation. However, she could not establish a line of communication with Jeff.

Betty had been so proud of Jeff. He'd made the Dean's List and was working very hard for his degree. Since Jo Ann did not return to Jackson for Jeff's high school graduation she had promised Betty she would go to his college graduation. She planned to keep that promise.

Although she'd overheard Bill tell Jeff not to worry about the money for his schooling she still didn't believe anything he said. If he hadn't said it with that cocky big-man attitude of his, as though he was trying to impress her, she may have not worried about it. She wanted to be sure Jeff was financially all right, but whenever she called Jeff he was distant, giving short answers to her casual questions about school or how they were doing, until Jo Ann finally gave up.

"I'd already asked Dick if we could fund Jeff through his school if Bill wasn't doing it. But Jeff was so short with me and would barely talk. There was definitely a strain between us."

All she could say now was, "Sorry Betty, I've tried."

Four months after her mother was murdered Saralyn began to have some grave concerns about her father's innocence. She was more in control of her emotions now that she was married and less under the control and influence of her father. She was beginning to think more rationally and factually than with her heart.

Just about the time she was certain of her father's innocence and put it out of her mind some little thing would come back to start her thinking about it again. Her father had displayed no signs of remorse over her mother's death. His rage was not directed at some unknown person for taking the life of his longtime wife and companion, but was still more directed at Betty herself for stealing from him and being unfaithful.

Saralyn had certainly been in a state of denial. If she fought back, if she believed it wasn't true, then it wouldn't be true. The loss of her mother hurt her much more deeply than those around her knew. She was ashamed for the things she had said about her mother for she knew in her heart they were not true. She also was becoming very curious.

It was a surprise to Jo Ann when Saralyn brought up the subject during a telephone conversation just after Thanksgiving.

"Saralyn wanted to know what was going on with the investigation and if the detectives still thought her dad did it.

"Well they're still pursuing it Saralyn," I told her, "but there's something that's really been bothering me. Don't you want to know who killed your mother? Do you not care at all?" She said yes, she wanted to know who killed her mother and she definitely wanted them punished for it.

"Then why don't you ever call the detectives and ask them how they are doing on the case? Are they still working on it? Do they have any suspects? You know, it's real strange. The Roundy family calls them weekly. I talk to them all the time but they say it's very strange that your father has never called them. And neither you nor Jeff have called and asked one question about how the investigation is going. It's like none of you care."

Now on the defensive Saralyn retorted, "Well my dad told us that we couldn't call."

"Why Saralyn, why can't you call?"

"Because Dad said the attorney didn't want us to call. They have misconstrued everything we say and twist it around and we're not to be in contact with them."

"That's baloney Saralyn. Do you still feel your dad is innocent?"

"Yes," came a meek reply.

"Then why don't you try to help these police, help them out, answer their questions, whatever it is they need to find out, so maybe you can shed some light on something they can investigate?"

Christmas of 1989 came and went, and for the first time since Bill and Betty bought it, the house at 435 Stacy Lane went undecorated. There was no Christmas music, no homey smells of cookies, cakes, sweets and treats baking, no elaborate decorated packages under a tree. For the Gray children it was an especially sad time and their thoughts often turned to their mother's enthusiasm for this holiday which had always generated laughter, happiness and family togetherness.

For Bill it was business as usual, and on December 30 he filed a police report saying he'd discovered $6,000 worth of his valuable coins missing and stolen from his home. To anyone who would listen he complained that "those dirty bastards who searched his home" had taken his coins. He referenced more than once it was Detective Rodriguez and Lt. Foster who were responsible. This was a natural accusation for Bill Gray as it was these two officers in particular that he had total animosity for. He knew they didn't buy his story and he knew they could be a threat to his freedom.

Although Detective Rodriguez was disappointed that the prosecutor refused to file charges he respected his decision. If Mason felt that strongly that he couldn't win in court, he probably wouldn't. If that happened it would surely be costly to the taxpayers and Bill would walk out a free man, never to be charged with these murders again.

Rodriguez had been getting some pressure. A lot of people wanted to know why that man wasn't behind bars. Jo Ann in particular, was calling constantly, passing on any information she could gather. She wanted to know what they were doing to go forward with this case. She wanted to know why they wouldn't prosecute, she wanted answers. Most importantly she wanted them to know she was not giving up. She was determined that her sister's murderer would not remain free.

The next phone call Jo Ann got from Saralyn left her concerned for her niece. "She said, 'Give me that detective's name and phone number. I can't handle this anymore. I'm having these dreams. It's Mom, and she's telling me that I must get to the truth of this. When I reach out for her I wake up. She wants help and I can't help her. Aunt Jo Ann, I think I'm going crazy. I've been to the library and I've got books to find out what these dreams mean. I'm trying to figure out what she's telling me.'"

I said, "Saralyn, if you want to know the truth call the police, talk to them, don't attack them. Don't be so hostile and listen to what they have to say."

Detective Rodriguez felt from the very beginning that the Gray children could have been the key to breaking this case but he had not talked to either one for eight months.

"It had been no use." he said. "That's the father they've had all their life and they loved him very much. I accused their father, I openly accused their father, and it got ugly. They were mad at me for accusing, even thinking, he did it."

Obviously he was quite surprised and a little cautious when he got a call from Saralyn Hoffman.

Normally another officer was designated to field questions

and keep the families of victims informed of the case status, but outside of Jo Ann's phone calls no one from the Gray family had been in contact with the department. Rodriguez took this call. She said she was having second thoughts about her father's guilt. Her father made some statements that had been bothering her. She wanted to know what they knew. What did they have on her father that made them so sure?

After making an appointment to meet with Saralyn at her home, Rodriguez called Jo Ann.

"He was really shocked. I told him I knew she was going to call. He wanted to know if I thought she was really sincere and I said Victor, I think she is. I think she really wants to find out."

Saralyn told her dad they were coming, and she told Rodriguez and Cowden when they came, that her father knew about their visit and would probably be talking to her about it afterwards. She wanted to know why they believed her dad did this. If he was their only suspect she wanted proof.

Because she had refused to listen to investigators when they tried to talk to her before, the only information Saralyn ever had, came from her father; telling her only what would help his cause. There were some damaging newspaper articles but her dad blew it off because he was being framed. Since the authorities weren't competent enough to find out who really did it they were picking on him, he told her over and over again. The master manipulator had his daughter right where he wanted her.

The detectives told Saralyn the real truth of the interviews and how her dad had lied and got caught. She learned about Mackey seeing her father, picking him out of a lineup and the moving of the Travelall. She'd been so sure her father couldn't have ridden a bike because of his health. Now she was told they had witnesses who saw her father riding a bike in Jackson two weeks before the murders. They talked at length. Then she asked, "If you've got everything that you have just told me, why has my dad not been arrested for this?"

It was a good question. The answer was Kimball Mason's refusal to prosecute. If they had the clothing or the gun and they could be traced to Bill that might help to change his mind.

"If it is my father," she said, "you will never find the gun."

The most significant information learned from this meeting for Saralyn was the realization that her father had been lying to her. She had been furious with her mother for lying and hiding the truth from her. Now, she could not deny her father had been just as guilty, but for a far more sinister reason.

Saralyn had been led to believe her father was facing serious money problems. He'd told his children the bank was the beneficiary of the large life insurance policy on Betty's life, as security for the loan on the pawnshop. But these detectives, who had the original policy in their possession, were telling her that her father was the sole beneficiary of her mother's insurance.

Was he lying to her because he was planning to hide this money from his kids and continue to cry poverty, or was he lying because he wanted his children to think there was nothing to have been gained by the death of their mother? For Saralyn, putting all these lies in a pile produced a mountain of suspicion.

"I want to help you." she boldly told detectives. "I will work with you to find the truth."

Cautioning her to understand the consequences, "What if we are right? What if it turns out we are right and it is your father?"

Strong in her determination she said, "I can't keep going on like this and I can't live the rest of my life unsure. I must know the truth."

"My dad did it," she said to her aunt Jo Ann on the phone after the meeting. Sobbing and barely audible she poured out her fears.

"I'm so afraid he did it. Unless these detectives don't know what they're talking about, he must have killed Mom. It looks really bad. What am I going to do?"

Saralyn was completely open with her father when he came over that night. Both Jo Ann and the detectives advised her to tell him everything. Her father would already know what they would be telling her.

Now, she thought, it makes more sense why we made that trip to Cheyenne to see that attorney, why he'd been ranting about needing more money and why he had been hiding his assets.

Bill had been methodically liquidating his assets. Turning what he could into cash, putting the boat and trailer in Jeff's name with the understanding that if Bill ever wanted them back they were his. The more valuable items, the gun and coin collections and five paintings deemed to have value were taken to his parents' home in Visalia, California. He sent Jeff and Saralyn home with most of Betty's jewelry but made it quite clear it was to be returned when everything settled down.

Bill, himself, had been sure the evidence against him was overwhelming enough that he thought he could be charged with these murders any day. A consciousness of guilt, he was preparing for the worst.

Saralyn wanted answers to which Bill could only deny, blame others, or evade her pursuing questioning. Because Saralyn had so vehemently protected him before, it's a safe bet he still felt she would not abandoned him now.

Saralyn had been privy to several of her dad's off-the-wall remarks and strange actions. Only now did they seem to fall into place. She thought back to the day after she learned of her mother's murder when she accidentally came across her dad in the garage. He had a tool in his hand and appeared to be either taking something off her bike or putting something on. She inquired as to what he was doing with her bike, but before she got an answer they were interrupted when the pastor walked in from the street though the open garage door. Saralyn thought nothing of it, not until now.

On the surface, she stayed on the same terms with her father but she was listening more acutely and posed supposedly unmeaning, unimportant questions to him, hoping he would not detect what she was up to. She went to the bank and confirmed what she'd been told. The bank did not have, and never had, first rights to Betty's current life insurance. Her father denied moving the Travelall, but Lloyd Laker, someone she knew well, told her otherwise. Lies!

By March it's likely that Bill was a bit suspicious of the questioning by his daughter. They had seen less and less of each other but it had not yet turned to open warfare between them. Bill came to the hospital to see Saralyn when Christopher was born, but he was hesitant to come in the room.

"Come in Dad and see your new grandson," Saralyn encouraged, but he stayed near the door as though he was going to turn and run. Both were sensing a major strain in their relationship.

Since Betty's death, Bill made it known nothing was to be removed from the house. Saralyn wanted her mother's cookbooks. She was in no hurry, but she didn't want her Grandmother Gray to have them. Several months later she was allowed to take them home, but nothing else of her mother's was to be taken. Most everything of any value had gone to California with the understanding it would come back when this was over.

Now that Saralyn was beginning to understand her father's greed and compulsion for money and possessions, she knew the things in California would not come back and he would never let her have the things that were always intended to be hers.

An aunt gave Betty an antique bedroom set just after Saralyn was born. It was always intended by the Hale family for Saralyn to have it when she had a family of her own. Having observed the methodical shuffling of things from her parents' home to her grandparents' home Saralyn made the decision to regain her bedroom set, now over 60 years old, before it went to Visalia with everything else.

Using her key to enter her father's house, Saralyn, Kent and another helper took the bedroom set and the matching antique clock. Saralyn was certain it would be sometime before her dad would even miss them since he seldom went to the basement. She was mistaken. Two days later Jeff confronted her about taking the bedroom set and clock.

Bill knew the minute he came home someone had been in the house. Within minutes he knew what was gone. The sprinkler and garden hose, set precisely in place on the porch, had been disturbed. He'd set up little traps outside as well as inside the house to alert him if any one unauthorized entered his home. Jeff, of course was told the traps were set for the cops.

Did Bill truly believe the police would break into his house without a search warrant or did he just want Jeff to be that much more cautious and afraid of the authorities? Saralyn believes the traps were deliberately set for her. She was the only person, besides Jeff, who would have had means or a reason for entering the house when her dad was not home. Why was her dad so sneaky? Why was her dad so greedy? Why was her mother dead? She knew the answers ... she just couldn't allow herself to admit it.

"We had always had a very happy family life and my parents were very giving of themselves to each other and I couldn't believe that my father would do this to my mother because at the time of my mother's death she was the glue that held our family together. My father was unable to work and my mother had her own cake business. She ran the pawnshop on her own. She had no time for herself because the time that she was not working, she was taking care of my father. I could not believe that he would be so hateful and so cruel as to do that to her when all she did was help him," said Saralyn.

On Betty's birthday, June 12, 1990, the *Post Register* newspaper in Idaho Falls published, at Jo Ann's expense, the following tribute:

> In Memory of My Sister Betty Lou Gray on
> Her 50th Birthday
> What a treasure to my life she was, my sister.
> She's my definition of love and sweetness and understanding, all wrapped up in one wonderful person.
> That's my sister.
> She's the best there was, the absolute best.
> And I appreciate everything about her; her beautiful spirit, the intertwining of our lives and the way she brought so many smiles my way.
>
> There will never be a day in my life when I will not love her, be thankful for her, admire her and simply think about her with happiness deep inside me. I'd give anything if she could know this. She's

someone who means more to me than she will ever know.

That's my sister, and what a wonderful sister she was.
I miss her so.

To Betty, with all my love!
Your sister,
Jo Ann

Almost a year to the day after the death of her sister, Jo Ann contacted the Idaho Attorney General's Office in Boise. She insisted that the attorney general look into this case. Specifically she related the refusal of the Bonneville County prosecutor to seek charges. She wanted them to review the case and hopefully find there was enough evidence to override Prosecutor Mason, forcing him to seek an indictment, or removing him from the case.

The attorney general has the power to take a case over from a prosecutor but rarely does. It's done only when it can be shown the prosecutor grossly abused his discretion. Deputy Attorney General Russ Rennau said they would look into it and review the files. Detective Rodriguez readily agreed to a review saying it would be a good idea to see if they could give them some fresh new ideas on the case. Jo Ann was encouraged, until she heard from Joy Ufford.

Joy Ufford, reporter for the *Jackson Hole Guide* took a special interest in the Gray case. She tracked down every story and kept the case alive in the papers until the court records had been sealed and the investigation came to a standstill. Lucky to have a confidant associated with a newspaper, Jo Ann kept Ufford apprised of the case status and Ufford contacted Jo Ann with information she gathered.

Ufford wrote a lengthy article pertaining to Jo Ann's soliciting the aid of the Attorney General's Office and their refusal to look into the case. Although this was the first indication Bill had that Jo Ann was actively pursuing the case, he must have been relieved to read his sister-in-law had run into a brick wall.

In the Guide, Ufford quoted Jo Ann's frustration with the legal system. "The last time I talked to Rodriguez he told me things were looking good, but I don't know what that meant. When I contacted the Attorney General's Office they said they would come in on it right away, so I just assumed they would follow through. I don't know why they keep refusing to; I just keep feeling like my hands are tied. It absolutely tears me up. Every time I try to find out something I just get knocked around, right and left. They'd just keep switching offices and they'd say, 'Oh you need to talk to Kimball Mason,' and I'd say no, I don't want to talk to Kimball Mason, so they would put me through to another office, and then another, and never any answers. Every time I get a little glimmer of hope Kimball Mason's name comes up and I get shot down. I'm sure there's no cover up, but why isn't it getting solved? I used to cry often that my sister's murderer would go unpunished, now I'm to the point where I'm just angry. I can't give it up. I'll keep it in their minds. I'm just not going to give it up. I promised my sister."

Through that summer and fall Jo Ann talked to Russ Rennau three times, each time becoming more frustrated.

"I was getting and angrier and angrier. I had to be a little cool with the press so as not to give out something that might harm the case, but I figured this was the Attorney General's Office and what I said would remain in confidence."

Much more bold and determined, she went step by step through the evidence and Kimball's refusal not only to prosecute, but to even talk to her or her niece.

"Kimball will never find the clothing. He will never find the gun. This was well planned. My brother-in-law planned these murders. He's bragged how he can do things and get away with it. If Kimball needs to have this, he will never have it."

In his defense Rennau told Jo Ann they had planned to go to Idaho Falls but Mason called it off.

"Well I want it recalled," she demanded. "I was never told it was called off. I found out through the press. Kimball isn't doing one thing on this and I want it investigated."

Unfortunately, Rennau informed her, "We cannot come in on the case by your request. If the detectives or Mason requested it we would come, but no one seemed to want them there now."

When hostile Jo Ann Buccola got Detective Rodriguez on the phone, she was ready for battle.

"After I hung up with Rennau I called Victor and read him the riot act. Why did this happen? Why didn't you tell me?"

Trying to reason with her, Victor told Jo Ann that Mason had led him to believe he was going to take this to the grand jury so they called off the dogs. I said, "Victor, you know darn well he didn't want to be investigated and have them find out there was enough evidence. It was you who told me your hands were tied and to go for it. You'd better call them back and get this thing started," she threatened. "Somewhere, somehow, this case is going to trial."

"My dad would have a fit if he knew I was talking to you," Saralyn said to Jo Ann in one of their now more frequent phone calls.

"He's absolutely furious over your contacting the attorney general. Dad said you were out to get him and he forbids Jeff and me to even talk to you."

No wonder Jeff was acting so cool, Jo Ann thought. But Saralyn needed to keep in contact with her aunt. There was no one else she could talk to, share her fears and gain emotional support. Saralyn wanted so much to believe in her father's innocence. Jo Ann continued to encourage her to seek the truth, only then could she be free of the burden she carried.

Already teetering on the edge, the turning point came when her father came to her home one afternoon. Boldly confronting him Saralyn took her father's head in both hands, made him face her and said, "I've got to know. Look me straight in the eye and tell me you did not murder my mother."

Withdrawing from her grasp and turning to leave, he huffily said, "That question doesn't deserve an answer."

But Saralyn reached out, turned him around confronting him once again, "Tell me you did not kill my mother," she screamed. As he wheeled around heading for the door he heard his daughter shout to his back, "You just answered my question. You killed my mother!"

Bill Gray's strongest ally just became his worst enemy.

It took a lot of persuasion to convince Jeff of her suspicions. Kim had feelings of Bill's guilt shortly after the murders. But she would not say anything to Jeff. She would not attempt to influence her husband's thinking. If Jeff was to decide his father was guilty he must come to this conclusion by himself. Just as Saralyn had, Jeff needed to believe that his father could not have committed this horrible crime. All the little things he'd heard and observed while he was in Jackson that pointed suspicion, were offset and rationalized by his fierce determination of innocence. Possibly his father could kill in the heat of anger, but it would be impossible for his dad to put a gun to his mother's head while she was sleeping and coldly pull the trigger.

Saralyn and Jeff talked about what she'd learned at great length and Jeff finally had to admit it sure didn't sound very good. Although Jeff was not happy, and quite reluctant, he too "had to know" and would accompany his sister to meet with the detectives.

Meeting in Detective Rodriguez's office in Idaho Falls, Saralyn told her story. All the strange statements her dad had made came pouring out. Although Detective Rodriguez knew this was damaging information, another "thread in the rope," he knew it would not be enough. Taking a chance, he brought out pictures of the crime scene being extremely careful not to let them see pictures containing the bodies.

"When I showed them that crime scene it was to pick out personality traits in that scene. I showed them photographs because every time you commit a homicide you leave your traits in that house. Your personality is in that house and I wanted to see what they had to say about that," Rodriguez said. "And it worked, the footprints, the Handi Wipes wrapper, Mountain Dew can, Betty's purse, and they began to add it up."

Indeed they began to add it up. Mountain Dew was their dad's favorite drink. His refrigerator was full of it. Saralyn and Jeff remembered their mother wouldn't let them or their friends drink the Mountain Dew. Their father would get real mad if it wasn't there when he wanted one.

When Saralyn noticed the pull top missing from the can in the picture Saralyn said her father always pulled the tops off of cans. Some time ago he was saving tops for a Kidney Foundation fund raiser and he just got in the habit and never quit.

The Handi Wipes wrapper found behind Betty's car near the footprint in the gravel was just like the ones they had seen in their father's home when Bill was going through peritoneal dialysis. The hospital supplied him with special sterile wipes, however they contained a red disinfectant which stained everything they touched. After enough permanent damage had been inflicted on clothes and sheets Bill switched to a generic wipe and added his own colorless disinfectant. The Grays never threw out the hospital wipes but Bill bought the generic kind by the case. It was the red hospital wipes the officers noticed on the first search of Bill's house.

The footprints in the carpet and scaled drawing looked identical to the sole of tennis shoes they'd seen their father wear when he was propped "feet up" in his recliner, and no, come to think of it, they had not seen those shoes since the murders.

"But the purse, Betty's purse. It wasn't what was in it, but what was not in it," Rodriguez recalled. "See, nobody would talk to us. We didn't know what Betty normally carried in her purse and then the kids said that she should have had her gun in her purse. They said their father gave her this small gun a long time ago and insisted that she carry it. Betty never went anywhere without it.

"Well we didn't know it then, but we found out that the gun we took from Bill the night of that first interview on July 24 was the gun Betty had always carried in her purse. We didn't know whose gun that was. We thought it was his. It didn't surprise me, with his fondness for guns. When he went for the money in Betty's purse he probably saw it and decided he just couldn't leave it behind."

As Saralyn held her mother's purse her eyes filled with tears. A woman's purse is such a personal and cherished possession, her mother's cherished possession. Zipping and unzipping compartments, two bracelets fell out in her lap. The bracelets, including the heart shaped bracelet Bill was searching for, had been placed in Betty's purse at the time of the autopsy. Saralyn put them back in the purse. She did not want her father to have them now.

When she realized her mother's address book was not in the purse she said, "Oh my God, I didn't even think about it. My mother had her address book with her all the time, but Dad was using her address book to notify all the relatives and friends right after we found out Mom was dead."

"They had been suspicious and had made up their minds when they came to talk to me," Rodriguez said. "I only helped confirm their feelings."

Detective Rodriguez had been quite put-out with Saralyn in the past. Having been on the receiving end of her anger and sharp tongue he'd written her off as somewhat neurotic. But as hardened as he was to the cruelties of life he couldn't help but feel a deep sympathy for these kids. They had lost their mother to a most heinous crime and now they shouldered the anguish of knowing their own father was responsible. Their pain was now doubled. He admired them for having the courage to come forward. He had no idea how truly courageous they were.

As vehemently as Saralyn protected her dad before, she was just as determined to see him brought to justice now. She still loved him in a sense, but could not excuse what he had done, not only to her mother but to their entire family. There could never be a relationship between them now.

She kept thinking about the premeditation. Saralyn would have been able to forgive him if her mother's death had resulted from a moment of heated anger where he wouldn't have had time to think about it before it happened. But her father had planned to kill her mother for a long time. He'd planned her murder, at the very least, thirty days before he carried it out because he bought the Travelall for only one reason, to cover himself when he went to kill her mother. He stalked her mother, and he cruelly killed her, without giving her any chance to save herself.

He had every opportunity to change his mind. He was a coward and thought only of himself, not caring how painful their mother's death would be to his children. Saralyn would never forget, and she would never forgive.

Men weren't supposed to show their feeling and Jeff kept his bottled up inside. This young man had been very close to his mother and he missed her so very much, but he'd always loved and trusted his father as well. He could never understand why someone would have wanted to kill his gentle mother who was so good to everyone. The fact that it was his own father was almost more than he could bear.

"When he killed my mother, as far as I'm concerned, he's dead too."

And Kim? She'd supported Jeff through all of this. She had determined that Bill was still Father unless, or until, the police could prove to them Bill was the killer. Now she knew, and she harbored a deep anger.

"I could never forgive his father for how he has changed my husband's life. I will never forget the pain in his voice or the look on his face, when he received that phone call that his mother was dead. We will never have the opportunity to have

Betty as a grandmother to our children, and out of a sense of duty we felt so bad for poor Bill that Jeff stayed there the whole summer and we spent our first anniversary apart, which we will never get back."

Coinciding with Jo Ann contacting the Attorney General's Office, a little over a year after the murders, Teton County Judge Terry Rogers unsealed the Gray case search warrant affidavits.

"At some point it's got to be a public record," he said. "I felt enough time had gone by and it shouldn't be sealed."

For the first time readers of the Idaho Falls and Jackson newspapers were privy to more specific information investigators had withheld from the public nearly a year ago. Headlines proclaimed "Murder Victim's Spouse Placed Near Crime Scene" and "Travelall Linked to Gray Seized" The affidavits revealed that Gray had been picked out of a photo lineup by two witnesses, the Grays were having "marital problems" and Betty was planning to get a divorce. Details of the murder scene, writings in blood, candles, footprints, the attempted hiding of the Travelall and all the evidence establishing cause to search were laid out to the public.

This set off a barrage of phone calls to the Jackson Police Department. With this information that appeared to be so damaging toward Bill Gray, the residents wanted something done. They were uneasy that a suspected killer was free to live among them and some wanted vengeance for Betty.

When news reporters asked Bill if he would discuss the affidavits, he refused, saying past coverage of his wife's death was unfair to him and he questioned whether the newspapers should have access to the affidavits.

"I have nothing to say to you people after you crucified me last time," he said. "It's the shits the way I got whipped in the press before. Looks like it's going to happen again."

It had been so quiet, for so long. He'd almost talked himself into believing nothing further was going to happen. After all, if the Idaho prosecutor said he wasn't going to prosecute he need not worry. The August 22 article in the *Guide* headlined "Murder Victim's Sister Persists in Lonely Vigil," which detailed Jo Ann's anguish and failure to get officials to take action on the case, confirmed that thinking, Then just days later, on the heels of anticipated liberation, Judge Rogers lets the cat out of the bag by unsealing the warrants and he's headlines once again.

Bill had been playing it pretty low key, tending to business, a Vegas trip now and then, but mostly biding his time until he could get Betty's will back from Idaho authorities and collect the insurance on Betty's policy. So far, all his efforts to that end had been rejected. He'd planned to sell the pawnshop but he wasn't in any hurry. He would have to wait out the courts and insurance companies before he could get on with his life.

Launching an investigation of her own, Saralyn tracked down a florist who said her dad called him twice the night before Reeda Roundy's funeral, first begging, and then threatening him to get flowers to Reeda's funeral. What got the florist's attention was Bill's attitude. Rather than sending flowers as a sympathy gesture to a grieving family, he was ranting. "I just found out her funeral is tomorrow. I've got to cover my ass. I don't give a shit what kind you send, but I've got to have flowers there in time." A far cry from damaging evidence it still indicated Bill's thought process in the days after the murders.

When Saralyn complained to Teton County Prosecutor, Tim Day that the Bonneville County prosecutor would not take the case to a grand jury, he said he certainly would. He felt the existing evidence was enough for a conviction. If the murders would have happened in his jurisdiction, he said, her father would be in jail. It was a very frustrating situation for Saralyn. It seemed to all depend on one man, Kimball Mason, and that man wasn't budging.

She knew they needed the murder weapon to change Mason's mind and she'd given it a lot of thought. If her father was to have buried the gun, or parts of it, or even the clothing, she thought he would do it in the back yard where the family buried pets that died. As she gathered her information she passed it on to the detectives. She was of the impression they were going to get another search warrant and either dig in that area or use metal detectors. Saralyn was geared to help move this case to its fullest extent.

When she heard reloaded ammunition may have been used in the killings she knew her dad's garage was full of reloads. That was one of his hobbies.

"What kind do you need? I need to know exactly what you need. If I get them will Kimball Mason file criminal charges?" she wanted to know.

Assured it would certainly help, but scared to death, she drove first to the pawnshop to make sure her father was there, and then went to the house. Scared enough to leave the car running with her two small children in it, she ran through the house to the cabinet she knew would contain the reloads, gathered thirty-two assorted cartridges and rushed home to call Detective Rodriguez.

"I've got them," she said. "Now come get them right away."

The September 11, 1990 ballistics report on the shells Saralyn collected stated, in part, "The bullets found near the victims were 9mm cartridges, reloads; and the box of 32 shells sent were also reloads, not substantially different, they may have originated from the same source."

The FBI Laboratory report also stated, "The bullets found near the victims had been fired from a weapon with a silencer attached." Some of the officers that worked the search warrant July 28, 1989 at Bill's house, mentioned they noticed a book about silencers. It had not been listed on the original warrant, nor was anyone aware that a silencer was involved at that time, so the book was never taken.

Saralyn was asked if she remembered seeing a book like that at her dad's home. Yes she had, although he always had lots of books around about guns, she remembered a green book sitting by her dad's recliner and was sure it dealt with silencers. Interesting, no one had mentioned the color to Saralyn, but the book described by some of the officers was also green.

Even with the new circumstantial evidence and the cooperation of Saralyn and Jeff, Mason remained steadfast. He did not have enough concrete evidence to prove guilt beyond a reasonable doubt. Until he did, he would not file charges.

"This is not the kind of case you want to rush into without adequate evidence," he publicly stated. "It has been some months, but as homicides go I don't think it's extraordinary. Some cases never get solved."

That was not what Saralyn wanted to hear. Like Jo Ann, she'd made every attempt to convince Mason there was enough evidence to prosecute and win. Kimball had been a recipient of Saralyn's abrupt temper. Now he set out to avoid her entirely. He was always out of the office and later in court, a meeting or otherwise unreachable when she called. Unrelenting she left message after message until one day he called her back and rudely told her he was not going to take this case to the grand jury, and now he'd returned her calls and he didn't want to hear from her again. Testing the system she called again and was told "I'm sorry Ms. Hoffman, Mr. Mason refuses to talk to you."

Having joined their aunt's campaign, Saralyn in particular, was in constant communication with Jo Ann. Together they were determined to somehow find a way to go over Kimball Mason's head, and force an arrest.

Everyone involved was frustrated over the Gray case. Detective Rodriguez and Lt. Dave Foster were certain Bill Gray killed the two women. There was a strong motive, they tied him to the Travelall, he tried to hide it when he knew he had been seen in it, Steven Mackley's sighting of Gray and picking him out of a photo lineup. In the July 28 interview, he lied about the Travelall. He admitted he lied, and then he lied about his reasons for lying.

Never giving up, Detective Rodriguez decided to use the information given by Saralyn to request another search warrant. Listed on the search warrant was the book on silencers, wet wipes, disposable rubber gloves and turf shoes. The affidavit specifically detailed Saralyn's knowledge of these items.

A second search was conducted at Bill Gray's home. None of the listed items were found. While conducting the search Detective Rodriguez couldn't help but notice the plastic box on the fireplace mantel containing Betty's ashes and the bizarre shrine. The mantel was covered with family pictures of Bill and Betty together, family pictures when Saralyn and Jeff were little, Bill and Betty's wedding picture, Jeff and Kim's wedding picture; a memorial to a family that once was. A vase of flowers taken from Betty's service was placed next to the box of ashes.

The flowers were now dead and dried. The entire setting was covered in thick dust seemingly abandoned and forgotten.

Unquestionably, the constant pressure brought by Jo Ann and Saralyn had Kimball Mason on the defensive and ready to fight back. He'd heard about all he wanted to hear about this case unless the detectives had something new for him. Detective Rodriguez badgered him so much about the case Mason threw him out of his office. Tension was high among the department heads. Everyone wanted this case resolved. No one but Mason could understand why it wasn't getting done. Two prosecutors from other counties looked at the evidence; both of them felt it was enough.

By now she was thinking there was either a major cover up going on, or everyone in Bonneville County was passing the buck. Jo Ann Buccola was a woman possessed. She spent untold hours every day on the phone, writing letters and talking about the case. She encouraged the Roundy family to write letters and make phone calls. She asked everyone she knew if they had suggestions that would turn her in the right direction.

She went to the Orange County Detective Division and asked for information and advice. Discouraged, but never giving up, Jo Ann hired Detective John Cowden, who had recently retired, as a private investigator. She'd hoped on private retainer he could devote himself to the case full time and uncover something that may have been overlooked.

She talked to Roy Leavitt frequently. He was still traveling to Jackson for Fanning Wholesale and had been trying to do some investigating of his own. She hoped he would find something out or at the least mention something in their conversations that he'd forgotten before.

Jo Ann's close friends, husband and sons surrendered to a constant assessment of events. For Jo Ann there was no other subject. From her family and friends, there was understanding, admiration and total support, but they all wished something positive would happen soon. Jo Ann needed to have her life back. By now anyone who spent much time with her could recite the case verbatim.

Son, Dennis, was almost as knowledgeable about the case as was his mother. Since this subject had consumed the entire household for over a year he was prone to discuss the problems his mother was having, hoping someone might have something to offer that would help. During a workout at the gym a casual acquaintance overheard Dennis discussing the case. Approaching Dennis, he said, "Do you know where I'm from?" Quite by accident, hundreds of miles apart, Dennis found the son of the founder of the *Post Register* newspaper in Idaho Falls. Through this contact Jo Ann not only started receiving the Post Register every day but was given ideas for additional contacts.

She started with the Idaho Bar Association but quickly found they gave names of attorneys by who were next on the list, not who would be more qualified for what she wanted. Given the names of two judges, the first was running for re-election and was impossible to reach. The second, Judge Ted Wood, could not talk to her. If Bill was ever charged, it was quite possible he would end up in Judge Wood's courtroom. Then it was the City Council. Everyone wanted to connect her to Mason's office.

"I said, are you guys all in cahoots or something? Kimball Mason is not who I want to talk to. I want him off this case."

Given the name of the previous Bonneville County Prosecutor, Jerry Wolf, she contacted him. Wolf was interested, thought there was something that could be done, but wanted to wait and see what the attorney general's investigation turned up. Unwilling to sit it out waiting, Jo Ann sought help from a local California attorney who advised Jo Ann to seek her counsel outside of Idaho Falls.

He cautioned problems with loyalty. A local attorney may be reluctant to make enemies of the prosecutor. Taking his advice Jo Ann started writing to attorneys all over southeastern Idaho to see if they could give her an opinion. Most responses were the same, they felt she might have a case but if the prosecutor didn't think he had enough evidence he had a reason.

Through a suggestion of DeeDee's, Jo Ann found Tom Dial. Attorney Dial, from Pocatello, Idaho was very interested. He already knew a little about the case. After being retained by Jo Ann he made appointments with Saralyn and the Jackson detectives. He went through all the Teton County case files. Everyone in Jackson was most cooperative, but Dial was met with total resistance when he asked to look at the case files held in Idaho Falls.

Sitting in on the meeting with the Bonneville County detectives, Mason told Dial to do what he had to do, but if he wanted to see the files and evidence he was going to have to get a subpoena. From what he'd learned in Jackson, Tom Dial was convinced there was sufficient evidence to file a wrongful death suit. If Saralyn and Jeff would file suit against their father he felt it would put the case in the public light and they may be able to get the case to a criminal court.

Jo Ann was not receptive to Dial's suggestion. "All I wanted was to get Mason off the case so someone else could take it to a grand jury. When Dial told me the kids would have to file a suit I said, 'No way, I'm not going to do that to my niece and nephew. This would be pitting them against their father.' As determined as I was to get Bill to trial, I would never do that to Saralyn and Jeff."

She'd spent well over $5,000 in her combined efforts, not to mention $200 to $300 in monthly telephone bills and she still wasn't hearing what she wanted to hear.

Detective Rodriguez was well aware of Jo Ann Buccola's pursuit. She called often sharing with him her trials and ever so small triumphs. This time she pleaded with him to give her a name. Tom Moss's name had come up before but Jo Ann was of the understanding he was a prosecutor and therefore couldn't take her case. But Rodriguez informed her Moss had a private practice as well.

"He may be able to help you. I don't know if he will even take the case Jo Ann, but he's a good man. You've got nothing to lose by talking to him about it."

She made several phone calls and was unable to reach him. Preparing to leave town for a few days she called Saralyn.

"I'm giving you this number, his name is Tom Moss. He lives in Blackfoot, Idaho which isn't far from Idaho Falls. Call him and tell him what we want. See if he can help us with this and if he says yes, give him my name and phone number. Tell him I'll pay his fees. We've got to get something going for us."

He received his license to practice law in 1966, was elected to the office of Bingham County Prosecuting Attorney in 1967, left the office in 1971 and was talked into running again in 1978. Winning that election and every one thereafter, Thomas Moss was a much practiced attorney and prosecutor, well respected by his peers and his community. Moss had his share of difficult cases. His first murder case came just a little over a year and a half after he received his law degree, and just five months after becoming prosecutor in 1967. It was a first degree murder case, which he won, and he felt it set the precedent for what was to come. Tom has successfully prosecuted so many cases he doesn't even know how many. He's been told he has prosecuted more murder cases than anyone else in the state of Idaho, but then he says, "It's because I have more longevity than anyone else in Idaho. Most prosecutors don't want to remain in office as many years as I have."

Moss was familiar with the Gray case, at least to the extent of what he read in the papers, saw on television and what he learned from his good friend Kimball Mason when they talked about it at a meeting in Boise. But when he got a telephone call from Saralyn Hoffman in late October, 1990, he had no idea who she was.

"She called and said, 'Mr. Moss, my name is Saralyn Hoffman and my brother and I want to hire you to prosecute our father for murdering our mother.' I asked her to tell me a little about the case and realizing it was the Gray case I told her I was a little familiar with the case. But I said, Ms. Hoffman, I can't prosecute that case, you will have to get the prosecutor in Bonneville County to do that. 'Well you don't understand,' she said. 'We will pay you to take over the prosecution.' and I said, Well you don't understand, it doesn't matter whether you pay me or not, I don't have the authority to go up there and prosecute a criminal case, only the elected prosecutor can do that. She said, 'He won't do it. We can't get him to do anything. We've contacted the Attorney General's Office and they won't do anything. We just want something done.'"

Moss went on to tell Saralyn there might be other alternatives he could help them with. She wanted to know what kind of alternatives. "I said well, a civil suit. I said this might be a means whereby you could get your story out to the public."

"That's what we want," she said. "We want to get our story told."

"She asked me what was done in a civil suit and I told her it was just like any other death action, you would sue for damages."

"We don't want money" she said. "We want our story told because he killed our mother and it looks like he's going to get away with it."

"Well, this is the vehicle you go by if you want your story told. Was there any insurance?"

"Oh yes," Saralyn replied. "There is a large insurance policy and the company has refused to pay my father because of the murder investigation, but they're gonna pay him if there isn't something done on the murder case."

Tom told Saralyn that they could certainly bring an action to intercept the funds and prevent their father from profiting from his crime. Saralyn said she wanted to think about it. This wasn't what she had expected to hear and she needed to confer with Jeff and Jo Ann.

Once again a wrongful death suit was mentioned to Jo Ann as the means to achieve her goal. Once again she was ready to reject it. She would not place her niece and nephew in jeopardy only to keep a promise. However, Moss had given her a lot to think about. If she was eventually successful in forcing the prosecution of her brother-in-law, he would undoubtedly spend every dollar he had defending himself. Any inheritance his children would be entitled to would be gone. The insurance money that her sister died for would be used to defend her killer.

For Saralyn the buzz words were "profiting from his crime." She knew her father killed her mother not for jealousy, but for her insurance and assets. Even if he was never prosecuted criminally, she would go to no end to see he did not live the good life on the blood money from her mother's death.

Jeff just wanted this nightmare to be over. He was still talking to his dad, barely. He wanted so desperately to believe his dad could not have killed his mother, but in his heart he knew.

With all the pros and cons thought out, Jo Ann gave in. If this civil suit would get enough attention and get the facts out to the public it might put enough pressure on Kimball Mason to force him to take it to the grand jury. Then if he still wouldn't, they had a better shot at getting the attorney general involved. If that failed, at the very least, Bill might be prevented from squandering and gambling away his children's inheritance. An inheritance their mother would want her children to have.

When Saralyn called Tom back she said, "If this will get it all out in the open we want to go through with it. We don't want our dad to make money because he killed our mother. But my brother is extremely upset about this, he doesn't want any money out of this." Moss assured her he understood what they wanted, but going after the money was the only basis they could start with.

Moss and his clients could not wait for Bonneville County to sort out their problems. The statute of limitations on a civil suit runs out after two years. There were only seven months left and Kimball Mason was still very positive on his decision not to file criminal charges. The children of Bill Gray would sue their father for the wrongful death of their mother and their mother's sister would foot the bill.

"I want to tell you," Detective Cowden said to Jo Ann over the phone, "You've got some happy detectives up here. Guess who showed up at our door today?"

When Victor came down the hall and saw Tom Moss he

jumped in the air, clicked his heels together and exclaimed, "Hallelujah, it's Tom."

This time Kimball Mason was very cooperative. He invited Moss to look at anything he wished to see. Moss returned to his office with a stack of files more than 18 inches deep. He set out to educate himself on the Gray case. Taking this wholly unorganized stack of papers he categorized them in precise detail. Where one report might contain several items or names he would make as many copies of that report as necessary to ensure each newly labeled file contained every piece of information pertaining to it. With a yellow highlighter, he highlighted all the information that was relevant to that particular file. Files labeled bullets, hair, footprints, Travelall, each individual involved, eventually equaled more than a large two-drawer filing cabinet. It was a very time consuming and sometimes boring job, taking him several months to complete, but when he was done the entire case was at his fingertips.

There were four different insurance policies on Betty's life. Dated in 1959 an amount of $3,000, 1972 for $14,516, 1980 for $10,000, and the last, which raised some eyebrows, was a large policy taken out in October, 1987 in the amount of $250,000.

Unproven, but certainly questionable, was the signature on this policy. Having access to samples of Betty's signature it was debatable if Betty had actually signed this policy. However for that amount of insurance Betty would undoubtedly have had to pass a physical examination and therefore be a willing participant in the purchase.

Ultimately an insurance examiner, a registered nurse, was located and verified she came to the pawnshop in August 1988 and gave Betty a cursory examination. Betty was fully aware of the large policy on her life. In the nurse's statement she recalled Bill was there that day to take care of customers while she was with Betty. Bill offered coffee and was very pleasant and courteous toward her. She remembered Betty as being in good health, a lovely lady.

"It's was just terrible what happened to her."

Bill told detectives the insurance policy was taken out because he was uninsurable and the lending institution from which they borrowed money on the pawnshop required a sizeable policy to support the loan. But the large loan had been made years before the insurance policy was bought. It could have been however, the excuse Bill used to talk Betty into willingly getting the policy on her life.

The simple fact that he felt he needed to lie about the policy beneficiary raises questions. Considering that Betty was seeing Leavitt at the time they took out the policy and knowing Bill's fondness for collecting insurance payoffs, the most chilling scenario comes to mind.

Could Bill have been planning to eventually collect on that policy when he bought it, as much as a year and a half before Betty died? Was he only waiting for an appropriate amount of time to pass between purchase and collection? Would Betty have eventually met an untimely death even if she was not planning to divorce Bill?

What is known about Bill is the unlikelihood he would be willing make large insurance payments for something as unforeseen as Betty's natural death at then age 47. Certainly with his health problems Betty would outlive him anyway. His pattern would be to insure something he fully intended to collect on, another fire may have been just one too many coincidences. It's highly probable Bill had been incurring mounting gambling debts. Certainly Bill was hooked. He admitted he was in such poor health he could not stand at the crap table for long periods of time, he used a chair on occasion, but still he went, and he gambled. And the odds are he lost. Bill needed money, big money, and when Betty signed the insurance papers, she may well have been signing her own death warrant.

All four insurance companies were appreciative to hear from Tom Moss. In this case there were concerns of paying one party only to be sued by the other party and ending up paying twice. Although they would be named as defendants in the civil suit, resolution of the suit would have a court decree to which the money should be paid. By voluntarily joining the suit, they need not send, or hire local attorneys for the litigation process. Moss and his clients stipulated to allowing the insurance companies to pay the insurance proceeds into a court controlled escrow account where it would remain until the civil suit was decided.

Bill had no idea his children were consulting an attorney, let alone planning to file a civil suit against him. But the relationship between him and Saralyn had taken a turn for the worse after she confronted him face to face. Bill knew his daughter doubted his innocence and began to drop little hints that she should stay out of it.

Like her mother, she began to sense strangeness in her father that was unsettling. Saralyn found herself looking over her shoulder, jumping at the slightest thing and extremely nervous if Kent was not home at night. As the time drew closer to the filing of the civil suit, Saralyn was a bundle of nerves. Taking her son, she flew to California to visit her aunt. Leaving a note for her father she explained she was going out of town for a few days.

"Don't try to find me, I just need to get away for a while."

At first the messages on her answering machine were, "I know you're there, pick up the damned phone. Answer this ... I want to talk to you." Then the messages became more demanding and nastier. Still not believing she was out of town, he went to her house, pounded on the door shouting for her to come to the door.

Saralyn was hysterical when the phone calls started coming to Jo Ann's. One or two a day, the caller would say nothing; remain on the line for a few seconds, then hang up. The Buccola's had not previously been subjected to hang up calls. They were all sure it was Bill. Finally in desperation Dick took the phone.

"Bill, if it's you, say something. Don't do this. Talk to us."

The phone calls stopped but Saralyn felt sure her father was trying to send her a message, "Keep your mouth shut."

On December 18, 1990 the civil suit was filed in Bonneville County. On December 19, Detective Rodriguez and Agent Kotrason personally served Bill Gray a summons notifying him of the suit which required Gray to answer the complaint within 20 days. He was surprised but very quiet for Bill Gray. He took the papers and walked away.

The wrongful death complaint alleged that William L. Gray shot and killed Betty L. Gray with a handgun. The conduct of defendant William L. Gray was wanton, malicious and outrageous in that it was done intentionally and without any justifiable provocation.

"The children are entitled to damages for the loss of support, care, society, comfort, love and affection permanently lost as a result of their mother's death. Said beneficiary, by willfully killing the insured, forfeited any interest he may have had in insurance policies."

The action was twofold, damages for the loss of their mother and for the insurance under the "slayers statute" which is an Idaho law that says if you are the beneficiary of life insurance and you intentionally take the life of the insured, you are not allowed to receive the proceeds. Gray hired the services of a local law firm Fix and Mulligan.

Christmas 1990 came and went and neither Bill Gray nor his children had much to be cheerful about. Saralyn and Jeff's world had totally collapsed. They lost both parents in the home on Crowley Road that night.

"I started having my doubts in early spring because too many things were not right," Saralyn told reporters. "Now I don't think he did it, I know he did it. I know without a doubt my father did this or I would never have brought this suit against him. This is something that takes a lot of thought and it wasn't a hasty decision."

Obviously very concerned she expressed her fears. "My home is only a few miles from my dad's. When you live in the same town, you're always looking over your shoulder. If he is capable of committing this crime, what is to say that in a fit of anger he couldn't do the same to me? I've become very bitter and I don't know how I feel. It's impossible to explain. This whole thing needs to be cleaned up and put away so I can get on with my life."

It had been extremely hard on Jeff to sue his father. He had stuck up for his father long after Saralyn became convinced of his guilt.

"It was pretty hard, having to come to the conclusion that he did it but I just couldn't deny it any longer; there was no other explanation for this." he said. "It's a long story that has taken its toll on us over the past year and a half. We've been dealing with it, but it isn't going away." Resentful of the legal system he vented his anger.

"We were forced into doing the civil suit because Kimball Mason wouldn't try the case. It wouldn't have had to be this way."

Although the focus was on the Gray family, the Roundy family had been suffering their share of grief and pain over the loss of their mother. It's impossible to weigh a level of anguish but one can imagine that the Roundys were especially traumatized by the fact that there was a reason, regardless of how evil it was, behind Betty's death but Reeda had died for no other reason than Betty was her friend. Urged on by Jo Ann, Reeda's sister, Evelyn Hamilton, had also asked the Idaho Attorney General's Office to investigate the case. She was justifiably as upset as everyone else by Mason's lack of interest. Besides, she wanted to continually remind them that two people were killed that evening and there was another family that cared and wanted the killer brought to justice.

Gray's attorneys, Richard Mulligan and William Fix filed a cross-claim and a counterclaim to the wrongful death suit asking that the insurance proceeds be paid to Gray and asked for his children to return their mother's jewelry. He contended he gave them the jewelry to hold for safe-keeping until such time as he requested its return. Now that the family was divided he wanted it all back. Bill had gone to a lot of trouble gathering Betty's jewelry after her death. He wasn't about to just turn it over to the kids without anticipation of getting it back. Saralyn was firm in her convictions.

"He said he was going to sell it to retain legal counsel for himself. He's not going to take my mother's jewelry."

When interviewed by the *Jackson Hole News*, attorney William Fix proclaimed Bill's innocence and charged that Mason's investigation was hiding information that would likely clear the cloud of suspicion surrounding Gray. He claimed there were other people involved that the police had not investigated. They were confident the lawsuit could help Gray.

"It's Bill's chance to prove his innocence." Going after Saralyn he said, "The civil suit was just an attempt by Gray's daughter to get money."

But Saralyn fought back saying money was her father's motive, not hers.

Bill's attorneys had taken every opportunity to portray Saralyn and Jeff as greedy children, willing to sacrifice their father for their personal financial gain. Residents of Jackson were divided. Saralyn received phone calls from supporters, as well as calls and personal encounters from those who did not understand. Most did not know the trauma Saralyn was suffering.

Her mother was still coming to her in horrendous nightmares that left her unable to sleep and unable to think rationally. Torn between the guilt she was suffering for being so flippant with her mother in the months before she died, then trying to live with the fact she was helping to imprison her father, or worse, were taking a toll on her mental stability. She couldn't remember things. On one occasion she couldn't remember picking up her son up from nursery school that very day. She'd start out to do something, then just that quickly, forget what she was going to do. Saralyn was headed for a mental breakdown.

Tom Moss was so concerned he had her placed under a doctor's care. Only then was she able to sort through the consequences of her actions and come to terms with herself and her convictions.

With the issues identified, both sides began a legal battle that would ultimately rival any other in the history of Bonneville County. Beginning the discovery process common in any civil suit, both sides began taking depositions. Saralyn, Jeff and Kim were the first to give their depositions. Bill was present for each deposition as the accusers gave their accounts under the cold glaring stare of the accused.

Now under oath, with every word being recorded, the story of a once happy family, now divided, began to emerge. Over a period of several days, Bill's attorney, William Fix, challenged their accusations and credibility, determined to elicit information he could use in defense of the charges against his client. The matter at hand was defending the civil suit, but if criminal charges were ever filed against Gray, what was said in these depositions could certainly be used as a foundation against Gray in a murder trial.

He had to know what would be said when they were called as witness. He would hear what they had to say, then would work very hard and patiently to find flaws in their stories. He would try to paint a picture of a malicious and greedy intent to destroy their father. But it's difficult to sway the convictions of truth and Fix found little he could effectively use against his client's accusers.

Jeff's deposition revealed that Lee Brown may have known much more about Betty's murder than anyone thought. Jeff made several references to his dad's best friend including his participation in trashing of the Jeep several years ago. Lee Brown may well have been privy to most all of Bill's suspicious activities. Tom Moss would be very interested in placing him under oath to find out what he had to say.

With Bill scheduled to give his deposition on April 18, his attorneys tried desperately to stop it. The day before, Fix argued before Bonneville County Judge Wood that a deposition would violate Gray's Fifth and Fourteenth Amendment rights. The Fifth Amendment states a witness cannot be compelled to incriminate himself, and the Fourteenth Amendment states that citizens have the right to "due process of the law." Fix also argued that a civil suit deposition could be used against Gray in a criminal investigation.

But Judge Wood, stating that there might not ever be a criminal charge filed, turned down the request, as well as refusing to grant a 60-day extension. Fix asked for a one-day extension so he could get a protective order from the Idaho Supreme Court which was also denied.

In another valiant effort to protect his client from being deposed, Fix sent his request by fax to the Idaho Supreme Court. A panel of five justices unanimously refused, without explanation, to grant the delay. Bill Gray was given nothing protecting him from having to give his deposition.

But appearing and answering the questions is one thing, the other is appearing and invoking the Fifth or Fourteenth

Amendment and not answering questions that were too close for comfort. With his children in the room, Bill Gray, on advice of his attorney, invoked one or the other Amendment on at least 80 percent of the questions asked.

Tom Moss couldn't help but wonder how much information Gray had really shared with his attorney. William Fix did not know the importance of some of the questions asked by Moss and allowed his client to answer. Several of these questions were directed at Ron Mitchell, the phantom buyer of the green Travelall. Asked who Ron Mitchell was, Gray gave an answer and several more in conjunction. But when Gray admitted he'd forged Mitchell's name on the title, his attorney quickly advised his client to take the Fifth, putting a stop to any more questions in that direction. But Moss now had an admission of forgery.

Unsatisfied with the outcome of Bill's deposition Moss filed a motion to force Bill to answer his questions. He spent a great deal of time researching the law and the law was quite clear. A person may claim the Fifth legitimately in a civil case, but they can't claim the Fifth during the discovery stage of the investigation and then testify at the trial. If Bill Gray wanted to testify in his own defense at the civil trial he would have to answer questions asked under deposition now.

In a criminal case, a murder trial, the defendant does not have to give a deposition. In a murder trial, if the defendant testifies in his own behalf, it is most often the first time the prosecutor has heard his story. But a civil case is much different.

Tom Moss argued before the court. "Judge, I don't care whether he answers my questions or not. All I care about is that he either claims the Fifth or he doesn't, and if he does claim the Fifth he's got to claim it all the way through and he can't testify at the civil trial. If he doesn't claim the Fifth then he's got to answer my questions."

The judge agreed and gave Gray 30 days to make up his mind. Later Attorney Richard Mulligan told reporters his client planned to testify because he was innocent, and is therefore going to comply with the judge's order and give a deposition.

Gray's attorneys argued profusely, and throughout the entire case, that the civil suit was a "sham attempt," that it was brought only to force Kimball Mason, who did not feel he had a case, to bring criminal charges. They argued that Gray's deposition could be used against him if a criminal charge was later filed.

"In the entire jurisdictions of America I've never found a case like this," Mulligan charged, referencing the filing of a civil suit prior to the filing of criminal charges.

Tom Moss acknowledged, "It was an unusual situation. No doubt about it, it's very rare, but there are other cases like it. I researched it and cited some of them to the judge. Our case was like an automobile accident. If someone hits you and kills you there may eventually be a criminal action but you don't have to wait and see. In fact you can't wait more than two years. If you've been damaged, you've been damaged. There may never be a criminal action. My people are entitled to their day in court."

Investigation by the *Jackson Hole Guide* regarding the filing of a civil suit prior to a conviction on a criminal charge found it was "extremely rare." In most circumstances, a lawsuit that alleges criminal activity, like a homicide, is filed after a defendant has been convicted on criminal charges.

"In my experience, this is highly unusual," said Sanford Kadish a law professor at the University of California at Berkley. "It is common to have wrongful death action without charges, but that's because usually the suit is based on negligence, not an intentional death."

Charley Whitebread, a law professor at the University of

Southern California and an expert in criminal procedure said, "Even though children frequently sue their parents, the Gray children's suit is a rarely used political tool. Obviously they did the only thing they could to get the case into a court."

With the ink barely dry on the previous motions, all the players were back in court. This time there was a motion from Deputy Prosecutor, John Stosich, as well as the defense. Stosich was asking for Bonneville County Sheriff's detectives to be excluded from testifying in the civil suit. He argued divulging evidence discovered in the criminal investigation would enable Gray to perfect an alibi and/or destroy incriminating evidence in his possession. But in Judge Wood's decision he said, "Detectives have already allowed Gray, Gray's children and their lawyers access to the evidence. The seal of secrecy has been broken."

Was this an indication that Stosich was attempting to protect the evidence in anticipation of criminal charges being filed? If it was, Judge Wood didn't see it that way, as his next ruling on Mulligan's motion indicated otherwise.

Mulligan was asking to delay the civil suit until the criminal investigation against Gray was either dropped, or a trial was held. But Wood denied the motion stating, "Idaho does not have a statute of limitations for murder. Granting a stay may be tantamount to dismissing the heirs' civil case. Further, a stay of these proceedings until Gray is either convicted or exonerated of criminal charges would be similarly inappropriate. It may be years into the future, if ever, before the state decides that sufficient evidence exists to justify bringing Gray to trial." The judge ruled on what was certain, not what may, or may not, happen in the future.

Bill had gone to the absolute extreme measure to be rewarded with the financial gain of his deeds. Now his children were not only threatening to block his path to the money but could very well be instrumental in blocking his path to freedom. Authorities were concerned he may threaten Saralyn and Jeff and wisely advised them to tape any phone calls that they might receive from their father. If he was going to threaten them, they wanted it on tape.

Just as was anticipated, Bill called Jeff. He tried the "poor me" routine, then "nothing could bring Betty back now," and finished by leaving the impression that "someday they would regret what they were doing." This statement may well have been made in the context that someday they would find out that he wasn't guilty of killing their mother and therefore they may regret what they were putting him through, however most tended to believe it was a threat against Jeff and Saralyn's safety.

Then Jeff received another phone call, a most disturbing phone call from Lee Brown. First he wanted to know if Jo Ann was involved in the civil suit.

"Read the papers and see who's name is on them," he snapped.

Jeff, as well as Kim who was on another phone, was sure Bill was standing next to Lee. Lee's voice would fade as though he was turning away from the phone, and he paused as though listening to someone give more instructions.

"Under the circumstance," Lee said, "knowing your wife was having an affair you would have done the same thing."

"Oh, no I wouldn't," Jeff fired back. "I would never do that."

Lee went on, trying to tell Jeff that even if his father did kill his mother he should give it up, he should stand by his father. Nothing good could come of this. It was not too late to save what was left of their family. Jeff felt strongly Lee knew what happened to his mother. Jeff mailed a copy of the tape to Tom Moss.

Less than a week after that phone call Lee Brown was dead. Jo Ann knew about it before the Jackson detectives did. Reporter Joy Ufford caught wind of it as it was unfolding, she called Jo Ann, Jo Ann called Saralyn, and Saralyn called Officer Chris Bracken. Suicide was the official ruling by the Sheriff's investigators, but there were many who felt Bill Gray claimed his third victim.

According to Cheryl, Lee's girlfriend, she and Lee had an argument that morning. Cheryl and her son left and did not return until late afternoon. She noticed Lee's wallet lying on top of the lampshade and knowing he was going to Las Vegas that day with Bill, she became concerned.

Why would he go to Las Vegas and not take his wallet, she wondered? Cheryl called the police telling them about the fight and quickly concluded Lee committed suicide. Although the Sheriff's Office immediately sent officers out to look, Cheryl actually found him. She said she drove around, spotted his truck on Teton Pass, walked into the woods and found his body.

Sitting up, with his back propped up against a tree, a gun by his side it appeared Lee had shot himself in the mouth. Lying beside him was a piece of paper with two stick figures drawn on it. One figure was in a kneeling position looking up at the other figure which was standing. The consensus was the kneeling figure was begging the standing figure for forgiveness. Since Lee was barely able to read or write most assumed he drew the picture in lieu of writing a suicide note.

Jo Ann will always believe, and she had many supporters, the picture was drawn in lieu of leaving a handwritten note which could be traced to the real author ... the real author being the person that killed Lee Brown.

The detectives working on the Gray case rushed to the scene when notified by Saralyn, but by the time they arrived the ground had been trampled and the body removed. If there had been any evidence linking Bill Gray to this death it was gone now.

Bill knew if Lee was called to give his deposition and eventually be forced to testify it could crucify him. Even though Bill knew he would lie for him, with Lee's limited capacity he could easily get confused and end up incriminating Bill. The phone call to Jeff certainly indicated Lee Brown knew much more about Betty's death than anyone thought. But investigators could find nothing to indicate anything other than a suicide.

"That was a Sheriff's Office case," said Lt. Foster. "They felt it was a suicide and not anything suspicious and so I can't really question their decision on that, but certainly interesting that he happened to choose to do that. It could be maybe he knew too much and just couldn't handle it anymore."

If Bill didn't actually pull the trigger, Jo Ann is convinced he was the force behind it.

"Lee really, really liked my sister and he was extremely upset when she died. But he was the type of person Bill could control, just like he did Betty, so he remained true to Bill even after he knew Bill killed her. I think Bill told Lee he was going to be called to testify and he'd better keep his mouth shut or was even told to leave town. I don't know if that would have been enough for Lee to kill himself or not, but it sure was a convenient thing to happen for Bill wasn't it?"

And so, the case closed on Lee Brown's death. Bill would not need worry about a Lee Brown testimony, and a year later he would try to use Lee's death to his advantage as he used him in life.

Lee's death prompted the Jackson Police to have Cheryl

come in and tell them what she knew about Bill and Lee's relationship. She said Lee was very distraught over Betty's death and just as disturbed about the police questioning Bill all the time. But when Cheryl said to Lee she thought Bill was innocent she had a small surprise.

"That's all you know," Lee snapped at her. "He probably did kill Betty." No doubt Lee was struggling with his suspicions.

Cheryl Carson was no friend to Bill Gray she told the police. She couldn't stand him. He was arrogant and she had been ashamed of Lee for hanging around him. But three days after this conversation, the Jackson police were advised that Cheryl and Bill had been seen together having dinner and dancing at the Elks Club. On three occasions thereafter the police were aware Bill and Cheryl were spending time together. For a woman who so vehemently despised Bill Gray, this was indeed strange behavior.

On the advice of their attorney, and in agreement with Jeff, Saralyn petitioned the 9th District Court of Teton County on July 5 for appointment as administrator of her mother's estate. Citing the charges against her father and that he had failed to file probate action.

On June 14, 1991, Gray's attorneys filed an objection stating that they were not aware that Saralyn had filed her petition until June 6 and asked the court to set aside the appointment of Saralyn Hoffman as administrator. The objection cited that Gray had made demand for the return of Betty's original will from the Bonneville County prosecutor and the demand had not been complied with. Gray intended to file a probate action as soon as the will was returned. For the first, but not the last time, they contended the civil suit was "mere allegations" and no criminal complaint had been filed and therefore there was a valid presumption that Bill Gray was heir to Betty's estate and competent to administer the estate. The court upheld Bill's objection and appointed him personal representative of his wife's estate.

Bill couldn't out wait authorities much longer. The legal battles were wearing him out. Few things were going his way and he was particularly upset about the insurance money being held in escrow by the courts. If Saralyn and Jeff hadn't interfered he would have been paid off by now. His attorneys were working hard for him getting extension after extension on the civil suit, filing petitions, motions, taking depositions and familiarizing themselves with the case. Understandably Bill needed money. His legal bills were rising more rapidly than homemade bread on a hot stove.

Although he had previously intended to sell the business, he'd planned to keep the building. By leasing it back to the new owners he would receive a monthly rent check he could count on and still have the investment and ownership of the building.

But with this civil suit in progress he had to have more money than monthly rent checks would provide. Without the insurance money he would have to sell it all. On July 5, 1991, Bill sold the business for $500,000. After the mortgage balance and closing costs were paid the profit on the sale was $396,000.

Two days prior to the sale, Saralyn and Jeff's Wyoming attorney Frank Hess had filed a lien against the pawnshop. The Teton Land and Title Company withheld half the profit from the sale in Betty's escrow due to the lien, and then paid Bill $198,000 plus a previously made $10,000 deposit.

Bill didn't waste much time. With $208,000 cash in his

possession he drove Betty's Subaru to Las Vegas and on July 10 he traded the Subaru and paid $32,000 in cash for a brand new, fully loaded, 1991 Cadillac. However, in the eyes of the law Bill Gray was not the owner of this new Cadillac for it was titled to his parents. He wasn't taking any chances. From now on his parents would hold titles and care for Bill's possessions safely out of reach of anyone who threatened them. He may certainly have had a premonition of what was to come for when he got home he was faced with yet another devastating blow.

Tom Moss was certain Bill would eventually sell off, dispose of, or hide, every asset Betty and Bill had as a married couple if he was not stopped. Through local Attorney Hess, Saralyn filed a petition for heirship and successfully obtained a temporary restraining order which forbid Bill from selling or disposing of anything that was part of her mother's estate.

Bill was ordered, by the court, to account for the money derived from property already sold, and the whereabouts of assets transferred or disposed of. Money received from the sale of any property, including the pawnshop, was to be held in an escrow account until the outcome of the civil suit. Bill was further ordered to post a $5,000 bond.

Filing an objection, Gray claimed that since the sale of the pawnshop occurred before the court order he should be entitled to keep all the proceeds from the sale. He further argued his attorney's fee would be in excess of $100,000 and the ruling would not allow him to obtain money for his defense of the pending civil suit. The court ordered an audit of all of Gray's assets and valuable possessions.

Undoubtedly the pressures were getting to him. Bill's Cadillac had been seen parked in front of the local Elks Club on numerous occasions, sometimes in early afternoon as well as late into the evening. Jackson police officers were keeping a light watch on his activities and they, as well as Saralyn, were somewhat surprised he hadn't left town. When they thought about it later it made perfectly good sense that Bill would not leave town without first fighting tooth and toenail for the insurance money he wanted desperately enough to kill his wife for. Bill knew Saralyn, more than Jeff, was responsible for his problems and would surely have a deep-seated animosity toward her.

Saralyn had a valid point when she said she was afraid of him, for one evening in early October, after midnight, officers came across Bill sitting in his car across the street from her house, sweat dripping off his face, a loaded revolver in the front seat. Officers talked to him, asking what he was doing.

He mumbled something about not being able to get the doors unlocked and the officers advised that he better go home. They watched him as he left the area and made a note to keep a much closer eye on Bill Gray. Saralyn was scared, as she should have been, when she learned about the incident. Oh, how she wished they would arrest her father and provide safety for her and her family.

On October 16 the Cadillac was once again parked in front of the Elks Club. Officers, having been advised to keep a closer eye on him, were watching as Bill left the area. The direction he was taking was not the direction to his home, but more toward Saralyn's. Making a turn without signaling was enough for the officers to stop him.

When Officer John approached the car, Dobbie the large Doberman Pinscher, stuck his head out the window barring his teeth, snarling at the officer. Having Bill get out of the car they noticed an odor of alcohol and asked him if he had been drinking. He said he'd had "two or three." When he couldn't pass the coordination or verbal tests given, Bill once again used his health as an excuse for his actions. He argued he was a kidney recipient, was on heavy medication and had bad knees. That's why he couldn't pass the tests.

Deciding to arrest him on a DUI (Driving Under the Influence) they put him in the patrol car then searched the Cadillac. After getting Dobbie under control, the officers found three fully loaded handguns, a colt 10mm semi-automatic pistol, a Smith and Wesson .357-caliber Magnum and a .22-caliber revolver, concealed under the seat. Carrying a concealed weapon inside a vehicle is not illegal in Wyoming.

Officers also found a paper bag stuffed with hundred dollar bills. Bill wanted them to leave the money in the car and have his renter, Shawn Jamison, pick up the car and the dog. But the officers took the weapons, the money and Bill to the station where he was formally charged with a DUI.

When the money was counted it added up to $32,884.18, a large sum of money to be carrying around in a paper sack.

At the station, under the normal DUI booking rules, Bill was asked if he would like to be taken to the hospital or a clinic to have his test taken, to which he replied, "I'll let my lawyer decide that." For the second time, he was advised verbally and by written form, that as a matter of Wyoming law, he had no right to contact an attorney before deciding to submit to, or refuse, a chemical test of his blood, breath or urine.

"The hell I don't," Bill challenged. Bill was booked at 2:14 a.m. Sometime after 4 a.m., after a little less than two hours in a cell he was ready to be taken for his tests. Then, posting a $500 cash bond, his attorney bailed him out and took him home. Bill left the station with his now unloaded weapons and his paper sack full of money.

After months of extensions and extensive legal fireworks Tom Moss finally got a defiant Bill Gray under deposition. Saralyn and Jeff were present but silent. They were very curious as to what their father had to say. Taking two full days, November 5 and 6, 1991, Moss worked at getting Bill's version of the story. In trial, if Gray told any other story than the one he was telling now he would be caught in his lies.

When asked a question he was uncomfortable with, he would in turn ask a question. Bill thought it was giving the appearance of not understanding the question, but in reality it was stalling for time to think about his answer. Moss would have to rephrase question after question. Occasionally, when Moss wouldn't let him off the hook, Mulligan would interject rephrasing it once again, then Bill would finally come up with an answer.

For Bill it was a sparring game to be evasive as he could get away with, but Moss stayed on him and eventually pinned him down. Slowly, methodically, patiently, Moss took Gray through events before and after Betty's death, covering every subject from his checking Betty's purse to the DUI arrest. Although it didn't make perfectly good sense, his story varied little from the one told over and year and a half ago. But when Tom Moss wanted to know where the money from the sale of the pawnshop was Bill said he only had about $200. Moss pressed on.

Moss: Do you have any other money besides that?
Gray: Do I have any other money?

Moss: Yes, other than the $200 you said you have in your checking account.

Gray: A little bit.

Moss: How much?

Gray: Do you want to know to the penny?

Moss: Well, as best you can, within a $100 or a few dollars.

Gray: Probably a little over $300.

After receiving $208,000 on the pawnshop sale Gray now tells them he has a total of only $300 to his name. Moss asked if he was receiving any other income and Bill said he was getting $682 a month disability from Social Security. Then Moss asked about the $30,000 plus, Bill had on him the night he was arrested on the DUI. Bill was reluctant to identify it as money from the sale of the pawnshop. Moss knew where it came from and he wanted him to admit it, but it had to come from Bill's lips, not Moss.

Moss: And where did that money come from?

Gray: Where did that come from?

Moss: Yes.

Gray: Money that I had.

Moss: Well, where had you been keeping it before you had it in your immediate physical possession in cash?

Gray: I had it with me, I told you.

Moss: Okay. Let me rephrase it. Where did that money originate from, where was it before you got it in your physical possession?

Gray: It was either from money that I had or money from the sale of the business, one or the other.

Moss: Well how long had you been carrying that $30,800

around with you?

Gray: Quite a while.

Tom had to ask several more questions to get a definite answer and finally Bill decided he'd had the money about four months.

Moss: And four months, or five months ago, whenever it was, where did you get it from, where was it before you had it?

Gray: It could have been in China. I don't know where it was before I got it.

Moss: Who did you get it from?

Gray: I told you, it either came from the sale of the building or it was money that I had.

Mulligan: (interjected) Or a combination thereof?

Gray: Or a combination thereof.

More questions met with more evasive answers.

Moss: Are you telling me as you sit here that you don't know where that money came from? Is that what you're telling me?

Gray: I don't keep money separate from this money. I don't know ... don't know. It came from the sale of the store.

After four transcribed pages, Bill finally admits that the large cash amount he had been carrying around came from the sale of the pawnshop. Then after much effort to get Bill to identify the exact amount he was paid from the sale, Moss wanted to know where the other $160,000 or so went.

Gray: I spent it.

Moss: What did you spend it on?

Gray: I lost it.

Moss: Well, that's a difference. Did you spend it, or did
you lose it? Where did you lose it?

Gray: In Las Vegas.

And so Bill went on trying to make every one believe he lost it all gambling in Las Vegas. Asked specifically where he lost the money he said, "Boy, oh boy, where didn't I." Then he named four casinos where he spent most of his time.

Moss: So you're telling me that you gambled away over a
$160,000 in Las Vegas?

Gray: More than that.

Moss: How much more than that?

Gray: All of it.

Moss: Did you gamble away the $30,800?

Gray: Yep.

Moss: When did you do that?

Gray: On this last trip. I just got back two days ago. I
didn't lose it all there. I lived on some of it.

When asked if he recently purchased a car Bill said he did not.

Moss: Do you own a Cadillac?

Bill: No I do not.

Moss: Are you driving a Cadillac?

Bill: Yes, I am.

Moss: Whose car is that?

Bill: My parents'.

His parents purchased the Cadillac, did not write a check but paid cash. They came to Las Vegas, paid cash from their own funds and bought him this car. Bill knew they weren't buying his story but what did he care. It would be difficult, if not impossible, to prove otherwise. Whatever cash he did have left after his major purchase and gambling escapades was undoubtedly in a safe deposit box in Las Vegas under another name, or in safe keeping with his parents.

For a while there was some excitement in the family's camp for there were rumors Prosecutor Kimball Mason was going to file the criminal charge. In support of the rumor, Mason contacted Tom Moss and Moss invited him access to his files.

"He'd always had access to all those files he'd given me, but now that it was organized. Well, I invited him, I said, Kimball if you want the benefit of what I've done you're welcome to it. When all you've got is a stack of papers it's awful hard to understand what your case is, it really is, and even to read through it one time is hard to understand. This case was very complicated. So, he came and copied all my files. Mason told me they were going to go with it, and everyone was pretty anxious, but then he didn't do it. It got put off and then he got put off, and it didn't get done."

On December 2, in Teton County, by previous order of the court, Attorney Richard Mulligan filed an auditing report prepared by Thompson, Palmer and Associates, a Jackson accounting firm. Their charge by the court was to file a verified and audited accounting of all items of real and/or personal property in the estate inventory that had been disposed of in any manner since Betty's death. The audit for the period of July 24, 1989 to November 22, 1991 began two years after Betty's death.

The firm reported they had to rely on unsubstantiated verbal information of the defendant William L. Gray as to valuations, disposals and proceeds, and further stated that they were unable to satisfy themselves as to the items discussed. Jackson CPA, George Thompson said; "It was not possible to reconstruct an audited beginning balance based on Gray's records. The scope of our work was not sufficient to enable us to express, and we do not express, an opinion on the schedule of the Inventory Analysis of the assets of William L. Gray."

The inventory listed the home at 435 Stacey Lane as valued at $118,000 in 1989 and deemed to be valued by Bill Gray the same in 1991. Details of the pawnshop sale were listed with the notation, "Under representation of Gray, the $208,000 received by Gray from the sale of his business, was spent on gambling activities in Las Vegas, Nevada. As we have not been able to confirm this information directly with the casino involved, we disclaim from making any opinion at this time as to the proceeds of the commercial property sale. We will however, continue our efforts to confirm this activity with the casino." Throughout the rest of the document in most cases, they had to disclaim from making opinions due to the reliability of their source, Bill Gray.

The document addressed property in California which Betty and Bill had sold prior to her death and disclosed a note balance of $23,500 to which monthly payments were still being made. Another piece of California property valued at $19,000 on July 24, 1989, was still valued at $19,000 in November 1991. In a sworn statement Jeff said he received the title to the boat and trailer from his father as well as certain articles of his mother's jewelry. The disposal of the Subaru as a trade-in was also acknowledged.

Case Backhoe: Under representation of Gray, this item was sold after July 24, 1989, for approximately $10,000. We have been unable to locate any documentation on this transaction and, therefore, disclaim from making any opinion on this article.

Coin Collection: The collection was valued at $20,000 by Gray, less a $6,000 amount that was reported stolen. Again they could not give an opinion.

Gun Collection: Valued by Gray in excess of $30,000. The majority of these guns are located either in California or with the Jackson Police. Because of the impracticality of any further verification procedures, we disclaim from making an opinion.

Oil Paintings: Under representation of Gray, five oil paintings were in his possession on July 24, 1989, of which one was given to his father.

Gray's Personal Jewelry: Gray retained all his jewelry on his person. These were not itemized, nor was a value given.

Decedent's Jewelry: Under representation of Gray, all of decedent's jewelry was given to his children and their spouses except for a gold chain given to his mother.

The CPA firm established that at the time of Betty's death there was $14,000 in the business checking account. In the six months after her death, $139,000 had been deposited to the account. In January 1990, after various business expenses and Gray's personal draws, the account balance was $0 and subsequently closed.

They did not deem it necessary to audit Betty's sterling silver set, Betty or Bill's clothing, household furnishings, tools, fishing equipment, or various other personal property because of the immaterial dollar amount involved and the impracticality of any further verification.

If all the assets could have been accounted for, or properly valued, the Gray estate, although sizeable, would have fallen well short of the multimillion dollar estate Bill bragged about to Roy Leavitt and the detectives who interviewed him in 1989. But what there was, was now dissected with pieces in California, pieces claimed held by the Jackson Police, hidden funds, stolen property and funds held in escrow. Bill was still determined to have it all.

Money was what Bill wanted, and he could hardly stand it that $198,000 had been withheld from him. He killed his wife of 29 years and her innocent friend for it, he wasn't about to give it up.

His attorney filed a petition to induce the court to release the $198,000 from the sale of the pawnshop held in escrow by the title company. At the December 10 hearing in Jackson, Richard Mulligan reminded the court once again, that Gray had not been charged and convicted of the crime of murder. Mulligan also cited that Gray's legal fees were getting very expensive and it would be appropriate that some funds should be turned over to him so he could pay for his defense. Without access to the funds Gray would be limited in his ability to defend himself. Filing this petition could have been a grave mistake for it ignited Attorney Moss and Judge Rogers' patience.

Moss blasted Gray's accounting of his property.

"The man didn't gamble the money away; he's got it hidden away from this court. I don't know that I've ever seen such a flagrant violation of a court order, of such magnitude."

Lt. Dave Foster had flatly denied the Jackson Police Department was holding any part of Gray's gun collection and Moss insisted the fifty-six guns were all in California with Bill's parents and were worth twice the estimate given by Gray. Moss also attacked Bill's business practices in that Gray never kept track of cash transactions.

"I don't know how this man has been in business all these years. He continually hides his assets. He should be held in contempt of court and punished."

Teton County 9th District Judge Terry Rogers was in total agreement.

"He has been running around this town with over $30,000 in a brown paper bag, driving a new Cadillac and says he lost all his money gambling. I don't believe him for a minute."

Judge Rogers not only denied the petition to release the funds to Gray, but removed Gray as executor of Betty's estate. One could assume that Rogers was about fed up with a lying, deceitful Bill Gray.

"That accounting isn't suitable to be used in an outhouse as far as its validity is concerned. I'm not having the fox in charge of the chicken coop. In Wyoming, we are concerned about the estate of Betty Lou Gray."

Judge Rogers didn't rule out a contempt of court charge either. "That door may still be open too."

Less than a week later on December 16, Gray's attorneys filed another petition with the court this time seeking release of enough funds to pay for the cost of the court ordered audit. Asking for $1,718.40 the motion stated, in part, "William L, Gray is presently without adequate funds in which to support himself and to pay this additional expense which has been incurred pursuant to the court's order."

On December 20, Moss responded, "William L. Gray asserts that he lost $208,000 gambling in Las Vegas. This claim has not been adequately substantiated to this court. Counsel would not object to the payment of the accountants from the $198,000 estate money, provided Gray give adequate proof he actually lost the $208,000 and that he has no other funds available."

Once again, Judge Rogers denied Gray's motion.

No one was feeling sorry for Bill Gray. The general consensus among the family was if his parents could pay cash for a new expensive Cadillac, certainly they could take care of their son's bills. All joking of course, for they knew full well that Bill had money stashed somewhere.

Authorities had been unable to locate safe deposit boxes or bank accounts in Bill's name in Las Vegas, but that didn't mean he didn't have those in another name or a different town. Some speculated he could even have money hidden in Oregon because his Cadillac bore Oregon plates. When asked about that in his deposition he said his parents also had a place in Oregon and had licensed the car there. Saralyn scoffed at that. She maintains he probably got his plates there because they would be cheaper. Nonetheless, Bill had connections to three other states, Nevada, Oregon and California. It would be next to impossible to track down the stashed money. This was a secret Bill may be able to keep.

The third Christmas without Betty came and went. Everyone who loved and cared for Betty thought of her often during the holidays. Those had been her fun times and her enthusiasm carried over to everyone her life touched. She had sent cards and made cheerful holiday phone calls passing on her excitement. Now she was silent.

Betty's mother was still extremely depressed. The senseless murder of her daughter would not leave her thoughts and it haunted her to know her killer was free and had every chance of remaining that way. Dorothy called Jo Ann almost every day wanting to know if there was anything new to report. She was concerned for the safety of her grandchildren, Saralyn and Jeff, and if Bill ever found out how directly Jo Ann's influence had contributed to his problems she might well have reason to fear for her safety as well.

Everyone who really knew Bill Gray knew what he was capable of. Even before Betty's death they were afraid of him. Now they had every reason to be extremely fearful of him. They were sure he was the type who would seek revenge.

In late January 1992, Moss was called and asked if he would come to a meeting in Idaho Falls. Detective Rodriguez set up the meeting with all the detectives involved in the case, including Foster and Bracken from Jackson, and the Bonneville County Prosecutor's Office. They wanted to go over everything about the case to see if they could pull it together. Each person had segments of it but no one person had all of it. Kimball Mason wasn't present, but Moss recalled that one or two of his deputies were there and they were real excited something was being done on this case. The meeting lasted for three days. The rewards were plentiful.

Early in the discovery process of the civil trial, Moss found an interview conducted on July 26, 1989 where the detectives ran out of tapes. Aware Bill had been recording the interviews, Tom received through a court order under the discovery process Gray's tape and was able to complete the entire transcript.

Ironically, Gray thought he was so clever to tape his

interviews and now it was coming back to haunt him. Although there was nothing major discovered here, it was interesting to listen to his voice as he rambled on about Reeda's boyfriends and how he thought they, or Leavitt, would certainly have had reason to kill the women.

He laughed when he told detectives he thought they were all done with him when they said they were bringing back his guns, he'd thought it was all "cut and dried" and they were done with him.

Bill thought he had beaten the system. But all he did was confirm what detectives already knew; his greed. His undivided interest when told about Betty's safe deposit box and his derogatory remarks about Betty unraveling his money and "Damn her." Damn the wife he loved two days after her violent death!

Clearly there was no emotion or remorse in his voice as he confidently talked to the officers. Clearly, if Bill had not taped this interview, or if he would have destroyed or hidden it, prosecutors would not be listening to it now.

But the squad room filled with excitement and astonishment when it was discovered that the most damning interview of all had never been made available to Tom Moss or anyone else. The officers who were present at the July 28 interview of Bill Gray were all aware of what was said in that interview and this is the reason they were so certain of Gray's guilt. However, the Prosecutor's Office had never heard the tape or ever had a transcript.

The original files Tom Moss received had been a disorganized mess, undoubtedly due to investigators searching and researching through them for 18 months. The prosecutor had not taken the responsibility himself, nor did he direct any one person from his office to take charge and sort it out. The missing interview would have been discovered long ago if he would have.

"I had transcripts of all of Bill Gray's interviews in one file," Moss recalled, "and I said, 'Gentlemen, there's a problem here. I have been told there was an interview that took place on the 28th where Bill Gray lied, and it's not here. I've got a second interview where he admitted he lied, but I don't have the first interview, did you not record it?' 'Oh ya, it's in there,' someone said, and I said, 'No it's not."

I remember Victor saying, "Well then I've got it, I'll get it for you." Then there was a big scurry. We must have spent a half hour, everybody looking for it, and nothing. Finally somebody said, "Here's the tape."

Detectives always had the original tape but it had never been transcribed. Recorded on a special machine that ran very slowly, it could only be heard in that type of machine which Bonneville County did not have.

Lt. Foster always recorded his interviews on a long running tape as he wanted to be sure he got the entire interview without interruption. He'd never had a problem with it, but then he'd never had a case quite like this one. This case was different than most that crossed state lines. They immediately dispatched the Bonneville County plane to Jackson to pick up and bring back the special recording machine.

"We sat down and listened to it. Man I just ... just ... my heart started pumping," recalled Moss. "I knew there had to be something because everybody was talking about it. I'd been told about it, but there it was and it was real damning evidence."

Yes, it was very damning evidence. The interview that had escaped them for so long was the July 28, 1989 interview where Gray was read his rights and Foster and Cowden got right down to business facing Bill with what they knew about the Travelall and the witnesses who saw him in Idaho Falls, both in the Travelall and on a bike. They confronted him with attempting to hide the Travelall and caught him in lie after lie. This was the interview when Bill Gray, knowing he was trapped and in trouble, asked for a lawyer.

The second interview Moss referred to having, was the interview conducted after Gray talked to his father and came back to lie about all the lies he had just previously told. Everyone in the room that day felt this was it. There would be a criminal charge filed.

It had been over a year since the civil suit was filed and the civil trial date had been continued by Gray's attorneys time and time again. The new trial date was set for March 3, 1992. Tom Moss and his clients were well prepared and anxious to get it over with. With no other petitions before the court from all appearances, the March 3 trial date would stand. Moss was beginning final preparations when he received a phone call from Richard Mulligan who wanted to know if they would settle the suit out of court.

"Tell me quick," Tom said. "I don't think my clients are very interested in trying to settle but I'll listen."

Mulligan made an offer. Moss rejected it. Most attorneys are receptive to talk of settlements of law suits but Tom knew how Saralyn and Jeff felt and what reasoning was behind their actions. Unless they were more than reasonably assured criminal charges were going to be filed, Saralyn and Jeff would not be receptive to settlement. Their first and foremost intent was not for the money, but to bring this case to the attention of authorities who would take action to bring their father to justice. Only a public trial would do this.

Tom advised his clients of the offer and, not to his surprise, it was rejected. They wanted to go to trial. But within days, Saralyn was notified that she would be testifying at a grand jury hearing. By then, Tom had heard rumors a grand jury was going to be called and so he advised his clients to settle. He told them if they didn't, all that was going to happen now is their dad would spend everything he's got defending himself and then he's going to ask the judge to invade the insurance proceeds to help pay his legal fees. Reasonably assured a criminal charge was coming, they took their lawyer's advice.

But their father wanted stipulations placed upon the settlement. Moss and his clients must agree they would not give copies of the depositions to the prosecutor and they would not cooperate, or do anything further, to push the criminal charges.

"That's why I rejected that first offer right away," said Moss. "I told Mulligan that cannot be a consideration. We will do everything we can to pursue criminal charges. We will cooperate fully and I will give all of my files and everything we have to them. I made that very clear to him."

Bill must have felt a trial would be very damaging to him. He had to give it up. He had to go forth with the settlement. Minus the original conditions, Mulligan, Moss and their clients arrived at a settlement. Papers were prepared which included an agreement that the terms of the settlement would not be divulged by either party.

On March 9, 1992, Moss had an appointment with Judge Wood to have him approve the settlement. However, that morning while Tom was en route to Idaho Falls to meet with the judge, his office received a fax from Mulligan which stated in part, "This is to confirm that you said you don't know of any criminal charges pending." Tom's office forwarded Mulligan's letter by fax to the Bonneville County Courthouse. Tom dictated a response to his secretary to be typed and sent back to Tom for his signature, which he in turn faxed to Mulligans' office.

Moss's response was, "No, that is not part of the deal. I cannot say that I am not aware of criminal charges pending and furthermore we would not settle this case if we did not believe criminal charges were imminent.

"I thought that would put the whole kibosh on the settlement. I also said in that fax that I wanted him to confirm the fact he understood this condition in writing before I submitted this to the judge, and asked him to fax me a letter to that effect to the Bonneville County Courthouse. I waited and waited and no response, so I called Mulligan's office. Mulligan said, 'Oh that's all right Tom, I've got your letter, don't worry about it.' But I said, 'No, I've got to have a letter from you confirming there is no deal related to any such terms.' There was silence on the phone. Then, 'Well, I'll have to talk to my client before I can do that.' And I said. 'Well talk to your client because I'm not going to submit these settlement papers to the judge until I've got something in writing back from you."

About an hour later Tom received a one sentence letter saying essentially, OK, go ahead, submit the papers, we will agree with what you are saying.

"I am certain that if I hadn't done that, that letter to me would have been shoved in our faces at the criminal trial," recalled Tom.

Gray misjudged his children once again. He was so certain they were doing this for the money, and only the money, that he felt sure if they got what they wanted they would drop everything else and back off. They would not.

On March 11 Saralyn and twelve other witnesses testified

before the grand jury. Among them were, Steven Mackley, the security guard at the hospital; Investigators Rodriguez, Kotrason, Foster and McCandless; Patrolman Greg Black who saw Gray on the bike that night; Mike and Sherrel Coy who sold the Travelall to Gray; forensic expert Don Wycoff and ballistics expert Wally Baker.

The grand jury's duty was not to find that the accused was guilty beyond a reasonable doubt. Their task was to determine whether the evidence established was enough for probable cause to believe an offense had been committed, and the accused committed it.

Prosecutor Kimball Mason had finally taken the Gray case to the grand jury four months short of three years. All the pressure he'd received from family members on both Gray and Roundy sides, the public, detectives and some officials had never moved him to action. But as Teton County Sheriff Millward and others believed, the suit may have been the latest in a series of mounting public and professional moves that pressured Mason into changing his stance.

"I think he [Kimball Mason] is afraid the lawsuit might make him look dumb," Millward told a *Guide* reporter. "I think it's what changed his mind." But there were a few who stood by Mason's earlier decisions.

"I kind of think it wasn't time. I look back and think that if we would have charged Gray three years ago we wouldn't have gotten a conviction. Something was wrong in Kimball that he didn't think we should file charges, but thank God he didn't because we would have lost it sure as hell. It wasn't ready. It wasn't right," recalled Detective Rodriguez.

When Tom Moss was asked his opinion he said, "One of the things I told the family up-front was if you're on a crusade against Kimball Mason you've got the wrong guy, 'cause I'm not going to do that. I don't think it does any good for your case. Besides that, he's my friend and I won't go after him. That doesn't mean I agree with everything he does, or every decision he makes, but I have also been a prosecutor long enough to know how I dislike other attorneys second guessing my decisions. It's real easy for someone out there who doesn't have to do the case to say how good it is. I always believed he would do it, but I figured it would be done in his own good time."

On March 18, 1992, the grand jury handed down a three-count indictment against William L. Gray. Count 1: murder in the first degree, for Betty Lou Gray's death; Count 2: murder in the first degree, for Reeda LaRene Roundy's death; and Count 3: burglary in the first degree, for entering a home with the intent to commit the crime of murder; and a firearm was used while committing the crime. The next day prosecutor Mason formally requested the court to issue an arrest warrant and further requested that no bond be set. Both requests were granted and the wheels of justice were set in motion. Betty Gray and Reeda Roundy would finally have their day in court.

Bill's attorney, Richard Mulligan, was understandably upset. Plaintiffs in a lawsuit have greater information gathering latitude than a prosecutor does and he believed Idaho authorities unethically relied on the suit to do the work for them. By having Gray's testimony from the civil suit depositions they could build their case against Gray knowing what his defense strategy would be.

"They take this guy, sue him through his kids and then they've got his deposition," Mulligan said. "I would argue that is a violation of his civil rights."

But it wasn't the information from the depositions that started this chain of events, nor was it the additional information Saralyn gave. It was information that the investigators and the prosecutor had in their possession all the time. It was the un-transcribed tape of the last interview with Gray. It was Gray himself that gave it up. The cunning and confident killer had tripped over his lies when confronted with fact. He had just been lucky, real lucky, and on the opposite side of the fence, so had Jo Ann, Saralyn and Jeff.

Gray had three years of freedom because of a combination of errors and events. Betty's family and children were lucky to have found Tom Moss.

Finally Jo Ann had some good news to report to her mother. Bill Gray would be arrested. He would stand in judgment for killing their sister and daughter. Saralyn and Jeff had successfully befriended their mother as far as they could. Now it would be up to a jury to see that justice was done.

But Saralyn and Jeff weren't celebrating, they were deeply saddened. Now that authorities believed what they knew, it made the whole thing seem a little more real, a little more sinister. They would all rest easier if Bill were behind bars. But no one had seen Bill Gray in Jackson since he was observed loading a trailer outside his home around 10 p.m. March 16, the same day the civil suit was settled. Gray signed the deed to his house over to his attorneys, loaded what possessions he could get in the car and trailer and quietly left town. He knew he had lost the battle. He knew the grand jury would indict him. Bill Gray was now a fugitive on the run.

4

ON THE RUN
LEGAL MANEUVERS

No one knew Bill's exact movements after he left Jackson. Undoubtedly retrieving all, or part, of the pawnshop money would have been first on his agenda. Then he most likely contacted his parents. When in trouble it was always his parents he ran to for help and guidance. This was something he had intentionally and maliciously taken from his children. There were no parents left in their lives to guide and help them through their rough times. There was no mother to love and play with the grandchildren. There was no father to look up to for strength and support. The Gray family was shattered and utterly destroyed.

But Bill still had his parents. Although William and Sara had always been there when their son needed them, there was little they could do now. If money would have helped, as it always did in the past, they would have given everything they had to save their only child. But first degree murder charges were beyond the scope of their help. All they could do now was worry, hope and wait.

A once happy home, surrounded by pretty flowers, decorated

to the nines for the holidays, the house at 435 Stacy Lane, had been stripped and abandoned. Bill took everything he could pack in the small trailer; photos, silver, dishes, appliances and clothing, the last remaining personal possessions accumulated from a 29-year marriage, the last remaining possessions that proclaimed Betty Lou Gray had even existed. What he couldn't pack, was left behind and put in storage at the direction of his attorney. Not unlike a fire which destroys irreplaceable memoirs, Saralyn and Jeff would have few physical remembrances of their mother.

Sometime after leaving Jackson Bill bought a Winnebago motor home. Warily, he wandered around Oregon and north central California. He would not leave the country, in fact he would not leave the west. He was very hesitant to get very far away from the one thing he had to have, the medications that would sustain his life.

Eventually, Bill was camping near Hemit, California just miles from the old worm farm. Setting his well-thought-out plans in motion, he recruited a past bait customer to accept and hold mail for him. Why he told the woman Betty had been murdered, is a bit surprising. Certainly he could have thought up several stories to tell. But most likely Bill was seeking some sympathy when he went into his "poor me" routine and assumed it would go no further.

It was a stupid thing to do, for when the bait store owner had a little time to think about it she became uncomfortably suspicious. For reasons of her own she opened a package when it came and discovered the contents to be the birth certificate and Social Security card of a Lee Brown. The more the woman thought about it, the more uncomfortable she became. If indeed something was wrong she could be considered an accessory. She wanted no part of it. She went to her attorney.

After several phone calls, her attorney discovered Bill Gray had been charged for murdering his wife and was running from the law. The envelope and its contents were mailed to Detective Rodriguez. Now authorities knew Bill had been in the Hemit area and was attempting to pass himself off as Lee Brown.

Whether Bill paid Cheryl for Lee's identification or there was some sort of relationship between them, or both, is mere speculation. Nonetheless, when Bill requested Lee's identification she sent it. Although Cheryl knew Bill was on the run, and she knew where to find him, she said nothing to the authorities.

When her dad left Jackson, Saralyn was cautiously relieved. Common sense told her he would not come back to harm her, but she was still gravely fearful of her father and what he might yet do. This once happy young woman who thought her father could do no wrong had now come to believe he would stop at nothing to get what he wanted. Not only had she been aggressive and successful in blocking his access to the money he killed her mother for, Saralyn was now a serious threat to his freedom. He had to fear she could be successful at that too.

She'd been the recipient of his cold, icy stare when she gave her deposition, relating the incriminating statements he'd made to her. Would he go to the extreme to prevent her from ever telling this to a jury? Would he send someone, someone whose new face in town would blend in with all the other thousands of tourists? She knew he still had a lot of money in his possession. She knew there are people who will do anything for money. After he was caught outside her house in the middle of the night with a loaded gun, she had to believe anything was possible. Saralyn would be restless and wary until her father was caught. After that she would have to deal with her fluctuating emotions.

Detective Rodriguez wasn't really concerned about catching his man. It was just a matter of time and Gray would have to surface. As an organ recipient he would need his medication to ensure the organ did not get rejected. He would need this and periodic biopsies for the rest of his life. Bi-annual checkups would be required to get his medicine. Even if he tried to seek out a new doctor in another state, his records would have to be transferred and that would be enough to lead authorities to his whereabouts.

There was a flurry of excitement when Bill did contact the University Hospital in Salt Lake indicating he would be in for an appointment. The FBI was waiting. Bill was a no show. But his doctor, Karen Servilla, had left the University Hospital in Salt Lake and was now practicing at the Presbyterian Hospital in Albuquerque, New Mexico. When Bill found this out, he changed his mind about going back to Salt Lake. He called Dr. Servilla in Albuquerque giving his name as Lee Brown, who needed to pick up some medication for Bill Gray. Dr. Servilla knew it was Bill on the phone and set an appointment for the next day, and then she notified the FBI.

Federal officers, hidden throughout the hospital parking lot, watched as the motor home pulled into a parking space. Almost an hour early for his appointment, Bill sat in the motor home reading a newspaper as a dozen men surrounded the Winnebago. He came out quietly when ordered, even though they had been warned he may be heavily armed and had once stated he would not be taken alive. Bill Gray was taken into custody on Monday April 6, 1992.

"How did you find me?" he wanted to know as officers shoved him up against the motor home and put him in handcuffs.

For Bill it was unimaginable he could be captured. Although he thought the authorities were a bunch of fools, it wouldn't have taken a rocket scientist to figure out where Bill ultimately would have to go. It was Bill who was the fool, a fool for thinking Rodriguez would not use this perfect opportunity to get his man. Bill's "How did you find me?" statement would aid the state when fighting to deny Gray bail. It clearly indicated he thought he had been cleverly concealed from the eyes of the law.

When the Bonneville County Prosecutor repeatedly stated in the newspapers, as much as two and a half years earlier, that he did not have enough evidence to charge anyone with the crimes, Bill must have felt invincible. When he went on the run, plans were devised that he thought would be clever enough to safely hide him from the law. Having hidden enough money to live on for a long time, switching from the Cadillac to the motor home where he could live comfortably away from prying eyes and using a dead man's name and identification, led Bill to believe he would be hard to find.

This was why he was not only surprised, but curious as to how they found him at all, let alone so quickly. But years ago when Bill Gray sat at home in his recliner recovering from real or feigned sickness, watching detective movies on television and plotting the perfect crime, he didn't take into account that he was different than the average killer. He carried within him a kidney, a kidney given to him by the death of its donor so he would live, a kidney that would require him to seek medical attention for the rest of his life. It was the organ transplant that allowed Bill to live to commit his crimes, it was also the transplant that tracked him down to answer for those crimes.

Motel and campground receipts found in the motor home were signed with the assumed names Elvis Morgan and John Morgan. Surprisingly only one gun, an unloaded .22-caliber pistol, was found along with a not surprising $27,000 in cash. Cassette tapes and notebooks having reference to the investigation of the murders and the civil suit were taken and forwarded to Idaho. Just as everyone suspected, a key to a safe deposit box in a Las Vegas casino was discovered, however authorities were never allowed to seize or even view the contents. Nevada protects their gamblers as well as their gamblers' privacy.

Although there had never been any previous indication Bill was into drugs, nor had there been any drugs found in the searches of his home and business, a significant amount of PCP (phencyclidine), a recreational drug known by a number of street names including angel dust, super grass and killer weed was found in the motor home. Bill possessed enough PCP to prepare more than 800 ordinary packets of solid material, or 40 to 50 vials of liquid PCP solution. The street value was estimated at between $4,000 and $7,000. If Bill was dealing no one knows. For sure, if he could make a buck, regardless of how ... he'd do it. Authorities felt the amount was sufficient enough to suspect an intent to deliver, however considering the more serious charges against him, no drug charges were ever filed.

There was real joy in the Buccola household for the first time since her sister died. Dick opened a bottle of champagne while Jo Ann called her family and close friends who had shared her swinging emotions though this two year, nine month ordeal.

Jo Ann had also been very apprehensive while Bill was unaccounted for. She knew how vehemently he resented her for her part in the civil suit and subsequent murder indictment. She didn't think for one minute he wasn't capable of harming her or her family, so much so, that she had offered to pay for a private detective to keep track of him before the indictment was handed down. But the Idaho Sheriff's Office had assured her they could keep an eye on him until they could legally and officially detain him, but obviously they did not do it. Jo Ann had long ago passed the class of Frustration 101 over this case but this lesson had her on pins and needles for the past three weeks.

Jo Ann was on her third glass of champagne when reporters called.

"I'm greatly relieved that he has been caught," she said. "We will all breathe a little easier. Now it will be up to a jury to see that justice is done for my sister."

Evelyn Hamilton, Reeda's sister was happy for all concerned as well as herself.

"It took a big load off of me," she told the *Jackson Hole News*. "Reeda was my little sister and I've been waiting for some justice."

Saralyn told reporters she was also greatly relieved her father had been captured and especially that no one had been hurt.

"I will sleep a little better now, for everyone."

Jo Ann had always been confident that if they could get her brother-in-law to trial he would be convicted, but she had little confidence, or respect, for Prosecutor Kimball Mason. Now that there would be a trial she wondered if Mason's resentment of her would influence his handling of the case. Their mutual dislike for each other would undoubtedly make it more difficult to work together through the process and subsequent trial, and what about Saralyn? Her testimony would be important to the prosecution. With Saralyn's volatile temper and her open animosity toward Mason, combined with her immaturity and his poor handling of victims, Jo Ann wondered if it might come down to open warfare between them.

She didn't know Kimball Mason would be up for re-election that fall, with the primaries just three months away. This time he would not be running unopposed. He'd taken some heavy hits in the newspapers over this case and her family wasn't the only one upset with him. If Mason was to win this election he needed something bordering on a miracle to come his way.

Bill was held in New Mexico's Bernalillo County Detention Center without bond until his fugitive arraignment on April 10. There he waived his extradition rights and agreed to be returned to Idaho. But Gray's extradition touched off a political controversy that had been simmering for some time in Bonneville County. There'd been many debates previous to Gray's arrest regarding the airplane Bonneville County Commissioners purchased. Idaho Falls Police Sergeant Byron Stommel, a candidate for sheriff in the 1992 elections, made a campaign issue over the purchase of the airplane as a waste of taxpayers' money. He charged that the 1969 Cessna Skymaster had a history of fatal accidents.

Gray's attorneys didn't want Gray on that plane for health reasons as well as safety. They argued that Gray should be transported back to Idaho by commercial airliner, citing that it would be safer and less taxing on Gray. The Skymaster did not have bathroom facilities and because of Gray's kidney condition he needed rest room facilities frequently.

"Due to his poor physical condition, transportation in the county's small airplane could cause him great distress and could result in an adverse reaction to his physical well-being," argued Idaho Falls Attorney, John Radin. "The small antiquated airplane is in a very used condition and therefore more susceptible to mechanical problems and air turbulence."

Comparison of costs against the Skymaster and commercial air travel proved less costly to use the county plane but Bill's attorneys maintained the cost was not an issue. The defense offered to pay a $300 difference. Based on Gray's medical condition Bill would be allowed to fly back to Idaho by commercial airline.

Distress, air turbulence, less taxing? Now that he was a prisoner, Bill's health had apparently deteriorated dramatically. He would use his health problems as a catapult that would ultimately strain the Bonneville County jail system and Judge Ted Wood's patience and wisdom to the maximum.

While Bill was sitting it out in an Albuquerque jail his attorneys stepped up their efforts on his behalf. Besides the lengthy battle over Bill's transportation back to Idaho they made application for the firm of Fix and Mulligan to practice law in Idaho. Hiring a local Idaho Falls attorney, whom they had previously used, Attorney John Radin would sit in counsel and advise the team on Idaho law. Disclosure of fees revealed that the firm of Radin and Webb charged $75 an hour for their services while the firm of Fix and Mulligan charged $150 per hour for research and preparation of any written memorandums and $200 an hour for court appearances. Considering the hours previously spent and what was yet to come, the combined legal fees would be astronomical. Tom Moss's advice to his clients to settle the civil suit was well founded.

The house on Stacy Lane was gobbled up in attorney fees way before this case would go to trial. The Fix and Mulligan firm already held title to it. With all the legal fees, litigating the civil suit and now facing a criminal trial, Bill would undoubtedly have to dig into his coveted rat-holed money. Even his own lawyers had to hope Bill was not telling the truth when he said he gambled away all of the $208,000 pawnshop money. One thing for sure, regardless of the outcome of the trial, Bill would never live the good life on the money he so wantonly killed for.

With his client charged with two counts of first degree murder, possibly punishable by death, Attorney Richard J. Mulligan would launch a valiant, aggressive defense for Bill Gray. Richard Mulligan was a very experienced trial attorney, well experienced in capital crime cases from both sides of the courtroom.

Admitted to the practice of law in 1968 in the State of New Jersey, Mulligan had been a municipal judge for two years, an assistant prosecuting attorney for three. He left the hustle and bustle of the East Coast for the more quiet solitude of Wyoming in 1981. Having over twenty years experience in criminal and civil law, Mulligan had all the qualifications and knowledge to launch a weighty battle in defense of his client. He'd already spent a year and a half in legal contests over the civil suit which gave him a good understanding of the case. However, Bill had been slow to educate his attorney with important details in the past. Mulligan could only hope his client would be up front with him now. But Mulligan also hoped to see to it that his client would never stand trial. Mulligan was convinced that a conspiracy had taken place.

He arrived in Idaho Falls on a late night Delta Airlines flight April 22. Reporters and television personalities were on hand to film a pale, somber, handcuffed and chained Bill Gray as he was brought into the jail section of the courthouse. Fully bearded, contrary to Saralyn's prediction that he would attempt to change his appearance by shaving off his beard, eyes down, flanked by two officers, Bill shuffled down the corridor presumably anxious to be away from the lights of the cameras and the small gathering that had awaited his arrival.

Originally scheduled for the next day, but postponed at his request, Gray would not be arraigned until a week later. On April 24 Mulligan began the fight for bail. In support, Bill's father wrote that his son had never been violent and had always been a loving and unselfish husband and father. If released on bail, he would be gainfully employed and would not flee.

Bill's parents would stand fiercely in support of their son. Having lost their only other child and all ties with Bill's children forever gone, all they would have left was Beverly's two children. It was a sad situation. They were at a time in their life where they needed family and their only son to be with them as their years passed. When Bill Gray put a gun to his wife's head and pulled the trigger he shattered the lives of absolutely everyone around him ... everyone who ever loved him!

Mulligan's affidavit proclaimed that Bill had been a reputable business man in Jackson Hole for 14 years, had been a bonded bail bondsman for ten years and had been cooperative with his attorney and the court, making all appearances required of him during the proceedings of the civil case.

According to Mulligan, Bill had not intentionally left town to avoid prosecution but had simply left town on vacation prior to his knowledge that a warrant for his arrest had been issued. After he became aware of the arrest warrant he was extremely frightened by the fact that he had been charged with a crime. He was concerned if he would receive proper medical attention if he was incarcerated.

Mulligan cited that he'd had several conversations with Bill after the arrest warrant had been issued, but prior to the arrest, and that Bill was willing and intended to turn himself in, but first he wanted to be assured that his medical needs would be adequately taken care of. Mulligan listed Bill's needs which included regular examinations by qualified doctors. He would have to have immediate access to his medication and a special diet designated by his doctors.

His doctor from Jackson confirmed he'd been treating Bill for more than five years and strongly recommended Bill be given the immediate opportunity to consult with an internist and be given every consideration for his medical needs. He listed the medications Bill was taking and the reason for their use.

Cyclosporine – to prevent kidney rejection

Imuran – to prevent kidney rejection

Prednisone – to prevent kidney rejection

Furosemide – for edema and blood pressure

Coumadin – to prevent blood clots

Ranitidine – to prevent ulcer

Cholybar – to reduce cholesterol

Nifedipine – for blood pressure
Valium – for back pain
Percocet –for back pain

In the months to come, Judge Wood would be well-educated in the requirements of an organ recipient, compounded by the demands of an out-of-shape, overweight, spoiled, middle-aged man who would play the system for all he could get.

If the defense had any chance of getting their client out on bail they needed to portray Bill as a very sick man who would have a valid concern for not coming in on his own. If Bill was granted bail, he could reside in his motor home in Jackson, where he already had a pad site or would move it to Idaho Falls while awaiting trial, Mulligan told the court. Although Mulligan was now the legal owner of the house on Stacy Lane his client could certainly live there if he wanted.

It was a good story, but unbelievable. Logically, a person would not use phony names if on vacation, nor would they be inquisitive as to how they were found if they weren't intentionally trying to be lost. Using assumed names supported his intent to cover himself. The judge was not convinced Bill had the slightest intention of turning himself in. Bail was denied.

It was a totally different Bill Gray than the one captured from the comfort of his motor home that appeared before Judge Wood on April 28. Hunched over, walking with a pronounced limp, huddled beneath a heavy wool blanket, presumably to ward off the chills, he gave the appearance of a sickly old man. Staring at the judge, showing no emotion, the charges were read. Two counts of murder in the first degree and a third count for burglary, carrying and displaying a firearm, in the first degree. If found guilty of these charges Bill could be sent to the state prison for a maximum sentence of death or life imprisonment on the first two counts and fifteen to thirty years in prison for count three. Having viewed a video tape regarding his rights, then signing in acknowledgment that he understood those rights, Bill pleaded, not guilty. The jury trial was scheduled for September 15, 1992.

Ironically, the prosecutor, who three months ago didn't feel he had enough evidence to even charge Gray, now goes for the throat ... murder in the first degree. First degree murder under the laws of Idaho is the highest degree crime with which an individual can be charged. The jury deciding this case would be given only two choices, guilty in the first degree, which could carry the most severe penalty of all crimes, or not guilty, which would set him free. There was nothing in between. Nothing for the undecided or squeamish juror to hold him accountable, yet spare his life. It was the ultimate or nothing. Although the jury would not be charged with setting the penalty, once they rendered their verdict it was out of their hands. They could not even render a guilty verdict with a recommendation of life over death. The judge would decide his fate. All that the defense needed was one juror who would not take the chance that their guilty vote could put Gray on death row.

Bill had a visitor that day. One woman all alone stepped into the courtroom and slipped into a corner. No one knew what her business was, and no one, besides Bill Gray, knew who she was, except *Jackson Hole Guide* reporter Joy Ufford. Approaching Cheryl Carson, Joy fired questions at her.

"What are you doing here? How did Bill get Lee's

identification? Did you know where he was when he was on the run?"

For the most part she was saying this to Carson's back for Cheryl jumped up and fled the courtroom. Carson left Jackson shortly thereafter.

The Bill Gray and Cheryl Carson association was more than interesting. The circumstances surrounding Lee's death continue to have bizarre implications with rampant speculation. Idaho authorities maintain Bill was in Las Vegas when Lee died. However Lee was to have left for Las Vegas that very day with Bill. It was for that reason, Carson told police, she became immediately alarmed when she found his wallet at home.

For her to instantly jump to the conclusion Lee might have killed himself because they had an argument that morning, when they had fought on several other occasions, was an extremely quick assumption. Then, considering the vast amount of wilderness within miles of Jackson, in any direction, it seems incredible Carson could have located Lee's body within a few hours of telephoning the police. Given every benefit of doubt, Cheryl may have known of a place Lee liked to go which sent her in that direction first. Their argument may have been much different than others. Something may have been said which left her somewhat apprehensive and concerned for him. Yet, she went out shopping with her daughter, not concerned enough to take any preventive actions.

If this had been the end of it, it could be chalked up to an incredible set of circumstances. But then she is with Bill several times, after she told police she despised him. While Bill was on the run, she was spotted unsuccessfully trying to get into an old pickup of his. Then she mailed Lee's identification to Bill in California without alerting authorities where he was. Cheryl wanted something when she showed up at Bill's arraignment, presumably money.

"It all connects," Jo Ann speculates. "It would have been extremely damaging to Bill if Lee would have lived to testify. I will always believe Bill killed him. He could have killed Lee before he left for Las Vegas and paid Cheryl to not report him missing until Bill was safely tucked away in Las Vegas with a solid alibi."

At the very least, Carson was undoubtedly offered money to send Lee's identification. If Bill remained true to form, he did not pay Carson the money he promised and she was in court to collect. She would not have fled the courtroom when noticed if she was nothing more than a curious spectator.

Fully prepared and in fierce defense of his client, Mulligan wasted little time. He filed an affidavit alleging among other things, that certain officers entered into a conspiracy with Gray's children to deny his client's civil and constitutional rights. In part, the 16-page affidavit read:

"Based upon my background and experience, information acquired as counsel in this matter, and belief, I allege the following by way of affidavit which is intended as an offer of proof. I believe that each of the following allegations can be established at an evidentiary hearing in the event they are controverted by plaintiffs.

"The genesis of this instant lawsuit was on July 24, 1989, when Betty L. Gray, the wife of the defendant, William L. Gray, and Reeda Roundy were shot to death at Ms. Roundy's residence in Bonneville County, Idaho. The bodies of these homicide victims were discovered by Mr. Leroy Leavitt, Betty

Gray's current paramour. Mr. Leavitt contacted police and told them of his relationship with Betty L. Gray and suspicion was immediately focused upon the defendant William L. Gray.

"Almost immediately thereafter, William L. Gray became the subject of an intense investigation by Bonneville County Prosecutor, Kimball Mason, the Bonneville County Sheriff's Department, with the assistance of other law enforcement agencies, the Jackson Police Department, Jackson, Wyoming. Gray was interrogated at great length, without counsel, by Bonneville County detectives, including Detective Victor Rodriguez and members of the Jackson Police Department, including Lt. Dave Foster. William Gray answered all of their questions. Contemporaneously herewith, a search warrant was issued by Honorable D. Terry Rogers of the District Court of 9th Judicial District, Teton County, Wyoming located in Jackson, Wyoming, which authorized searches of Mr. Gray's home, business and vehicles. The affidavit upon which the search warrant was issued was the affidavit of Detective Victor Rodriguez.

"At the same time as the above events were occurring, there was an intense investigation in Bonneville County, Idaho and in Teton County, Wyoming, relative to the homicides. Law enforcement officials conducted searches for and collected forensic evidence, including blood, fingernail scrapings, hair samples, fingerprint identification and other evidence from the person of William L. Gray. Various interviews were conducted and reports prepared by law enforcement officers from both the state of Idaho and the state of Wyoming.

"The Plaintiff, Saralyn Gray Hoffman, who resides in Jackson, Wyoming, and Jeffrey Gray, who resided in Portland, Oregon, at the onset of the investigation vehemently and steadfastly, supported their father's innocence regarding the double homicide allegations. It was their position that the defendant could not and would not have murdered his wife, their mother.

"It was at this juncture that any pending criminal prosecution against the defendant for murder by Bonneville County Prosecutor Kimball Mason came to a dead end. Detective Rodriguez realized that he did not have sufficient evidence to convince the county prosecutor that Mr. Gray should be formally charged with the homicides. Victor Rodriguez has complained throughout his involvement in this matter that Mason, without substantial additional evidence, would not bring this matter to prosecution.

"It was the expressed opinion of Rodriguez that the defendant was guilty of the crimes and should be prosecuted. Accordingly, he engaged in a course of conduct in hopes that the defendant William L. Gray would be prosecuted.

"Accordingly, Detective Rodriguez developed a scheme to bring about the prosecution of defendant William L. Gray by conspiring with other persons to obtain evidence against the defendant outside of the criminal justice system and in violation of defendant's rights under the Constitution of the United States of America, the state of Wyoming, and the state of Idaho.

"Detective Rodriguez, on various occasions after the murders, in the company of other law enforcement officers, went to visit the plaintiffs Saralyn Gray Hoffman and Jeffrey Gray at the respective residences in Wyoming and Oregon. In an attempt to convince the plaintiffs of their father's guilt, Rodriguez shared with them police department information, photographs and other evidence that would not be available to non-law enforcement personnel outside the law enforcement or judicial process. In addition, he consulted on a frequent basis with Jo Ann Buccola, Betty Gray's sister, who assisted in financing the civil lawsuit against my client.

"It was the intention of Rodriguez to cause plaintiffs to enter into a conspiracy with him which had as its objective the violation of defendant's constitutional and civil rights and the criminal prosecution of William L. Gray for the murders of Betty L. Gray and Reeda Roundy.

"Initially, plaintiffs were reluctant to seriously consider Officer Rodriguez's attempts to have them re-evaluate their former position regarding defendant's complicity in the subject murders. Officer Rodriguez pointed out to plaintiffs that if they were to change their position and file a lawsuit against their father the following mutual benefits would occur to Detective Rodriguez and the plaintiffs.

"The plaintiffs would obtain over $1,000,000 in assets owned by their father by virtue of filing a wrongful death action. Detective Rodriguez, by virtue of the discovery that would flow from such a wrongful death action, could obtain sufficient evidence for criminal prosecution against the defendant. If the civil action were successful, the defendant would be stripped of the assets necessary to defend him against a criminal prosecution.

"Prior to the above-described events, Victor Rodriguez had made the acquaintance of Thomas E. Moss, the plaintiffs' attorney herein. I believe that Mr. Moss became acquainted with Rodriguez when Moss was hired as a special prosecutor in Bonneville County, at which time Moss and Rodriguez worked together in the prosecution of Paul Rhoades and possible other criminal matters. In my opinion, Moss is basically a criminal attorney, who is relatively inexperienced in regard to civil trials and civil procedures. Rodriguez encouraged and conspired with plaintiffs to seek the services of Moss to affect the objects of the aforementioned conspiracy. Thereafter, Moss conferred with

Rodriguez and was shown all of the information contained in Rodriguez's investigative file of William L. Gray which would not be ordinarily available to him. Moss joined in the conspiracy with plaintiffs and Rodriguez, caused to be filed a wrongful death action against William L. Gray alleging therein that the defendant murdered his wife; which is the complaint pending before this honorable court.

"In furtherance of this conspiracy, the plaintiffs, by and through Moss, noticed the deposition of defendant pursuant to the pending civil legal action. When defendant asserted his constitutional right to remain silent, the plaintiffs brought a motion compelling him to testify. This Honorable Court ruled that the defendant had an election to either testify in his own defense or remain silent at the time of trial. Defendant appealed this ruling and as a result of said appeal, by way of writ, was placed in the untenable position of abandoning his assets or waiving his rights, so defendant William L. Gray was forced to waive his rights and testify by way of deposition, answers to interrogatories, answers to request for production of documents and answers to request for admissions. In fact, the defendant had an election to either testify in his own defense or remain silent and lose his assets and ability to adequately defend himself.

"In all my experience as a municipal judge, assistant county prosecutor and criminal defense attorney, I have never seen a suspect in a criminal matter, such as William L. Gray, before the court as a defendant in a civil case defending against the very same charges that he is suspected of committing in the criminal investigation. If such conduct were in fact permitted by law enforcement and/or heirs, then these lawsuits would be common in major metropolitan areas, as well as other jurisdictions, and I know that prosecutors would be using that as an effective tool in the criminal prosecution of many individuals. I know of no such cases throughout the United States of America and cannot find any because there are simply none since it constitutes unconstitutional, inequitable and illegal conduct by the plaintiffs, their counsel Thomas Moss and cooperating law enforcement officials such as Detective Victor Rodriguez."

It certainly was an unusual set of circumstances. But that's exactly what it was, circumstance, a chain of events that unfolded over a period of time ... events that would have followed a normal prosecutorial pattern if Mason would have filed criminal charges prior to the civil suit. Granted, the finding of the most damaging tape came from the civil suit lawyer's efforts, but the tape had been in Bonneville County's possession since it had been recorded. If Mason himself had , or if he would have directed another deputy in his office to sort through the available material years ago, the tape would have been discovered then and Mason would have undoubtedly filed criminal charges.

Discovery of the tape caused two things to happen almost simultaneously. Bill Gray decided to settle the civil suit with his kids in anticipation they would back off and Mason elected to file criminal charges, most likely based on the discovery of the tape, which caught Bill in his lies and his telling an incredibly unbelievable story.

To give up the large amount of money he killed his wife for had to have been a painful decision for Bill Gray. The mere fact that he elected to defend himself against the civil charges, rather than attempt to settle quickly, thus quietly, indicates he was going to give himself every chance and take every risk to keep the blood money. Only when he finally came to realize that it might come down to either the money or his freedom, possibly death by lethal injection if convicted, did he decide it wasn't worth it.

Although the prosecutor now had Jeff and Saralyn on his side and their testimony would be powerful, Mason would have brought the criminal charges without them. The gift was the missing tape; the kids were just the wrapping paper.

The judge would not take Mulligan's charges lightly. He would read sworn statements of the accused conspirators and weigh all elements before he would determine that a conspiracy to strip Bill Gray of his rights had not taken place.

Bill would not be released on a technicality or because of Mulligan's charges, he would remain in custody, but how long Bill would remain in the county jail would become another battle of outstanding magnitude.

Undeniably, the Bonneville County Jail was overcrowded. A facility rated to house forty-nine inmates was currently housing an average of 76.8 prisoners a day. Where the Idaho State Penitentiary in Boise averaged sixty square feet of space per inmate, the Bonneville County jail was averaging twenty-four. Due to Bill's unique medical condition and having been advised by the jail doctor of Bill's need for exceptional sanitary conditions under normal circumstances, doubly necessary due to the overcrowding of the facility, extraordinary measures were taken to protect Bill from infection that might pose a risk to his transplanted kidney.

A four-cell block that formally housed women prisoners was cleaned, painted and sanitized. Housing fewer prisoners, the women's block was much quieter and Bill would have the luxury of four times more space than any other inmate. Here he would be distanced and isolated from the general population who might carry disease. The larger cell would also afford him more area to walk around, thus help to keep the swelling in his legs to a minimum.

But almost before the paint was dry on Gray's new cell, he and his lawyers were back in court. This time Bill was not wrapped in wool blankets and there was no mention of a problem with the temperature in the courtroom. On May 8, a hearing was held on a seven-part motion filed by the defense requesting modification of the conditions of Gray's confinement. If the court would not grant bail, Gray was asking to be removed from jail and placed under house arrest. The reason was simple, the argument lengthy; jail conditions were detrimental to his health.

A large private cell and isolation from the other prisoners would not be enough for Gray. They wanted the jail population to be reduced and capped at the required forty-nine. Judge Wood was well aware of the overcrowding situation in the Bonneville County jail. Commissioners were certainly aware of the problem but it would be several years before the situation could be rectified.

Jail Administer, Lt. William English testified that "Overcrowding negatively impacts virtually every condition of confinement, sanitation, security, supervision, recreation and most importantly, the physical and mental health of the inmates."

Dr. Douglas Smith in a sworn affidavit said "Gray, who has a reduced immune system and was in precarious health before being incarcerated, is now subjected to a substantial increase of infection and possible death each day of his continued confinement in that grossly overcrowded facility."

To add a little padding to the argument, Defense Attorney Radin advised the court that inmates from a bordering Idaho county sued their county commissioners and Sheriff's Office seeking to rectify inadequate staffing, inadequate recreation, poor lighting and plumbing. In 1991, more than a year before this case was before the court, Lt. English addressed this very situation in a letter to Sheriff Ackerman. "I do not want to sound like an alarmist, but to wait for an inmate, or someone else, to file a law suit is to invite disaster. It appears we have one last opportunity to do it our way within a very short time, or after a law suit have a court order do it someone else's way."

The need to either increase the size of the facility and staff, or reduce the population, had begun ten years earlier and was worsening as the years went by. Although prisoners were transferred to other counties it was very costly and most counties were experiencing overcrowded situations of their own and were unable to accept Idaho's second largest city's inmates.

Bill's list of needs, more appropriately called "wants" continued. Bill wanted his own microwave oven and a refrigerator. He should be allowed to get his groceries directly from the market and be allowed to prepare his own meals. The jail diet was not sufficient to meet his requirements and he must take some of his medicine with food or milk and could not depend upon jail personnel to provide these in a timely manner.

Bill's attorneys argued for his personal watch so he would know when to take his medicines, Ivory Soap in a plastic container, Selsun Blue shampoo, his own hairbrush and a new mirror. He also asked to be allowed to obtain and wear a knee brace.

He must have a personal television. He could not watch the community television in the jail library with other inmates without having contact with them and catching their infections and disease. If he had his own television he needed a weekly *TV Guide* and because of the boredom he wanted personal delivery of the local newspaper and magazines.

"If he gets his own refrigerator, his own microwave, gets to prepare his own meals, gets his own newspaper, magazine subscriptions, they're going to have a riot down there," stated Kimball Mason.

"We cannot treat this inmate that much differently. It causes problems for the jail. Some of the inmates already consider Gray a special case and they don't like it, and so there's the possibility that when he's passing through the common area to go out for recreation he could be assaulted."

Quickly picking up on that statement, Mulligan said that was exactly what he was concerned about. Because of the blood thinning medicine Gray was taking if he got into a fight he could bleed to death. Further, Mulligan didn't want his client locked down in his private cell at night.

"What I would like to see, since he's already confined in a cell block, is to have him have access to a recreation area after lock-down. Since Bill doesn't sleep very well at night, I'd like him to be able to come and go out of his cell to watch television, go to the bathroom or take a shower and maybe he could ease back into some drowsiness and go back to his cell and sleep."

"I'm surprised they didn't ask for an overstuffed couch and a leather recliner," quipped Jo Ann. "He always got his way with my sister and it looks like nothing is going to change."

The prosecutors and the defenders argued their positions. It was the sparring game, each side sizing up the other, flexing their muscles to see who would be victorious. The prosecution would go through the motions and play the game very aware that every consideration would be given the defendant to protect his health as well as his rights. Bill got the knee brace, his watch, bottled water and a personal television. He would not get a refrigerator, microwave or a special menu other than what his doctor ordered for him.

If he wanted to pay for his personal items he could have them and he could order, at his expense, the *TV Guide* and magazines sent to general delivery at the jail. There would not be special delivery of the newspapers. He would have the same access to them as all the other inmates. Gray would not be locked-down.

Idaho law provides neither that prisons be comfortable nor that they provide every amenity one might find desirable. Bill Gray put this law to the extreme test.

Asked by the *Jackson Hole Guide* if Gray's requests were out of the ordinary or unusual, Deputy Prosecutor John Stosich replied, "Gray's requests are extraordinary. It's very unusual, very, very ... yes! No other Bonneville County Jail inmates charged with first degree murder and awaiting trial has made similar requests. They have not found anything wrong with the accommodations. Of course, the others had not been kidney transplant recipients either," he quickly added.

Within a week after Gray was placed in the women's cell block Judge Wood received a copy of this letter signed by four female inmates.

BONNEVILLE COUNTY INMATE REQUEST FORM
From: Females
To: Lt. English
We the females due to the circumstances of Mr. Gray not

having to be locked down which creates the task of opening the doors and closing them each and every time rounds are made are being woke up. This makes for a very restless night and we do not feel it is fair. We do not feel we should be subject to this each and every night because of one person.

Following on the heels of that letter, came a written report entitled Warning to Judge of Inmates Serious Medical or Psychiatric Problem. The report signed by the jail nurse and two jail supervisors stated:

"Based upon the following reasons we feel that inmate William L. Gray may have a serious medical and/or psychiatric problem which may be a serious danger to his health or life.

1. Mr. Gray has apparent multiple serious medical and/or health problems.
2. The jail is overcrowded and there is a serious lack of segregation available.
3. Overcrowding adversely effects the ability of the jail staff and jail to deal with extensive ongoing medical issues without subjecting inmates to higher risk.
4. Alternatives to housing in this jail may be indicated."

No one wanted to deal with Bill Gray, not even the inmates. No one wanted the responsibility if he should suffer rejection or have a blood clot break loose. Bill was a sick man, undoubtedly made sicker by the fact he had been captured and incarcerated but because of his high priority status, he demanded, and got, the staff running for his every need or whim depending on how one viewed it. However, Bill was not a convicted killer. He held all the rights to the presumption of innocence until proven guilty. Having been considered a flight risk by the court he was merely being detained in the Bonneville

County Jail until his peers determined his innocence or guilt.

When bail is denied most often it's because that person poses a threat to society or there is evidence to suggest that person may flee from prosecution. It's called preventive detention. The person is a pretrial detainee. The question: Was Gray's preventive detention tantamount to punishment? Judge Woods' 17-page memorandum decision addressed this question.

"Even though Gray has not yet been convicted of any crime, it is undisputed that the state may permissibly detain him prior to a formal adjudication of guilt. The state's right to interfere with the personal liberty of pretrial detainees is much more limited than its interest in dealing with convicted prisoners. The law is clear that a defendant who is being detained pending trial on criminal charges may not be punished while in detention. It must be determined whether the conditions existing in that detention facility, as they specifically relate to Gray, amount to punishment of Gray. If those conditions do amount to punishment, then Gray's continued pretrial detention in jail would violate his constitutional right to due process. If the government could confine or otherwise infringe the liberty of detainees only to the extent necessary to ensure their presence at trial, house arrest would in the end be the only constitutionally justified form of detention. In deciding whether jail overcrowding constitutes punishment the following factors are to be considered:
1) the duration of the prisoner's confinement
2) the degree to which the population exceeds the institution design capacity
3) the size of the inmate's quarters and the number of hours the prisoner must spend in those quarters
4) the effects of the prisoner's mental and physical health

5) the relative permanency of the crowded conditions"

Having thoroughly reviewed each of these factors and reviewing testimony of Dr. Smith and Lt. English, Judge Wood resolved that the severe overcrowding would result in a form of punishment for Gray which was the basis for his final decision.

"No evidence was presented which purported to show that Gray is a violent person or that he poses a risk to the public. The fact that Gray has been charged with two counts of murder and one count of burglary cannot be considered in this proceeding as any evidence of violence. However, evidence was presented which convinced this court that there existed a substantial risk of flight if Gray were to be released on bail. The purpose for detaining Gray before trial can best be achieved and, at the same time, eliminate the risk to his health caused by institutional confinement, by detaining Gray, without bail, on house arrest monitored by electronic device. By using an electronic monitor, law enforcement officers can regularly check to ensure that Gray is within the house arrest premises and immediately detect any attempt to flee. Further, the evidence indicates that Gray will die if he fails to take numerous drugs prescribed by his treating doctors. Since those drugs cannot be obtained without a valid prescription, the risk that Gray may try to flee before trial, even with the electronic monitor, can be further minimized by limiting the quantities of the prescription drugs that Gray can have in his possession at any given time."

The date was June 12, 1992. Betty Lou Gray would have been celebrating her 50th birthday; instead her killer would be allowed to leave the confinement of jail and rest comfortably in the privacy of a rented home.

Jo Ann was outraged. She didn't think the electronic

monitoring device was foolproof. She still had concerns for her niece and nephew's safety as well as her own.

"It's ironic," she added, "that Bill would be cleared for house arrest today of all days."

Bill would be released to house arrest as soon as housing was found and the electronic monitor was fitted to his ankle. The monitor, waterproof allowing for bathing, undetachable by Gray, would send a signal to the Sheriff's Office if he strayed more than 150 feet from the center point of his telephone. If the ankle monitor was tampered with, cut or removed, the telephone would automatically dial a national monitoring center in Dallas, Texas. The signal would be red-flagged immediately and the center would notify Idaho authorities. Officers would be at his house within minutes.

The electronically monitored house arrest program had been in use in Bonneville County since 1990 primarily as an alternative to jail sentences for DUI convictions. It wasn't 100% effective. There had been some offenders who had abused it and took off. It wasn't a tracking device; it merely told authorities he was gone. Aware of the fallacies of the program, even the judge knew it wasn't fool proof. He told Bill if he really wanted to escape he would be able to do it.

The state was directed to pay all costs associated with the monitoring system but special privileges would not come without some cost to Bill. He would have to pay for his new found comfort and privacy. He would pay all his living expenses, rent, utilities, food, personal items and all cost associated with his medical care including medical examinations, doctor bills and the daily medications he required. Bill was to place his order for food and other necessities through his attorneys, they in turn would be responsible to have it delivered to the Sheriff's Office. Everything going into Gray's house would then be checked and taken to Bill by an officer. In particular they would be inspecting his groceries for weapons. He could eat whatever he wanted to pay for, he could have his cigarettes. He would not be allowed any form of alcohol. Unmonitored and accompanied by two police officers, Bill could even go shopping if he so desired.

Stosich had fought valiantly to keep Bill in jail. Having lost that battle, they fought to make him post a $1,000,000 bond. If Bill wasn't going to be securely locked up behind bars they wanted additional insurance he would be around for his trial. They lost that battle too. But when the judge did not allow a three-day supply of medication to be in his possession at one time they fared a little better. After extensive argument Judge Wood directed that only a one-day supply of medication be allowed and it was to be delivered between 8 and 9 a.m. each morning. For the state it was a small victory, for the Sheriff's Office it was just one more Bill Gray headache.

Setting the rules for house arrest would be argued in court on several more occasions. The state wanted a visitors list in advance and to have an officer present at every visit. Bill's attorney, John Radin, didn't think it was necessary to account for visitors or to have officers present. Unquestionably, Bill could have consultation with his attorneys at any time of the day or night, but ultimately Bill would need to get permission to have any other visitors. The judge allowed that an officer may be present at all visitations. This was now at the discretion of the state. If they wanted officers present they were allowed to do so. Authorities could enter the house at any time, without permission or warning. They could search and seize. They could be all over Bill Gray like paint on a fence if they so desired. But even though the Gray case was a priority case, it wasn't the only one sheriff's officers had to contend with and it was doubtful they would make many waves as long as the monitoring device remained silent.

Those closely associated with the case openly laughed at the argument of his not mixing with the jail population. In the early days after his transplant when he was even more vulnerable to infection he had no qualms about crowded airplanes or standing elbow to elbow with strangers at the crap tables for hours on end. Bill had not previously had any problems mixing with the public as long as it was at his own choosing.

Reeda's sister, Evelyn Hamilton, was as outraged as Jo Ann over Bill's house arrest. Although Evelyn had never been afraid of Bill, knowing he had no animosity toward any of the Roundy family, she couldn't understand why he deserved such preferential treatment and pampering.

It had been one month short of three years since her sister had been murdered. Her killer had roamed free for most of this time and she was anxious to see him suffer some of the consequences for what he had done. Because of all the past events, pointedly Mason's refusal to prosecute, the legal system in Idaho was very suspect in her mind and she wrote of her displeasure in a letter to the editor, published in the *Post Register* on June 22, 1992, questioning the wisdom of the judge's actions. She wanted to know if Bill Gray was ever going to be brought to trial or was he going to be able to squirm out of that too?

Saralyn was outright bitter over the house arrest. She was not surprised that her father found a way out of jail.

"My father is used to getting his own way. He paid dearly to get out of jail. He'll do what it takes to get his own way. He is no sicker than I am."

But she also couldn't help but be a little amused at her father's release to house arrest. He'd gotten out of jail, in part, because it wasn't sanitary enough. The last time she had been in the house at 435 Stacy Lane it was a filthy pig sty. Dirty dishes, dirty laundry, counters covered with encrusted food, slop on the floors, and smelled like something between a stale bar room and a hobo camp.

"It was a mess. It was gross. He wouldn't even take out the garbage. My cat box is cleaner than his house was," she added.

In the months following her mother's death Saralyn had tried to help her dad keep up the house, but she was pregnant, working full time and couldn't do it all. She tried to get her dad to hire a housekeeper but he wouldn't. He didn't seem to care. Unsanitary conditions didn't seem to bother him much. Bill had a special gimmick and he was using it to its fullest extent. Bill checked out of the Bonneville County Jail on June 23.

Although the location of Bill's house had not been made public, most of his neighbors knew who he was and they weren't at all sure they liked the idea of having a suspected strike-in-the-night killer in their midst. The Sheriff's Office received a call from a woman complaining that Bill was loose and walking around the streets. If he was very far from the house, his signal should have gone off alerting authorities, however, when officers were dispatched they found him at home caring less about what the neighbors thought.

"I guess he's got to live somewhere," said another neighbor. "You would think that normal people would know not to do anything when they are being watched that closely, but if he's done what he's accused of, he's not too normal."

But not everyone felt threatened. The owner of a daycare

center in the area probably put it in the best perspective when she said she believed he was a person who would not go out and look for just anybody to murder.

"If he is guilty of the crime he is accused of, that stemmed from a domestic problem within his own environment. He's not going to go around murdering strangers."

The Sheriff's Office was deluged with phone calls the first week of Bill's house arrest, and then it was quiet until a brazen news anchorwoman for a local television station found the house and tried to interview Bill. This prompted him to file a report with the Sheriff's Office.

"Laurel Porter knocked on my door and wanted me to make a statement that would put my neighbors at rest. I told her I couldn't talk to her, but the neighbors don't have anything to fear from me."

Bill was big news for this mid-sized town. Residents had followed the case not unlike a soap opera. From the discovery of the bodies, through the investigation, the civil suit and now most recently on their minds, the capture and release, to house arrest. Laurel wanted something special for her viewers. She contacted Radin and Mulligan asking for an on-camera interview.

Denied cooperation, she interviewed several neighbors. A camera placed out of sight caught Bill on the sidewalk in front of his house a few days later. This film was shown on the 6 p.m. news promising more exclusive footage to be shown on the 10 p.m. news. As their lead story, the late news once again showed the footage of Bill on the sidewalk and an interview with a neighbor expressing fear of Gray's presence in the area. Mulligan was furious. Before he could even argue the subject, the television station's attorney filed a petition with the court, requesting release of the grand jury transcripts.

Exploitation of Gray could be held to a minimum by the courts but the news media has rights to freedom of the press. There will always be debate on the moral and ethical conduct of the media, but as proven by the sensationalism of the O. J. Simpson case in 1994, the media will obtain whatever, and however, the stories and pictures that will attract listeners, readers and viewers.

"As with many rights of constitutional magnitude, the public's right to know is not without limits," Judge Wood said, "particularly when other fundamental constitution rights are implicated. Here the defendant was tracked down at his house out of sheer media curiosity and for sensational purposes of publicizing the current custody circumstances made necessary by the unfortunate health restrictions the defendant suffers. While the use of a normal beat reporter to cover the proposed story would still be prejudicial, the use of a "media personality" demonstrates a level of commercial motivation incompatible with reasonable avoidance of prejudice to a defendant's right to a fair trial." Having said this, Judge Wood imposed a gag order on the news media, the prosecution, defense attorneys, detectives, witnesses and the victims' families which included Saralyn, Jeff and Jo Ann.

For the judge, the final straw had been the television personality's disruption of the house arrest. The rumblings over Gray's receiving a fair trial in Bonneville County had already started. He was concerned about pre-trial publicity compromising Gray's rights. The gag order would compel everyone named to remain silent or be subject to retribution by the court. The media would be allowed to report on documents and statements made during court hearings. Court controlled press releases would be allowed periodically.

There had been several instances of inflammatory remarks

about Bill made by Jo Ann and Saralyn to the media and Mulligan took every shot at lambasting them in the press. Stosich had been complaining for some time about Mulligan's press remarks and the judge had admonished Mulligan to cease on several occasions. And even though one of the terms required by Gray for settling the civil suit, demanded that Moss and his clients not disclose the amount of the settlement, Mulligan told the *Jackson Hole Guide* the children had obtained $1,000,000 of their father's assets. In fact, Jeff and Saralyn received less than half of that amount and paid expenses including to their aunt Jo Ann for Tom Moss's fees. For the state, the gag order would be a blessing.

For a while everything settled down to a semblance of normalcy. Bill would be transported, on two occasions, to Salt Lake City for his check-ups and biopsies. He would travel by automobile with two officers and was allowed to remove the monitor from his ankle. He petitioned to be released on his own recognizance to go to California for six days for a family get together, but that produced nothing more than additional time spent in court by his attorneys and the state to argue about it. Bill was victorious when he requested that his parents be allowed to stay with him.

Bill's parents were driving the same motor home Bill was arrested in and the monitoring device did not prevent Bill from leaving the house and entering the motor home. The Sheriff's rights to search and seize did not encompass a motor home owned, on paper, by Gray's parents. One wonders how important the Sheriff's Office check of Bill's groceries for concealed weapons was now. If he wanted guns, alcohol or anything else, he could undoubtedly convince his parents to get it for him. His loving and devoted elderly parents had long ago ceased to deny their son anything within their power to give.

Over the next few months there would be motions to keep witnesses out, motions to keep witnesses in, motions to keep specific statements from being heard by the jury, a motion to throw out the photo lineup, two motions for change of venue and motions to extend the time to file more motions.

On August 18, Bill waved his rights to a speedy trial and requested the trial date be set back so he could file more motions, petitions and extensions. His attorney complained that the prosecutor had not yet supplied them with records, reports, evidence and tapes for its pre-trial discovery process. The defense wanted more time to review those materials, locate and coordinate expert witnesses and read instructions given to the grand jury that indicted their client. They felt the pre-trial publicity would likely diminish during the period of continuance. The trial was rescheduled to February 16, 1993.

Kimball Mason was defeated in the May primaries. He would be leaving the office of Bonneville County Prosecutor in January. Fully intending to still be in office at the time of the Gray trial, originally set for September, he and his staff had proceeded on this case as they would have on any other case, if not more so. It had been an extraordinarily demanding case requiring his office's full attention, resources and experience. After the date was extended to February 16, 1993 Mason, knew he would not be around to prosecute this exceptionally borderline case.

The foundations for which he'd based his reluctance and refusal to prosecute Gray before were still valid. Nothing would positively, absolutely, without a doubt place Bill in the Roundy home on the night of the murders. To convince twelve people of Gray's guilt with irrefutable facts, combined with enough circumstances that the jury could recognize there was no other rational conclusion but that Bill Gray murdered the two women, would take a very experienced criminal litigator. A thorough understanding of this complex case would be essential to its outcome.

Deputy Prosecutor John Stosich had primarily taken over all aspects of the Gray case. He'd filed, answered and argued all the briefs and motions before the court for the past six months. John was familiar with the case and could have adequately prosecuted the Gray case. But John had previously determined to leave the prosecutor's office, taking a job with the public defender. John, as well as Kimball Mason, would be leaving after the first of the year. In fact, this was a year of major changes in Bonneville County. After eleven years in office, Sheriff Richard Ackerman retired and former Idaho Falls Police Sgt. Byron Stommel won the election for sheriff. Previous loyalties and other job offers would reduce the experienced prosecutor's staff to a trickle. Five of the six attorneys in the Bonneville County Prosecutors Office would be gone by January 11, just one month before the Gray case was scheduled for trial.

Faced with the realization he was leaving office, Mason had real concerns for this case. Early in September Kimball called Tom Moss and asked if he would assist Bonneville County in the prosecution of Gray. Tom readily agreed. As the events of the elections and the extension of the trial date had been unfolding, Tom was also experiencing concerns if a new, lesser experienced prosecutor could step in and try this case successfully after only 45 days in office. Tom not only agreed to sit in as special prosecutor, he agreed to do so at no expense to Bonneville County.

Unquestionably, this case was dear to him. Over the past two years Tom had grown very fond of Jeff and Saralyn.

"They're my kids," he said. "I love them as my own."

He admired their courage and could feel the pain and trauma present within their very core. If money was the only thing Saralyn and Jeff wanted, they already had that, but he knew their motivation went much, much deeper. Simply put, their mother's killer should not go unpunished. Yes, Tom would gladly give of his time and experience to help see this case to conclusion. Mason appointed Tom Moss as special prosecutor on September 14. The next day Mulligan and Radin filed a motion to disqualify.

The dispute over Tom Moss's appointment as special prosecutor was long and bitter. Conflict of interest, Mulligan argued.

"Moss's impartiality is called into question where his discretion may be influenced by having represented the Gray children in the civil suit. His impartiality may also be in question when he has some direct personal interest arising from animosity. The facts indicate Moss has a strong belief in Gray's guilt witnessed by his testimony at an evidentiary hearing where he stated, 'I am concerned that the man killed two defenseless women in their beds at night, and I think he would kill again if something angered him. Here's the feeling I have about Mr. Gray. I am convinced and the evidence shows that Mr. Gray murdered these two women. I think he should be prosecuted and held accountable, yes, I feel that strongly.'"

Mulligan went on to say Moss stated to him personally he would not feel secure until such time as he saw Mr. Gray placed behind bars permanently. Moss also expressed fear Gray was carrying guns to his depositions.

Tom had definitely felt uncomfortable when he deposed Bill Gray.

"He's a scary guy. I'll tell you. I sat across the table from him in the depositions for a couple of days and he'd wear me out. Number one he was so evasive, very hard to get an answer out of him and then he'd get mad, boy he'd ... boy you could see ... he scares me. I'm scared of the guy. I think if he gets off, I think Jo Ann would be in trouble and Saralyn would be in trouble and I think I would be in trouble."

But Tom's motivation for offering to prosecute without compensation was not out of fear, nor for the vindictive reasons Mulligan painted for the judge, he wanted the killer of Betty Lou Gray and Reeda Roundy prosecuted, and he was very concerned for the strength of that prosecution under the present circumstances.

Asked by Mulligan, under oath, why he would serve without compensation if it weren't for any other reason than a personal desire to vindicate his former clients, or personal vengeance, Tom plainly stated; "Well, number one I've been asked to, number two, I think that I've been asked by a county that needs assistance because of the limitations that they have in terms of their experience. There is a transition going on in this office."

Tom wasn't the only one concerned. Jo Ann was so upset she couldn't sleep. She'd spent almost every waking hour worrying over this case and now it turned into a 24-hour-a-day problem. She'd wanted to take out ads to campaign against Kimball Mason during the primaries but had been advised by Tom it would be unwise to do so. If he should win the elections she would still have to deal with him only under much more unfavorable circumstances. But now that every experienced prosecutor was leaving office she almost wished Mason would have won the election.

It took almost three months for the dust to finally settle on this controversy. Although Judge Wood held utmost respect for Tom Moss and believed firmly in his credibility, he could not deny that Moss could be placed in a compromising position with regard to his previous involvement in the civil suit. Therefore, Tom Moss was disqualified as special prosecutor. If Gray was to be convicted, Judge Wood was giving every assurance the conviction would hold up against a later appeal. If Moss was allowed to prosecute Gray, that in itself could be volumes of fuel in argument on appeal. The fact that Moss knew the grand jury was meeting, where Mulligan did not, could be an issue on appeal alone. But when Detective Rodriguez and Jackson Police Lt. Dave Foster were spotted in the halls outside the grand jury room on March 18, just about everyone including the press knew it was the Gray case the jury would be hearing.

Grand jury indictments are normally shrouded in secrecy until the defendant is arrested and appears at his or her arraignment. But this case had not been normal from the start. A criminal investigator with the U.S. Marshal's Office in another city leaked to the press that a warrant had been issued for Gray and anyone who read the paper knew Gray had been charged.

It is a misdemeanor offense to reveal the existence of an indictment. Mason considered filing charges against the *Post Register* and the investigator, but decided against it saying only that he had other things to worry about. A spokesman for the *Post Register* said he was flabbergasted that any sort of charges would be considered. This was a case of the newspaper aggressively pursuing information that was in public interest.

"Clearly the newspaper broke no law in pursuit of this information," he professed.

The defense was undoubtedly pleased that Tom Moss had

been disqualified. They had worked diligently to that end. Jo Ann felt the defense had purposely planned to extend the trial date until Mason would be unable to prosecute. Everyone knew the new prosecutor would be much less of an adversary than Kimball Mason or Tom Moss. Everyone involved in the case was concerned, everyone except Bill Gray and his defense team.

After Mason lost the primary election in May he told a reporter for the *Post Register* he would continue to work at the major cases pending in court, including the Gray case until he left the office. Taking a final jab at his adversary's experience he added that, Johnson didn't have the experience. He was not qualified to handle the Gray case.

But the Bonneville County voters wanted a change. Rookie David Johnson had easily defeated 11-year veteran, Kimball Mason in the primaries and ran unopposed in the November election. According to Johnson the people wanted justice. Mason had relied too heavily on plea bargains. Taking his pot shot at Mason, Johnson said he would certainly be more sensitive to crime victims.

Six days after Tom Moss was disqualified, David Johnson was officially elected to the office of Bonneville County Prosecuting Attorney. While David Johnson was a good lawyer, having a wealth of experience in the civil side of law, he'd had no previous prosecutorial experience in criminal court. Johnson would be butting heads with two very experienced and sharp criminal defense attorneys. He knew little about the Gray case and he had very little time to prepare for it. The new kid on the block would step into office facing, within a month, with less than half of an experienced staff, one of the most lengthy, litigated and controversial cases in Bonneville County history.

Everyone involved was concerned if Bonneville County would have sufficient resources to successfully prosecute Bill Gray, but no one was any more concerned than Tom Moss. He called his friend in Boise, Attorney General Larry Echohawk.

"I knew the state had a prosecutorial division which was basically one guy named Mike Kane. Larry was familiar with the case because the family had contacted him some time ago. I told him I had been disqualified and he was rather surprised. He didn't see any reason why I should not be on the case. But I said, 'Larry, you've got to assign Mike Kane to this thing.' He said depending on his schedule he'd sure do everything he could to get him up there but he would have to get a request from David Johnson. So I called David and said, 'David, you've gotta get some help,' and I suggested he call Echohawk and get Mike Kane and I said, 'I talked to Larry,' and he said he would assign him if you ask for it. Well, David asked and Larry assigned Mike."

Michael Kane came with a set of credentials that should have had Mulligan wondering if he should have fought so hard to have Tom Moss removed as special prosecutor. Mike Kane spent his first six months fresh out of law school in 1980 as a public defender. His knowledge and professionalism quickly catapulted him into the Office of Kooteani County Prosecutor for Coeur d'Alene, Idaho where he remained for eight years trying everything from traffic tickets to first degree murder. He chuckles a little when he remembers his trial before a jury for a traffic ticket.

"When I first started in this business you could actually demand a jury trial for a speeding ticket. I had to try one and the penalty was a $5 fine."

But Mike had a special talent for prosecuting the murderer. The tougher the case, the more challenged he became. His reputation and natural instincts for criminal law did not go unnoticed by the State Attorney General and in 1988 was appointed as Chief of the Attorney General's Criminal Law Division. Working diligently with the state legislature, Mike was responsible for amending and writing several Idaho laws, including a complicated Victim's Rights Amendment.

The Idaho Supreme Court was a second home to Mike, as his office handled all the appeals brought in the criminal justice area. He'd spent time with the head of then President George Bush's Drug Task Force and rubbed elbows with Cabinet members, governors and attorney generals all over the country. Mike had tried seven first degree murder cases winning convictions on all, getting the death penalty on two. Michael Kane was no average prosecutor. He was one tough cookie and Mulligan would have his hands full.

By mid-January David Johnson had been sworn into office and Mike Kane was in Idaho Falls preparing the case. He received Tom's elaborate set of files and the Sheriff's Office turned over more boxes of jumbled files containing everything accumulated in three years of investigation. If that alone didn't appear overwhelming, Mike still had to review mountains of court records from both Idaho and Wyoming as well as the stacks of files from Jackson. He'd have to talk to case investigators, witnesses, and the victim's families. Mike would be a busy man playing catch up. The trial was scheduled for just a little over a month away, the defense was well into their pre-trial preparations and Kane was just beginning to learn about a man whose premeditation, greed and utter disregard for human life was absolutely horrifying.

In late January 1993, Kane was successful in having the trial date set to March 2, based on the exceptional circumstances surrounding the prosecutor's office even though Gray's attorneys argued that his right to a speedy trial would be infringed upon. When this was over, it would be one of the most costly cases in terms of man hours in the history of Bonneville County, and if Bill had been upset over his wife "unraveling" the few dollars she was "stealing" from him, he must have been sickened over the mounting cost of his own defense.

But Mulligan was earning his money. He prevailed when he argued that Gray's rights were violated when he was placed in a position of having to give his deposition in a civil matter which he felt was directly related, and the basis for which Gray was even indicted. He vehemently charged it was a tactical maneuver to enable the state to gain advance information for the criminal case. To eliminate any possibility of violation of Gray's right to due process related to this charge, Judge Wood ruled that certain items discovered in the civil depositions, that had not been discovered through other means and/or in prior interviews, would not be admissible at trial.

The jury would never know that Bill professed to have gambled away all the proceeds of the pawnshop sale, all $208,000. They would not learn of his flight to avoid prosecution and subsequent arrest in Albuquerque. They would not know he used assumed names to avoid the authorities or of the items found in the motor home, the large amount of cash or the illegal drugs. As far as the jury was concerned, the DUI arrest in Jackson, Bill being found in front of his daughter's house late at night with a loaded gun or his refusal to take a lie detector test never happened. The prosecution could not talk about Gray's gun collection and his fondness for guns, or that he regularly had possession of loaded firearms in his home, car and on his person. No one could mention Gray's conspiracy to steal a backhoe, theft of a snowmobile, bringing a tape recorder to his interviews, undue interest in the time of the women's deaths or any statements made by Gray concerning the arson at the pawnshop.

All evidence surrounding the incident of the Pizza Hut employee hanging advertising on his door of which Bill said he better stop or he might "get blown away," his statement about taking a baseball bat to Leroy Leavitt and "breaking every bone in his body" and any and all disparaging statements made by Bill, as told by Leavitt, as referring to his wife as a "dumb fucking cunt," were suppressed. The defense was also successful in getting Jo Ann's testimony that "Bill carried a gun," that he was "capable of killing" and "displaying a gun to Betty" withheld, but her testimony that Betty feared him would stay.

Chipping away statement by statement, incident by incident, fact by fact, would tend to make one wonder what would be left to try Gray on. But the state had willingly agreed not to use several of these items. Mike Kane was confident of their case and was at ease in allowing suppression of some of the defense's demands, but not all. The prosecution would show photographs of the bodies to the jury, use Gray's statements, "This bracelet will hang me," and "If I only knew." They could show that the defendant bought and sold guns and therefore had access to them, reloaded 9mm ammunition, and would present all evidence surrounding the Travelall even though the defense fought bitterly to keep this information from the jury.

Mulligan maintained in newspaper accounts since Bill's arrest, that the investigators overlooked two other possible suspects, C. J. Walker and Howard Wilson. Wilson had motive caused by Reeda's undue pressure on him to leave his wife as indicated on Reeda's answering machine tapes, and Walker's threats against Reeda had been known by several people. If he could present these possibilities to the jurors he might cast a shadow of a doubt that would be just enough to free his client. Mulligan would have opportunity to go after Wilson when he took the stand but the defense also wanted the jury to hear about Walker. Reeda had told her children, her boyfriend Howard Wilson, and her employer's wife Vada Roberts, that she was frightened of him, he threatened to kill her and if anything happened to her, he should be investigated.

Radin argued for the opportunity to question the Roundy children on this subject and put Roberts on the stand. But the jury would never know about C. J. Walker and his threats to kill Reeda. Determining what these witnesses would say would be hearsay, the defense would not be allowed to ask any questions concerning Walker. Backing Judge Wood's decision was the unshakeable alibi and passing of the polygraph test which had eliminated Walker as a suspect.

Patti Donbeck who had been jogging in the vicinity of the EIRMC hospital the morning of July 24, 1989, had contacted the Sheriff's Department in response to their public request for information from anyone seeing a man on a bike near the hospital that morning. Patti said she saw a man on a bike around 6:45 a.m. Her description was vague but had similar characteristics to those of Bill Gray. When shown a photo lineup containing Gray's picture she picked him out as the man she saw on the bike, then after thinking it over decided she could only say Gray's picture resembled the man she saw.

Patti could not have seen Bill Gray on a bike in Idaho Falls at that time of the morning. Bill was in Jackson having blood drawn at 8:30 a.m. After the murders he would certainly have been en route back to Jackson or already home by 6:45 a.m. Because of the time frame, and her uncertain identification, detectives had taken the position it was not Bill Gray who Patti observed that morning. They would not dismiss her claim she had observed a bike and rider, only that it could not have been Gray. There could have been numerous bicyclists out at that hour on a warm July morning.

The defense however, was very interested in Patti's story. Mulligan wanted to show there had been a bicyclist who fit Gray's description close to the hospital at 6:45 a.m., a time when it could not have been Gray and therefore it could be highly probable the security guard encountered and identified this look-a-like. At the least, it would be cause to have a jury aware there was another person out there that could have been mistaken for Gray.

Patti could also lend to the defense's contention that the police pressured her into identifying Gray from the photo lineup before they found out the time frame wasn't conforming to their belief. If Patti had been pressured by the authorities, might not Mackley and Patrolman Black have been subjected to the same pressure?

But Patti had moved to Tennessee since Gray's arrest. If

Mulligan was to have a jury hear her testimony, he would have to go to Tennessee to get it. If her testimony was presented to the jury by video tape the prosecution must have the right of cross examination and therefore both Mulligan and David Johnson flew to Tennessee to take Patti's statement.

This was a high profile case for Bonneville County. The media had been reporting every detail. When the judge sealed the records the flow of information was curtailed to a trickle. When the media couldn't find out what they wanted to know, they tried the family, lawyers and investigators, but they could not, and would not talk, the gag order imposed by Judge Wood was still valid. The local newspaper had their attorney file a motion to unseal all the records. The judge would not budge, but the defense was adamant that enough publicity had already been made available to the public, prior to the gag order, to warrant a change of venue.

The double homicide and the civil suit had been in the papers for almost four years. Gray's children made various statements to the media including that "he always carried a gun" and "would not be taken alive," the defense argued. Particularly worrisome to the defense was the memorial by Jo Ann which they accused, was nothing more than a paid advertisement that she put in the *Post Register* for no other reason than to inflame the public.

"She knew the sensitivity of pre-trial publicity, but did it anyway. All of this would gravely impair the partiality of prospective jurors," Radin claimed.

Backing his statements, the defense introduced sworn

affidavits from two Idaho attorneys who said the case had generated more publicity than any other, except one, over the last 20 years. After careful considerations, Judge Wood wrote that he did not believe a fair and impartial jury could not be found in Bonneville County. He agreed the Gray case had generated a large amount of media coverage but it had been spread out over a period of almost four years, had been factual with the exception of some statements made by Jo Ann and Saralyn, and that any prejudice resulting from these statements will have dissipated by the time of trial. Wood further maintained that even though the media reported Gray would not be taken alive, they also reported Gray's capture was without incident and therefore should offset the inflammatory remark made by Saralyn Hoffman.

Although the judge denied the defense's motion, he did develop a backup plan in the event an impartial jury could not be found. The court would make advance arrangements for a backup jury to be called in a county where there had been little or no publicity. In the event they were needed, they would be brought to Idaho Falls, sequestered and would hear the case.

Bill Gray's attorneys, Judge Wood and two totally different sets of prosecution teams had been litigating the criminal case for nearly a year. Now both sides were stepping up their discovery processes, taking depositions of listed witnesses and compelling one another to disclose all pertinent records.

On February 12, this time waiving Gray's rights to a speedy trial, the defense requested another trial date extension. Attorney John Radin asked the court for the trial date to be rescheduled citing the prosecution's lack of providing materials requested by the defense through discovery. For the fourth time the trial date was extended. Gray was now scheduled to face a jury of his peers on May 11, 1993.

The Hales family a few months before the Grays moved to Jackson. (L-R back) Joe, Dorothy and Dan. (L-R front) JoAnn and Betty.

Betty and Bill going to a school dance.

(L-R) Betty, Dan and JoAnn on Betty's
graduation day from high school.

Bill and Betty getting married in Las Vegas,
June 13, 1960.

One of Betty's hand-decorated cakes.

Bill and Betty at their pawnshop prior to the fire.

Bill next to his recliner, several years before the killings.

(L-R) Betty and JoAnn during Betty's last California trip, four months before her death.

William Gray is escorted by a Bonneville County, Idaho, deputy to a pre-trial hearing.

A clipping from the *Post Register*.

(L-R) David Johnson, newly elected Bonneville County Prosecuting Attorney, Jo Ann Buccola, Tom Moss, Bingham County Prosecuting Attorney in Blackfoot, Idaho and Saralyn.

(L-R) Detective Victor Rodriguez; Rick Le'Gall, Boise Attorney General Detective; John Kotrason, Idaho State Investigator; and Michael Kane, Chief Prosecutor, Attorney General's Office, Boise, Idaho.

A gathering of the prosecution team and witnesses during a court break, Prosecutor Michael Kane, standing.

The home where Reeda and Betty were killed.

(L-R) Janice Roby, Saralyn, DeeDee Batson and Tom Moss.

(L-R) Saralyn, Prosecuting Attorney David Johnson, JoAnn and Jeff.

(L-R) Detective Victor Rodriguez and Lieutenant Dave Foster from Jackson Police Department.

(L-R) Steve Mackley, the security guard at the hospital who saw Bill put the Travel-all and Albert Thompson, an investigation detective.

Richard Mulligan, Jackson, Wyoming, Bill Gray's attorney, 2011.

The Travelall Bill bought and drove to Idaho Falls.

Jo Ann's gate was decorated in celebration when she returned home after the sentencing, "Jo Ann, Job Well Done!"

5

INNOCENT UNTIL PROVEN GUILTY

J ust one, just one is all I need, he must have been thinking as he scanned the faces of the 84 men and women who were assembled in Courtroom IV. It was Tuesday May 11, 1993.

"Good morning ladies and gentleman. Welcome to District Court and jury duty this morning," began Judge Ted Wood. "We'll take up case number 92-1586, State of Idaho versus William L. Gray."

Two months short of four years since the deaths of Betty Lou Gray and Reeda LaRene Roundy, Bill Gray was staring intently, and somewhat curiously, at the men and women who would decide his fate. Everyone was in their places as the swearing in and questioning of the jury pool began. A now fully bearded Richard Mulligan and John Radin, who grew beards on purpose for this trial because their client was fully bearded, were ready for the defense, David Johnson and Michael Kane for the State of Idaho.

A no-nonsense Judge Wood sent the sheriff to arrest the four potential jurors who failed to answer roll call.

"Now, aren't the rest of you glad you came in today?" he asked the rest of the assembly, reinforcing the seriousness of being called for jury duty.

In the first step of the elimination process several jurors were excused when they said that they did not believe in the death penalty. Another volunteered he'd been privy to information, otherwise unpublished, about Gray and his family.

"If you were sitting in Mr. Gray's position, knowing what you know or having heard what you heard about this case, would you feel comfortable with a juror of your frame of mind and with the knowledge that you have on your jury?" asked Judge Wood.

"No" was the reply.

"Excused," said the judge.

Having previously decided to assign jurors a number as they turned in their questionnaires to satisfy the random selection process as required by law, Judge Wood was immediately met with resistance from the defense.

"By assigning the numbers starting with the number one to the individuals as they complete their questionnaires, the first jurors we are going to get, and most likely the jurors who will sit on this case, will be those who are able to successfully complete the questionnaire in the quickest time," argued John Radin. This would lend itself to jurors who are perhaps more educated or certainly more adept at completing forms than other jurors. That would potentially compose a jury that is not representative of Mr. Gray's peers," he said.

Radin went on to offer another formula for numbering the jury pool.

Essentially, unconcerned how the court arrived at a numbering process, the whole of what was just implied did not escape Prosecutor Mike Kane.

"I'll just be brief Your Honor. I didn't know the defendant has a constitutional right to an undereducated jury."

The smoothness for which Kane delivered this statement was just the first glimpse of a man whose presence in the courtroom seemed to command respect and trust. Unlike those who demand attention from a loud and forceful approach or by the quantity of their words, Michael Kane was soft spoken, reserved and to the point. So much so, that when a prospective juror fired back all in one breath, "Is this during the day I'm expected to be here and participate? ... Is it all day and all night? ... How many hours do I put into this? ... Will I have time to take care of my personal life?" Kane simply answered, "We allow you to sleep," which brought slight smiles and served to break the somber tension in the room.

But the business at hand was one of grave importance to both sides. Appearance and relationships had to be established with everyone they questioned because 12 of these good people would ultimately end up on the jury.

It wasn't until they were finished with the second prospective juror that Gray's attorney asked for a blanket for his freezing client.

"We can turn up the heat, Your Honor," Mike Kane offered, "I'd rather see the rest of us a little too warm than these jurors perceiving the defendant is ill."

The Judge asked the elder Grays to bring their son a sweater and jury selection continued.

The defense lawyers probed the backgrounds of prospective jurors asking if they had ever been accused of something they hadn't done, or told they were seen someplace they hadn't been. Mulligan or Radin asked if they understood that the state must prove Gray guilty beyond a reasonable doubt.

"You might think it sounds pretty suspicious, maybe he did

it, even probably he did it, but if it's not proved beyond a reasonable doubt would you have any problem coming back and delivering a verdict of not guilty?"

One by one for the next three days prospective jurors were questioned. Some were easily excused, such as the 81-year-old woman who felt she could not serve because she had to take care of her 87-year-old husband, and the gentleman who had a sleeping disorder and if chosen, guaranteed he could not stay awake during the proceedings. The laborious process was aimed at determining the state of mind of prospective jurors, and whether there was something in their background that might make them empathize more with one side or the other. Some jurors were questioned for as long as 30 minutes.

Eighty-one out of 82 prospective jurors admitted knowing something about the case. All of them promised they could be fair, impartial and judge the defendant on the evidence rather than any preconceived belief they may have had. In agreement with both the defense and the state, Judge Wood stopped jury selection when 38 persons were passed. Each side had 12 peremptory challenges which could be used to excuse anyone without explanation. Assuming each side used all 12, the remaining 14 would be Bill Gray's jury of 12 and two alternates.

By 2 p.m. on Friday afternoon, five women and seven men were assembled in Courtroom IV ready to hear jury instructions. There were three engineers, radio news reporter, housewife, money lender, bank teller, store manager, communications programmer, management counselor, retired West Point graduate and a hunter education instructor.

Bill Gray needed only one of these jurors on his side. The state needed all 12. The law weighs heavily on the side of the accused. The fact alone that a guilty vote might cost Gray his life, regardless of the probability that he killed the two women, would be a tremendous burden on these jurors' consciences. Either way, they would have to live with their decision the rest of their lives.

"A defendant in a criminal action is presumed to be innocent. This presumption places upon the state the burden of proving the defendant guilty beyond a reasonable doubt. Reasonable doubt is not mere possible doubt, because everything relating to human affairs is open to some possible or imaginary doubt. It is the state of the case which, after the entire comparison and consideration of all the evidence, leaves the minds of the jurors in that condition that they cannot say that they feel an abiding conviction, to a moral certainty, of the truth of the charge," recited Judge Wood.

"The law requires your decision be made solely upon the evidence before you. Neither sympathy nor prejudice should influence you in your deliberations. Faithful performance by you of these duties is vital to the administration of justice.

"If I sustain an objection to a question, the witness may not answer the question. Do not attempt to guess what the answer might have been. Similarly, if I tell you not to consider a particular statement, you should put it out of your mind and not refer to it or rely on it in your later deliberations."

Juries are always instructed to listen to everything that is being said, but then to suddenly forget it, take it out of their minds, tell themselves they didn't hear what was just said if instructed to do so. Yet, human nature as it is, tends to seek out and retain more intensely that which is forbidden or made a point of.

The instructions took a total of 42 minutes covering the judge's duties in conducting the trial and witness testimony. The jury was forbidden to speak to any of the attorneys, visit any of the sites mentioned in the trial, talk to anyone about the case including other members of the jury and to read or watch any news pertaining to the trial.

"There is no magic formula by which you may evaluate testimony. You bring with you to this courtroom all of the experience and background of your lives. In your everyday affairs you determine for yourselves whom you believe, what you believe and how much weight you attach to what you are told."

It was a beautiful spring day in Idaho Falls. The morning air was fresh and clean, the sky pale blue and sunny with the exception of just a few puffy white clouds strolling lazily over the valley. It was the kind of day made for getting outside, working in the yard, washing the car, starting a summer tan. It was Monday, May 17, 1993.

The courtroom was small by some standards seating approximately 60 spectators comfortably, or more, by sliding closer together on the oak benches. Reporters from the *Idaho Falls Post Register* and *Jackson Hole Guide's* Joy Ufford were seated intermingled with a handful of interested trial watchers. There to represent Reeda Roundy were her sister Evelyn and two nieces who had driven over 350 miles to attend the trial. Reeda's first husband and father of her three children was there in support of his family. Taking as much time as possible from their daily responsibilities, the Roundy family would come and go as the trial progressed.

Reeda's children, Clayton, Paul and Ruth Ann would be testifying in the trial and could not join their father and step-mother in the courtroom. Saralyn, Jeff, Kim and Jo Ann were also scheduled witnesses and were forbidden to be present in court. Betty Gray's good friend and past neighbor DeeDee Batson, Rhonda Roby (Janis' daughter), and Jo Ann's traveling companion and roommate from California, Sandi, sat in the front row every day of the trial becoming the eyes and ears of the family members who could not be present.

Everyone noticed the tiny, impeccably dressed and groomed, grey-haired mother of Bill Gray sitting in the spectators' seats behind her son. Most of the time she sat alone, almost like stone, displaying no emotion of any kind. Occasionally she was joined by Richard Mulligan's wife. William senior would be testifying and was also banned from the proceedings, thus she represented Bill Gray's sole, unyielding support.

The courtroom had a warm, serene feeling derived from the carpeting and lightly stained oak prevalent throughout the room. But the large seal of the State of Idaho 7th District Court mounted on the back wall above the judge's bench, kept in perspective that this was a place of business, serious business. There would be tears and laughter, arguing and frustration, and there would be a judge who would control his courtroom, keeping the proceedings lawful and professional.

A half wall divided the spectator seating from the rest of the room. The defense table was on the far left, the prosecutor's table was left center of the room. The jury seats, on the right side, elevated higher than anything else in the room except the judge's bench, were comfortable padded arm chairs that swiveled and tilted.

The witness box also elevated, was between the judge and the jury. Behind and left of the judge's bench was a door through which the judge and the jury would enter and leave the courtroom. The defendant used a door behind the defense table which led to a prisoner holding room and another small room where physical evidence was kept under lock and key.

In charge of crowd control, the bailiff stationed at the entrance checked packages and purses of spectators as they entered. It was highly unlikely anyone would attempt to bring a weapon into court but Judge Wood would take no chances. Mulligan succeeded in getting the two armed officers who normally sat directly behind Gray to be backed off. One would sit behind and to the left, the other would sit in the front row of the spectators' seats. The house arrest monitoring device was removed from Gray's leg. The main show was about to begin and Mulligan wanted the first act to open with an untainted Boy Scout impression of his client.

Richard Mulligan cautioned the jury not to accuse the first suspect they found like the state did. There was a valid reason, regardless of how incredible it seemed, for everything Bill Gray did or did not do. Ron Mitchell was real, and Gray had good reason to move the Travelall considering the frame of mind of Mitchell. He lied about the Travelall because he knew he was a suspect and he was scared.

Attempting to discredit the forthcoming testimony of witnesses, Mulligan stressed that Gray's children were only in this for the money, attempting to sacrifice their own father and fabricate evidence toward that end. Jo Ann Buccola never liked Bill Gray and blamed him for something he didn't do. The detectives were in constant contact with the family. And the family, in their haste to incriminate their father and brother-in-law, told the detectives things that were not true. Steven Mackley identified the wrong man. The man he saw in the hospital parking lot did not have a beard.

Continuing, Mulligan contended the insurance company made a mistake in naming the beneficiary of Betty's $250,000 life insurance policy. It should have been in the name of the bank to cover a loan and not in Bill Gray's name. But when the policy came, Bill put it away without looking at it, therefore it was overlooked and never corrected. Bill was a sick man, so sick it would have been impossible for him to ride a bike 7.2 miles.

"He carries a pill box that looks like a tackle box," Mulligan told the intently listening jury.

Mulligan went on to suggest that although the other suspects, specifically Howard Wilson and Leroy Leavitt, had motives to kill, and even though they seemed to have good alibis for the time of the killings, they would not have had to actually pull the trigger to have been responsible for these crimes. He promised the jury they would hear from Bill Gray himself. He would take the stand and tell them where he was when his wife was killed. Mulligan addressed openly what the jurors were going to hear from the prosecution, then attempted to defuse each item piece by piece.

"In conclusion, I leave you with this thought. Mere suspicion does not support a finding of guilty. The mere possibility that the defendant could have done it does not support a finding of guilty. Only evidence which proves that the defendant committed the crimes alleged beyond a reasonable doubt can support a finding of guilty. The evidence cannot, and does not, support such a finding."

Opening statements went well into the noon hour. Michael Kane for the state, briefly told the story of a marriage on the rocks, money, murder and evidence.

Prosecutors Michael Kane and David Johnson were prepared to methodically, step by step, lead the jury through a strange and twisted story. The witnesses were chosen in precise order to lay the foundation of the state's case.

The first witness, Reeda's daughter Ruth Ann, talked about the loving and kind person her mother was, about her mother's divorces, her work, her love for the outdoors and how she cared for stray animals. The state introduced an 8 x 10 picture of a smiling Reeda, passing it through the jury. Now they had a face to the name of a person who vibrantly lived and violently died.

Jeffrey Gray would have preferred to be anywhere in the world but on the witness stand. He'd wanted nothing to do with the whole thing but knew he had a duty to his mother to be there. It was hard for him to look at his father. This was the man he once loved so very much. Jeff would never understand how this extreme cruel side could have emerged from within his father who had always been so tuned in to his kids, a great companion who was always there. Even though he knew the truth, he still had periods of denial. It was almost more than he could bear imagining his father standing over his sleeping mother and deliberately shooting her in the back of her head. It was so vicious, it was so cruel ... it was so final.

When Bill saw his son he momentarily showed emotion of watery eyes then slipped back into that piercing stare. Jeff had seen that stare before and he knew it was one of pure anger. It was a standoff. Neither would ever forgive the other. Each had his own burdens to bear. Each had to live with the consequences of his actions.

His voice was shaky in the beginning, gaining more strength with time. He established for the jury how familiar and proficient his dad was with firearms, and yes, his dad reloaded ammunition and had access to 9mm weapons. Discrediting the defense's contention that Gray's health was so poor he could not have ridden the bike to Reeda's house, Jeff said his father was physically able to go hunting on four-wheelers over rough terrain using his legs to help maneuver the machine through the forest and up steep hills.

Led expertly by Mike Kane, Jeff went through the events that happened after his mother's death, the fiasco at the mortuary, the fear instilled by his father that someone was out to kill the whole family, Jeff's later realization that his father must have done it, the civil suit and his memory of his mother.

"My mother had to kind of pick up the pieces after my father got sick. It was more or less expected of her to pick up the slack, depending on how my father was feeling from day to day. She had her own business as a cake decorator. I remember times when she would get up early in the morning and start baking her cakes, and then come 10 o'clock she would go down and open the store and work the store until 5:30 at which time she would come home and continue with her own things she normally had to take care of as well as cooking dinner, cleaning, cleaning up after dinner, doing dishes, cleaning house, doing the laundry and then would begin working on her cakes again later in the evening."

"What would your dad be doing all this time?" asked Kane.

"Usually he would be reclining back in his recliner with his legs up watching television."

"Are you prepared to tell us a little bit about your mother?"

"I'll try. She was a very loving and caring person ..." Jeff managed to say before breaking down and reaching for a tissue.

"She loved life. She enjoyed laughing and being with others and doing things with others, other couples as couples, going to a movie or dinner, to the Elks Club dancing. In her spare time she enjoyed watching old movies." When shown a large picture of a happy smiling woman ... "That's Mom" he said in a barely audible cracking voice. Once again, the jury viewed a photograph of a woman in the prime of her life, now dead and lost to her family and friends forever.

"Jeff," Mike Kane said, "This has gone on for four years now, and a lot of things have happened. Can you give the jury some idea of how you feel about your dad, now as you sit here?"

"I feel that my father has already been removed from my life. When he killed my mother, he had not only taken her away from me, but he had taken himself as well. And when I remember my father, I do not want to remember the bad things. I want to remember the good things. He was a man I looked up to and I regarded and loved very much, and I do not want to remember him for the person he turned out to be since July of '89. As far as I'm concerned, my father is just as dead as my mother, but his loving memory I'll keep in charge forever. And this is just something that ... the only way that I've been able to deal with things in my own mind, so I can continue with my life and my family, and so I have not gone insane over all this."

Most every female in the spectators' seats had tears in their eyes, the men were quiet and somber. Bill Gray was seen wiping tears and the eyes of jurors were clouded and emotional. This was the first glimpse of the shattered remnants of a once loving family utterly destroyed. Now sobbing, Jeff was given time to compose himself before cross examination by the defense.

Richard Mulligan would start out easy on Jeff. The last thing he wanted to do was turn the jury off by being too rough on him right after that emotional finale. Mulligan took Jeff into how much he'd loved and respected his father in previous years, how they'd enjoyed hunting and fishing together and how much his father had done for his family. Jeff said his father always treated his mother well, at least in Jeff's presence. Jeff answered questions about the pawnshop business, how sick his dad had been and how close he came to dying when his kidney started to fail.

Mulligan was able to bring out that Jeff, as well as Saralyn, owned guns and Jeff used to have a 9mm handgun. Mulligan tried to get Jeff to say his father learned for the first time about his mother's affair the day after her death, however Jeff would say only that he didn't know that for a fact, only that it was what his dad told him.

Wanting the jury to know just how much money was involved in the civil suit, the actual amount Jeff and Saralyn received from their father, Mulligan asked Jeff, "As a result of the civil suit you and your sister received a total of $520,000. Isn't that correct?"

A quick minded Jeffrey Gray replied, "It was discussed earlier that no information be divulged about the civil suit, which you are aware of, it was at your insistence, as well as my fathers. I don't feel that I can answer that."

Judge Wood immediately broke for recess. Once the jury was out of the room, the judge confronted Mulligan.

"Mr. Mulligan, you're asking this witness to breach the confidentiality agreement?"

But it was much more important to Bill Gray's cause to have the jury thinking Saralyn and Jeff went after their dad for money. When the civil suit was settled with the nondisclosure terms, neither Mulligan, nor Bill, thought criminal charges would be filed. Now Mulligan needed to use this as a tool to help his client.

When Jeff left the stand he didn't look at his dad. He knew he would either see hatred or pain and he didn't want either impression left on his mind. This was not a tremendous victory for him as some might have thought, this was not a "chalk one up for us and the prosecution" feeling. This was a beaten young man who had just finished airing his family's dirty laundry and all he wanted now was to get out of there and be left alone.

For four years Jo Ann Buccola had been living this case. She'd been strong and forceful, armed and ready to speak for her sister. But when she was called to the stand her legs turned to jelly. She thought the pills she had taken earlier to calm her down weren't doing their job. For a moment she even forgot what she was going to tell this jury, but Michael Kane would take her through the questioning making sure she told the jury what they could hear and stopping her if she went beyond. Placing her at ease with familiar questions about herself and her family, he then asked her to tell about Betty's early life, Betty's marriage, sibling closeness.

The jury learned about a despondent Betty Gray who had too much responsibility, a sometimes sick, and a sometimes not so sick husband, how unhappy she was in her marriage and finally her affair, discovered love notes, collect phone calls, keeping their divorce secret and all the events leading up to Betty's death. When she related the nightmare at the mortuary she was talking so fast she was almost hyperventilating.

"Jo Ann," Kane interrupted. "Take a deep breath and slow down a little." But it was her day, it was her last shot. It was so important for Jo Ann to make this jury understand that all the little things that happened added up to only one conclusion. Nothing else made any sense.

As Jo Ann held two bracelets, a heart-shaped and a chain style that had been taken from Betty's purse, she testified Betty had not been wearing either one of them when she was in California just a few months before her death. It would be left to the jury to decide if Betty wore it often enough to justify Bill's stating he knew she had it on because she always wore it, or did he see the bracelet on her wrist when he killed her?

Jo Ann returned the next morning to be questioned about her role in the civil suit. She finished her direct examination leaving the jury with the knowledge that the civil suit was brought for the purpose of forcing the previous prosecutor to look more closely at the evidence. She assured them she had gained nothing financially from the lawsuit. That certainly was not the force behind her persistence. Her motive was to have Bill Gray exactly where he was right now, afraid for his life just as her sister had been. Seeing Bill for the first time since she'd been in Jackson right after Betty's death, contributed to her early nervousness. But as his penetrating eyes flashed danger signs she only got stronger.

"You intimidated my sister all her life," she thought, "You will not do the same to me now."

Just as she did not let Bill get to her, she would not make life easy for Mulligan either. There was seldom a yes or no answer to any of his questions and she used her tone of voice as deftly as her interrogator did.

"All that we have with regards to all those conversations with Betty is your word. Isn't that true?" Mulligan said, his words dripping with sarcasm.

"Absolutely," Jo Ann said firmly and with total conviction.

"And with regard to the telephone conversations that you've told us about, as far as you know, the only people that were involved in those telephone conversations were you and Betty. Isn't that true?"

"Correct, because she made sure Bill was never around because he always listened when Betty and I had phone conversations."

"How do you know he was listening?"

"Because all of a sudden my sister would find out, and she would say, 'Bill, why don't you say something?' She told me she was never allowed to have a conversation with me in the 11 years that they lived there unless he was out of the house."

Now, through his own attorney, the jury learns that Bill is sneaky and has no respect for his wife's privacy. With the exception of a couple of pot shots at Jo Ann and Saralyn's early problems, Mulligan scored few points for his client but the truth is hard to suppress or disguise.

He managed to establish her awareness of Bill's failing health, but the testimony leaned more toward sympathy for Betty than it did for Bill. Mulligan may have been better served to keep the cross shorter. There'd been several objections raised, causing some disagreement among the attorneys. The jury had been sent out of the room twice, and Jo Ann broke down when she was asked about the last time she talked to her sister. None of these were very favorable to the defense. But then, the state's witnesses are not intended to be favorable to the defense.

"She wore the heart-shaped bracelet, oh, two, three times a week," Janis Roby said as she held the two bracelets in her hand.

"Not every day ... not all the time, no," Betty's best friend testified. Yes, she knew about Betty's affair and she was afraid for her just as Jo Ann had been. Now on the witness stand she educated the jury about a determined, but very nervous Betty Gray.

"I saw her hide her purse in the washing machine before we went out and walked. She hid it because she thought Bill might go through it."

Janis was revealing all the events that had been going on before and after Betty's death. Bill feigned anger, throwing a pen across the table when she told him about Roy Leavitt.

"Well to me, it was ... he wasn't angry when he threw the pen. He was trying to be angry, but it was, like I say, he got more angry at Betty and I when we went to have a cup of tea, when I would go get her from the pawnshop than he was that day he found out about Roy."

Bill had confronted her wanting to know where the money was. "Bill, I don't know what you're talking about. What money?" He also wanted to know what was in the boxes. "I didn't have the boxes, but it seemed very important to him to get them back."

A few days later Bill called Janis wanting to know if she knew anything about some silver. "He said Betty had asked for the silver after the divorce was final, and I assumed it was silver coins. He said it was worth 48,000 goddamn dollars."

No, he had never mentioned anything to her about the state of the investigation or suspects or anything like that. "What he really wanted to know about was some kitchen knives that were missing."

On cross examination, Mulligan spent most of his time with Janis bringing out as many sordid events about Betty's adultery as he could. He was also able to get her to say that she never saw Bill mean with Betty and he had been generous at times buying her jewelry and giving her money.

Janis told detectives in her early interviews, of Bill showing emotion after he found out about the murders. Mulligan wanted the jury to hear this from her but she fought back just as Jo Ann had. "Yes," she said, "but it was all an act. I didn't see him cry. I saw him make noises." No, she did not see any tears in his eyes.

"And do you recall telling Officer Cowden that Betty got diamonds and gold and she got anything she wanted. Do you remember saying that to him?"

"Yes," a somber Janis said, "Betty got lots of material things."

Kim Gray went through the phone call from her father-in-law notifying Jeff of his mother's death, Bill's attitude the week after Betty's death and how scared she became because of the things he was saying and doing. Seeing people in the yard, the house being bugged and turning on the water or going out to the patio to talk were prevalent in her mind. Kane led her through each day's events until she went back to Portland leaving Jeff to stay and help his dad.

She told of her viewing Betty at the mortuary and Bill telling her not to tell anyone what she saw. She said eventually almost everyone had asked her what she saw, everyone except Bill. which tends to confirm he had pulled the covers back when he went into the viewing room after Kim had verified it was Betty. The state however, was suggesting to the jury that Bill already knew what Betty looked like because he was there when she died.

Mulligan chipped away at Kim's testimony which was more a confirmation of previous testimony and future witnesses than earth shattering damage to his client. She said she saw Bill cry on Tuesday night and again on Wednesday after he found out about Roy Leavitt. He did not cry at the memorial services or any time thereafter that Kim witnessed.

Once again the amount of money received in the civil suit was brought up and caused objections from the state.

"She can answer my question, Judge. My client has authorized me to waive the nondisclosure agreement," Mulligan argued. The judge overruled the state's objection. Mulligan continued, "Did your husband ever discuss with you the amount of money he received in the form of a settlement?"

Quick minded and not about to answer this question without a fight, Kim directed her question to the judge.

"Do I have to discuss anything that my husband and I have discussed in confidence as husband and wife?"

"Yes, unless there is an objection," advised Judge Wood.

"Well in that case," Kane said, "I'll go ahead and pose an objection on the marital privilege."

Kim would not have to answer any more questions regarding the financial gain of the civil suit.

Mulligan wanted the mortuary viewing situation cleared up for the jury. To do that he needed to give another reason why Bill did not want the family, and especially Jeff, to know what condition Betty's body was in. Kim was forced to give the details of the viewing. Betty's thoracic cavity had not been sutured closed from the autopsy. The vital organs had been placed in a sack and the sack was placed in the cavity. But the funeral director had only advised Kim of this, she did not see this for herself, as Betty was in a body bag zipped up to her shoulders.

Obviously visible was the cut around the hairline where the skin had been pulled back to examine the head wounds, and then replaced so as not to disfigure her face any more than necessary. The mortician had pointed out to Kim the entry and exit wounds of the bullet that killed her.

"And would it be fair for me to assume that you would agree with the mortician that it wasn't something for Jeff or Saralyn or Bill to see?" pressed Mulligan.

"No," Kim replied, "I thought they could have seen her."

She couldn't look at her father as she passed the defense table on her way to the clerk for swearing in of the oath, but when Saralyn turned and sat in the witness chair, momentarily her eyes met her father's, causing her a slight uneasiness. Unlike Jo Ann, she was not so nervous about testifying in front of all these people, she was nervous about encountering her father face to face and having to tell what she knew and believed to be true. The accused has the right to confront his accuser. Saralyn would be testifying for the next two days under the constant intense scrutiny of her father's glaring eyes.

Skillfully Kane got her attention, settling her down with easy personal questions leading to life as it was in the Gray household a few years before her mother died. Then he took her to the reason she was there.

Yes, because of her father's having to undergo home dialysis she personally observed wet wipes and latex surgical gloves in their home. Her dad was still carrying around and using the same wet wipes in July of 1989. Saralyn told the jury about knobby soled shoes she saw her dad wearing, Mountain Dew pop, her dad's favorite drink, his habit of removing the pull top from the can. She knew nothing about her parents pending divorce even though she and her dad were extremely close. So close in fact, she was really surprised he hadn't told her about the divorce. Her mother seemed withdrawn in the last months of her life. She wasn't her usual happy self, but Saralyn chalked it up to the stress with running the business and taking care of her father.

Guns were just part of their family. Her mother carried one in her purse all the time because her dad insisted. She and her brother learned to shoot and handle firearms but were not as proficient at taking them apart and fixing them as their dad was. She described a hard covered green book on how to change a semi-automatic weapon to an automatic weapon and how to make silencers, lying on the table by her dad's recliner. She'd seen her dad working out on his Nordic Track but couldn't recall what he tended to look like if he overdid it.

"I don't recall," she snapped, "because I don't recall him overdoing anything."

The spectators had been eager to hear Saralyn's testimony. The courtroom was almost full. Tom Moss made a point of being there in support of Saralyn. A few investigators who were not testifying later came to hear her testimony. Saralyn talked about being notified of her mother's death and demonstrated her father's reaction after she said she was going to tell her mom that very night about marrying Kent and a new grandchild.

"Well my father was sitting there with his hands in his lap, and he raised his hands up to his head, (demonstrated palms of both hands touching the forehead) and he goes, 'Oh, my God,' he said, 'If I had only known! I am so sorry! If I had only known!' and then he turned around and gave me a hug."

"Did it make any sense to you, what he was saying?" prompted Kane.

"No, because I told him, I said, 'Dad, it's not your fault. Don't be sorry. It's not your fault! I just wanted to tell you.'"

"What did your father talk about regarding the killing or the affair, if anything?"

"My brother and I had made it known that we would like to call the police to find out what was going on. He forbade my brother and me to call the police or be in contact with them. He said he would take care of it, and that he had called them and they were giving him the runaround. When my brother approached him again he said, 'I'll take care of it. It is my responsibility. I will do it.'"

In her presence, and she was with him a great deal that first week, he never attempted to call and find out either about suspects or about where her mother's body was.

Once again the jury heard about the fiasco at the mortuary and Bill's determination to get the jewelry back. She told about her fear that a bomb was planted in the car and tires that were fixed to cause an accident. She also told of the phone call her father made from a pay phone in Swan Valley.

"'Jack,' he says, 'this is Bill, I'm not in town right now, I'm in Idaho. I need to talk to you about the Travelall.' He says, 'We need to get our stories straight. They're trying to frame me.'"

Saralyn explained what her father wanted Jack to tell the police. Bill had Jack repeat the story back to him three times then he said, "Jack, I do not want you to call me at home. I do not want you to contact me in any way. I will contact you. Do you understand?"

"I didn't know what to think" Saralyn said. "I was a little curious ... well, I was pretty curious and I asked my father what that was all about. He told me, 'Honey, I'm sorry, but I can't really tell you right now but someday I will explain it to you.'"

She'd been very protective of her father in the first few months after her mother's death, but at the same time she did not understand why he wasn't cooperating with the police to try to clear his name and find out who really did it. He showed no interest whatever in who killed her mother, but extreme interest and revengeful anger about the affair.

"I was very protective over my father. I felt sorry for him because I felt my mother was withdrawing not only from him, but from the rest of the family. I felt that my father was trying harder than he ever had in the past, and so I was kind of like being the parent and him being the child. I was like nurturing him and trying to comfort him and I guess I was just very protective over him."

"Are those the bullets that you removed from your dad's house?" Kane asked as he handed her a box containing bullets.

"Yes," she answered, her voice cracking as she examined the box.

"That's good," Kane said. "We'll go ahead and put them back. Did you feel ...? You're obviously having trouble with this. Is that something that you felt pretty bad about?" Kane asked when Saralyn started getting quite emotional.

"Yes, because I was hoping that I wouldn't find something, and I could prove to the police that ... I was hoping that I could still cast some doubt. But at this time it was pretty much confirmed to me that my suspicions were more than just a little bit strong, they were pretty realistic."

"Saralyn, it's been a long time since this whole ordeal began for you, and you've had to sue your father, and come into court and testify at the grand jury. Now you've testified in a trial. Can you give the jury some idea of what your feelings for your father are?"

Quiet, taking a moment, trying to collect herself, she cried, "I miss my father. I miss my family. My mother has been taken from me, but my father is still here. And it's hard, knowing that he's here and I'm not able to maintain a relationship with him because I miss him."

Turning toward her father and looking directly at him, now sobbing ... "And I do still love you, Daddy. I do love you. I don't condone what you did and I try to understand."

Still sobbing as she stepped down from the witness stand, passing in front of her father, she looked him right in the eyes wanting desperately for him to understand.

"I do love you." she cried, "I do love you."

It was a moment even Bill Gray could not contend with. In a silent whisper he mouthed the words, "I love you, too." Visibly shaken, Bill Gray cried tears ... this time for real.

After recess it was a more composed and somewhat defiant

Saralyn that squared off with Richard Mulligan. His job was to convince the jury of Saralyn's unyielding belief and persistence in her father's innocence until she found out there was a lot of money to be gained. Electing to go for the money and sacrificing her father to do it, Mulligan accused her of fabricating stories statements, evidence and conspiracy with Detective Rodriguez. If the jury would believe, even slightly, that Saralyn had motive ... the motive of money, for what she was doing to her father, the defense could then portray Bill as the innocent victim ... the victim of a daughter's greed.

But Saralyn, every bit as strong-willed and determined as her father, stood her ground. She wavered very little from her previous testimony, statements or deposition. Mulligan asked a considerable amount of questions surrounding the civil suit and her essentially breaking and entering into her father's garage to steal the reloaded bullets that were sent to the FBI.

Displaying her knowledge of ammunition Saralyn corrected Mulligan that the 9mm reload jackets were brass, not copper. When she was young she reloaded ammunition with her father and was told by him never to use others reloads because you never knew how hot they might be loaded and it could be highly dangerous. Thus she remained firm that her father did not, never would, purchase reloaded ammunition for resale in the pawnshop.

Mulligan introduced into evidence a pair of tennis shoes taken from the Gray home during the search warrant. Saralyn testified it was definitely not the knobby soled pair she had seen her father wear before. Obviously, everything worn by her father that evening in July 1989 would never be found, but she could not say that. It would be up to the jury to make that determination after they heard all the other evidence yet to be presented.

Having scored few points for the defense Mulligan attacked Saralyn herself, bringing out that she had been married and divorced twice, having two children by two different fathers.

Questions were asked about her mother's weight loss, then leading to Saralyn's complaints to her father that her mother was picking at her about her weight. Diving into the derogatory remarks Saralyn made about her mother after her death caused an objection from Kane and the jury to be sent from the room. Protecting Saralyn from what Kane believed to be inflammatory, irrelevant and prejudicial, he did not want this line of questioning to lead to a smear campaign against Saralyn. Kane's objection would be overruled and Mulligan could continue a limited line of questioning.

"Mrs. Hoffman, you had made some derogatory remarks about your mother in the week after her death didn't you? Could you tell me what some of those remarks were, or all of them, if you remember?"

"Well, I don't remember exactly what I said, but I know that it was to the effect that I was very angry with her because I felt that if she wasn't having an affair, that she would still be living."

"Okay. Do you remember any other derogatory remarks that you may have made?"

"I was upset with her because I felt that my mother and I had always had a very close relationship, and I was hurt that she wasn't able to come to me and explain to me why she had been so withdrawn because ... she was told by my father not to discuss the separation with my brother and myself, or with anybody for that matter. And I was just hurt that she felt she couldn't come to me and explain why she was acting the way she was so that maybe I could understand and help comfort her and maybe things wouldn't have taken this course."

"And apparently, your remarks were sufficient to have your

aunt talk to you about them and ask you to stop making them. Isn't that true?"

"Yes."

"And I think you testified yesterday that your father also made some derogatory remarks. Isn't that true?"

"Yes."

"Mrs. Hoffman, isn't it fair to say that despite these remarks that you made, you still loved your mother, didn't you?"

"Yes."

Regardless of the nightmares Saralyn had already suffered over her earlier anger toward her mother after her death, this was a humbling admission for Saralyn. It was also a score for the defense for if Saralyn could say the things she did, while still loving her mother, conceivably so could her father.

Mulligan semi-effectively, was able to bring out that through all his research he could not find where Saralyn had ever mentioned the book on silencers, the trip to Cheyenne, knobby soled shoes, her father's going to look for her mother at the time of the camping trip, or many other items prior to her deposition for the civil suit. His intent was to prove Saralyn began to fabricate and bring damaging things into evidence only after she was suing her father for a large sum of money, only after it would be beneficial to her cause to dredge up all this incriminating evidence. But Saralyn fought back. Sometimes she couldn't remember exactly when, and to whom, she'd mentioned these things. Sometimes she agreed some things had not been brought out because she hadn't remembered them until later, and sometimes she flatly denied having not said them before.

"Isn't it a fact that you didn't tell anybody about the fact that your father had gone to look for your mother on the camping trip. Isn't that true?"

"It's possible, Mr. Mulligan, but it's been a long time ago."

Challenging her on her statements, intending to identify a conspiracy with Detective Rodriguez, Mulligan pushed her hard.

"Well, when he showed me the photographs he didn't say anything about the photographs as he was showing them to me. Once I finished looking at them, he asked me if there was anything in the photographs that stood out in my mind that might put my father at that place."

"He showed you some pictures of the Mountain Dew can. Isn't that true?"

"He showed me some pictures and the Mountain Dew can was in one of the photographs that he showed me."

"And you thought because there was a Mountain Dew can on Crowley Road, that perhaps this would link your father to the crime?"

"No, I did not."

"Didn't you make a statement to the effect that your father drank Mountain Dew?"

"No, I did not. What I said was the pull tab on the Mountain Dew can was missing, and it was ... my father had a habit of removing pull tabs from cans that he drank out of, because he used to save them for a dialysis treatment center in California. And when I saw the can, I noticed that the pull tab was missing, and I had made that comment at the time."

"Now when you talked about the Mountain Dew can in front of the grand jury, you didn't mention the pull tab did you?"

"I probably did."

"And when you talked to me in your deposition, did you mention the pull tab."

"I don't recall, Mr. Mulligan."

"Now Ms. Hoffman, a review of my notes indicates to me

that you never mentioned the Mountain Dew can before the grand jury. Is it possible that you did not mention the Mountain Dew can to the grand jury?"

"I believe that I did."

"And do you feel that you mentioned the Mountain Dew can at any time during your deposition?"

"I believe I did, but I wasn't focusing on the Mountain Dew can, Mr. Mulligan. I was focusing on the pull tab that was removed from the Mountain Dew can."

Saralyn's utter defiance led more to confusion than anything else. Mulligan could not rattle this defiant and determined young woman. At best, he could show the jury she was relentless in the pursuit of her father. But if Saralyn's only motive for condemning her father had been for the money she could have certainly relaxed her fiery testimony and attitude for the criminal trial because she had already received the money. But she did not. She glared back at Richard Mulligan just as intensely as the man with the beard sitting at the defense table glared at her.

Reeda's oldest son, Clayton, testified to his and his brother's encounter with Bill at their mother's home while they were packing her belongings. This testimony served to establish Bill was so greedy that his main concern, in the few days after his wife's death, was to recover small insignificant items Betty may have removed from the Gray home and items she might have purchased. He wanted them back. He left a list of what he was looking for.

"Mr. Roundy, I notice that some of these items on that list are less than $10. Does that kind of strike you as odd?"

"The whole discussion seemed a little bit odd about the material items in general. I mean, I was very upset, both my brother and I were hysterical at the time. It seemed like it was more of an issue on material items than there was on the actual murders, you know ... what had taken place there."

Clayton pointed out on a large diagram of the floor plan of the house, indicating how Bill went directly to Betty's room while Clayton and his brother followed. The brothers thought it strange that he should know exactly which room Betty died in. Both brothers were relieved when the sheriff's detectives showed up to take Bill for his blood test at the hospital.

John Radin would chip away at Clayton trying to cast a cloud over his mother. He worked at suggesting Reeda may have been a drinker solely because liquor bottles were found in her home. But Clayton said his mother was just a social drinker. Then Radin tried to slide in testimony surrounding C. J. Walker even though the judge had previously ruled there would be no reference to Walker admitted.

"In fact, had your mother expressed to you and your sister some concern about an individual whose name was given ... "

"Objection."

" ... to the police?"

The jury was removed from the room while the subject of C. J. Walker was rehashed ending in the judge upholding his prior ruling. This jury would not know about the man who told Reeda he was hired to kill her.

Had Bill Gray been in his mother's home before?

"Yes, as a matter of fact, the Thanksgiving before I was up there with my girlfriend. We had dinner, Thanksgiving dinner."

This was good information for the jury to hear and Radin would stretch it to Bill's sitting in the living room, but did not ask any direct questions that may have given Bill a reason to know which bedroom Betty was sleeping in the night she died.

Excused as a witness by both sides the judge informed

Clayton he could stay in the courtroom for the rest of the trial if he wanted to, but this had been enough for Clayton.

"I think I'll go home," he replied.

"We went fishing together. I taught her how to fly fish. She went to fly fishing school up in West Yellowstone which I started a number of years ago, and she went through that and was trying to improve her talents, so to speak," related Howard Wilson. "She wanted to know more about it, being as she was in the sporting goods business. She was a person who loved to hunt and fish. We fished quite a bit together on weekends and we would go on occasion out hunting. I'd been elk hunting with her. Black powder hunting, she wanted to get into that. She loved the outdoors."

They'd known each other in three different states over 15 years, but their relationship did not become physical until Reeda came to Idaho Falls in 1984. Reeda was the one suggesting they get married. They'd had so much in common, and he'd given it some serious thought even though he had been married to the same woman for 44 years. Wilson admitted he might have been less than truthful with Reeda. He was kind of playing both ends at his convenience. He really couldn't bring himself to leave his wife, yet he cared a great deal for Reeda too.

Wilson was absolutely shocked when he learned of her violent death, but was at home in the state of Washington the night of July 23. His daughter had already testified before this jury supporting his alibi and there were others who could be called if necessary.

Mike Kane only called this witness because he knew if he didn't, the defense would. The jury must know the prosecution had nothing to fear by the testimony of this witness. Kane knew there was little probative value in this witness towards establishing the guilt of Bill Gray, but the defense was intent on playing Reeda's taped conversations with Wilson to the jury.

The jury heard the conversations between Reeda and Howard where he lied to her telling her he was divorced and coming to her, then making excuses why he did not, which caused Reeda to pressure him for a commitment. Now Wilson had a motive, defense attorney John Radin pointed out. Howard Wilson had a motive to kill ... a reason to silence Reeda. The defense was very successful in establishing Wilson led her on, was deceitful, lied to her and was a first class predator of a lonely woman's emotions, but there was nothing to make him a killer. The jury would have to have a wild imagination if they would turn their attention away from Bill Gray because of this witness.

Betty and Reeda were joyful, smiled and talked openly, when Kay Gunderson saw the two women about 9 p.m. Sunday night. He'd taken them fresh raspberries he had picked before he'd gone fishing. Betty wanted to see what his worm bedding looked like and Reeda was inquiring about the best places to elk hunt come fall.

Gunderson had a feeling he was the last person, except the killer, to see the women alive, so he went immediately to the sheriff's office when he heard of the murders on Monday. He did not see any cigarette butts on the kitchen table. He did not see any liquor bottles on the table. All he saw on the table was a basket of flowers. Gunderson had not used the bathroom, walked down the hall or entered the living room. He'd given hair, body fluid samples and footprints of his shoes.

Leroy Leavitt looked everywhere but at Bill Gray while he was on the stand. Leavitt was now humbly paying the consequences for loving Betty Gray. Further compounding his misery, the media would thrive on his admission of sexual encounters, love notes, deceit and adultery.

A story unfolded before the jury of a salesman calling on a business where he became friends with the owners. Even though he'd had a good friendship with the proprietor, the salesman eventually entered into a sexual relationship with the proprietor's wife.

"Before the fall of 1987 it was just friendship. I wanted to help her as much as I could. She was working in the store basically alone and needed a lot of help. So I would help her all I could. As we grew together with our relationship being friends, I helped her a lot with her own personal problems. I was a listening post for her. When she had a problem I would listen."

"How did it begin that you and she began to have more of a relationship," Michael Kane asked. "How did that begin?"

"She told me how lonely she was and how she needed someone to hold her. And I guess that's how it got started from there. Then as time went on working with her, I fell in love with her after that."

This love was mutually shared for their plans soon turned to divorcing their spouses so they could eventually get married. Betty had been certain enough of their plans that she started buying and laying away small household items for an apartment and had been having Roy deposit money and coins in a safety deposit box, all in preparation for their future together. Roy identified the love notes and cards he'd sent to Betty. Those without fingerprint dust on them were passed through the jury for a closer look. After viewing the heart-shaped bracelet he testified that he'd never seen Betty wearing it before.

Bill Gray's health couldn't have been too bad in May of 1989 Roy said. Lee Brown, Roy and Bill had been fishing in the Memorial Day fishing derby at Jackson Lake. On their way out, the boat trailer slipped off into a wash, digging the axel into the mud.

"So we moved rocks, pieces of log and dirt and Bill worked right along with us, shoveling the dirt, grabbing rocks, filling in the hole so we could get the trailer up. He appeared to be working right along with us, just as hard as we were."

Roy had seen knobby soled tennis shoes on Bill Gray that were the same pattern as the footprints he saw in the carpet in the murder house.

"Bill was walking on this snow and ice and he slipped. He said, 'I didn't think these would slide on the ice.' And he said, 'Look at the bottoms of these.' And he showed me the bottom. I said no, I wouldn't think those would slide on ice either."

Leavitt related the events of seeing the women briefly the night before the murders and the last memories of affection between him and Betty.

"She had me sit on the chair and she sat on my lap, just basically talk, you know, I love you, and that type of stuff there. And then she said that when we got together the next day she had something to tell me."

Roy would never know what it was she would have told him the next day. That secret went with Betty.

You could have heard a pin drop in the courtroom as Roy related the events of finding the women dead that Monday morning. Spectators and jurors alike could virtually feel the extreme eerie quietness in the house in response to Roy's repeated calling out the women's names as he made his way through the kitchen and down the hall. All previous testimony had been directed at before and after events and the defendant's strange behavior. This testimony struck at the heart of why the defendant was there. Roy had to work to keep his emotions under control as he was called upon to relive his horrible discovery. Bill Gray sat emotionless, staring insolently at his wife's lover.

Richard Mulligan needed to leave the jury with the thought that Leavitt would have had a motive to kill the women. To win this case, he had to flash possibilities of guilt by others just enough to create a "shadow of a doubt." He pressed hard on Roy's not being as gung ho to get a divorce as Betty. He implied that Leavitt was being pressured, boxed in by Betty's demands on him to get his divorce, maybe before he wanted to, or maybe he never did plan to get one?

Using Leavitt's interviews as proof, Mulligan seized upon his lie to the detectives.

"You lied, didn't you? You lied to the officers when they asked you if you were having a sexual relationship with Betty Gray. Is that not true?"

"Yes," he lied at first he had to admit, but he and Betty had a secret. A secret Leavitt would have liked to have kept but realized the investigation would eventually bring everything out and he decided the next day he might as well face it head on.

Mulligan's tone of voice was sarcastic and his questions purposefully derogatory as he grilled Leavitt about sexual encounters, sleeping with another man's wife, where they would meet for sex, how often? When he used the term "lovers" it came as if Roy and Betty, by their actions, were unfit for the human race. It was a subject that he kept coming back to, pressing upon the jury that a sin was committed, in his view, the worst kind. But this was what he was hired to do, this was his job and he did it skillfully.

Trying to soften Mulligan's caustic blows, on redirect Kane asked Roy if Betty was making demands on him to divorce his wife.

"No, she wasn't making demands on me. The pressure I had

was pressure within me. I had problems within myself on how I was going to tell my fellow workers, how I was going to tell my wife and my two boys. I knew it had to be done, but I wasn't sure how I was going to do it. I didn't want to hurt anybody's feelings any more than I had to." This woeful admission kept the room quiet while all pondered the predicament this man got himself into until Mulligan on re-cross woke everyone up with a booming, "Apparently, you were not worried about Bill Gray's feelings, were you?" A subdued and barely audible "No, sir," came from the beaten man in the witness chair.

Almost everyone has some sort of secret, some of more consequence than others, but few people end up telling it all, under oath in front of strangers and the news media who will make it their business to inform the entire community. Quiet, mild-mannered Roy Leavitt was believable, even pathetic at times. The more soft hearted could even feel sorry for him. Roy left the stand, the courtroom, the courthouse and probably wished he could leave the country.

A brave and special woman who stood by her husband through all this, LaDeana Leavitt informed the jury Roy had been home all night after he returned from Reeda's about 7:30 p.m. She usually heard Roy get up at night to use the bathroom, but occasionally she slept through and wasn't aware if he got up or not. But nothing was out of the ordinary that would have led her to believe Roy left the house that night.

Mulligan jumped on the chance to pursue that "sometimes" she slept through without hearing Roy get up in the night. She had to admit it would be fair to say she wouldn't have known if her husband was in bed or not if she had been in a real deep sleep.

Roy called LaDeana at 10 o'clock that Monday morning and

asked her to meet him at the warehouse at noon. There he told her of finding Reeda's and Betty's bodies but did not tell her about his affair. It wasn't until Wednesday evening he confessed all. This witness's testimony was sort of mundane overall. Kane gained a sort of alibi for Roy on that Sunday night, Mulligan cast the thinnest thread of doubt on that alibi.

If anything, LaDeana's appearance in the courtroom served to leave the impression that Roy must have been a decent person if she would stick by him under such traumatic conditions.

Sergeant Kevin Cox, the first officer on the scene, checked Reeda for signs of life then searched the home for possible other victims or a suspect.

"Was there a reason you did not check the other victim?" David Johnson asked.

"It's reactionary to check a victim. But just by looking at the two victims, it was obvious from the time factor and the time lapse that they were both deceased. What made it obvious was a large amount of blood was dried and coagulated. And when I checked the first victim, the body temperature was considerably lower than normal. It was apparent that whatever transpired in that residence had transpired considerably earlier."

He described the scene and his observations but spent most of his time on the stand answering questions for both the prosecution and the defense, about the footprints he'd observed both inside and outside. He identified photographs, some of which had a tape measure depicting the length and width of the footprints. His testimony would serve to support testimony yet to come.

Sergeant Morgan Hendricks described an aerial photograph showing the murder house in relation to the hospital. He testified that he'd driven the distance between the two points and concluded it was between 3.5 and 3.7 miles each way. Describing what he'd observed in the house matched previous testimony, burned down red candles, writing in what appeared to be blood, saucer with cigarette butts, liquor bottles, women's purses in the kitchen and the bodies in the bedrooms. He remembered the house to be very neat and clean except for what obviously had taken place there.

Hendricks had taken a complete video of the crime scene. The video would be shown on a television set placed in front of the jury causing the defense attorneys and the defendant to leave their table and stand somewhat behind and left of the jury box, in front of the spectators' seats, so they could view the video. Apparently Bill Gray could not stand for very long because he elected to take a seat in the front row next to a female spectator. It was a strange situation for this spectator to suddenly be seated next to the defendant. Since the spectator was I, the author of this book, I had an unexpected, but perfect opportunity to observe the defendant up "close and personal." Gray was wearing his normal trial attire, western cut dress jeans, a western styled jacket, bolo tie, socks and sandals on his feet.

"As the video methodically took us through the house, pausing and capturing each item of importance, I found myself torn between watching Bill Gray or viewing the crime scene. I did a little of both, but concentrated more on Gray. I stood up so I could see over John Radin and Richard Mulligan who were standing directly in front of me. I moved slightly to the right so I might turn somewhat toward Gray without being overly obvious. At the beginning of the tape, Gray seemed more interested and curious as the camera panned the center island with the satanic scene, and the other items in the kitchen. The camera zoomed in on the footprints in the carpet then down the hall to the bathroom showing the toilet seat in the up position and the footprint on the bathroom rug. As the camera started farther down the hall, Gray's breathing became heavier, certainly audible, and as the camera went into Betty's room Gray reached for a handkerchief.

The next morning the newspaper stated that Bill Gray cried and was wiping his eyes free of tears. On the contrary, I was looking down and directly at him at this highly charged moment. I did not see Bill Gray wiping tears ... he was wiping the sweat from his brow. The veins in his forehead were standing out like they might burst, the pock marks on the face were bright red, almost like a rash. His breathing was very labored.

Later, after the trial, I watched this video twice without interruption or distraction, thus enabling me to give a complete and accurate accounting of the crime scene.

With the playing of the tape, suddenly everyone in Courtroom IV was taken inside the murder house. They saw what the investigators saw, they saw what Leavitt saw, they could probably feel the unnatural quiet Leavitt must have felt as he went down the hall, then focusing on Reeda sitting up in her bed and then Betty, blood trailing from the wound in her head onto the pillow then down her side.

When the video was over there was a stunned silence in the entire courtroom. Everyone apparently lost in their own personal thoughts. This wasn't a movie where bodies and blood are abundant. This was the real thing. This was strangers intruding on the violent deaths of two human beings. The judge called for an immediate recess. The courtroom emptied in silence. No one spoke. Suddenly no one had anything to say.

After the recess, Michael Kane went immediately to the business at hand. He went through photograph after photograph with Sergeant Hendricks, passing each to the jury for closer examination. Every detail of every item was shown and discussed, Betty's open suitcase on the floor of her bedroom, Reeda's packed suitcases in her bedroom and her briefcase in the kitchen chair. There were large blown-up pictures of newspapers on the kitchen table, cigarette butts in a saucer, a bullet hole in the mirrored wall, a heart shaped bracelet on Betty's wrist. Everything was photographed including the recliner in the living room, the footprints leading to it, from it, and the bodies from different angles. Then on a large diagram of the house Hendricks marked where each of these pictures was taken so the jury could put them all in their places.

"Now officer, when you first observed the scene did you think anything about the 'Satan Loves You' writing and the candles? Did you believe immediately that it was a ritualistic killing?"

"No, I did not. From my training and from the things I have learned and read there were many things absent from this scene. Some of the things that would be included in a ritualistic-type worship service or anything of that nature were missing. What was left there, the candles, the numbers, and multiplication of six's could have been picked up from any movie or any book on the market that deals with Satanism."

On cross examination John Radin went directly to the satanic implication left at the scene. But it was doubtful the defense made many points in this area as Hendricks said people sent him photographs to find out if they were linked to Satanism and he had gone to locations where satanic graffiti had been left. He felt he was quite knowledgeable with the subject. He was not aware of any organized satanic groups working in the area and he was certain these killings were not linked to the occult.

Before the trial John Radin and Richard Mulligan had been submitting motions and arguing admissibility of Reeda's interest in psychic readings, tarot cards and astrology. According to the defense she subscribed to related magazines and newspapers. Some tarot cards were found in her purse. But they could produce nothing to tie her to actual involvement in the occult.

The jury was sent out of the courtroom while Mulligan once again argued this point.

"A lot of people can be interested in astrology but that does not make them a devil worshiper. I don't think it's relevant," stated Kane.

"I agree," said the judge. "Mr. Radin, motion overruled."

Picking up from there, Radin worked hard to confuse the issue over footprint impressions and footprint size. Was Hendricks talking about an 11-inch length of the prints or size 11? Although Hendricks referred to size previously, in fact he meant length, but he cautioned the jury that he had not taken the actual measurements himself. What was in his notes came through other sources. The defense would not dwell further on this subject now. They had a witness scheduled who would do a much better job of adding to the confusion over the shoe size of the footprints.

"An autopsy is a medical investigation into the body, what we call a total examination of the body," testified Forensic Pathologist Dr. Charles Garrison. "In general terms, you do an external examination, looking at the body, any marking the body may have on it. And then you open the body, opening the chest in a Y-shaped fashion so you can expose the entire thoracic contents. And then you also open the abdomen in a similar fashion where you can see all the abdominal contents. The organs are then removed and examined individually. One then also opens the cranial cavity by making an incision that goes over the top of the skull so that the incision is hidden by the hair. The scalp is then removed or peeled back, the skull cap removed and the brain is then examined. And all of these organs or portions thereof are taken for microscopic examination."

When the medical examiner testifies it is almost always a gruesome testimony. It's where the information given isn't fluffed up and smoothed over. This portion of the trial can be troubling not only to family members but to the jury panel as well.

One gunshot wound to the head of each victim was the cause of death, he told Prosecutor David Johnson and the jury. Shown large drawings of head diagrams depicting the entry and exit wound locations he affirmed the diagrams were accurate with his autopsy findings.

"The wounds on Betty Gray began in the posterior portion or the back part of the right side of the skull. And then the bullet tracks through the skull, going from the back to the front, where it then exits the head at the left temple. The bullet track is essentially at the same level in the head so the bullet enters and exits at a point parallel to the ground. Reeda Roundy's wound entered from the left side of her head, exiting on the right. For all intents and purposes, again this bullet was also a fairly flat trajectory to the head."

On cross examination Radin wanted to know about powder burns and Garrison gave a lengthy lesson about gunshot wounds.

"If you put a gun tightly against something, all of the material goes inside whatever you are firing into. So if we have a weapon fired close to the head, the smoke, the unburned powder and so forth should go inside the head, inside the tissue, and also inside the bone. The further back you come, the wider the area on the body in which you have deposition of material. You can determine part of the distance that the weapon was fired based upon the pattern one gets on the body. Things that can interfere with that could be hair or clothing. If those things are present at the site of the entry wound, you may not be able to determine distance."

The doctor's best guess at estimating the distance of the gun when fired at Betty and Reeda's heads was between 18 and 24 inches which he stated was "sort of an off-the-cuff estimate."

Further contributing to a more accurate measure, was Dr. Garrison's testimony that if a silencer was used it should effect the distance. A silencer essentially lengthens the barrel of the weapon and then the weapon could be fired closer to the body without depositing powder. Given all the variables, use of a silencer and hair present at the entry site, the shot to Betty's head could have been much closer than originally estimated.

In addition to educating the jury on autopsies and gunshot wounds Dr. Garrison confirmed there was nothing sinister or incriminating in that Gray had his wife cremated. The doctor had taken all the required forensic evidence before her body was released.

Partially digested raspberries were found in the stomach contents confirming the fact the women had eaten some of the fresh berries Kay Gunderson had brought them that evening. The stage of digestion of foods known to be consumed at or near a certain time have accounted for fairly accurate determination of the time of death in many homicides, but this pathologist would not give either an estimation or professional guess at the time of death. Undoubtedly, he could not be certain how long after Gunderson left that the women ate the berries.

Betty had a very minor .01 percent alcohol content in her

body fluids while Reeda had none. The women certainly weren't having a party that night or would they have been responsible for the decrease in the liquid content of the liquor bottles Roy said were less full the next morning than they had been the night before.

This witness's testimony was short and to the point. The bodies revealed facts and the facts were given to the jury.

Through Sergeant Kent McCandless, the state introduced the wet wipe wrapper which was found near the Crowley Road home's logical exit from the property if going toward the hospital. The Mountain Dew can with the pull top missing was shown and noted that it was found about 20' from the wet wipe.

For the first time the jury and spectators were looking at actual physical items taken from the murder scene. Besides the wet wipe and Mountain Dew can, they viewed the plaster cast of the footprint found outside near the carport, a saucer used as an ashtray covered with fingerprint dust and a cup found next to the saucer on the kitchen table with a small amount of liquid in it, believed to be alcohol but never tested. Partially filled bottles of gin and vodka, and a newspaper were also presented to the jury. Everything had been tested for fingerprints. None of the fingerprints found were Bill Gray's.

A sense of personalization hung in the air when Sergeant McCandless held and identified two women's purses. Women's purses are so very cherished, often almost a part of their owners. On this day, the purses with fingerprint dust covered contents were present in the courtroom displayed to all.

Defense Attorney John Radin asked many questions surrounding the sergeant's previous testimony. In his best sarcastic voice he pinned the witness down to some possible sloppy detective work when the liquid in the cup on the table had not been tested, in fact, McCandless had not bothered to even smell it. Further, a recorded tape made by Reeda to Howard was missing and this witness not only testified he heard it but was in charge of the evidence locker where the tape was supposed be kept safely.

Discussing the footprint pictures, Radin just added confusion as to how the detectives went about placing a tape measure near the print which was intended to show the size of the print in a photograph. They discussed the various angles photographs were taken from, discovery of other prints in the area with one believed to be Kay Gunderson's and the testing of them in the Boise forensic lab.

But the highlight of this cross examination was bringing out that if as much liquid had been drunk from the liquor bottles as Leavitt thought there was, the person drinking it would have been very intoxicated. Although Kane stopped this line of testimony before it went further, Radin left the suggestion in the jury's minds that since the medical examiner testified the women had hardly touched the liquor and Kay Gunderson testified he did not have a drink, whoever drank the liquor was the killer and could not have ridden a bike to the hospital as the prosecution was contending. Reasonable doubt or mistaken identification of the liquor bottles contents?

After a lengthy testimony comparing six human hairs recovered from the recliner in the living room at the murder scene with hair taken from Bill Gray, Supervising Criminalist for the Idaho State Crime Lab Don Wycoff could only say the hairs were substantially similar. Using charts and blown up pictures of both sets of hair fibers, Wycoff pointed out numerous characteristics Gray's hair had that matched the hairs found in the recliner. However, unlike fingerprints, the science of matching hair is not positively identifiable.

Neither woman had intercourse shortly before their deaths, Betty's blood, type O, was a match to the bloody words left on the center island and the cigarette butts were contaminated to the extent that no saliva typing could be obtained.

Radin's cross examination jumped quickly to the hair testimony. He dwelled on the fact that hair matching is not an exact science and the only type words the examiner could possibly use legitimately were "similar," "approximately the same," "consistent with," "some variation."

In fact, if they were Bill Gray's, the hairs could have been transferred via Betty's clothing or even by Reeda after she visited the Grays. Stretching as far as he could, Radin reminded the jury through this witness that it was no secret Gray had been in Reeda's home just months before and could have deposited his hair then.

Questioning Wycoff on various types of hair testing such as chemical testing (drugs and medicine), neutron activation tests (metals in water used to wash hair), isoenzyme test (a form of DNA), which were never taken by this lab, may have left the jury wondering if the lab hadn't made some mistakes. However, Wycoff stayed firm that these type tests were not necessary for this situation.

"They wouldn't have been done that way simply because we do not, as a routine course of analysis, send hairs out to be worked up through the methods that you're talking about," Wycoff stated defending his position.

Donna Shepardson from the Idaho Bureau of Forensic Surfaces underwent a short examination by Mike Kane and a rather lengthy, confusing, cross by John Radin. When all was said and done, the cast taken from the footprint in the gravel near the car port was not complete enough to give an exact size. Her best guess was between size 9 and 10½ but there was no certainty since among other things she was unable to identify the manufacturer of the shoe in question.

In less than 15 minutes the fingerprint specialist, Robert Kerchusky, was on and off the stand. There were no fingerprints belonging to Bill Gray anywhere in the Roundy home. Curiously though, the liquor bottles surfaces would usually bear excellent fingerprints. Betty's or Reeda's prints logically should have been found, however, there were none, no prints whatsoever on the liquor bottles. The expert, in his opinion, felt the liquor bottles had been wiped clean. Reeda's prints were found on some of the saucers containing the wax, Betty's were found on the phone, but not Leavitt's. The surface of the phone had numerous smudges most likely caused by sweat on Leavitt's hands as he excitedly called 911.

The bullets that killed the women were fired from the same gun the state's firearms expert, Wally Baker, testified, but none of the weapons he received from Bonneville County could be positively identified as the one that fired the fatal shots. Two of the guns, a Browning 6 Saur 9mm and an Interarms 9mm pistol could not be excluded, or included.

Yes, there are elements that could have happened to change the striations that would normally match the bullet markings. Repeated use, debris in the barrel or intentional scarring can alter the microscopic or test fired characteristics of a bullet. The prosecution did not have the gun that killed. The prosecution knew it, the defense knew it and the jury knew it.

Normally when Jason Perry came home from work he

parked his Fastback next to an old bluish-green Travelall, but on Sunday night July 23, 1989 at 11:30 p.m., the Travelall was not there. Perry, who rented the apartment below the pawnshop, thought it had probably been sold.

He heard the dog moving around in the pawnshop upstairs when he went to bed at 1 a.m., then when he got up in the night to go to the bathroom somewhere between 3 a.m. and 6 a.m., he heard someone upstairs hushing the dog. This testimony certainly raised some questions as to Bill's whereabouts on that Sunday night. But defense attorney Richard Mulligan blew Jason's credibility sky-high.

"Do you recall telling me that you saw the vehicle missing on the night of the crime?"

"Yes."

"And when I asked you why, do you recall what your response was?"

"Yeah, I said something about the tracks in snow, or something like that."

"And I said to you, but this happened on July 23rd, in the summertime. And what was your response to that?"

"I guess I just screwed up."

Jason told Mulligan this same "tracks in the snow" story not once, but twice, once in May 1993 and again in July 1993.

The witness admitted he'd been smoking marijuana that night, had a couple of beers and fell asleep on the couch. Mulligan preferred to use the term "passed out" on the couch, but either way Jason's entire testimony was now very questionable.

Wounded, the prosecution could only hope the jury would take Jason's sketchy testimony as a confirmation of testimony by his roommate, Shawn Jamison, who also heard the dog walking around in the pawnshop at 1 a.m.

When Security Guard, Steve Mackley, rounded a corner inside the hospital on August 2, 1989 and saw Bill Gray, he ducked back. It not only startled him but momentarily scared him. By now he'd identified Bill Gray as positively being the man in the Travelall the night of the murders and he had to assume Bill Gray knew it. Momentarily Mackley was concerned for his safety.

"What's he doing here?" "Has he come to get me?" were his first thoughts. "Is he asking questions about me?" "Is he trying to find out what my shift is?"

When he saw the two officers with Gray he relaxed. Gray had only come to have blood drawn.

Now on the stand, Mackley was telling the jury, the court, the spectators and the press about the man who put a bicycle into the back of a green International Travelall with Wyoming license plates and identified himself with a medical-alert bracelet, the same night a woman from Jackson, Wyoming was killed.

"Oh, yes," he was positive that was the man, Mackley said, as he pointed to Gray who was seated at the defense table. Four years had passed but Mackley had the same conviction as he did two days after the murders.

Steve Mackley was the single most important witness for the prosecution and Mulligan had to do everything he could to discredit this witness. He stirred confusion surrounding Mackley not mentioning the beard that the man he pointed to in the courtroom had worn for many years. He held up the composite sketch Mackley helped prepare and made an issue over the fact the composite showed a beardless man. Mulligan drove home the point if Mackley was mistaken about the beard he could be mistaken about other things as well.

The notes the detectives asked him to make after Mackley

contacted them bore some question marks. Keys, what did that mean? Glasses, what did that mean? Mulligan wanted to know. He picked and picked at every word, statement, notation, interview, deposition and grand jury testimony, and anything Mackley appeared to be a little vague about. But Mackley saw what he saw, a Travelall with Wyoming plates, a man with a pock marked face, and a man with a medical-alert bracelet. Bill Gray had all three.

The security guard was on the stand most of the day. His testimony was incriminating and extremely damaging to the defense.

The morning of trial day seven, the defense came in outraged. They demanded the judge declare a mistrial. The television news, as well as the newspaper, chose this time to sensationalize Bill Gray as their number one story. Reeda's son Clayton gave an interview to the television media in which he stated he'd reviewed the evidence himself and it was enough to put Gray away. He believed Gray was guilty and he believed Gray pulled the trigger. If that had been the end of it the defense wouldn't have been quite so steamed, but it was not.

Bill Gray's picture was next to a picture of Paul Rhodes, who was convicted of the most gruesome murderer in Bonneville County's recent history, and both were displayed large and prominently on the front page of the paper. Almost the entire page was devoted to the Gray trial and the Rhodes case, dredging up old memories of the sensational triple murder spree two years before.

The defense contended it was outrageous to do this to a

presumed innocent man in the middle of his trial.

"The entire article was designed to sell newspapers based upon something that occurred in our community years ago, and caused such fear in our community that everybody literally relates to that particular case," Radin told the judge.

"As the court is aware, we did previously request that the jury be sequestered in this matter. The court denied the motion, and as a result, we're left with a situation where we have 14 jurors, I submit, most of whom receive the *Post Register* nightly and many of whom watch the evening news broadcasts, and who have potentially been exposed to these two very prejudicial and outrageous aspects of journalism in this case."

With agreement from both Mike Kane and Richard Mulligan, the judge chose to poll the jury. If the jury was contaminated, if they had heard or read any trial publicity, Mulligan might well get his mistrial. However, 12 of the 14 said they had not heard or read anything. One saw the pictures and headlines of the paper in the coin machine at the entrance to the courthouse, but did not stop to read it. Another glimpsed the taping of Clayton's interview on the front lawn of the courthouse but heard nothing. The judge denied the motion.

Officer Delano Dixon did not tell Steve Mackley the person whom the police suspected was in the photo lineup. He said the suspect "may or may not" be there. He asked Mackley to look and see if the man he talked to in the Travelall at the hospital was there.

"He [Mackley] immediately focused his attention on number three and after a minute, two minutes of viewing it, he said the person in number three was the person he had seen that night. No, I did not prod him. Just the opposite I told him to take his time and make sure."

Mackley's identification of Gray in the photo lineup was so positive, the best effort by the defense was to taint the photo lineup itself, pointing out the lineup was prejudicial toward Gray. Officer Dixon prepared the photo lineup. He picked the pictures he would use. He chose to put six pictures on the photo board and he used pictures from the city detectives' division, one of which Steve Mackley knew personally. In fact, this then left Mackley with a choice of only five individuals. Yes, Dixon could have used ten, 15, or more, photographs. He could have made more than one set, one of which did not have Gray's photograph at all. He could have prepared the photo lineup in several different ways, but he used six because it was kind of standard practice in the department to use six.

John Radin pushed the witness to say he was aware Mackley had identified a man with glasses and therefore Dixon put Gray and only one other person in the lineup with glasses, once again limiting the number of persons Mackley could easily relate to. But the witness said Mackley could not recall if the man even had glasses. This was a direct contradiction to Mackley's earlier testimony and on re-direct Mike Kane quickly led Dixon to establish why.

"Mackley first indicated that he didn't recall whether or not the individual was wearing glasses because he remembered seeing his eyes and focusing on them," Dixon said. "After seeing the lineup and picking out Mr. Gray, he indicated that the individual was looking over his glasses rather than through the glasses, which is why he remembered his eyes so distinctly."

"When I went to notify Gray of his wife's death, I recorded

the conversation because that's, in my opinion, the best way to record what was said, so they [Idaho investigators] could form their own opinions about what took place," testified Lt. David Foster. The tape recorder was in his pocket and Gray did not know he was being recorded.

Having the benefit of written transcripts, as well as listening to the tape, the jury could get a true feeling for what transpired in that notification. The jury heard Bill's instantaneous wailing when told of Betty's death. They also heard his quick recovery and inquiries of the whereabouts of Betty's jewelry. Then he went through his "poor me" routine, followed by a rehearsed-sounding statement of how he and Betty were going to "sit back and clip coupons and enjoy what they had left." They did not hear him ask how his wife died.

On cross examination, Mulligan was quick to point out that Bill asked "What happened," "Where it happened," and "When it happened." He also cried and sobbed as everyone heard for themselves. Mulligan did not dwell on the length of the crying, the quick recovery, or the fact that Gray did not once ask Foster whom to contact in Idaho Falls to find out more information about the killings, or where Betty had been taken and when he could get her home.

Of all the detectives, officers, investigators and experts having some part in this case, Bill Gray despised no one more than Victor Rodriguez. While Rodriguez was on the stand Bill glared intensely at him. If looks could kill ...

The detective identified a picture of a medical-alert bracelet on Gray's wrist and the photograph of Gray, still wearing the bracelet, taken with Bill's permission at the first interview.

Given Betty's purse, Rodriguez was asked to take out Betty's wallet. There were pictures of her grandson Cree, Jeff, Kim,

Saralyn and carefully hidden between those pictures was a picture of Roy Leavitt. These were all the people she loved so much. The moment was not lost on the spectators, or the jury.

Rodriguez explained in great detail the attempts of both Idaho and Wyoming officers to find a "Ron Mitchell." They found some Ron Mitchells but none were the Ron Mitchell who Bill Gray claimed bought the Travelall.

"Where is that Travelall now?" asked Kane.

"It's being held in our Bonneville County Road and Bridge Department which it has been there for four years." replied Rodriguez.

"Has anyone under any name, let alone Ron Mitchell, attempted to obtain that Travelall back from your office?"

"Nobody, sir."

On cross examination Mulligan used his best sarcastic approach to impress upon the jury he had no use for this detective. His voice booming, he asked his questions in rapid fire as though it didn't matter what the detective said, it would all be false anyway. Emphasis placed on the end of his questions of "Isn't that true?" literally defied the detective to answer his questions any way other than in the affirmative.

"And Mr. Gray indicated to you, and you testified on direct examination, that Mrs. Gray wanted a civil divorce. Isn't that true?"

"I believe the defendant made mention that he wanted a civil divorce, sir."

"Well your report says that when Betty came back from San Diego, she told William that she wanted a divorce because she did not love him anymore. She wanted a civil divorce. Isn't that what your report reflects? Would you like to see it again?"

"That does say that. However, it is the defendant that wanted the civil divorce."

"Okay. So then this report is not accurate. Is that what you're telling me now?"

"No sir, it is accurate. However maybe I just didn't word it the way that you wanted it to read."

"Don't argue with me detective!"

"I'm not, sir."

"Don't try to be cute," Mulligan retorts. "What we're saying here is that it says she wanted to have a civil divorce. Isn't that what it says? Do you want to see it again?"

"No sir, it's not necessary."

Mulligan abruptly changed the subject. But after a brief recess, when Mulligan continued his cross examination, forthright and up front he admitted he'd made a mistake.

"Initially, Detective Rodriguez, I want to tell you that I did review your handwritten notes and I found that phrase in those hand written notes. So you were right."

"Thank you, sir," replied Rodriguez.

Mulligan went to Rodriguez's statement of Bill having had bloodshot eyes, complained his legs hurt, his back hurt, his knees hurt, when he was interviewed Monday night, just five to six hours after he was notified of his wife's death. The detective agreed Gray's eyes could have been bloodshot from crying. He also agreed it was fair to assume Bill had been through a lot that day. Mulligan did not get into anything that would cause the detective to say he felt Gray's legs and back hurt from riding a bike 7.5 miles some 12 hours ago, had been up all night and could have had bloodshot eyes from lack of sleep.

Since Kane had mentioned the medical-alert bracelet Mulligan had no choice but to face the bracelet now, implying to the jury the defense was not concerned with the bracelet because it didn't mean anything significant. However, it backfired on him.

"And in fact, to the best of your recollection, Bill Gray wore that medical-alert bracelet every time that the police officers talked to him in that first week. Isn't that true?"

"Well, up until the time that he actually became the suspect in this case and he found out the man identified in Idaho Falls that night had a medical-alert bracelet, then the bracelet became lost ... disappeared."

Mulligan pressed on, hoping to show Gray had nothing to fear by wearing the bracelet throughout that first week because he was innocent, however the damage was done. Bill Gray did not remove the bracelet until he knew he was a suspect. Then it could not be found.

Mulligan was successful in pointing out minor mistakes in reports and pressuring the memory of an officer who investigated this case almost four years ago. But unless Mulligan had a dramatic courtroom finale which would catch the detective in a major mistake, Detective Rodriguez's testimony would go down as credible and believable.

Idaho Bureau of Investigation Officer, John Kotrason, told an attentive jury about love cards found in the Roundy home, "Love Ya, hope you have a wonderful birthday, X,O,X,O's," signed Roy. He told of the interview held on Wednesday the 26th where Bill talked at length about searching Betty's purse. A blow up of Bill's personal inventory of Betty's wallet and lay-away receipts was presented to the jury.

It's interesting to ponder Bill's thought process. Bill couldn't wait to show the detectives his inventory of Betty's purse, so much so, he sent his son immediately to get it. He was proud of this inventory. Look here, here's proof, look what she was doing too me. Poor me, my wife took some of my money. He had truly never really shared anything in his entire marriage. It had always been, me, me, me ... mine. Then the hunt. He was real proud of the hunt, searching until he found the purse, even to the depths of the washing machine in the basement. The greed ... counted even the change. He is so outraged at his wife for what she did to him he has no grief over her death. Even though he planned her death and intentionally killed her, there should have been some sense of loss, but no ... she stole from him!

Bill thought these men who were listening to his story would understand. In his mind it was perfectly normal to go through your wife's private things, sneak, betray, degrade, blame. He never once considered this action, this inventory, something he should keep private. He could not fathom that others would be disgusted, repulsed even, for his caring more about these small amounts of money than the fact his wife had just died a violent death.

Yes, Gray had been wearing a medical-alert bracelet every time he saw him that first week and Gray did not appear to be trying to hide it, Kotrason said in answer to Radin's question.

John Kotrason agreed with the defense attorney that Bill voluntarily brought up the pending divorce and the hopes he could win Betty back. Gray also volunteered the notes of the inventory of Betty's purse and yes, he could have destroyed them if he'd wanted to. The defense chipped away bringing out every item that might put their client in a favorable position.

Presumably it was difficult for Jack Hurley to tell his story about receiving and storing the Travelall on his ranch. Bill and Jack had been friends and traveling buddies for many years. However, Jack was a little put out that Bill brought the Travelall to him under the circumstances. On the stand, he said he did not remember talking to Bill on the phone at all that first week after the murders. But Kane brought out Jack's interview from August 1989, where he said he had talked to Bill on the phone several times that week. After Kane read several statements Jack made to the police along those lines, Jack's memory was still not refreshed and his only answer was that he "didn't remember having any phone conversations with Bill the week after Betty's death."

For the defense he remained firm he'd not had a telephone conversation with Bill about getting their stories straight. He could have hidden the Travelall in some out-buildings but Gray didn't ask him to hide the Travelall, just store it. Jack Hurley seemed confused, or nervous, or caught in the middle, or all three. It was hard to tell if he was a prosecution witness or a defense witness. Clearly, he found himself in an uncomfortable, compromised position.

Michael Coy testified about selling the Travelall to Bill Gray, leaving the title blank except for his and his wife's signatures as the sellers. Shown a blowup of the title, Coy said it did not have either Ron Mitchell's name or the reading of the odometer on it when he turned it over to Gray. The spare tire was flat and it was easy to see it would not be useable. It had pulled away from the rim and was easily visible it could not be used. Yes, Bill Gray knew it was flat when he bought the vehicle.

He then told his story of the Travelall having been gone the early hours of Monday, July 24, 1989, but it was there that afternoon when he went by the pawnshop.

Mulligan brought up nothing regarding the title but scored a small victory with Coy's testimony. In his previous deposition Coy said he went by the pawnshop every day. Both he and his wife had a natural curiosity about whether Gray was ever going to do anything with the Travelall so they were very aware of the

Travelall's presence until Monday morning when they noticed it gone. Still checking on the Travelall each time they passed, they again noticed it had been returned by Monday afternoon. However when Mulligan asked if he remembered seeing the Travelall Tuesday or Wednesday parked at the pawnshop, he said he did not. The last time he saw the Travelall was Monday about 3:30 p.m. as he went to pick up his wife. In fact, Mulligan was able to point out the Travelall had been parked at the pawnshop all day Tuesday and all day Wednesday.

Coy's testimony had a hole in it. He either was aware of the Travelall at all times as he testified, or he noticed its presence selectively. Therefore, could he be believed when he said the Travelall was missing Monday morning? Then, add his statement of how surprised he was when the cops came to his trailer.

"Sherrel said, 'The cops are here, and I said well, what in the hell do they want, I haven't been drinking today.'"

By his own admission, he had a tendency to have a few drinks during the day so one would tend to think he might have an alcohol problem. The jury would have to weed out what they could believe of this witness's testimony and what they could not.

William R. Gray, Bill's father, took the stand for the prosecution and testified about taking the Travelall to Bondurant Wednesday night. His story was no different from what his son had told authorities. The senior Gray did go to the police station where his son was being interviewed. Upon speaking privately with Bill, William advised him the Travelall had been impounded and was enroute to town at that very moment. Yes, his son did return to a room with detectives and they talked again for some time. That's all Mike Kane wanted from him. He did not want to place the father of the defendant in any more compromised position than he already was.

On cross-examination, under the guidance of John Radin, Bill's father insisted his son had been very emotional over the loss of his wife, breaking down frequently, seemingly torn up. When somebody mentioned Betty's name, he would just come apart. Sometimes he would cry for two or three minutes at a time.

Contrary to what others had testified to, William Gray believed his son had been very interested in the whereabouts of his wife's body. He called police every night but was always told Betty's body was out of town for an autopsy. On and off the stand in a heartbeat, the elder Gray could still not join his wife in the courtroom for he was subject to recall, presumably by the defense.

After lunch, Elmer Beal, who owned the only odometer calibrating machine in Idaho Falls, testified the odometer on the Travelall was working accurately and the speedometer had not been tampered with.

Then Lt. Dave Foster from the Jackson Police Department was recalled to the stand. This time he was there to introduce the tape recording of Bill Gray's July 28 interview.

Following along with written transcripts, the jury heard Bill lie to the officers about moving the Travelall, then returning to admit his lie after he talked to his father. This was the missing tape that kept Bill free for so long. This was extremely damaging evidence against Bill Gray.

All Bill would have had to do was mention one word, the word "lawyer," at the onset of his interrogations, and in all probability he would have been out fishing on this beautiful spring day instead of sitting behind the defense table defending against first degree murder charges.

James Corbman, mechanic at the Jackson Service Center, fixed the wheel cylinder and the brakes on Bill Gray's 1971 International Travelall. He identified the work order he'd prepared, identified his handwriting and testified he wrote in the actual mileage of the vehicle when he did the work on July 3, 1989. The work order appeared to be exactly the same as it was when he prepared it and had not been tampered with.

The spare tire was not flat when Mary Lou Royce, crime scene analyst, processed the Travelall. She identified her pictures, and said she had taken them because there appeared to have been scuff marks on the top of the tire as though something had been rubbing back and forth over it, a bicycle perhaps? The interior of the Travelall was very dirty with thick dust throughout except for the driver's side. The armrests, door handles, steering column, dashboard, windows and the rear view mirror were very clean. Those areas as well as the exterior doors appeared to her to have been wiped down.

"It looked like it had been cleaned in specific areas. The floor boards were very dirty. There was lots of dirt in the bottom of it, and the seats, if you were to smack the seat, dust would rise. So it seemed odd to me that some areas were very clean while some areas were very dirty. The dashboard had white rub marks like cleaning marks on it. If you were to take a wet rag and rub it across something dusty it would dry and leave white streaks. That's what was on the dashboard."

She found no fingerprints at all, not even smudges.

Royce worked both searches of the Gray home and the pawnshop. On the first search she saw wet wipes of the normal ordinary Kentucky Fried Chicken variety in several places including on the night stand next to the bed in the master bedroom. On the second search there were none in the house. A book on how to make silencers was shown to her but it was not seized.

The bailiff wheeled in a bicycle taken from the side of the pawnshop on August 10, 1989. The examiner's fingerprint was the only identifiable print found on the bike, other prints were smeared and therefore unidentifiable. The bike did not have a light. Although the presence of a bicycle in the courtroom was intended to be dramatic, in reality it was nothing earth shattering. The state could leave the impression they had the right bike, but could not prove it.

Attorney Tom Moss took the stand on the ninth day of the trial. In detail, Moss explained how and why Saralyn and Jeff contacted him. They were not after money, he told the jury. They wanted the Bonneville County prosecutor to file criminal charges against their father for the killing of their mother. That was the only reason a civil suit was filed.

Reading from the deposition Moss took of Gray in preparation for the civil suit, Mike Kane asked the questions and Moss read Gray's answer.

Through Moss, Bill told of a Ron Mitchell who was average height, a little taller than Bill, of average build, brown hair, in his the late 30s, early 40s, who wore ranch clothes, boots, Levi's and a western shirt. Bill did not notice his eyes. Mitchell came into the shop before Bill bought the Travelall. Then after Bill bought it he came back to look at it. They went outside and looked at the vehicle. Mitchell drove it then brought it back and left a $200 deposit. Then Mitchell came back but he didn't have any money. Bill had Mitchell sign the title so if Bill got stuck with it, he'd have open title on the vehicle. The next time Bill saw Mitchell was the Friday or Saturday before his wife was killed. He paid Bill the remaining $200. Mitchell took the vehicle then came back bitching. He wanted more work done to the vehicle. Bill said he was not going to do anymore work on it and they got into a big argument.

"I told him, I says, if that's the way it is, you can pay me the repair bill that I paid on it, too, if you're going to be that way. So I didn't let him take the vehicle. I kept it on the lot," Moss read.

Bill intended to absorb the cost of the repairs already done on the Travelall, until they got in the argument. Since they argued outside, the only people who would have observed this argument would be coming and going from his shop. Bill had given Mitchell a receipt for the $200 down payment. The pawnshop receipts were numbered in sequence but when a transaction was completed he always destroyed the receipts.

"Just like a lay-away," Bill had said. "When it's finished being paid for I don't keep the receipts. They are no longer of any use to me."

Eventually, Bill admitted to signing Ron Mitchell's name on the title, writing in the mileage of the Travelall, filling in all other requirements, taking it to the courthouse, paying the taxes and having the title put in Mitchell's name.

When his association with the Travelall turned out to be by far the most critical piece of evidence the prosecution had against him, Gray himself admitted to forging the title. This was Bill's deposition, taken under oath, one and a half years before this jury was hearing it. Bill never dreamed criminal charges would ever be filed against him then. The defense had no questions for Tom Moss. The state rested its case.

Friday morning May 28, the tenth day of the trial, the defense was prepared to present witnesses to support Bill Gray's claims of innocence. Robert Gray came from Minnesota to testify for his first cousin, Bill. Since school teachers have the summer off he decided to spend a week with his cousin Bill in Jackson Hole. Arriving on July 11, 1989, he stayed at Bill's home.

"Did you ever have an opportunity to visit with Bill in his bedroom while he was in bed?"

"Yes, Billy's medical condition at this time forced him to get comfortable by having all kinds of pillows around him. He needed the water bed. And so he would always try to situate himself to get as comfortable as possible."

"Okay. And did you do any activities with Mr. Gray during that week you visited with him?"

"Yes, he took me around Jackson Hole and showed me, you know, the sights that were there. We couldn't travel long because he would become tired and he would have to go home."

On the last day Robert Gray was in town Betty's friend, Reeda Roundy, came to stay the weekend.

"Did you have a chance to see her before you left?"

"Yes, the arrangement was that we would go out Saturday night to the Elks Club for some dancing, if that was possible. They heard there was going to be a band there and we were going to find out. Billy, Betty, Reeda and I sat at a table out by the bar. I had a blackberry brandy and Coke, and I believe Billy had a 7-Up. And the girls, the ladies, were drinking Long Island

Iced Teas."

"Okay. How long did you stay at the Elks Lodge that evening?"

"We stayed several hours. We moved into the dance area and they played some old '50s tunes and I'm a '50s dancer so I danced the fast dances with both ladies. Billy was ... seemed to enjoy himself. And we talked about the last time he had danced. He ended up with a blood clot and ended up in the hospital. So he was sensitive about going out and dancing. And I tried to persuade him to try it at least once, a slow one. And they played a nice, very slow dance and Bill danced with Betty and I danced with Reeda. It was a nice slow dance and they embraced and danced very well together. They seemed to be enjoying themselves. There was a smile on Betty's lips. And it was just an all-around good time. Bill only danced that one dance. He was pretty tired after that."

Bill and Betty had taken their guest out to dinner twice that week. On the other occasion Saralyn went along.

"Could you describe to the jury what her mood, or attitude was, please?"

"Well being a teacher, I'd have to say she appeared to me to be a little bit spoiled, a little bit snippy. She did not seem to appreciate her mother."

Mike Kane immediately objected to this line of questioning.

"That's totally irrelevant."

The judge agreed.

"When we went driving around we used an old blue pickup," he told Kane on cross examination. "It didn't run very well but it was comfortable, and we usually had the dog. We rarely got out of the pickup except for lunch and that seemed to tire him out."

Kane wanted to know how Bill looked when he got so tired.

"Slack in the face," Robert said. "More slack, than flush faced."

He didn't recall him sweating. Yes, Bill spent most of his time when home, laid back in his recliner and he did notice his feet. He was always wearing slippers.

Dr. Karen Servilla possessed a long set of credentials establishing herself as qualified transplant nephrologist. A nephrologist primarily takes over after a transplant, managing medical problems and medication related to the transplant. She had been treating Bill since his transplant in April 1988.

The doctor took the jury through the peritoneal dialysis process, establishing that Bill would have been in possession of, as a matter of necessity, surgical wet wipes and disposable gloves. She had seen Bill approximately 50 to 75 times, both through his dialysis and subsequent transplant. She had treated close to 300 transplant patients, but Bill Gray was one who stood out in her mind.

"Bill had problems almost immediately after he was sent home, and returned to the University of Utah, I believe within weeks of his discharge, because he had a blood clot in his leg. He'd currently complained of some cramping in his leg. About mid-May he returned with this clot in his leg and complaining of shortness of breath. The clot broke off from his leg and went into the lung. He was hypoxic. That meant he wasn't getting oxygen in his blood from his lungs. The clot blocked some of the blood supply to some of the tissue on the right side of his lung. That is quite painful, and some of the tissue dies and it's not uncommon for people to have problems with oxygenating their blood well after that. He was on oxygen while hospitalized but did not require it at home.

"Bill had a history of smoking. He had a history of previous lung trauma related to one of his episodes of infection that he had in his belly, requiring him to go on hemodialysis for a short period of time. And to put somebody on hemodialysis, which is the form of dialysis where we take the blood out and put the blood back. You have to put a big IV in the neck or the groin and the one that was put in the vein in his neck resulted in his lung being punctured. This happened actually in Idaho Falls, and if you puncture the lung, air leaks out of the lung and so it can't expand. He had several reasons to have difficulty with providing enough oxygen to his blood, and I think that the smoking and the number of insults at the time he was discharged from the hospital after his blood clot to his lungs, his ability to oxygenate was very borderline."

In April 1989, Bill was back in the hospital with yet another blood clot. "For some reason, his blood likes to clot. He will be on blood thinning medicine the rest of his life."

Dr. Servilla and John Radin discussed all the clots, pneumonia, infections, high blood pressure, reduced heart rate and the trauma to his kidneys when he was in the automobile accident in 1971. She explained every medication he was taking and went into detail on what each did for him. It would be very common for Bill's legs to swell and the best relief, in addition to reducing his salt intake and using water pills to flush his system, was to elevate his feet.

"Doctor, based upon all you have just told this jury, do you have an opinion as to whether or not William Gray would be able to ride a bicycle 3.6 miles one way, rest for a period and then a return ride of 3.6 miles?"

"Yes I do. Based on his medical condition at the time I was taking care of him and my exposure to Mr. Gray, my opinion is that he could not ride the bicycle that distance in a short period of time. As I've told people in the past, anybody can ride a bicycle a distance, given enough time, and I could conceive Mr. Gray doing it if he stopped, rested, got back on the bicycle. Just walking down the hall of the clinic in Salt Lake, it was maybe a block from the parking lot, he would be huffing and puffing when he would get to the clinic. So conceivably, yes, he could do it but it would take time and it would take resting."

Even the fact that Gray was seen riding a bike before the murders or the fact he had an exercise bike did not sway her opinion. In fact, quite honestly she said, most people have exercise equipment in their homes but never use them. When she saw him he didn't look like he was doing any exercise. He was gaining weight and it wasn't good for him. She had been working with him to get him to do something about his weight.

On cross examination Kane went right to the heart of what he wanted to hear.

"All right, now we're not talking about whether it's a good idea to ride a bicycle for this length of time, but there's no question in your mind he would be capable of riding a bicycle that far?"

"With resting."

"How would you expect him to look after riding a bicycle for a period of time?"

"Short of breath. As most people notice, Mr. Gray is a little ruddy complexioned."

"Would he be a little more red in the face and cheeks, perhaps?"

"The whole face."

"How about sweating. Would you expect him to be sweating?"

"I would some. You know when we talked previously, you asked me about sweating, and as I recall Mr. Gray, you know, yeah, he always looked like he was sweating, but looking at him today, the sweating was his oily ... I mean, he has an oily complexion, a wet looking complexion. To me, he looks like he's sweating now."

On re-direct Radin asked one question. "Doctor, have any of the questions that Mr. Kane has asked you caused you to reconsider your opinion about Mr. Gray's need to rest 10 to 15 minutes every two blocks in July 1989 on a bicycle ride?"

"No."

The defense team reached deep into Bill Gray's pockets to have the presence of this next witness in court. The witness charged $250 an hour for her services. She had already received $2,500 and now she would charge additional for her transportation, travel time and expenses, plus her appearance in court.

Dr. Elizabeth Loftus, a professor of psychology, had enough credentials, experience and degrees to outweigh a train. Dr. Loftus was a celebrity in the small town of Idaho Falls, Idaho. The Department of Justice, the General Services Administration, the FBI and the Internal Revenue Service were a few of the clients she had consulted for. She had appeared on television talk shows, not only as an expert in her field, but in promotion of her books. Dr. Loftus either authored, or co-authored 16 books, many of them on the subject of eyewitness testimony. Three of those books were sitting on the prosecutor's table in front of Mike Kane.

"We use a method called the simulation method, where we present people with simulated crimes or simulated accidents or simulated events of some sort, then later on we'll test people's memories for what they saw, and then we can find out some things about the ability of people to accurately remember past events. I've been very interested in the factor of post-event information, which means new information that a witness gets after the event is completely over. And in order to study the effects of getting new, particularly erroneous information, we've done literally hundreds of studies where we take people that have seen, let's say a simulated crime. One group gets new information and the other group doesn't. Then we test the memory of both groups.

"What the work has shown is that by exposing people to erroneous information, you can alter, contaminate or distort a witness' recollection and get them to believe they saw things that they did not actually see."

The implication was certainly there. If Bill had any chance at all, the defense must discredit the security guard Steve Mackley's eyewitness identification of Bill Gray, for without his credibility the state had a very weak case. In fact they really wouldn't have a case.

The photo lineup was attacked at length.

"Sometimes even the slightest variation in the tint of the photograph could cause an eyewitness to erroneously retain that picture in memory as the person they saw," she said.

"Could you tell me what the confidence factor is doctor?"

"My studies show that people are very confident when they're wrong, as well as at other times being confident when they are right. So in the language of psychology, we say that the correlation between confidence and accuracy is a very weak one. And in lay language, that means that confidence is not a very good indicator of accuracy. The finding about the confidence factor is that it tends to grow. It can grow with successive identifications. The more you see someone, the more familiar they get and the more confident you become. All exposure could be attributed to familiarity, the television, newspaper pictures as well as appearances in court."

Loftus' answers to almost every question Mulligan asked were answered in depth and detail. Her direct examination lasted for hours, sometimes repetitive, sometimes too involved for the average person to retain every scenario or implication provided.

The cross examination was as difficult to follow as it was when Mulligan was asking the questions. Mike Kane had done his homework and pointed out statements in her books that tended to disagree with some of the theories given now in her direct testimony. Dr. Loftus was quick to point out the book he was reading from was 12 years old.

Kane did not lack for knowledge in the field and he fired questions of complex content which she answered in succession, short answers compared to the lengthily answers given Mulligan.

"In the Ted Bundy case basically you described it as having caused you something of a moral dilemma, and do you remember writing at that time about a conversation that you and your husband had in which the following statement was made? 'You're a scientist, you're not a mind reader, and it's not your job to pronounce guilt or innocence on another human being. It's your job to testify what's going to be true.' Do you still feel that way about your work?"

"I do, yes."

But for all the questions asked and answered, the ones that summed it up for the prosecution were, "I guess what I want to get across is that you're not able to come into court and tell this jury that any particular witness is good, bad or indifferent?"

"That is correct."

"Nor would you ever even make an attempt to make that kind of statement?"

"Right. It would be, without corroboration or some other information, it would not be appropriate."

On Tuesday morning the 11th day of the trial, anyone coming into the courthouse from the rear parking area would have had to walk past an old beat-up green International Travelall parked near the back door.

In a few minutes the jury would be taken downstairs to view the Travelall, then loaded onto a bus that would take them to the hospital, then to Reeda's home on Crowley Road and back to the hospital. The defense had worked hard to get the judge to agree to this jury excursion. This was the only way they felt the jury could get a feel for themselves of how far Bill would have had to ride a bicycle. If the jury could see this distance for themselves and believe what Bill's doctor said about his health, they might find it impossible to believe Bill was the man on the bike that night.

After lunch, back in the courthouse, the trial continued and the first witness called was Alice Clark. On the morning of Monday, July 24 between 6:30 and 6:45 a.m., she saw a

Travelall with Wyoming plates pull out in front of her. In fact her sister who was with her commented that those out of town drivers don't know how to drive in the big city. It wasn't shiny, in fact it was quite corroded and it was either green or blue. The driver was neat looking. If he had a beard it was neatly trimmed, "like Mr. Gray's is," she said. She was quite sure the driver was not wearing glasses and when she pulled up alongside him he put his hand up so as to hide his face.

But Alice was somewhat confused. She'd been in Idaho Falls Sunday afternoon as well, and had gone shopping. But she was quite sure, with the aid of her sister, that it was Monday morning when she saw the vehicle.

"Okay, I want to get this as straight as possible if we can," said Kane on cross examination. "Are you just not sure which day you saw it on?"

"I'm just not sure, it's been too long."

"Okay. Do you remember telling us when we were talking to you that you might have been going to get your niece a birthday present?"

"Yes, we did. One of those two days we went to get her a birthday present. Her birthday is the 23rd."

"The 23rd? Um-hmm."

"Would you have gotten her birthday present after her birthday, do you think?"

"I don't know. My sister does get birthday presents late, so I don't know."

Kane was gentle with this witness. Clearly she was a little confused. She was right, it had been a long time.

The defense called two additional witnesses who saw a green or dark colored Travelall or Suburban in the area near the hospital. Both sightings occurred at a time that would not fit the prosecution's time frame. One sighting was at 7 or 8 p.m. Sunday, the other at 1 a.m. Monday. Both witness saw more than one person in the vehicles. Neither witness was absolutely positive it was the Travelall in question.

If the jury was waiting for something concrete, something they could use to give this defendant the benefit of the doubt, so far they were sorely disappointed. But the defense was attempting to show there were other vehicles similar to the green Travelall and other persons resembling Gray spotted in Idaho Falls on the night of the murders. Mulligan and Radin were taking every opportunity, regardless how slim it might be, to cast a shadow of doubt for their client.

"Rose Kienlen saw a man on a bike around 11:30 the night of July 23rd. The rider was coming from the direction of Crowley Road toward the hospital by way of 17th Street.

"Let me ask you, can you describe to the jury what you saw as far as the bicycle and the individual riding it?" asked Radin.

"Like what?"

"What did the person look like, if you can tell us?"

"Just a person, a man."

"Okay, could you tell what race the person was?"

"No, it was too dark."

"And did you get any kind of look at the person's face?"

"No. He had his head down."

"Can you tell us what type of clothes the person was wearing?"

"Just dark clothes."

"Can you tell me whether or not the person had a beard or anything about the hair?"

"No."

"Can you tell me anything about the bike?"

"A bike is a bike."

And so Rose Kienlen's testimony went, bringing smiles to the otherwise somber courtroom. The prosecution had no questions for this witness.

John Cowden, second detective in command under Detective Rodriguez, now retired, was called to testify for the defense. It is not unusual for the defense to call an officer directly involved in the case. It is unusual for the officer to passively answer the defense's questions without the least bit of resistance.

Cowden was present at all interviews of Bill Gray but did not read or review any of the interview transcripts prior to testifying at this trial. Consequently he failed to remember some things, and on most other questions simply agreed with John Radin as Radin brought out all the favorable actions and statements given by Gray in his interviews.

So Cowden agreed Gray was cooperative, "Very cooperative," he added, at all of his interviews. He agreed that Gray did ask about where his wife's body was and he agreed Gray asked about the status of the investigation. By the time the defense was finished with Cowden, Bill Gray was that Boy Scout the defense wanted the jury to see.

Kane moved swiftly to turn this testimony around.

"When you talk about very cooperative, I take it that means that he was he was willing to talk to you?"

"That's correct."

"Whether what he was telling you was true or not, you didn't have any way of knowing?"

"No, that's right."

"Would you call him very cooperative when he started lying to you about the Travelall?"

"Well, up to that point, no I wouldn't."

"Would you call him very cooperative when he started lying about Lloyd Laker seeing him in the Travelall?"

"No, I wouldn't."

"Tell me, if you remember, if he asked you if you knew how his wife had been killed."

"I don't recall him ever asking me that."

"Did he ever ask you if she had been raped or not?"

"I don't believe so."

"Did he ever ask you if she had been mutilated?"

"I don't recall that either."

"Did he ever ask you what condition the body was found in?"

"No, I don't believe so."

"Did he ever ask you how Reeda was found?"

"No."

After a few more housekeeping questions retired detective Cowden was excused.

The prosecution had made a major issue over the fact that the phantom "Ron Mitchell" could not be found. If Ron Mitchell did exist, as the defense wanted the jury to believe, the defense must have a plausible reason why Mitchell could not be found.

On the witness stand was a private investigator hired by Mulligan to find Ron Mitchell. The witness went into lengthy detail how he searched records, made personal inquiries, checked several areas and states, but could not find Mitchell.

At the onset this seemed like it would serve to confirm the prosecution's contention that Mitchell did not exist. However, the point of his testimony was centered around the probability that Ron Mitchell gave Bill a phony name because Mitchell had something to hide. He could have been running from the law for all they knew or could have been put in jail and thus unable to claim his vehicle. All they had to go on was Bill's description which could fit a large portion of Wyoming residents. Without the real name it would be next to impossible to find this man, especially if he didn't want to be found.

June 2, day 12 of the trial, the courtroom was packed. Extra chairs were brought in and, amazingly, everyone who wanted in, was seated. Detective Victor Rodriguez, agent John Kotrason, and attorney Tom Moss were among the additions to the people in the spectator seats. Joy Ufford from the *Jackson Hole Guide* and all the Roundy family were back in the courtroom, in addition to the familiar faces of DeeDee, Rhonda and Sandi who had sat through every minute of the trial. Although Mike Kane had fought hard to have the judge allow Jo Ann and Saralyn in the courtroom since they had already testified, the judge would not budge.

On this day Bill Gray would take the stand and testify in his own defense. This is a rare event in most first degree murder trials. Either Gray's attorneys felt it was their only shot at an acquittal or Bill was still confident he could beat the system and win the sympathy of at least one of the five women and seven men seated in the jury box with his personal charm and "poor me" testimony. Just as he had been convinced his full cooperation with the police at his interviews would show innocence, obviously he felt testifying at his trial would give the jury cause to believe he had nothing to fear because he was innocent. Bill Gray was sworn in and limped to the witness chair.

"Mr. Gray how old are you?"

"I'm 53."

"A little bit nervous?"

"Yeah."

Mulligan went on with the help-to-relax type questions, where he lived, how long, birth place, the loss of his sister and his years in California.

Betty was 14½ or 15 years old when he met her, he was 17. Bill's version of inviting both sets of parents to the Las Vegas wedding was directly opposite to Jo Ann's remembrance of Betty eloping and her parents knowing nothing about it. Bill claimed her parents were invited but elected not to attend.

Step by step Mulligan and Gray went through the process of taking a gun in for pawn and the paperwork associated with it. He did not have a Class Three Firearms License so he was not allowed by the ATF (Bureau of Alcohol, Tobacco and Firearms) to sell or take a silencer in for pawn. They spent a considerable amount of time discussing the average pawn transaction and procedure for redemption of a pawned item.

Then Bill was asked to tell the jury about one of his favorite subjects ... his health, starting with the broken collarbone when he was in second grade, to his kidney transplant and swelling knees. The jury learned all about peritoneal dialysis and the need for disposable gloves and Betadine medical swabs, not the average run of the mill wet wipes; never did use that kind, never had them in his house.

The recovery from his transplant had been long and slow, aggravated by the swelling in his legs. His wife had everything dumped on her and she became depressed. He tried to help her but really the only thing he could do was to get well and get back to work. He was not aware of Betty's affair with Leavitt until Janis Roby told him after Betty's death.

Their relationship was real good the weekend before Betty went to California, Bill thought. They went out and did things. Just before she left for California they went out and had a good time.

"When I got home from Las Vegas, my wife and I and another couple went down to the Cowboy Bar to listen to a band they had there. And we had fun. We enjoyed the music and we danced quite a bit together that evening."

Shortly after Betty went to California he ended up in the hospital with a blood clot.

"I did not ask Betty to come home, no. She says, 'Do you want me to come home?' And I told her, I says, heavens no. I says, you're on vacation. Enjoy your vacation. Everything is locked up. The season hasn't started. Don't worry about it. Just you know, enjoy your vacation. I'm just calling to let you know I'm not at home if you can't get me. I'm in the hospital."

"After Betty returned from her visit in California did anything unusual occur between you and her and your relationship?"

"Yes, it did. It was a while after she came back home. It would have had to have been at least three weeks, because we were up that morning getting ready to go to work. I approached her when we were getting dressed ... and we had relations the evening before. And I approached her and snuggled up to her back and I says, How about a little before work? And at that time she just became rigid."

It wasn't until the day after Betty's birthday, June 13th that a divorce was discussed. They discussed very calmly about how things would be split, they both cried tears.

"Who's idea was it to keep the divorce a secret?"

"That was my suggestion."

"Why?"

"Well, we had put the business up for sale and anytime a buyer thinks, you know, that there is something wrong in a relationship or somebody is sick and the business is being sold over that, it kind of affects your bargaining power. They seem to have the upper hand at that point."

"Okay, was that your only reason?"

"Yes, it was."

"But Betty betrayed their agreement and told someone."

"I steamed open a letter Betty wrote to her mother."

"Why?"

"Well, there had been money missing from the business. The accounts were screwed up. And I had found out that Betty had been taking money from me. And I didn't know why she was taking this money. And I thought maybe I might get a hint out of the letter to her mom, you know. Who are you going to talk to if you don't talk to Mom?"

Mulligan led him through his discovery of the boxes Betty brought home and filled, then the questioning went to the missing money and the subsequent inventory.

"No, I never said anything to Betty about it. When I discovered it and found out, you know, what was going on, I told Betty that I was going to have to start making up a till every night, because I was screwing up. The checkbooks were off, and I told her that I was either putting money that belonged to the pawn account into the general account, and that I was going to have to start making up a till until I got this thing straightened out."

"Why did you tell her that?"

"So that she wouldn't think that I knew that she was taking money. I didn't want to make an issue of it."

"But at the same time let her know that you might have known?"

"Yes, a little bit."

"Did you start checking anywhere to see where the money was going?"

"Yes I started checking her wallet regularly then."

Unlike the interviews when Bill dwelled on his inventorying of his wife's purse and every detail of his written record, the subject was brought up, a somewhat conceivable reasoning given, then quickly dropped.

When the boat slipped off the trailer on that fishing trip with Leavitt and Brown, he assisted in getting it unstuck.

"I did what I could do."

"What did you do?"

"I picked up some small rocks on the bank and put them in the hole, went up, and we had to gather some ... well, they were gathering pieces of blown-down quakens. And there was a rotten log up there and I carted down some small pieces of rotten log, drug them down, rolled them over the bank so they could pack it in."

He knew nothing, "absolutely nothing," about love cards and notes. He did not leave a card on the floor for Betty to find.

"Did you in fact ride a bicycle into Mr. Oetting's gas station two weeks before Betty's death?"

"It may have been a little earlier than that, but yes, I did ride a bicycle. I'd been out in the garage puttering around, and I noticed that the gears on the ten speed, the bike had either been dropped or something in the garage had fallen against it, and they were bent slightly in. I bent it back out and adjusted it somewhat, and took the bike for a little ride to test it out."

He went through a rather extensive story of having to get off and push the bike three different times before he could get to Oetting's station. The total distance from his house to Oetting's he estimated at a half mile.

"It was a ten-speed boy's bicycle. It had a baby carriage rack mounted over the back wheel that my daughter put on it when she was using it. There is a light on the front part of the bike, a headlight. And that bike is equipped with a narrow seat like you see on all ten speeds. That was the only bike I have been on since 1986."

"Did you ride that bike, or any other bike on the night of July 23 or morning of July 24?"

"No, I did not."

"Have you ever ridden a bike in Idaho Falls, Idaho on the night of July 23 or July 24 of 1989?"

"I have never ridden a bike in Idaho Falls at any time."

"Did you ride a bike from Eastern Idaho Medical Center over to Crowley Road for the purpose of killing someone?"

"No, I did not."

Asked about the Sunday morning before Betty left for Reeda's, Bill gave his version of Betty planning to go to the Wilson Chicken Fry then changing her mind and deciding to go to Reeda's. When it was time for him to go to work he recalled the event.

"We gave each other a hug and a kiss, and that was the last time I saw her."

Bill's voice was shaky and he appeared emotional. Mulligan advised him to take a couple of deep breaths then asked if he could go on. Bill said he could.

Then Bill was asked what he did Sunday afternoon and evening. Bill repeated the same story he'd given the investigators of going home around 3 or 3:25 p.m., propping himself up with pillows in the recliner to get his feet up, trying to call his parents and Jeff but no one was home, watching some television then falling asleep until about 10 p.m. Well, it was probably closer to a quarter to 10 because he tried to reach Jeff again at that time. He then went down to the store to check out for the next day, get the cash box ready and whatever else had to be done. He must have arrived at the store around 10 p.m., he thought.

"Do you remember ... do you recall how long you stayed there?"

"On an easy night when everything goes all right, you don't have to run through things twice, usually it takes 35 to 45 minutes to run through everything."

"Did you go down to the store alone?"

"Yes, I was alone, other than my dog. He went every place with me."

"What time did you feel you left the store?"

"I wouldn't have left the store any sooner than a quarter to 11 to 11 o'clock, someplace, would have been the soonest I would have been out."

He went straight home, got back in the recliner and didn't get up until "my Dobbie woke me up to go outside." When Dobbie came back in he crawled into his own bed and spent the rest of the night there.

"Did you go to Idaho Falls on the evening of July 23?"

"No, I did not."

"Did you kill either your wife or Reeda Roundy?"

"No, I did not. I could never hurt my wife."

"Did you have anything to do with her death?"

"No, I did not."

468

The questions led to Monday morning, Bill getting his blood test then opening the shop. Detective David Foster and Police Chief Dick Hayes came to tell him about Betty a little after noon.

"Was it unusual for the police to come in?"

"No, it was not unusual. They came in periodically if they were looking for something that had been stolen or a house had been broken into or got a report from another state of someone that had stolen something or committed a burglary that was headed in our direction. They would stop in to see if I had picked it up or if I'd seen it. A lot of times they'd just pick up the telephone and call and ask me. Police officers just stopped in. They bought tackle there, and once in a while they would just stop to shoot the breeze."

Slowly Bill was grinding out his story. A fragile story at best, but certainly the way Bill wanted others to perceive the events in contrast to all the witnesses before him.

"Now there was some testimony that when your daughter told you she was pregnant, you exclaimed something to the effect, 'Oh God, if I only had known.' Did you say that?"

"I did say those words, but not in the expression my daughter went through."

"Would you explain as briefly as you can why you made that statement?"

"Okay, Saralyn had told me that she had made plans with Mom to go over on Monday evening for dinner at the house, her and Kent. And Saralyn told me that it was their intention at that time, at the dinner, to let us know we were going to be grandparents again and that her and Kent were going to get married. And when she told me that I made that statement of 'oh my God, if I had only known,' meaning to my daughter that if I'd have known that she was pregnant, I would have told my wife so my wife would have treated my daughter differently, because at that time they were pretty much down on one another."

"And by being down on one another, what was going on between them?"

"They weren't getting along at all at that time. I think it was just that Friday Saralyn had been in the store in the afternoon and Betty had made the comment to her about she was sure getting a rear end on her, she was putting on weight and she was getting heavy. And if Betty would have known that Saralyn was pregnant she never would have made that comment to her and they would have been getting along instead of arguing."

Yes, he did have a medical-alert bracelet but now he was wearing a necklace. Why? Because he'd lost two of them. They wouldn't stay on so he thought he'd try a necklace instead. Innocently lost or conveniently lost? Who would the jury believe?

When Bill entered the courtroom after the noon recess he stopped dead in his tracks after he looked up and saw Dick Buccola and son Rick seated in the courtroom. They flew in from California that morning and went directly to the courthouse. Since Jo Ann was not allowed in the courtroom she was determined that someone in the family, who knew the truth, was present while Bill testified. She was sure it would make him quite uncomfortable as he conjured up all his lies. She may have been right. As soon as Bill saw Dick he had a flurried conversation with John Radin. Thereafter, Radin tried unsuccessfully to have the judge remove the Buccolas from the courtroom, but they had every right to be there. Judge Wood upheld that right.

Mike Kane introduced himself to Dick and moved them to the front row of the spectator seats. Bill never once looked at Dick as he re-took the stand and continued his testimony. Dick sat in amazement as Bill cranked out lie after lie, just as Jo Ann knew he would.

Bill went through Betty's purse looking for money, he kept an inventory of the amounts he found. He did not see a picture of Leavitt.

"No, I did, you know squeeze the pictures to see if there was money folded up in them. There wasn't any money and I didn't see anything else."

They discussed his interviews.

"And in that interview [July 27] did you ever make any inquiries of the facts surrounding your wife's death?"

"Many times."

"What generally would you ask?"

"Well, I called the police department daily, or the sheriff's office. I guess it was over in Idaho Falls, trying to find out when we could, you know, find out where Betty's body was so that we could take care of it."

"Did you ever ask specific details about whether or not the bodies were mutilated or whether the women were raped or anything like that?"

"No. After they told me how they had been killed, I wanted to remember Betty like the last time I had seen her, and I really didn't ask any detailed questions along that line, I don't believe."

"You didn't want to know?"

"I really didn't want to know."

Bill was well prepared to face the Travelall and Ron Mitchell. He knew his story could not stray far from his interviews and deposition or Mike Kane would crucify him unmercifully before this jury.

Ron Mitchell came by the pawnshop to drive the Travelall before it was repaired and left a $200 deposit. Then he came back after it was repaired, sometime after July 3, and drove the Travelall again. He said everything was satisfactory and he would return to get the vehicle when he got paid and left. The Friday or Saturday before Betty's death, Mitchell paid the balance on the Travelall and left with it. Within the hour, while Bill was in the parking lot looking at someone's pawn, Mitchell returned. This time he wanted more work done on it.

"He wanted the steering fixed because it was bouncing around all over the road. He was also pretty insistent that I have it tuned up. And we got into a pretty heated argument over it before we were done. At one point he was insistent that I do the work or that I buy the vehicle back from him. At that point in time, when he expressed that if I wasn't going to do the work, he wanted me to take the vehicle back. He reached in his pocket and pulled out the title and held it out. I took the title from him at that time and we argued some more and I told him I didn't intend to do any more work to it."

"Did he leave at that time?"

"Shortly after that, yeah. We grumbled some more and he did leave. He was pretty grumpy when he left. And he left and he said, 'I'll be back.'"

Bill did not ask Mitchell for any identification and Bill never heard from him again. Bill had made his own efforts to try and locate Mitchell through the bail bond company and by making inquiries of various people.

"Now you apparently moved the vehicle just shortly before midnight on the 26th. Why did you move it?"

"Why did I move it? Because Ron Mitchell still owed me some money, as far as I was concerned, on the repairs. And when he left, he had a set of keys to it, and I just had the feeling that he was going to come back and take it without paying the repairs."

Bill repeated his story of moving the Travelall to Bondurant, telling Hurley he was being framed. They discussed his interview of July 28 and then he explains why he lied to the detectives.

"And you lied to them?"

"Yes, I did."

"Why did you lie to them?"

"Because I was afraid."

"Why were you afraid?"

"Because when ... I mentioned before the reasons that I thought that, you know, I was definitely a suspect."

"Well did you in fact have anything to do with the murder of these two women?"

"No, I did not."

Bill wrote the mileage on the Travelall's title which was more mileage than the Travelall had on it when it was repaired. His explanation was simple. He made a mistake.

"Was it possible that you made a mistake, Bill?"

"It's possible, very possible that I made a mistake."

"Have you ever made mistakes before when you have written

down numbers?"

"Yes, I have, several times. It was pointed out to me on inspections by the ATF, to where we had inverted numbers on our yellow sheets when we had been ... when we would pull a yellow sheet out of our book that we kept them in, the top was numbered. When we took one out, we put the next number on the next sheet, so we didn't have to look them up, and there were numerous occasions that those numbers were messed up."

"Transposed?"

"Transposed, turned around. The last three numbers turned around."

The mileage put on the title by Bill was 73,406, the mileage from the repair bill was 73,158. Just the last three numbers!

Bill was very despondent over the loss of his wife, depressed, devastated, he missed her very much and he cried "a whole bunch that week."

"Were you still in love with her?"

"Very much so, I still am today."

Performing adequately for the jury, Bill became emotional as he talked about the autopsy being completed in one day and he could have had Betty back much sooner but the police would never tell him where his wife's body was.

"After Betty was cremated, did you get an urn containing her ashes?"

"They gave me a container. It was in a plastic container with her ashes."

"And at any time did you threaten to flush her ashes down the toilet?"

"Never."

"What did you do with her ashes when you got them?"

"When I got them, I put them on the mantel next to a wedding picture of ourselves. They remained there for a year ... I couldn't let go."

"Then what did you do?"

"She wanted her ashes scattered where she could enjoy the fall colors. I took her up to Jackson Lake, out on Elk Island, with a beautiful view of the Tetons looking out over the lake, and the fall colors are always pretty, very pretty there, and scattered her ashes there."

In answer to his daughter's accusations Bill admitted he'd made a phone call to Jack Hurley on the way home from paying his last respects to Betty, but their conversation was not about getting stories straight. Bill went into a rather lengthy explanation of calling Hurley about the electrical work for his addition on the pawnshop. It was all about business. But why did he call from there on a day he had just spent in a mortuary where his wife was lying dead?, Mulligan inquired.

"Because I knew that I could reach him at that time, I figured he would be home at that time. And the next day was going to be Sunday, and I didn't know if he would be home. My schedule was very, very busy."

The jury learned when Bill and Betty applied for a Small Business Administration loan on the pawnshop the bank required life insurance policies on both Betty and Bill. Applications were filled out and each received a $100,000 policy. Mulligan admitted the two policies and the application for the loan into evidence.

But, according to Bill, his policy was quickly canceled after they checked his medical records. Then one day in October of 1987, they received a renewal slip on Betty's policy and were discussing it at work that day. A customer in the shop overheard their conversation and he guaranteed them he could get a better price for more insurance than they were getting. So Betty canceled her policy through the bank and took out a new one for $250,000. When the white envelope came Bill looked in it just long enough to see it was the policy, then he put it away and did not look at it again until after Betty's death, therefore he did not know he was the sole beneficiary of her policy. He thought the bank owned the policy until he paid off the loan on the pawnshop.

Bill had a reason or excuse, no matter how lame or unbelievable, for every item of a suspicious nature. He hadn't been intent on getting back Betty's minor purchases because of their value. All he wanted to do when he gave the Roundy brothers the list of missing items was to make sure Leavitt didn't get anything.

He was "flabbergasted" when he found out his children were suing him. This subject led to another rather lengthy story of Saralyn's running away.

Not even having the guts to leave them a note, he said slamming his daughter.

He continued his Saralyn bashing until Kane raised an objection.

"Your honor, I'm going to object to this. This is totally irrelevant. It's got nothing to do with the case. What he's trying to do is massacre his daughter in court here. It's got nothing to do with it."

The judge agreed and Mulligan moved on.

"Now, the fact that you decided to settle the civil suit, did that reflect anything on whether or not you committed these crimes?"

"No, it did not."

"Why did you settle that suit?"

"One was my health. It was, you know, affecting my health. The other one was ... how do I want to put it? I was advised by my counsel that with the civil case, with them not having to ... how is it, prove beyond a reasonable doubt that there was a possibility, you know, that we could lose the case."

"We talked about the terms and the fact that a civil case takes preponderance versus proof beyond a reasonable doubt," interjected Mulligan quickly.

"Yes, it was."

Bill claimed he knew nothing about a warrant being issued for his arrest before he left Jackson. He spent some time in Las Vegas and then in northern California, then he called his attorney and found out about the warrant. He bought a Mini-Winnie motor home in the town of Paradise, California then worked his way south to see his doctor, then he was going to go back to Jackson and turn himself in.

Over the objections of Mike Kane, Mulligan managed to inform the jury that even while Bill was incarcerated defending himself against murder charges, he paid $41,000 to the IRS, implying only a man expecting to be acquitted and set free because he was innocent would pay his taxes.

Bill Gray never reloaded 9mm ammunition.

"Never in my life," he said.

He used to reload other types, but not 9mm. The shells Saralyn found in his garage came from a merchandise purchase for the pawnshop. Some of the merchandise was stored in his garage. Contrary to his daughter's testimony, Bill did sell reloads in the pawnshop. He said the price of a brand-new box of ammunition was $12 to $18, while the price of reloaded ammunition was approximately $6.30 a box. His pawnshop customers liked a choice of less expensive ammunition and they got a $1 if they brought back a box of 50 spent casings. Bill in turn sent them back to the reloading manufacturers and saved some money on his future purchases.

Would anyone think the killer of the two women spent extra time in the murder house going after the spent casings because they could be traded for money? Was it more a habit, like saving the pull tab on pop cans, to gather spent casings after firing a gun?

The only time Bill drank Mountain Dew was when his parents came. If they couldn't get 7-Up at the market they got Mountain Dew, he said. It was a long, long time ago that he saved pop can tabs, way before his dialysis. Once they got the kidney machine in Visalia he quit saving them. Saralyn certainly had not agreed with that statement.

Yes, he printed in capital letters just as Saralyn said he did. He denied writing "Satan Loves You" on the countertop.

Bill didn't own any other tennis shoes in July of 1989 other than the two pairs Mulligan entered into evidence. These two pairs of tennis shoes were taken from his home during the search warrant. They were size 12.

Bill had a reason or explanation, no matter how lame, for everything others thought were incriminating. Most all of his answers had been long and rambling and some were very hard to swallow. If he was attempting to talk his way out, he was stretching at best. He'd shown emotion at all the proper times, he'd smiled and grinned and found humor in all the right places.

But it was impossible to believe a word he'd said.

It is very rare for a prosecutor to have the opportunity to cross-examine a defendant charged with first degree murder. Mike Kane would relish this opportunity. He would pounce on Gray like a cat on a mouse. Firing questions in rapid succession his voice would not boom like Mulligan's when he examined Rodriguez, but it would be authoritative, demanding and unbelieving.

"Good morning, Mr. Gray. Let's begin with some easy things. First of all, you owned a 9mm pistol?"

"Yes."

"You owned more than one?"

"With the business, yes."

"You had several at your pawnshop?"

"Several, I had some."

"Yeah, and you had bought guns regularly?"

"Yes."

"You pawned guns regularly?"

"Yes."

"You traded for guns?"

"Yes."

"And I guess we have been talking about a pawnshop as if that was the beginning and the end of things. There was nothing to stop you from going out and buying a 9mm pistol anywhere you wanted, was there?"

"No."

"Anywhere, including Las Vegas or Idaho or anywhere else?"

"With my license I can buy weapons any place."

"You heard Saralyn testify that there was an empty box in the garage and she took the 9mm shells from three different boxes and put them in that one?"

"That's what I heard, yes."

"Apparently you had three boxes of reloaded 9mm ammunition in your cabinet?"

"I had several boxes in my cabinet."

"Right, and I guess that's the point I want to make here, Mr. Gray. Whether you were reloading them yourself, or you bought them, you don't deny that you had access to 9mm reloaded bullets, do you?"

"No."

"When you obtained a weapon through the pawnshop you were responsible to write up that weapon in the ATF book."

"That would be correct."

"Now in 1988 do you remember being advised by the ATF that your books were so bad that you were admonished by the Bureau of Alcohol, Tobacco and Firearms in writing for some of the problems?"

"That is correct, because at that period of time, I was so sick that I wasn't going into the store."

"Well let's talk about some of the problems that they found. Three guns had not been written in the book at all at that time, you sold handguns to people under 21, failure to execute the yellow forms you were describing to the jury, failure to record disposition of three firearms in the book and failure to report multiple handguns sales. Do you remember that?"

"I was not even there."

"But you were going down to the store regularly and checking the records, weren't you?"

"Not at that time, I wasn't able."

But Kane continued to pin him down. Gray finally couldn't deny he was going to the store regularly in 1990 and it was in 1990 he had been cited by the ATF for failure to record 22 weapons. Gray had no recollection of this happening. Kane changed the subject.

After establishing the Grays had a sizeable estate that would have to be split down the middle if they divorced, Kane wanted to know if it was Bill's idea to keep it secret.

"I guess so."

"And what you testified to is that's it's because of the bargaining power of prospective buyers."

"That is correct."

"So you didn't want this secret to get out so a prospective buyer would learn about this?"

"I didn't want anybody to know about it, because I had no doubt in my mind that whatever was wrong would be resolved."

"You wanted it kept secret from even Betty's own mother. Everyone, children, aunts, friends you knew, everyone was supposed to be kept out of this decision?"

"That's correct."

"Okay, but would you agree that some of these people had nothing to do with bargaining power. The people in California, for example?"

"I explained why."

Kane handed Bill a wallet which Bill identified as Betty's wallet. He had Bill go through the wallet and show the jurors where he found the money. Bill showed each compartment and talked about how the money would build up, this spot here in the back, that's where she kept the larger bills. She kept the smaller bill right here, then she would put it here, then it would be gone. He was pumped up just talking about the search. He was eager to show the jury all the hidden compartments.

No, he didn't go through her purse many times, not two or three times a day, as Kane accused.

"No sir, there was sometimes that I checked it in the morning and in the evening but not anymore than that."

Bill denied being mean with Betty about the boxes she was removing from the house. Reading to the jury from an interview where Bill jumped Betty about the boxes, where he cussed at her, making her cry and telling her to get the "goddamned boxes back," Kane thought that indicated that he "jumped all over her."

"I guess I was a little harsh in my phrasing it, but I wouldn't say I jumped all over her."

"Okay. You confronted her about the boxes and letting the secret about the divorce out, and you did not confront her about the money?"

"I didn't care about the money."

"You didn't care about the money?"

"No."

"What was the chart for, then?"

"The chart was so I knew how much she was taking, but I could have cared less."

"Okay, you cared about the boxes but you didn't care about the money. Now, just for the record, you were going to Las Vegas regularly?"

"Yes, I was."

"And you were gambling obviously?"

"Yes."

"You're a craps player?"

"Yes."

"And you were betting pretty heavy, weren't you?"

"What do you call heavy?"

"At one of your interviews you complained about Jackpot, Nevada because it only has a $200 limit on the tables. I assume you were spending hundreds of dollars gambling?"

"I believe my reference to the $200 limit at Jackpot was to a conversation I had with the investigators. I told them that was, you know, a poor place to gamble because if they got to you,

you couldn't come out."

"Mr. Gray, I've got your briefcase that was seized. It has reference to hundreds of dollars worth of gambling. You remember that don't you?"

"Yeah, sure."

"So you were betting pretty heavily?"

"There again, I have to ask you what you're asking me is heavy."

"Several hundred dollar bets on the crap tables."

"Several hundred?"

"Mr. Gray, please, what amount of money were you betting at the crap tables?"

"Okay, when I first started going over there, I played with $1 and $5 chips until I definitely had a system that I had there, and at that time I started betting with $25 dollar chips."

"And it went up considerably from there didn't it?

"No, I stuck with it. I would play $25 chips, $100 chips, and they would give me some. It depends what I bought into the game for, the denominations of chips I got."

"Okay, the point of all this is that basically you were gambling a large amount of money. Correct?"

Mulligan rose to rescue his client. "That's been asked and answered."

"It's been asked and has not been answered," retorted Kane.

Kane changed the subject. Yes, he had lied to the police about being on a bike a couple of weeks before the murders.

"I guess I really didn't consider that a ride. It was a ride, yes, but not in the sense of going out and riding a bicycle."

Getting to the subject Bill knew was coming and prepared for, Kane asked question after question about the Travelall.

"You're saying the moving of the Travelall had nothing to do with being questioned by the police. Is that what you're saying?"

"None whatsoever."

"You moved the Travelall about midnight and you didn't get to Hurley's until about 1 a.m.?"

"It was pretty close, yes."

"And you are saying you did this to stiff Ron Mitchell out of $58.13?"

"Yes."

"So let's make this absolutely clear. This is the amount of money you moved the Travelall for?"

"That is correct."

"But you also said the $58 didn't even come up until this so-called argument between you and Mitchell?"

"That's correct. Up until that time it was my, well, that was the deal we made. He was going to pay for it up until that time."

"It was never part of the original deal, was it?"

"It was part of the original deal. I was going to pay for the repairs myself, originally."

"So Ron Mitchell was going to pay you $400 and that was going to be it?"

"That's correct."

"So, Ron Mitchell never owed you that $58 until you say he changed the deal?"

"Yes, when he changed his deal, I changed my deal, yes."

"So basically, what you're telling this jury is that two days after your wife is dead, at midnight, you move a Travelall 30 miles to save $58 that was never owed to you in the first place?"

"That's correct. Wouldn't that be three days? Monday, Tuesday, Wednesday?"

Bill had no clue. What's two days or three days? The implication is the same. It was his mouth that got him in trouble to begin with. He had not learned his lesson and this was only the start of his cross-examination.

Kane established that Mitchell would not have known where Bill lived, so was there any reason Bill couldn't have taken the Travelall and put it in his own driveway?

"There's a big reason why I couldn't."

"Let's hear it."

"We had more cars there than we can park on the driveway and I had to park some cars in the street."

"Okay, so you could have parked it on the street then couldn't you?"

"I'd never take a crummy vehicle like that and park on our street."

"You could have parked it almost anywhere in Jackson couldn't you?"

"Yes, I guess I could have. I guess I could have, you know, left it someplace in town. It just never occurred to me."

"Pinedale is closer to Bondurant than to Jackson isn't it?"

"I don't know."

"Well there was no reason to move it closer to where you thought this Ron Mitchell might be is there?"

"I don't know which is closer."

"I guess Mr. Gray, let's stop beating around the bush. This Ron Mitchell just didn't exist, did he?"

"Yes, he did, most definitely."

"You said you were so sure that Ron Mitchell was going to buy the Travelall that you had the Coys sign the bill of sale before Ron Mitchell ever saw it?"

"That is correct."

"Once the Coys signed over and gave you that title you could have just turned that over to Ron Mitchell, couldn't you?"

"I could have, yes."

"There was really no reason to go down and pay money and basically forge his signature, was there?"

"No, only like I say, I had told him I would do that for him."

"You needed to register the vehicle in order to get the plates, didn't you?"

"I don't know if you have to or not."

Referring to the odometer reading on the title, Gray said that yes, he could have been wrong when he wrote that in.

"Where did you get that information from?"

"Off the speedometer."

"The speedometer didn't read that. You would agree with that wouldn't you?"

"I have been told it's a different reading than the one the garage had."

"Do you disagree with that?"

"One of them is wrong."

"Right, you're saying that you don't know which one is wrong?"

"That's what I'm saying, yes."

"Do you have any reason to believe that the garage made a mistake?"

"No reason to believe that."

"And yet, you tried to tell the police that if they would just check the mileage, they'd see that the Travelall couldn't have gone to Idaho Falls. Do you have any explanation how 400 miles gets on it between July 3rd when the shop worked on it and the date it was picked up by the police?"

"Other than the times Ron Mitchell drove it, and the time I drove it to Bondurant no, I do not."

Mike Kane would not let up and continued questioning Bill about the Travelall and then summed up the facts.

"Okay. So what you've been saying is Ron Mitchell and you

got into an argument out in the parking lot and he pulls out the title and starts waving it around and you take it?"

"That's correct."

"And when the argument is over, you wind up with the Travelall, the title, the money and a set of keys?"

Kane hammers and hammers.

"You paid taxes on it, you get plates on it and you've got nothing in the way of receipts or documents to back this up except for these documents here, the title, registration."

"I had the sales set off the cash register to show where I rang up the money."

"You had it?"

"Yes, I did."

"Well, do you have it now?"

"I don't have it now. Would you like to know where it went?"

"Tell me where it went."

"I had a bag, by a bag, I'm speaking of a grocery sack, plastic sack, from the store. I had put that in there with some other things that I had, a calendar, and it has some other things in there that I was saving for the, what was the first case called?"

"The civil case."

"Yes the civil case."

"Did you give that to your lawyer?"

"No. It was missing from my home when I came back from one of my trips."

"It was stolen?"

"Yes, it was."

"You aren't trying to tell the jury that one of your kids stole it, are you?

"They were asked about it."

By now it's a safe bet Mulligan was rethinking his decision to allow his client to testify even if his client had insisted.

"You have said basically that you didn't say some of the things that Saralyn talked about?"

"My daughter worked very hard to try to bring evidence against me."

"So you're going further, you are saying that she's manufacturing evidence?"

"Yes."

"And of course they sued you civilly?"

"Yes, they did."

You paid money to your kids even though you are saying that they were lying?"

"Yes."

"Because you stood to lose a lot more than $500,000?"

"If we were to lose the case, yes I stood to lose everything, all of my assets."

The next question was about the Travelall again. Just that quick Kane puts Bill in the hot seat again. Kane fires question after question.

"But the point of the fact, the bottom line, the truth is, that you did have the Travelall the night of the murder, in your possession?"

"Yes, he had brought it back and it was at the store, yes?"

"Now in your deposition you said that you lied because the police were pressuring you. Is that still your statement?"

"That, and you know, I was scared at the time of the interview."

"You heard the tape. You feel that the police were pressuring you?"

"Yes."

"But knowing you were a suspect you would lie and not tell the truth?"

"I lied because I was afraid, you know, with what I had done on my own, I guess you could say. The first question off the bat was, 'Do you own a Travelall?' And it just, you know, knowing that I had moved it just two days prior to that, I told them no."

"You were basically trying to protect yourself, basically?"

"Like I say, I felt that ... definitely felt that, I was being framed at that time and I knew that I had definitely moved the vehicle on that Wednesday night or early Thursday morning."

"So you were trying to protect yourself?"

"Yes, I didn't want anything to do with it."

"To throw the police off track?"

"Not throw them off track. I guess I just didn't want to have anything to do with it because like I say, I knew that I moved it that night, and the first question off the bat. There hasn't been anything said about a Travelall, and then boom, Travelall. And I thought, you know, I started lying."

Kane dropped it there. It was enough about the Travelall. If the jurors hadn't got the message by now they never would. Then Kane asked several questions about who was telling the truth. Who should the jury believe? Through his answers, Gray had said his son, his daughter and his daughter-in-law had all been lying.

"Was everyone else," Kane asked. "You're saying Steve Mackley is wrong?"

"Most definitely."

"And Paula Lesinger is wrong."

"Who? Which one is that?"

"That's the lady that spotted your truck in Jackson."

"Most definitely, yes."

"Jason Perry you're saying is wrong?"

"Yes."

"The Coys are wrong about them saying the vehicle was missing?"

"I can't say that they were or weren't. I know that the vehicle was there when I came to work. I'm sure of that."

"Is Janis Roby wrong when she says that you told her you knew your wife was having an affair?"

"Yes, I never said anything like that."

"Okay, I guess you're saying that Roy Leavitt was wrong about the tennis shoes?"

"Correct."

"Okay, I guess Saralyn is too, because she testified to that also?"

"Correct."

"Okay, and Saralyn and the police are wrong or lying about the book on silencers?"

"Most definitely."

"And Jim Corbman on the mileage may be wrong. You don't know?"

"I don't know."

"Richard Oetting is wrong about the bike?"

"The bike that I described, he's wrong about."

"And Mary Lou Royce is wrong about the wet wipes?"

"That is correct."

"But Ron Mitchell really exists?"

"Yes, he did."

"That's all I have," Mike Kane said as he disgustedly turned his back on Gray and walked away.

The centerpiece of the defense's case had been on the stand for almost seven hours. He'd called everyone, except himself liars. He had a story, but was it believable? Bill Gray never expected to have to answer questions about bicycles and Travelalls. He was caught off guard so swiftly he'd had no time to prepare. The first lie required the next, then the next, until nothing he said made any sense. The house of cards came tumbling down and Bill was caught in the rubble.

Several more witnesses were called to add minor housekeeping items to the record. Then the defense rested. They had given it their best shot and soon the jury would determine if they had been successful.

On Monday morning, June 7, the hall outside of Courtroom IV was full and noisy. Everyone who had previously attended the trial sporadically, was now back in court to hear the jury instructions and closing arguments. All the Roundy family had come back from Utah, a full contingency of media reporters was present, officers and investigators who worked the case including Rodriguez and Kotrason were there, as was Tom Moss. The troop of trial watchers who had been in attendance every day and had made friends with one another were anxiously wondering if there would be enough seating in the courtroom for them now. The testimony was over, the evidence had been presented. Now Jo Ann Buccola, Saralyn Hoffman, Jeff and Kim Gray and William Gray would be allowed in the courtroom.

"Good morning ladies and gentlemen. We're convened this morning before reading the final jury instructions and before closing arguments to put on record a waiver. We met on Friday to hold a jury instruction conference, and at that time counsel for the defendant was prepared to waive any right he might have to have the jury instructed on a lesser included offense, second degree murder."

Bill was going for broke. On the surface one might think he should jump at the opportunity for a lesser charge. However, it would be much easier for the jury to return a guilty verdict on second degree murder than first degree murder, which could impose the death penalty. Assessing the evidence presented against him, Bill and his attorneys must have felt the odds were the jury would be more inclined to render a guilty verdict on second degree than they would a guilty verdict of first degree. Therefore, if found guilty of second degree murder as they were sure the jury would find, Bill would spend some time in jail, but if found not guilty of first degree, as they were also sure the jury would find, Bill would walk out of the courtroom a free man. Considering the state's case was all circumstantial, Bill could not be connected directly to the murder scene and the squeamishness of juries to convict when the death penalty is associated, Bill chose to take his chances.

The jury instructions took less than an hour. Then the attorneys, Richard Mulligan and Michael Kane, rose for their final performance. The room was exceptionally quiet as each side told its story interpreting the various testimonies to their advantage and dwelling on the stronger points of its case. At 2:23 p.m. the jury was taken to the jury room to start their deliberations. There was nothing left for anyone to do but wait.

The jury deliberated until late that Monday night and now sequestered until they reached their verdict, retired for the night at a local motel. By 5:30 p.m. Tuesday, a verdict had not been reached and the rumors around the courthouse indicated the jury would soon go to dinner and retire for the night. Those who felt strongly about Bill Gray's guilt were becoming more concerned as the hours passed. A quick verdict would certainly have been in their favor, now they were downright worried.

Jo Ann couldn't control her emotions years later as she remembered her fears. "I was so nervous. My hands were so wet. I walked off by myself and my husband came up putting his arms around me, asking what was wrong. I said I was just so scared. Dick, I cried, what will we do if that verdict comes in not guilty? I'll never, ever forget that feeling."

The judge's previous remarks weighed heavily on her mind. If the judge felt there was not enough evidence to convict, maybe the jury wouldn't either.

"Frankly," Judge Wood had said after the jury was absent from the room, "I've been very troubled throughout this case as to the strength of the state's evidence. It is obvious that someone committed these terrible crimes, but the state's evidence linking the crimes with the defendant has been minimal.

"There is evidence, of course, that the hair that was left on the recliner matched or was similar to the hair of the defendant. But the evidence also indicated that the experts could not state with certainty that it was Mr. Gray's hair.

"None of the footprint evidence really tied the defendant to the scene of the crime, other than Saralyn Hoffman's testimony that her father did have turf shoes with knobby soles and that's what the footprints in the carpet were from. We've got Mr. Mackley's testimony wherein he see's someone whom he identifies as Mr. Gray, an individual riding into the parking lot of the hospital at 2 a.m. or 3 in the morning, and then he identifies him later in the hospital.

"So the big problem for the state is frankly, convincing the jury beyond a reasonable doubt that it was Mr. Gray that did this. There's been no turf shoes recovered. No fingerprints found on anything that positively identifies Mr. Gray as the perpetrator of these crimes. We've got the story on the Travelall and intrigue and deception that went along with that. The question that I have to decide is whether or not any reasonable jury could find beyond a reasonable doubt that the defendant committed this crime."

Clearly, the judge did not feel the state had proved their case. He did not say Bill was not guilty, only that there had not been enough evidence to convict him. This was a strong statement for the judge to make. It would be printed in the newspapers the next day and those who were feeling smug for a guilty verdict were not so sure now.

The jury had not heard the judge's remarks but they had heard Mike Kane address this issue in his closing statement.

"No guns, no shoes, no prints. Homicides are meant to be committed in secret. They are designed so you don't get caught. There is no doubt whatsoever that the defendant did an awful lot to cover up. Of course, he's not going to leave his fingerprints behind. Of course, he's going to get rid of the gun. Of course, he's going to get rid of his bloody clothes. But if all you've got to do is get rid of the gun, get rid of the shoes, get rid of your clothes and not leave any fingerprints to get away with murder, if that's all it is going to take, then whose life is safe, whose life is ever going to be safe?"

The families left the courthouse as soon as they learned the jury would soon be quitting for the night. They retired to their motel rooms and motor homes. Clayton and Paul were especially disappointed for they had commitments in Utah the next morning. When they heard the news, they left town.

Reeda's children and Betty's children had never known each other before their mothers were murdered. Now they were linked together by a common bond of grief and quest for justice. There had been some phone conversations between them in the months before the trial began but they did not actually meet until they were all present at the courthouse for the beginning of the trial. The first time Saralyn saw Clayton Roundy she went up to him, put her arms around him and said, "I am so sorry my father killed your mother."

She knew firsthand the grief they were experiencing, and she felt the guilt was hers. Saralyn knew the Roundys were there because of the problems of her family, she knew there was absolutely no reason their mother should be dead. These young people who lived states apart became friends for the three weeks of the trial, sharing the same goal, sharing the same empty place in their hearts for their mothers.

Two dedicated women trial watchers stayed in the courthouse long after all the others had left, the only two people in the quiet lonely corridor. One was knitting, the other reading, neither able to concentrate wholly on what they were doing. They kept talking about leaving after they heard the jury was going to dinner and retire for the night, but decided to stay until the jury physically left the building. But the jury did not leave at 5:30 p.m. and were still there at 7:45 p.m. when Prosecutor David Johnson came running down the hall announcing a verdict had been reached. The jury had deliberated for a total of 17 hours.

Soon the courthouse was ablaze with activity. Several newspaper reporters, three television channels, with their crews, lights and cameras were among the first to arrive. Then family members, trial watchers, detectives and investigators began arriving. Tom Moss made the 25 miles from Blackfoot to Idaho Falls in record time, but he would have to wait, everyone would have to wait. The State Police had been sent to intercept Clayton and Paul who were enroute to Utah and escort them back to Idaho Falls.

It was after 8:50 p.m. when Judge Wood sternly advised his packed courtroom that he would not tolerate any talking, whispering or demonstrations when the verdict was read. There were to be no displays of emotion and no outbursts of any kind, and the bailiff was instructed to immediately remove anyone who disobeyed those instructions.

Jumping at any and every conclusion Jo Ann was convinced the judge was specifically directing his statements to the families in anticipation of a not guilty verdict. Reeda's children, Clayton, Paul, Ruth Ann and Betty's, Saralyn and Jeff sat together on the front row. They all held hands, each working hard at controlling their thoughts and emotions. Jo Ann, Dick and their son Rick sat directly behind them with Tom Moss and Detective Rodriguez. This was it. It was time to put the events of July 23, 1989. behind them, one way or the other.

Whatever the verdict, they could then put their lives back together and begin the healing process. They had been waiting for this day for a long time. For four years they had been held hostage by a judicial system that would not act. In just a few minutes they would be liberated.

Bill looked for his parents the minute he entered the courtroom giving them a wink of encouragement, then shared a slight smile with his attorneys. He would not look at anyone else in the spectator area, especially those seated in the front row. Bill and Mulligan spoke briefly and Mulligan put his arm around his client squeezing his shoulder in support. The bailiff who normally wore a jacket covering his holstered gun was now jacketless, gun exposed, standing directly behind Bill Gray. The second uniformed officer stood close by.

Mulligan and Radin stood with their client while the verdict was read. Saralyn was visibly shaking as she waited for the words to be said. Jo Ann, without realizing it, grasped Tom Moss's knee so tightly her fingernails dug into his skin. He hardly noticed, for even though Tom was accustomed to the tense moments before a verdict was read, this one seemed more personal. He'd mentally adopted Saralyn and Jeff, he knew what they had been through and the torment they'd suffered because it was their father who stood before this courtroom now, his destiny just a few seconds away.

The clerk read the verdict, with all the legal jargon attached to it, and it seemed forever before she said the first "guilty," then the second "guilty," and then the third ...

When Bill heard the first guilty, his shoulders slumped. Jury Foreman, Richard Schwartz said in a later interview that Gray slammed the table with his fist. "He hit it hard enough and loud enough that I'll never forget it," recalled Schwartz.

As the jurors were polled to confirm their guilty verdicts Bill glared at the jury as each juror solidified their decision. The judge was talking, finishing up his duties, but no one really heard him.

Bill Gray was remanded to immediate custody, immediate incarceration. Just that quick he would not be going back to the comfort of house arrest. Bill's parents sat in stunned silence undoubtedly their hearts filled with rage and loss. Jo Ann's eyes filled with tears. Tears of relief, tears of release from her long ordeal and tears for her sister. But regardless what the judge had instructed, Saralyn lost it. She completely broke down. She cried uncontrollably, her entire body shook. Jeff put his arms around her and held her tight.

Tom Moss and Jeff helped Saralyn out of the room.

Everyone in that room, except her father and grandparents, hurt deeply for Saralyn. Either way she could not win. In a twisted way, her father was just as gone as her mother.

Saralyn and Ruth Ann exchanged hugs and tears. Their mothers could rest now.

"He's going to be punished for what he did, which he deserves," Ruth Ann cried, "but we still don't have a mom."

Would Bill die by lethal injection for the murder of his wife and her friend? Would he spend the rest of his life in prison? Or would he be out on parole in 10 or 15 years? The sentencing would take place on November 1, six months after Bill became a convicted killer.

All family members of both Reeda and Betty would write lengthy letters to the pre-sentencing investigator. Each would give their reasons why Bill Gray should not ever be free. Most pleaded for death, a life for a life; in this case, for two lives.

Working equally as hard to save their client, the defense sent letters to almost everyone Bill Gray knew who they felt would be sympathetic toward him. The defense was asking if the recipients of the letters would testify in Bill's behalf at the sentencing.

When the letters started showing up in Jackson, they became the subject of much humor among the townsfolk. Jokingly several people asked Janis, "Did you get a letter? Did you get a letter to help save Bill Gray? Ha, ha?"

The reasoning behind the letters was not lost on anyone. Bill Gray did not know, or have enough real friends who would come forward on their own to help him. Using all their resources, markers were called in by the elder Grays, demanding that family members write letters and go to Idaho to help Bill. And they would. The William Grays held a financial leverage sufficient to see to their demands.

Three seasons, spring, summer and fall, had passed since the Gray trial and subsequent guilty verdicts. Now on this cold, crisp winter day of November 1, most of the players who were present at the reading of the verdicts were back in Courtroom IV for the finale.

The defense found three Jackson Hole residents who had known Bill through the pawnshop. They said he had always dealt fairly with them.

Two deputies who worked at the jail confirmed Bill had not given them any trouble and had not been written up while he was jailed. The deputy who was in charge of the monitoring system saw Bill almost every day while he was under house arrest. He'd gotten to be friends with Bill and said he never tried to abuse the system. On the contrary Bill called in and reported when the system malfunctioned.

A neighbor of Bill's, while on house arrest, said he visited with him often, and that his wife sent over meals occasionally, he shoveled Bill's sidewalk and Bill gave his kids each a Christmas present.

Bill's brother-in-law and nephew, Beverly's husband and son, and an aunt and uncle all vouched for Bill and told of all the good deeds Bill had done over the years, what a wonderful family man he had always been, how much he loved his wife, how much he loved his children.

His father and mother said Bill had always been a thoughtful and loving son. He had always been a hard worker, a good provider for his family, and his family was his whole life. In all,

16 people stood up for Bill at his time of need.

Bill Gray gave a lengthily prepared statement on his own behalf. Extremely emotional his voice was barely audible and hard to understand. He paused to wipe tears from his eyes when he said he had sorrow "from the bottom of his heart" for Reeda's family, as well as his own. But, "I've been wrongly accused," he cried.

He strongly professed his innocence and his voice gained strength when he targeted Detective Rodriguez, Jo Ann Buccola and his kids for framing him.

"The jury, although well meaning, never comprehended the meaning of 'beyond a reasonable doubt' and when my attorneys polled nine of the jury members and from their remarks there was no way possible that they should have arrived at the verdict they came to," he said. "Since the jury is held unaccountable to anyone for their verdict, nothing can be done. They will have to live with their decision, and sadly enough I, too, am burdened with that decision.

"My life and everything Betty and I accomplished in our 29 years of marriage has totally been destroyed. I did not have to testify at my trial, but took the stand to prove to everyone that I had absolutely nothing to hide. When I stood fast and told the truth about what the police had stated as facts, it all fell on deaf ears. Now I just pray to God that I don't become one of the many lost souls that I am sure are locked up in prison. I know someone, somewhere out there, knows they have gotten away with it. But God will sit in their judgment. It was a total shock to me. I was deeply hurt and I called her some pretty rotten things that I'm sorry for now. Betty deserved better than that. There were no words to describe the loss that I will always feel, not only for the loss of my wife, but the loss of my children. It turned out that out of all the suspects, I was the only one without an alibi. If my dear old Dobbie could have only talked, I wouldn't be here today."

Sensing the "poor me" routine surfacing and that Bill was beginning to ramble, Mulligan called for a recess. When court reconvened Bill was finished and so was the defense.

Michael Kane gave an eloquent final speech. He had a job to do and his job was to speak for the two dead women. If ever there was a defendant who deserved the death penalty, Michael was sure it was Bill Gray and he would pursue that belief to no end.

"Reeda Roundy has been the forgotten woman in this case. Virtually the entire trial centered around the relationship with Betty and the defendant, but she was a human being. She had friends and she had a family. Her only crime was being Betty Gray's friend and that's why she is dead. The law says that if you kill somebody and you do it in certain ways, the death penalty is proper. One is obviously when more than one killing is committed at the same time. The second one, whereby the murder or circumstances surrounding its commission, the defendant exhibited utter disregard for human life.

"All I can do is ask the court to rethink what that scene looked like, that murder scene on that tape. We have two women shot in the head and then someone, the jury says the defendant; then goes about dipping a pot scrubber in one of the victim's blood and writing words with that blood. This was a well-planned, well thought out, cold calculated murder. And that is the kind of murder that the Idaho Supreme Court talks about when they use the term, utter disregard for human life, the utmost callous disregard for human life, the cold blooded pitiless slayer."

After a recess, Judge Wood was ready with his decision.

"Mr. Gray, would you please stand? Now Mr. Gray do you know of any legal reason why I should not sentence you today on the charges for which you were convicted?"

"None other than if you have to do it," replied Gray.

"Alright, Mr. Gray, if you wish you may have a seat for the moment. As the state has pointed out in its comments, it has now fallen on my shoulders to decide the fate of William Gray. I want you, Mr. Gray, to understand, and everyone else here today, that I do not relish that task. Some states require that the jury that convicts the defendant also determines the sentence for that defendant. Today I wish Idaho had such a system. It would be a lot easier for me. But we don't, so it is my job to determine what sentence should be imposed in this case. I don't take this task lightly. And it's on days like this that I wish that I were not a judge. Nevertheless it is my job."

After reviewing everything he had taken into consideration for his determination, he continued. "Now in this case the murder of Reeda Roundy is not the result, in this court's view, of hot blood. It was a conscious killing of a human being. William Gray had no personal interest in Reeda Roundy at all. Her offense and her mistakes would simply be she was at home when the murder of Betty Gray was committed. Her mistake was to be in the wrong place at the wrong time. After the murder the evidence indicates that Mr. Gray calmly went about the business of attempting to falsify the scene to make it look like a cult killing and attempting to set up an alibi. Therefore, the court finds beyond a reasonable doubt that the murder of Reeda Roundy was performed by a cold-blooded, pitiless slayer.

"Now, having found two statutory aggravating circumstances to exist beyond a reasonable doubt, this justifies the death penalty. Where the court finds statutory aggravating circumstances, the court shall sentence the defendant to death, unless the court finds mitigating circumstances outweigh the gravity of any aggravating circumstance and make imposition of the death penalty unjust."

Judge Wood listed the mitigating circumstances. Bill Gray had no prior history of conflict with the law, no prior history of violent acts, has been a productive law-abiding citizen, a good provider for his family and enjoyed a good reputation in his community for truth and honesty and veracity. The defendant obeyed all court orders and did not try to flee while on house arrest.

It seemed the judge had arrived at a great deal of his decision through the testimonies of the character witnesses who had earlier testified. This was a certain plus for the defense.

Then once again the judge went through the holes in the prosecution's case causing a residual doubt. Lack of a murder weapon, lack of fingerprints, no matching hairs, unidentifiable footprints; the eyewitness saw no facial hair, no conclusive evidence which placed the defendant at the scene and lastly, the defendant steadfastly maintained his innocence.

"Now, having said that, Mr. Gray would you please stand? As I stated earlier Mr. Gray, the law in Idaho requires me to weigh all the mitigating circumstances in this case against each of the individual statutory aggravating circumstances. Having done that, this court finds and concludes that the mitigating circumstances do outweigh each of the aggravating circumstances that the state has proved in this case. Therefore, based upon Idaho law, this court finds that the imposition of the death penalty would be unjust. However, this court also finds and concludes that the mitigating circumstances which weigh against imposition of the death penalty, do not weigh in favor of your eventual release back into society. Therefore, it is hereby ordered, Mr. Gray, that you be sentenced as follows:

"As to the conviction for the first degree murder of Betty L. Gray, you are hereby sentenced to the Board of Corrections for the state of Idaho for a fixed term of life.

"As to the convictions for the first degree murder of Reeda Roundy, you are hereby sentenced to the Idaho Board of Corrections also to a fixed life term.

"As to the conviction for the crime of first degree burglary, you are hereby sentenced to the Idaho Board of Corrections to a fixed term of five years and a maximum term of ten years. That will be the sentence imposed. Mr. Gray, do you have any questions?"

"How long did you just give me, Your Honor?"

"I gave you two fixed life terms for the two first degree murder charges, and one fixed five-year term for the first degree burglary charge, followed by an indeterminate ten years."

"I'm sorry. What is a fixed life term?"

"A fixed life term, Mr. Gray, means that you will be in prison for the rest of your life without the possibility of parole."

"No matter how much you fold, mutilate, spindle the truth, no matter how much you sugar coat it, and throw up smoke; the truth has a way of coming out."

Michael Kane in closing arguments.

6

EPILOGUE

everal weeks after her father's sentencing and prior to his transfer to the Boise State Penitentiary, Saralyn tried to see her father. She had a Bible in her hand. Undoubtedly she was driven to give him something to hold comfort in and to help him through his long ordeal. Bill refused to see his daughter. He said, "I don't have a daughter."

He's still her father; she can't change that.

"And I do still love you, Daddy, I do love you. I don't condone what you did. I try to understand."

ABOUT THE BOOK

by author Dixie Murphy

Crime puzzles have always been a fascination of mine ... the desire to know why crimes are committed, the events that lead up to them and eventually the hunt for the guilty. Some are obvious and some require a great deal of investigation to uncover the truth. Now that premeditated killers know how damaging fingerprints and DNA are, they don't leave them behind. Killers  who plan their kill well in advance tend to leave the barest of clues.

But as smart as they think they are, they always leave something of themselves, if nothing more than a good motive or the lack of an alibi. It is my interest in the investigation and the smallest details forensic experts uncover that lead me to the true crime section of every bookstore.

The murders in this book were committed in my hometown where murder is rare. The fact that this case went unsolved for so long piqued my curiosity. After sitting through a three-week trial, I spent countless hours sitting on a hard bench in the hall of the courthouse pouring through stacks of documents that revealed additional information into the personality of Bill Gray.

I did not know anyone involved in this crime, but as the story unfolded, it became apparent that it was so cold blooded and destroyed so many lives, the story had to be written.

I traveled and interviewed family members, detectives and others, transcribed the cassette tapes and then put the information in order of events for this story to emerge. Ultimately, all the pieces came together and the puzzle fell into place.

However, I wrote this book 20 years ago and left it residing in my computer. Early on, I was reluctant to pursue it as I felt the families had been so traumatized through the trial, I did not want to add further grief. When I believed enough time had passed, I then found it impossible for unknown, first-time authors to get published, so it stayed in the computer. Over the years I had several friends read it and offer editing help. All encouraged me to go forward. And then finally technology caught up and allowed this first-time author to turn this story into a book.